REGNUM STUDIES IN MISSION

Resources and Opportunity

The Architecture of Livelihoods in Rural Kenya

REGNUM STUDIES IN MISSION

Series Preface

Regnum Studies in Mission are born from the lived experience of Christians and Christian communities in mission, especially, but not solely, in the fast growing churches among the poor of the world. These churches have more to tell than stories of growth. They are making significant impacts on their cultures in the cause of Christ. They are producing 'cultural products' which express the reality of Christian faith, hope and love in their societies.

Titles in the Regnum Studies in Mission series are the fruit of rigorous research to the highest international standards and always of authentic Christian engagement in the transformation of people and societies. These books have been created for the world. The formation of Christian theology, missiology and practice, in the twenty-first century, will depend to a great extent on the active participation of growing churches contributing biblical and culturally appropriate expressions of Christian practice to inform World Christianity.

Series Editors

The publication of this title is made possible through the generous financial assistance of The Commission on Theological Education of Evangelisches Missionswerk in Deutschland (EMW, Dr. Verena Grüter), Hamburg, Germany

REGNUM STUDIES IN MISSION

Resources and Opportunity

The Architecture of Livelihoods in Rural Kenya

Edward Ontita

First published 2012 by Regnum Books International

Regnum is an imprint of the Oxford Centre for Mission Studies
St. Philip and St. James Church
Woodstock Road
Oxford, OX2 6HR, UK
www.ocms.ac.uk/regnum

09 08 07 06 05 04 03 8 7 6 5 4 3 2 1

British Library Cataloguing in Publication Data
A catalogue record for this book is available from the British Library

ISBN 978-1-506477-40-4

Typeset by Words by Design Ltd

Distributed by 1517 Media in the US and Canada

Contents

List of Figures

List of Abbreviations

AD	Anno Domini
BBC	British Broadcasting Corporation
BC	Before Christ
Cap.	Chapter
CBS	Central Bureau of Statistics
CEE	Common Entrance Examination
CNN	Cable News Network
DC	District Commissioner
DFID	Department for International Development of Britain
DO	District Officer
ECA	Economic Commission for Africa
EIU	Economic Intelligence Unit [of London]
GATT	General Agreement on Tariffs and Trade
GDP	Gross Domestic Product
Ha	Hectares
IBEAC	Imperial British East Africa Company
ICA	International Coffee Agreement
IFIs	International Financial Institutions
IMF	International Monetary Fund
KES	Kenya Shilling
KETEPA	Kenya Tea Packers Ltd
KJSE	Kenya Junior Secondary Examination
KNA	Kenya National Archives
KTDA	Kenya Tea Development Agency
KUSSTO	Kenya Union of Small Scale Tea Owners
MOA	Ministry of Agriculture
MP	Member of Parliament
MOPND	Ministry of Planning and National Development
ODA	Overseas Development Agency
ODI	Overseas Development Institute
PC	Provincial Commissioner
RNFE	Rural Non-Farm Employment
SACCO	Savings and Credit Cooperative
SAPs	Structural Adjustment Programmes
SCDA	Special Crops Development Authority
SDA	Seventh Day Adventist Church

SSA	Sub-Saharan Africa
TBC	Tea Buying Centre
TBK	Tea Board of Kenya
USA	United States of America
WTO	World Trade Organisation
ZD	[KTDA] Zonal Directors

Approximate Exchange Rates (KES to USD[1])

1976	KES 8.16[1]
1985	KES 16.00[2]
1995	KES 56.00[3]
1996	KES 55.00
1997	KES 63.00
1998	KES 61.00
1999	KES 74.00
2000	KES 78.00
2001	KES 79.00
2002	KES 80.00
2003	KES 76.00
2004	KES 76.00
2005	KES 72.00
2006	KES 70.00
2007	KES 61.00
2008	KES 74.00
2009	KES 73.00
2010	KES 77.00

[1] Heyer, J. JK Maitha, and WM Senga (1976) Eds. *Agricultural Development in Kenya: An Economic Assessment.* Nairobi: Oxford University Press. P.XV.
[2] Orvis, S. 1977. P. 60.
[3] http://www.oanda.com (rounded off for a random December date from 1995 – 2010).

Preface

> With all my resources I have provided for the temple of my God—gold for the gold work, silver for the silver, bronze for the bronze, iron for the iron and wood for the wood, as well as onyx for the settings, turquoise, stones of various colours, and all kinds of fine stone and marble—all of these in large quantities.
>
> (1 Chronicles 29:2, New International Version)

> Be very careful, then, how you live—not as unwise but as wise, making the most of every opportunity, because the days are evil.
>
> (Ephesians 5: 15-16, New International Version)

At the beginning of my PhD studies an experienced researcher looked at my research proposal and quipped, "It is difficult to study villagers without reference to some intervention so that you describe and explain their interactions with it and the ensuing social changes or lack of them". In retrospect I agree with the advice in the context of a PhD research project with its time and resource constraints. Nonetheless at the time I did not follow the wise counsel and went ahead to focus my study on villagers' resources and livelihoods.

Resources & Opportunity is one of the outputs of that research project. This book serves at least three purposes. First, it contributes to the livelihoods debate in several respects. In terms of advancing the argument that assets/capital as resources should be conceptualised as both material and non-material. By exploring processes of actor co-production of resources in league and/or contestation with their physical and social environment. In locating villagers' non-material livelihood objectives; thus re-affirming the view that livelihoods constitute more than just food, income, shelter and environmental sustainability.

Second, at a theoretical level the book brings out the actor – structure tensions and local – global interactions/contestations in everyday practice. An elaborate exposition of the theoretical perspectives provide a sound backcloth for the analysis that follows. Third, in terms of methodology the book offers an opportunity to fruitfully grapple with the concept of households and its application in the cultural context of the study areas. An ethnographic approach brings out the complex and multiple relationships characteristic of villagers and a blurred 'household', in the western sense. Extended case studies are developed. Excerpts from those case studies and local popular music are then used to tell the story of villagers' struggles to co-produce resources and construct livelihoods. Some excerpts are presented more than once and looked at from a variety of perspectives in search of holistic meaning. This approach to data analysis and writing up is deliberately followed to clearly provide the contours of the journey from fieldwork to written work. A major aspiration of this work is to simplify this journey and attract more researchers especially PhD students in East Africa to qualitative research. However, research methods *per se* – qualitative or quantitative are beyond the scope of the book.

Resources & Opportunity is the result of subtle public policy evaluation from below. It shows what happens to ordinary souls when the smallholder tea sub-sector is liberalised without robust safeguards from emerging corruption and the penetration of multinational corporation interests. It also explores the multiple dimensions and complexities of rural economy, exposing the lack of traction that characterises rural development policy organised almost solely around agriculture. And it delves into varied improvisations, creativity and ingenious endogenous livelihood constructions occurring in everyday lives often running counter to or even without policy specifications and in the face of uncertainty and risk. The book invites the state to view the rural economy with wider lenses.

Principally this book addresses undergraduate and graduate students of Development Studies, Sociology, Anthropology, Extension, African Studies, Public Policy and Mission Studies. Teachers and researchers in the foregoing fields will also find the book useful.

Acknowledgements

Many people have contributed to the completion of this book. It is difficult to list all of them in these pages, because the journey has been long. The journey started with my parents' decision to send me to primary school in the early 1970s. That is when they embraced their dream, planted the seed and set me off to search for knowledge. I hope I have lived their dream, and so to you mum and dad – Sibiah and Nelson – a big thank you. I grew up in a large, supportive family – my siblings Agnes, Elijah, the late Tabitha, Dan, Periah, Hassan, Yabesh, Nelly and Gideon have, over a long time, provided the support that has culminated in the completion of this book. Their families have equally been supportive, especially during the fieldwork for this book. They have been a blessing and I thank God for them and their help in accomplishing this work. I thank my wife Catherine and the boys: Kevin and Rodney, for their love, prayers, patience and encouragement as I spent many months in the field in Nyamira and later in The Netherlands and in Oxford writing up.

The idea of undertaking PhD studies at Wageningen started on February 21, 1997, when I met Dr. Paul Hebinck at the Mayfair, Nairobi. We discussed many issues some of which have shaped the arguments in this book although it took another six years before I could commence studies at Wageningen. I thank Paul for his consistent counsel that I should visit Wageningen and complete a research proposal. I finally visited in 2002, completed and submitted a proposal to *WOTRO*– the Netherlands Foundation for the Advancement of Tropical Research. Subsequently the proposal was accepted and I commenced my studies in September 2003. I thank *WOTRO* for the funding which facilitated my fieldwork in Nyamira and studies in the Netherlands in general. I also thank IFRA – the French Institute for Research in Africa and the Deans' Committee, University of Nairobi for funding a survey on tea growing in Nyamira, some results of which have been used in this book. I am grateful to Prof. B. Charlery de la Masseliere of IFRA's Nairobi office for his interest, comments and support for my work.

The book could not be completed without the interest and support from my PhD supervisory team. This included my promoter Prof. dr. Leontine Visser, co-promoters Dr. Paul Hebinck and the late Prof. Mary Omosa; who put in many hours to ensure the completion of the work. Leontine spent most of her

2006 Christmas holidays reading portions of the work and held very helpful meetings with me during the holidays. Paul and Mary worked flexibly, allowing for meetings as was necessary and possible, in airports while on transit or at their homes. In particular, Paul liberally shared his personal library with me and held many fruitful discussions with me in Wageningen, Nairobi and in the field in Nyamira.

In Nyamira, I had a supportive fieldwork team comprising of Andrew Nyandieka, the late Grant Aming'a and Elijah Maera. Andrew worked hard, staying late in the field when necessary. I appreciate Tom Nyang'au's assistance with the survey. I would like to thank the people of Sengeta for their hospitality and support. They shared their knowledge, work and dreams with me freely with the customary Gusii generosity, I thank them abundantly. I also thank the then Nyamira DC in 2004, Mr. Baruga, the chiefs, their assistants and several village headmen for their cooperation. I appreciate the support received from the Ministries of Education, Agriculture, Livestock and Planning in Nyamira. I thank the staff at Kenya National Archives in Nairobi for assistance in locating some materials on Nyamira and Gusiiland, and Emma of CBS for availing some of the maps.

Several friends in Wageningen supported me in this work. I thank Dr. Sarah Southworld and Dr. Alberto Arce for their comments especially at the proposal stage. My office-mates Kei Otsuki, Martijn Koster, Pablo Laguna and Nienke Tander shared resources and ideas with me. Hennie van Ee, Vincente van Ee, Lucia Duncan, Yvette Jack and Emmanuel Bowyer and their families were good friends in the Netherlands. Their fellowship in church and invitations to their homes often gave me the much needed break from my work. My East African colleagues in Wageningen over the years provided a homely environment. They include Chairman Ayub Oduor, Benjamin Kibor, Nelson Mango, Pius Odunga, Michael Misiko, Daniel Sabai, Diana Okullo, Everlyn Kiptot, Moses, Winnie and Geoffrey Kamau. My dinner groups that included Kennedy Okeri, Roberta Gerpacio [Bobbie] and Ela Bosangit in 2003 and Lawrence Mose, Ciciliah Onyango and Pauline Andango in 2006/7 made my evenings worth looking forward to and I thank both groups for their incredible skills in the kitchen and for accepting the products of my rudimentary skills during my turns. In 2006, Samuel Guto acquired household items for me ahead of my arrival in Wageningen making my settling in unbelievably easy. I thank these men and women for their magnanimity.

Another group of people that has contributed enormously to my academic journey are my teachers, at all education levels; key among them my dad Nelson Ontita for his indelible arithmetic and *Ekegusii* home-schooling that gave me a head-start in regular school. On my first day in primary school I encountered and was settled in by Mr. Joseph Nyarangi and the late Mr. Kiriago. In the following three years I remember with awe the support I received from the late Mrs. Thresa Sereta, Mrs. Mellen Ming'ate, Mr. Joe Sereta, and Mr. Leo Magara, Mr. Matoke, David Nyatwang'a, Norah Bonareri and Florence Ado. Three teachers who made a lasting impression on me are the late Mr. Isaac Ming'ate, Mr. Samuel Otinga and the late Mr. Christopher Momanyi. In secondary school I remember Mr. Enoch Moenga, Mr. Daniel Ratemo, the late Mr. Z.K. Ontumi and Mr. Joe Nyataige, the latter especially for his daily evaluations and his incredible oppositional presentation of *Kiswahili* and *Ekegusii* sayings! I appreciate the support I received from my high school teachers; Joe Wangai, Mrs. Khaweza, Mrs. Musiga, Mrs. Gichui, Mr. Isabirye, Mrs. Kessio and Mr. Kiwanuka.

At the University of Nairobi I received academic and administrative support from many people as I planned for and undertook PhD studies. I thank Prof. Mauri Yambo for supporting my academic endeavors when he served respectively as Chair to the Department of Sociology and Dean of the Faculty of Arts. I would like to thank Prof. Gakuru and Dr. Mbatia, who as chairs to the Department of Sociology at different times, provided administrative support for the completion of this book. Prof. Roberta Mutiso and Prof. Preston Chitere initiated me into research work and I appreciate the opportunity and the collaborative work that ensued. I thank seminar participants at Wageningen and at the IDS, University of Nairobi for their comments on aspects of this work at different times.

I thank the Oxford Centre for Mission Studies (OCMS) for a fellowship to Oxford. This enabled me to live comfortably in Oxford in 2011 to revise and edit this book for publication. Many thanks to the OCMS Director Dr. Wonsuk Ma and the Academic Dean Dr Thomas Harvey for administrative support and to colleagues Dr. David Singh and Dr. Damon So for being collegial. I thank Parrizad Pound of OCMS for typesetting the book. Thanks also to Marslin Blanche and Carole Seward of OCMS Accounts Office for all the support during my fellowship period at the Centre.

Finally, I express gratitude to Jos Michel for her invaluable assistance throughout my studies both in Wageningen and while in the field in Kenya. Her institutional memory was an asset to this work and her invitations to dinner timely.

Edward Ontita
Oxford, England
October 2011

CHAPTER 1

Introduction: Moving into Sengeta

Introduction

How can we understand the continued survival and apparent social functioning of rural villagers amidst officially acknowledged absolute poverty and uneconomic land sizes per household? During my fieldwork in Sengeta Village, Nyamira District, mid Southwestern Kenya, I encountered villagers who were clear about their life objectives. They pursued them through working hard in their small fields and tea gardens, kiosks, open-air markets, livestock markets, in employment on other people's farms, at their craftwork or in some other activity in the village or elsewhere, which enabled them to eke out a living. For the villagers 'making a living' or 'a livelihood' means food, shelter, school fees, health care and other basics, and also perhaps more importantly marriage and bride price exchange, usually in cattle, and 'being able to share the little they have with others'. They share with one another at different sites in everyday life; in church, at beer drinking places, tea kiosks, with the bereaved in funeral and burial rites and during other rites of passage.

Yet, policy documents and expert opinion seem to write off such rural people. The Second Report on Poverty in Kenya volume one of June 2000 reveals that 67 per cent of the population in Nyamira District live in absolute poverty, which means an inability to access basic needs such as food, clothing, shelter, education and health (Kenya, 2002: 24 – Nyamira District Development Plan, 2002-8). The plan lists the major causes of poverty in the district as including impassable roads, population pressure and small land parcels, inadequate health services, inaccessible credit facilities, inadequate energy supply, laziness and idleness, insecurity and agricultural decline – low rates of technology uptake and poor marketing systems (cf. Kenya, 1999c – National Poverty Eradication Plan, 1999-2015; Gitu, 2004: 13). Consequently, they see solutions as lying with improved 'access' to essential services by low income groups within a strategy for broad-based economic growth. These have been the goals of development discourse and practice since independence in 1963 and nothing has changed or improved. The government appears to be "chasing the wind" as it has reiterated this approach in successive policy documents (Kenya, 1965 – Sessional Paper No. 10; Kenya, 1986 – Sessional

Paper No. 1; Kenya, 1987 – District Focus for Rural Development; Kenya, 1996 – The Policy Framework Paper). Each of these documents commences from the premise that the poor are powerless and helpless and in need of interventions to uplift them and especially to improve their access to certain 'essential services'. Each policy document acknowledges the limited success of the preceding ones and starts the circle again; while the poor continue with their lives as usual. These processes appear to hinge on what Haynes (2008: 187) calls a narrow conception of 'development' as mainly implying poverty reduction. A conception practiced without a clear understanding of how people experience and contend with poverty.

How then do villagers manage to construct livelihoods that apparently defy the official bleak descriptions? For instance, there are no householders in the study site of Sengeta Village living in deplorable conditions such as intractable hunger, lack of shelter and clothing, which is common in urban slum life. Do development experts understand resources and opportunities for making a living from the villagers' perspectives? In the field, I regularly encountered villagers partly relying on social ties to secure formal and informal employment and assistance or to strengthen their businesses. The avenues for securing credit to pay school fees or for health services exist in the form of merry-go-round clubs and self-help groups. Is it therefore possible that villagers construct their livelihoods in ways that are invisible to, or taken for granted, by policy makers? The study focused on villagers without qualifying them as poor or otherwise, because the label does not reveal much about what people do. It often points to what they do not have, hence my reference to villagers throughout the book. My fieldwork brought me face to face with the centrality of local brew production and trade as an important livelihood activity. This exemplifies how villagers combine agriculture with other activities in complex ways in order to make a living. Villagers are not fixed in agriculture, they move out of it when it does not work and they return when it is right for them and in line with their preferences and objectives.

Therefore, this book explores how rural villagers create and use resources to make a living. Hence, the central question is; *how do villagers in Nyamira District, mid South-western Kenya, create and use resources to make a living and with what results?* The book departs somewhat from previous livelihood or poverty studies that focus on poor people's incomes and the assets they own or have access to (such as Maxwell 1999; Ashley and Maxwell 2002; Ellis 2000), food security (such as Omosa 1998) or factors that hinder poor people from exiting poverty (such as Ellis and Kutengule 2003). Rather it focuses on villagers' lifestyles, how they mould and mobilise resources, conceptualised broadly to include both the material and the non-material. Furthermore, the book is premised on the view that it is more compeling, challenging and revealing to explore how villagers co-produce resources, improvise opportunities, spend their time, harness and disseminate information; and deal with their environments in order to meet their consumption needs and to enhance their identity and self-esteem than whether they own or have access to certain assets, such as land and finance.

The book is stimulated by the theoretical and practical challenges in understanding the multiple meanings of resources and the implications of this on livelihood construction. The theoretical challenge stems partly from the view in livelihood studies that resources are made of five forms of capital, which form the basis for constructing livelihoods. The book goes beyond, and challenges, this materialist view of rural life, by investigating villager's material and non-material resources and how they create and use them to make a living. This strengthens the view that livelihood is about more than just material resources and outcomes. The practical challenge that this book responds to, is the relative ignorance about poor people's resources and their lifestyles. For instance in a World Bank poverty assessment mission to Kenya, district officials linked poverty with illiteracy, drunkenness, and laziness, whereas villagers said that the poor were often educated, religious and hardworking (Narayan and Nyamwaya, 1996; cf. Chambers, 1995). The central question then is how do villagers create and use their resources. People's livelihoods need to be demystified and their resources and lifestyles explored to capture their view of what constitutes viable and improved livelihoods and how they pursue these goals. How do villagers evaluate viability or success? In addition, how do these occur or fail? Which lifestyles facilitate success and which ones constrain it? How is failure explained and how is it confronted in everyday life?

In searching for answers to the above questions, I started my fieldwork on one Friday morning in March 2004 at the Sengeta village headman's home. I left the market where I lived at about nine o'clock in the morning. On my way to the village, I saw several people walking toward the market. I gathered that some were going to the local branch of Nyamira Tea Savings and Credit Cooperative (Nyamira Tea SACCO) Society for banking services. Others were headed for a burial ceremony for a departed relative. On the main village track, a few groups of young men were gathered discussing in low tones. It later emerged from my discussions with villagers that some young men wake early to sell their napier grass (*pennisetum purpureum*) to dairy farmers and head to the tea kiosks to take tea and *mandazi* (modified doughnuts) for breakfast. After breakfast, they talk to each other before they go to weed the napier or to do other farm work. Those engaged in petty theft returned to the village shops at nightfall. Across the valleys in the village and beyond, people were on the farms weeding maize and beans while others were plucking tea. The villages were green as the ground was fully covered with maize and beans, tea, napier grass and other pastures. From this appearance alone, the village looked very prosperous.

At the headman's home, it was all quiet. A woman who turned out to be his wife was smearing the walls of the main house with clay soil mixed with cow dung and water. The house adjoins the main village track and appeared to have been used as a shop previously. She ushered me into the living room where her husband was seated next to a small table. I explained the objectives of my work in the village in detail and sought his support. The headman told me that his support for my work commenced when the local chief informed him of my plans and he pledged to inform as many villagers as possible about my work to ensure their cooperation.

After discussions on the logistics of my work in the village, I asked him to tell me the story of his life. Although he started his story from birth, I realised that the story thickened at the point that he started to discuss his marriage plans – putting together resources for the bride price, getting an intermediary to locate a bride and convince her family to offer her for marriage and the actual negotiations for and payment of the bride price. My discussions with other villagers and my observations around the village crystallised the view that livelihood pursuits in this village, and arguably in Gusiiland, commence around the time of preparations for marriage. Therefore, this is an eventful stage of life and it involves struggles for resources, which involve negotiations and contests.

The notion of commencement of life thus becomes a central one and a foundation to most of the analyses. This necessitates a detailed discussion at this point of the book, as it is the trigger for the pursuit of relationships beyond the household one was born in, as well as for the search, struggles and contests over resources. At this point, the meanings of resources undergo changes. Cattle and goats, understood thus far as sources of milk and prestige for the family, take on a new meaning as the fulcrum of marriage and the bridge upon which two hitherto unfamiliar families relate to each other as one and the same family. Land too, assumes new meaning as the groom relates to it with more passion.

Commencing Life: Cattle, Goats and Marriage

In commencing life, that is to say at marriage, men require resources mostly cattle and goats both for the bride price and an intermediary to locate an appropriate suitor. In the olden days, up to mid-1960s, the latter was the most important resource antecedent to marriage. In those days, resources were also required for ankle rings after the traditional wedding as well as for housing and household items.

The intermediary who literally brought together prospective husband and wife played a central role. In Abagusii society, the intermediary was from the man's side, because the onus was on him to find a woman to marry. The work of the intermediary was to find out as much as possible about the prospective wife to facilitate sound decision making by the bridegroom. Major considerations included the character of the woman in terms of inter-personal relations; not too stingy to embarrass and yet not too generous to be wasteful. It was also important to check out her dependability in tilling the land, milking cows and goats, cooking and other house keeping roles.

In order to unearth all these attributes, the intermediary employed a variety of artifices. S/he could hide in the bush or by the pathways as the girl tilled her mother's land and observe her abilities and how much farm work she did in a day. The intermediary would also observe as she fetched water from the wells or streams and even carry out espionage-like missions to find out whether she cooked nice maize meal (*ugali*), by asking the youngest and most innocent siblings whether their parents complained about the food their sister cooked. They could also rely on the girl's aunts or neighbours to get sensitive information about her.

Once an intermediary was satisfied that the girl fitted the bill, they reported to the boy's parents. If they agreed with plans for a marriage with a girl from this family, then the boy's father would go ahead (at least up to the mid 1940s) to negotiate bride price with the girl's father. After they agreed then the boy, in the company of one or two peers would visit the girl's home. This was probably the first opportunity that the girl would have to see her prospective husband. If she liked him, she gave him a wooden block to sit on and asked her mother to offer porridge made from millet (*erongori y'obori*) to him and his friends. If she did not like him, she started to sweep her mother's house, symbolically and literally sweeping them out. At that juncture, the boys left embarrassed and the prospecting exercise with regard to the girl ended.

If they were accepted and drank *erongori y'obori* that their mother-in-law to be had made, they happily reported this good news to the boy's father who then arranged to officially go to the girl's home to invite the girl's father to negotiate the bride price. Even if they had earlier discussed and more or less agreed on the number of livestock, it was an agreement that the cattle were available. With the girl's assent, the real negotiations commenced. The girl's father came with a group of negotiators, the best in his family and clan. On arrival in the boy's home before they went into their prospective *korera's*[4] house, the man then led them into the cattle pen or paddock to show them the cattle. They usually haggled over the number for hours before they agreed or totally disagreed and the prospecting was broken.

If they agreed on the number of goats, cows and bulls, then they went into the house, ate and drank over night. In the morning, boys from the man's side drove the livestock to the bride's home. Up until the 1950s between thirty or forty cattle, ten to twenty goats and a bull *(eeri nyagesicho*) for the bride's father to slaughter and get a skin (*egesicho*) for his clothing, constituted bride price. The bull was strictly reserved for the bride's father. The unmarried young men who drove the livestock carried twigs and leaves to signify that the livestock were a peaceful gift for marriage and not from a raid. The boys delivered the cows to the bride's home, had a meal there and returned to their

---

[4] *Korera* is the local title by which a man's parents, aunties and uncles and their counterparts in his wife's family and clan address each other.

home or if late spent the night at their nearest relative's home, but not in the home in which they had delivered the livestock as this was taboo.

Once the 'cattle had been taken[5]' the marriage was officially on. If the groom was not ready for an immediate wedding, he could assemble a band of strong young men from his village and clan to ambush the girl and forcefully take her home for marriage. If both parties were ready with food and drink, the man and his friends prepared to go to the girl's home for *enyangi y'ebitinge* (wedding). They drank and danced over night[6]. During the wedding night, the girl was fitted with thick ankle rings[7] - the last known wedding of this kind in Sengeta took place in 1943[8]. Then the groom's party wrestled and fought the local young men and took away the woman after defeating them.

The woman handed over easily; the young men had to struggle and wrestle to get her to demonstrate her value to their family and clan. Her brothers, cousins and young men from her clan had to prevent 'the intruders' from taking away their sister because she was precious to the family and clan. As the young men took away the woman, her mother would weep because her daughter's assistance in cooking, farm work, fetching water and firewood had come to a halt. In retrospect, this was a contest over a resource that had multiple meanings to the two respective parties. At the end of the haggling over bride price, the bride's father withdrew from the contest and perhaps shifted to prospecting for a new wife using his daughter's bride price. He left the rest of the contest in the hands of her mother and stepmothers and the young men in the clan. His only involvement would be his presence and participation with other elders during the wedding night (see Philip Mayer, 1950, for a detailed discussion on Gusii wedding ceremonies).

A few days after the girl went away into marriage via a wedding or ambush[9], her father would slaughter one of the goats given to him in bride

[5] All the livestock given in bride price were referred to as 'cows', in spite of the fact that they included goats and a bull or bulls. Any suckling kids or calves (*omobiaro*) among the number are not counted.

[6] This drinking and dancing that started at the bride's home and continued in the groom's home the following day required enormous resources. For this reason the transfer of bride price and the wedding night were often as much as a year apart to facilitate mobilisation of resources with the assistance of family and clan.

[7] From the descriptions of villagers *ebitinge* (ankle rings) were made of copper and bound with aluminum. They were painted red and metallic silver and were permanently worn by the woman until death, when they would be cut off and removed. After burial they were thrown on the grave to signify the end of a marriage.

[8] Elderly men and women in Sengeta named a number of villagers who married through enyangi y'ebitinge (wedding) between 1940 and 1943, but did not know of any such wedding afterward anywhere in Gusiiland.

[9] If the girl was taken into marriage via an ambush, her mother had to be sure that she was taken to the specific family that had delivered bride price so that the *ugali* and goat meat could be taken. Otherwise wayward young men could also ambush and forcefully take into marriage girls they had neither seen before nor paid dowry for, hence delivering the ugali

price. The meat was taken together with '*obokima bw'obori*' (millet *ugali*) to her daughter's new home. The bride's sisters and sisters-in-law carried the *ugali* and meat all the way to her new matrimonial home for consumption by the girl's parents-in-law and their peers. Her husband, his cousins and peers did not eat it yet; waiting another week for theirs to be delivered in the same way. On their return journey, the girl's sisters carried millet grain in *ekee* (a special kind of basket) in which the *ugali* had been delivered. This was Abagusii people's *omogiro* (appreciation) meaning that *ekee ngekoirana bosa* (the gift does not go unappreciated). The practice encouraged the next delivery of ugali and cyclical appreciation for both families over time and space. It was like *gosunera ekeumbu oboba, goteba ankio kande*[10]. According to local myth, their sister would put a stick in the millet grain as a message to her mother. If the stick was lying across in the millet, the message was that her husband was impotent and the girl was seeking her mother's counsel. If the stick stood vertical in the millet, then the message was that her husband was sexually potent and she was happy.

The issue of the stick in the millet throws up another dimension of the newly married woman as a potential resource. By the time, a mother sends *ugali* and meat to her daughter's new home her daughter's meaning to her has shifted from that of a resource and helping hand to an actor in procreation who will give her grandchildren. Her daughter's relatives-in-law are equally expectant of new momentum from the newly married woman in opening up new fields and before long a bulging belly to give them nephews and grandchildren. The valuation and meaning of the new husband also shifted from that of a village defender to that of a property owner and a worker through his wife. In their perspective, his livelihood trajectory had truly commenced.

Several issues surrounding marriage customs have changed. By the mid-1960s, the role of the intermediary in the marriage had greatly weakened and by the early 1970s, it had disappeared. This was the result of Christianity, education, migration and the media all of which, emphasised marriage as being between two people who needed to negotiate their terms and understand each other before hand. The notion of courting, which was very much in currency by the 1970s, turned the role of the marriage intermediary on its head. For the same reasons, the issue of wrestling and fighting over a girl for marriage also fell into disuse by the beginning of the 1970s. Quiet sobs by younger sisters and mum at wedding receptions or as a girl leaves her parent's home for

---

required due diligence lest a family be embarrassed. If it turned out that the girl for whom pride price had been paid was taken away by way ward men, all the bride price paid had to be returned.

[10] In a discussion with Mzee Jonathan (aged 83) of Sengeta on April 19, 2006; he likened the millet grain to the Abagusii practice of taking a small piece from the top of a mushroom and putting it back in the hole from which it had been harvested, thus symbolically appreciating the land for the harvest.

marriage, have replaced wrestling, struggling and weeping. Therefore, both sides of the marriage continually express the significance of the woman as a resource.

Another major shift in the marriage arrangement and commencement of livelihood is related to girls getting married or starting to 'live with men in marriage' before bride price is transferred. TSuch men enter into negotiations on bride price after the wife has given birth to several children, as and when they get livestock or money. This presents a contradiction as to when the momentous valuation, search and application of livelihood really commences. This is a crucial point as though the man appears not to have overtly mobilised resources in livestock for marriage; he and his wife have commenced a livelihood all the same in the sense of seeking resources for their own provisioning. There is pressure on the couple to create and recreate resources, which originates from their having to care for and provide for children as they arrive. Even in the absence of their own children, their cohabitation brings responsibilities for others, such as aging parents or parents-in-law, thus driving them to redefine resources and to apply themselves to life differently in order to function as expected in society.

In Sengeta Village young women married in the late 1970s and 1980s had no clue about the millet and stick in *ekee* except that the older ones among them said they learnt of it in stories from aunties and elder sisters who married in the 1960s or earlier. This form of messaging has been very rarely used if at all, since the 1970s. Interactions in the course of courtship have overtaken usage of the stick in the millet. However, the practice of the millet in the basket has persisted together with payment of bride price, although the number of livestock for bride price has dropped significantly since the late 1960s.

There are several reasons villagers advanced for the decline of the number of livestock offered and/or taken as bride price. The first is that Christian leaders especially Adventists, who are the majority in the village, have challenged the legitimacy of bride price beyond tokenism since the colonial times and with significant success. Second, there has been another more general fight waged by women's rights activists, especially since the early 1990s. These activists have linked violence on women in marriage with the 'payment of bride price'. Third, the value of livestock as wealth has declined over the years and the focus of value in bride price has centred on the quality rather than quantity of livestock offered. Those taking grade cattle agree on just one or two. Bride price is increasingly paid in cash with an accompaniment of a cow or two. Some of the villagers said that since the 1980s wealthier villagers negotiated bride price for their daughters secretly, unlike in the past when this was done in the presence of invited villagers and relatives. Villagers said this was mainly the result of increasing mistrust among people. Finally, the general poverty and unemployment in the villages explains the inability of many young men to pay bride price at all, let alone with fewer livestock.

Villagers said that some marriages were consummated after bride price was transferred but were not followed up with the delivery of *ugali* and goat meat as was traditionally the practice. There are villagers who have not received *ugali* in respect of their daughters-in-law and some who have not sent *ugali* in respect of their daughters, in spite of the payment of bride price. These omissions are attributed to declining interest in the practice and the couples often being absent from home. Despite this, I witnessed several *ugali* deliveries around Sengeta in the course of my fieldwork and on one such occasion a huge feast involving many invited villagers. The practice has thus declined but is not under threat of disappearance in the foreseeable future.

Scenarios in locating resources for marriage

There are several scenarios for creating the resources necessary for marriage, as demonstrated in various case studies in this book. The first is when a man who is ready to marry has sisters for whom bride price is due; he gets cattle depending on his birth position. In such a scenario, as shown in the case excerpt below, a sister's entire bride price is paid to a brother's bride's home. The key thing here is that the groom was the first-born son and has several sisters. By the time his younger brother was ready to marry all his sisters' bride price had been used up by his brother, so he had to buy cattle in order to be able to marry and commence life on his own.

> Petro joined the Adventist Church in 1950 got baptised and married in the church in the same year. The bride price for his wife was from his younger sister, and consisted of six head of cattle, a bull and a goat. The wedding expenses were low because people walked to the woman's home and to church as well as back to his home. His last-born brother married in 1974 and it was not until about 1980 when he paid the bride price. He raised a bride price of five heads of cattle plus a goat from his savings as a teacher and earnings from tea.

The younger brother lamented this:

> "You see my elder brother inherited a bigger piece of land than me and he used up all our sisters' bride price. In fact some were from the last born sister and I am the last born brother. I could have been given at least some for my own use."

The scenario in the marriage of Petro's younger brother may not have arisen if his brother Petro had followed custom. He would ordinarily have saved some of his sisters' bride price for his brother to use in marriage. Traditional canons about the use of bride price provide that a father uses that from the first born daughter and subsequent brothers use the bride price from sisters in corresponding birth positions. The case below roughly demonstrates this.

> Joshua was born in 1944 and has two brothers and five sisters. All the sisters are married and bride price has been paid. His elder sister's bride price was used by his eldest brother to pay his bride price. His elder brother married with their

second born sister's bride price and Joshua used his third born sister's bride price to pay for his wife.

Joshua had the support of his father in preserving his sister's bride price until he was ready to pay for his wife. His father gave him the cattle he received as bride price for Joshua's sister long before he was ready to marry. To a father, a son's marriage is crucial for the continuity of the lineage, hence the sacrifice to help him marry. Besides, there is always a lot of respect in the village for a man whose sons are 'properly married', that is, who have paid bride price. Parents-in-law on either side of the marriage refer to each other as '*korera*' confidently and respectfully because cattle have changed hands.

When the bride price of one's sister is not sufficient for a son's marriage, the son has to find a way of supplementing it, either by themselves or with the support of their parents. This is because bride price is negotiated, so a father may get less for his daughter while he is pushed by strong and adamant negotiators to pay more for his son's bride. For example in another case study, Nyandika supplemented the bride price from his sister with cattle he bought using earnings from his job in the Kericho tea plantations. He first used the earnings to buy goats and as they multiplied he sold them and bought cattle. Cattle were his priority in life at the time because he knew that his marriage depended on having them.

> Nyandika married his first wife from Bosiango Clan in 1951 and paid a bride price of thirteen heads of cattle. Nine of the cattle he raised from the bride price paid for his sister. He already had bought four cattle and two goats from his savings from work in the plantations and so easily met the bride price for his wife. Nyandika has two daughters by this marriage, both of whom are married but no bride price has been paid for them.

Another scenario for securing bride price resources is where there is one sister and two brothers and the parents have already died. The first son takes advantage of being ready to marry early and uses his sister's bride price. This is supported by tradition as the first son is his "father's first 'spear' into the future and in the advancement of his lineage". The second son must foresee this early enough and organise his manoeuvres in life in order to create resources for bride price in marriage. Nyagwanga's case illustrates this process.

> Nyagwanga was born in Sengeta village in 1936. He said, "My father was a peasant rearing cattle and goats. I have an elder brother and a sister who is married. My brother used the bride price her husband paid to us to pay for his wife. When the time came for me to marry, I bought cattle with the money I made while working in Kericho. This is because we had only one sister, if we had two sisters it would have been easier for me".

There are also situations where poverty is entrenched and marriage may be inhibited if a family has no daughters. The case study below shows that poverty may isolate a family and inhibit outside assistance even from relatives. Such isolation may only be changed through the marriage of a sister and subsequently a brother, opening up new possibilities and opportunities for the family.

> Jason and his brother never progressed much in school due to lack of resources. Jason went up to standard two and his brother up to standard three. During their brief stint in school, they used to cultivate their parent's fields and take care of cattle and poultry although their father's livestock died frequently. Jason recalls that they lived a difficult life. Nobody came to their assistance, except only one uncle whom they could visit and share in his resources.
>
> Jason married in 1968. His intermediary for the marriage was his maternal cousin who played an important role in linking the couple. He paid seven heads of cattle in bride price, which he got from his sister's bride price. His brother used to get his food from Jason' house since he was very young at that time. After marriage Jason' wife joined his mother in cultivating the fields to get food. Sometimes they had surplus, which they exchanged for goats in local barter trade.

Marriage presents itself as the first challenge in life for a man to mobilise resources; not just cattle and goats, but also relationships including intermediaries to consummate marriages and in this sense is the starting point of life. The man's parents, if still alive, play a key role in assisting their son to create resources and to negotiate a favourable bride price for their prospective wife. A sister's bride price is an important source of cattle for brothers' marriages, but due to competition, the brothers often have to look outwards to migrant work such as in tea plantations to raise resources for the bride price and commencement of a livelihood. The villagers also turn out at the wedding if it takes place, and support it with food and other material things such as firewood and seats as appropriate. Even in the absence of weddings, villagers come to the bride price negotiations after which they eat and make merry to celebrate the marriage.

Source: Laikipia D.D. Plan, 1997–2001.

Map 1: Kenya and the location of Nyamira District

What is a Village?

Kenya, like most former British colonies is divided into a variety of administrative units that originate in colonial administration. First, the country is divided into eight provinces, namely, Coast, Eastern, North Eastern, Nairobi, Central, Rift Valley, Western and Nyanza; each headed by a Provincial Commissioner (PC). Second, each province is divided into districts headed by District Commissioners (DCs). Third, each district is divided into administrative divisions headed by District Officers (DOs). Fourth, the divisions are divided into locations under chiefs. Fifth, the locations are divided into administrative sub-locations headed by assistant chiefs. All the administrators in charge of these administrative units are civil servants appointed by the Civil Service Commission to work under the office of the president and are largely answerable to that office. In particular, the chiefs and their assistants are civil servants and should not be confused with the hereditary chiefs in Southern and West Africa. The lowest administrative unit is equally a colonial relic but it is informal and the head unremunerated; it involves the division of the sub-location into villages under village headmen. Commenting on the significance of village headmen in British Central Africa, Gluckman (1949: 89) indicates that many (colonial) District Officers described them as the invaluable Non-Commissioned Officers of native administration although they did little to improve their situation. Post-colonial governments have not improved the position of village headman either. In Kenya the presence and strength of the institution of village head varies from one region to another depending on the historical importance of village leadership. For example, village headship is strong and contributes significantly to rural development initiatives among the Abaluhyia of Western Province (Chitere and Ontita, 1991). In Gusiiland, the institution was active during the colonial period especially with regard to enforcing law and order as well as tax compliance (cf. Silberschmidt, 1999: 42). During fieldwork, I learned that village heads were important in Gusiiland and were relied on mainly in local dispute resolution.

Sengeta village, the location of the study site, is located in Nyamira District, Nyanza Province. The village is about one and a half kilometres square and the village headman estimated the population at about 1250 people living in about 210 households[11]. The village boundaries include a valley on the east and another on the south, a rocky outcrop on the southwest and about halfway down the hill to the west and north of the main village hill. The main village track divides the village into two almost equal halves with the village shops (business centre) at the centre lined along both sides of the village track. Sengeta has a primary school as well as Catholic and Adventist churches, all shared with other surrounding villages. Therefore, everyday life is not bound up in the village; it flows in and out of it to neighbouring villages to deliver green tea leaf to the buying centre, for a drink, to the dispensary, to the market and in other ways. Fieldwork for this book also flowed in and out of the village following people as they related and interacted with others in neighbouring villages, for a variety of reasons and in different ways.

---

[11] In October 2005 the village headman had a list of 210 households known by the names of the men who had commenced them through marriage. Some of the households had with time been left with widowers or widows or sons.

Sengeta Village in a Wider Context

As indicated earlier most of rural Kenya is divided up into villages. However patterns of village life in Kenya are not homogenous. They are shaped by many factors, such as climatic conditions, culture, main economic activities and even distance and influence from major urban centres. Not many of Sengeta's particularities can thus be generalised for the country.

Sengeta Village, as a part of Gusiiland, largely reflects the conditions of rural life in the two counties occupied by the Abagusii people, namely; Nyamira, and Kisii. The culture and way of life of the people across the three districts of Gusiiland are similar in many respects. The kinship relations, the types of food consumed and the major struggles to earn a living all show similarities. However, there are differences especially regarding the main cash crops. Sugar cane dominates in the deep south-west of Gusiiland, there is more coffee in the western sides and more tea on the central highlands and eastern part. Maize, beans, bananas and cattle are widely found throughout Gusiiland. Sengeta Village is representative of rural life in Nyamira District, except for the former white settler areas on the eastern margins of the district where land sizes per family are slightly bigger. The villagers rear cattle, goats, sheep and poultry mainly chicken. They mainly grow tea, maize, finger millet, beans and an assortment of vegetables. Passion fruit, coffee and tobacco are also grown to a limited extent. Other activities in the village include operating tea and grocery kiosks, trade in vegetables, fish, tobacco, baskets, mats and other goods in demand locally. There are some people in the village with formal employment as clerks in government, teachers and other civil service or private sector positions. Others are cattle traders, brick makers, local brew producers and sellers, thatchers and crafts makers.

In general, life in Sengeta village is quite typical of that in Gusii villages in terms of social relationships, general climatic conditions and the main struggles to make a living. This is particularly true of Nyamira District, at whose heart lies Sengeta village and the tea-dairy belt that dominates the district. The particulars of Sengeta village are a good reflection of Gusiiland in general and Nyamira district in particular. This generalisation must however take into account area specific activities around major crops: coffee, tea and sugar cane, as well as people's idiosyncratic ways of making a living. Overall, as O'Loughlin (2011:82) argues with regard to different context of community; people in a community setting such as a village are not a collection of like-minded people. They present multiple and complex trajectories in many aspects of their lives.

Outline of the Book

This book takes the view that resources are dynamic and fluid. It argues that villagers create resources through redefinition in everyday practice and use them in various ways to make a living. The resource creation processes are anchored in social relationships that span local, regional and international borders. Arguments presented throughout the book aim at deepening our understanding about how rural villagers engage with their natural and socio-cultural environments to create and co-create resources and use them to make a living. In pursuing this understanding, the book first takes a general historical look at the study area of Nyamira District in the context of the Gusii Region where it is located; chapter 2 therefore presents an historical overview of the Nyamira landscape. The aim of the chapter is to bring out what people in the district have considered resources over time and how they have moulded them to make a living. This provides a setting for the book. It shows how, over time, cropping has dislodged herding as the main basis of livelihood, and that land for livestock and crop production has become increasingly scarce. However, such structural explanations of change leave the central question largely unanswered.

Consequently, a different approach is adopted to give more weight to villagers' agency and this implies a different theoretical choice. Hence, in chapter 3, the central question is subjected to the actor-oriented, livelihood and landscape perspectives to explain the processes of resource creation and use. Combining actor-oriented concepts such as agency, power and knowledge with the notion of livelihood and landscape as co-produced with the social actor as main player moves toward appreciating the idea of resource creation. The actor-oriented, livelihoods and landscape perspectives provide a partial account of resource creation processes. So it became necessary to shift the exploration to the field in order to fully capture, describe and explain the processes as they unfold. Chapter 4 describes and explains the research process and presents the key extended case studies (the corpus of data) that form the bases for answering the central question in the rest of the book.

In chapter 5, the central question is addressed using the case of tea farming, the dominant activity in Nyamira District, as the entry point. A detailed discussion of how tea farming entered the lifeworlds of villagers through migrant labour to the plantations beginning in the 1940s is provided. It also looks at how villagers have diversely moulded tea farming into livelihood opportunities and resources with varied outcomes. Against the backcloth of socio-cultural dispositions (part of lifestyle), villagers who mould tea and tea earnings into accumulation in land, cattle and children's education end up with viable livelihoods compared to those who mould it into entertainment and consumption, especially in local brew. The issue of villagers' efforts to re-work tea as a resource is however, more complex. Tea farmers face myriad problems in the handling of tealeaf beyond the farm and these constitute opportunities for resource creation and livelihood for other actors who may not be growing the crop or may only be growing a small amount. This complex and often invisible phenomenon is taken up in chapter 6, and presented in two simple folk concepts; *soko huru* and *mashabiki. Soko huru* is the alternative market for tealeaf and constitutes intermediaries taking advantage of conflict situations between the official tealeaf buyer (KTDA) and farmers, to buy tealeaf from farmers and resell it to multinational tea plantation factories in the neighbouring Greater Kericho. *Mashabiki* on the other hand, are KTDA tea buying centre clerk handlers. Some of them grow some tea and others are 'ghost farmers'. Both collude with and 'purchase tealeaf kilograms' from the clerk, who 'steals' them from *bona fide* farmers by cheating them on the weight of their tea leaf. It is concluded that the *soko huru* and *mashabiki* phenomena facilitate the re-creation of tea as a resource and a basis of livelihoods for different actors involved locally in the village and beyond.

Chapter 7 takes up the issue of the changing role of agriculture in resource creation and livelihood construction. Discussions in the chapter contribute to answering the central question by specifically tackling the questions of how and why people move in and out of agriculture over time, which resource creation processes ensue in the course of these movements and how livelihoods are constructed therein. It argues that some people leave farming from time to time for employment elsewhere, business or due to land disputes, and return to farming on retirement, retrenchment, the resolution of disputes or as lifestyles change to embrace farming. The process of deagrarianisation is thus cyclical and non-linear. Resource creation and livelihood construction depends on shifting lifestyles and gives rise to non-linear deagrarianisation. Besides moving in and out of agriculture over time, some villagers combine agriculture with other activities in order to make a living. Chapter 8 treats the issue of livelihood diversification, by identifying and discussing its various forms in Nyamira District. It shows that the various forms of diversification hinge on social ties and that some resource creation processes powerfully influence the landscape.

In the chapters so far outlined, villagers' efforts at creating resources through agriculture, occasionally without agriculture and through agriculture in combination with other activities in order to make a living are described and explained. Chapter 9 takes up the central question from another angle by explaining how villagers organise themselves in individual households or in league with others to protect their livelihoods and pursue the ever elusive social security. It argues that lifestyles and the social relationships they entail are crucial to the protection of livelihoods in Nyamira District. This is a common feature of the Sub-Saharan Africa, where formal social security arrangements are minimal or non-existent. The concepts of positive and negative linkages are deployed to demonstrate that emerging lifestyles (within which specific resource creation patterns exist) in livelihood protection, correspond to specific forms of livelihood strengths or weaknesses and are thus open to circulation of actors, depending on the success with which they create resources. Although implicit throughout the book, the notion of villagers' creation of resources is explicitly drawn out in chapter 10. This chapter looks back at some empirical instances of creativity in redefining and renaming resources in order to use them to make a living. It brings to the fore the interaction between policy and villagers' undertakings, which in some instances turn into conflicts. This chapter emphasises a central theme throughout the book, that social ties are the bedrock of household resource creation endeavours. It concludes that the creativity of villagers in producing and co-producing resources for their use in making a living is not without limits. It is circumscribed by 'nature' and other factors such as institutional arrangements. Finally, chapter 11 summarises the study findings and reflects briefly on their implications for theory and policy development.

CHAPTER 2

A Historical Overview of the Nyamira Landscape

Introduction

This chapter explores the evolution of the Gusii landscape in general and the Nyamira one in particular. It examines the changes that have occurred in the landscape and their implications for household resource creation and livelihood construction. In this way the central question, *how do villagers create resources and use them to make a living,* is placed in a historical context. The aim is to locate the debate on resources and livelihood within the landscape and to capture the historical struggles involved in making a living in Nyamira. The description of the landscape is also intended to provide a backcloth to the choices that actors make in their everyday practice, some of which are discussed later in this book.

Nyamira District is home to the Abagusii people. Their occupation of the Gusii Region was the result of protracted struggles with neighbours[12] as well as with colonialists[13] when they arrived to lay claim to the land. On arrival at their present settlements, the Abagusii must have encountered and displaced a significant hunter-gatherer population in the forests that covered the area between Kisii and Mau (Ogot, 2002: 23). Soper (1974) points out that some of Gusiiland may have been under some human settlement as early as the third century BC. Land is significant in Gusiiland as in many other African societies. 'Gusii', refers to the land that the Abagusii people occupy and the people on it, that is to the people in league with culture, 'nature' and space. Thus, when an

---

[12] The struggles of the Abagusii people to occupy their present land started much earlier. In the course of their early migration from Misri, probably to the Mt. Elgon area and Yimbo in Siaya they were often repulsed by intruders or neighbours (see Ochieng' 1974: 41-5).

[13] Establishment of colonial rule in Gusiiland was a fiercely contested and bloody affair. A key event in that bloody encounter, which was retold by adults during my fieldwork in 2004-5 was the attempt by a Gusii warrior called Otenyo to kill a colonial District Commissioner in the resistance of 1907. As Maxon (2002: 101) has indicated, the Abagusii were much slower than some of their Luo and Luhyia neighbours in accommodating the colonial system.

urban dweller in the diaspora such as Nairobi says that they are going to Gusii, they mean that they are going to their people, their land and their ancestors – *ase a'rorera*. In this sense, land is not just a physical and material resource, but home in the physical sense of dwellings or abode, and also more importantly in the spiritual sense in terms of final abodes of loved ones and ancestors in their graves, and the beginnings of life where the umbilical cord (*ororera*) and the first hair are actually or symbolically cut. In this perspective the land links life from cradle to grave and is a source of identity.

Landscape

Land in the Abagusii lifeworlds, considered from a landscape perspective, can be seen after Cohen and Odhiambo (1989: 9) as including "the possibilities and limitations of space: encompassing the physical land, the people on it, and the culture through which people work out the possibilities of the land. 'Landscape' means 'existence'". In the words of Cosgrove, (1984) landscape reveals how people see and remake the land. Landscape is always under creation and re-creation, because people live on it and by it. In other words, socio-cultural attributes are intertwined with the land, its use and even the identification and extraction of its potentials.

The notion of landscape and how it is claimed, constructed, defended and utilised over time is crucial in this book because it is concerned with how people create and use resources to earn a living. Earning a living is conceived broadly to include material and non-material domains and thus resonates with landscape both as a basis of identification, meaning and lifestyle, and as an arena for the playing-out of life or the pursuit of livelihoods. Groth's (1997) conceptualisation of landscape enhances this argument further. He posits that landscape denotes the interaction of people and place: a social group and its spaces, particularly the spaces to which the group belongs and from which its members derive some part of their shared identity and meaning. Landscape thus conceptualised, represents the arena for articulation of culture and aspirations, choice and limitation, knowledge, practice and strategic action. A landscape perspective of resources and livelihood therefore presents a fresh look at spatiality as contested and co-produced, but also more importantly as an indelible record of socially embedded action or of life generally. The notion of landscape is an appropriate point of departure as it captures villagers' perspectives of life as lived and their endeavours at co-production of resources through time and space. Such a perspective challenges the partial view presented by government statistics and reports since colonial times that focuses on some crops and livestock and ignore the multiple activities of villagers in everyday living.

Origins of Abagusii: Myths and Realities

Levine and Levine (1966) indicate that the people who occupy the western Kenya highlands 75 kilometres south of the equator, 60 kilometres north of Tanzania, and 45 kilometres east of Lake Victoria's Kavirondo Gulf call themselves Abagusii. They argue that the Abagusii identify a common ancestor called Mogusii, believed to be the founder of their society and from whom they take their name. Were and Nyamwaya (1986) point out that the Abagusii and other Bantu peoples such as the Kikuyu, Akamba and Bukusu with whom they are historically linked, originated from a place called 'Misiri'. While 'Misiri' is clearly an *Ekegusii* or *Kiswahili* name for Egypt, Were and Nyamwaya (1986) dispute that this 'Misiri' is the Biblical one i.e. Egypt and assert that the place referred to may be just North of Mt. Elgon in Eastern Africa. The actual origin of the Abagusii and other Bantu groups thus remains a contested myth.

Wherever they may have originated, their main dispersal area was around Mt. Elgon where they left the Bukusu and moved on to Yimbo in Siaya around 1560 AD (Were and Nyamwaya, 1986). Probably with the arrival of the more populous Luo, Abagusii left Yimbo and settled in Kisumu to escape cattle raids by their new neighbours. They stayed in Kisumu for about two generations (Were and Nyamwaya, 1986: 14) and Mogusii and his mother Nyakomogendi died there. That, coupled with famine in Kisumu, forced them to move eastward to the Kano plains under the leadership of clan leaders such as Mobasi, Oibabe, Mochorwa and Mogusero. Were and Nyamwaya (1986) put the migration from Kisumu to the Kano plains at around 1650 AD. Interestingly, the Abagusero clan, which had emerged around the time of migration to Kano, is a dominant clan in Sengeta in Nyamira District.

Even as the clan leaders emerged in Kisumu to lead their people to Kano, real leadership remained with family heads (Were and Nyamwaya, 1986: 15). In other words, then as now, centralised leadership of entire clans or indeed the entire ethnic group did not materialise (cf. Orvis, 1989: 117). The totems that now distinguish Gusii clans evolved in Kano with Abagirango taking *engo* (leopard); Ababasi, *enchage* (zebra); Abasweta including Abagetutu, Abanyaribari and Abamachoge, *engoge* (baboon); and Abanchari, *engubo* (hippo). Besides their spiritual significance, the totems were the bases of exogamous marriage among the Gusii clans. At Kano the Gusii mixed economy begun to evolve with *obori* or *wimbi*, eleusine, becoming their major crop (Were and Nyamwaya, 1986). The Abagusii have thus historically practiced herding and cultivation (cf. Glickman, 1974).

Were and Nyamwaya (1986) argue that the Abagusii subsequently migrated to Kipkelion (Lumbwa) in the Kericho area mainly due to pressure from the Luo and the Nandi. They settled at Kabianga where their respective clan leaders led them: the Ababasi by Ogichoncho, the Abasweta by Manyanta, the Abanchari by Oisukia and the Abagirango by Tabichi. The Luo completely assimilated some other Abagusii who remained in Kano. At Kabianga, the

Abagusii encountered the greatest misfortunes of their migration including famine and disease that resulted in the deaths of livestock and humans. This is why the place is called 'Kabianga' meaning 'where things refused to survive'. In addition, while nature was uncooperative their neighbours especially the Masai and the Kipsigis increased the pressure on the Abagusii through cattle raids and war.

Although they stood their ground against the Masai and Kipsigis for a time, they later moved on through Sotik, Gelegele and Ikorongo to the Trans Mara – Migori area and settled at a place called Nyangarora (Were and Nyamwaya, 1986). With more pressure from the southern Masai, some of the Abagusii moved further north towards Kisumu, settling at Nyakoe, Manga and Isecha, which became the nodal points of their present settlements. They are believed to have left behind some members of sub-clans such as Sweta, Nchari, Basi and Girango in the Trans Mara – Migori areas, and these people now form the Abakuria of present-day Kuria District in Southern Nyanza. From the three original settlements of Nyakoe, Manga and Isecha, different clans eventually dispersed to settle in various points in the highlands that have now become their home. Gusii occupation of the highlands was slow with pioneers leading their clans or sub-clans to occupy the land, ridge by ridge, due to intra-Gusii and inter-tribal hostilities that characterised the settlement process (Maxon, 1989; cf. Levine and Levine, 1966: 4).

Oral history accounts gathered from Sengeta indicate that on arrival in the Manga areas, the Abagusii grazed their cattle further afield during the day but retreated to below Manga Ridge for the nights mainly for the security of their livestock. Although they grew *obori*, at the time of their arrival and until the arrival of colonialists around 1905, the Abagusii were *de facto* pastoralists, patrilineal and organised around extended families and clans, without any centralised form of governance (cf. Mayer, 1965; Garst, 1974; Orvis, 1997). Levine and Levine (1966: 9-10) point out that economic aggrandisement was primarily in terms of the acquisition of large herds of cattle through breeding and raids on neighbouring clans or on other tribes. Land was abundant, homesteads were widely dispersed across the hillsides; and people undertook cultivation to supply *obori* necessary for daily living. The availability of land and the vaguely defined property regimes allowed lineage groups to move around considerably on the Gusii landscape rather than remaining fixed on a particular piece of land (cf. Levine and Levine, 1966).

Religion and Labour Organisation

In terms of religion, Abagusii believed in a supreme entity, *Engoro*, who guided and assisted them especially in their migrations, saving them from their enemies and calamities (cf. Were and Nyamwaya, 1986). *Engoro* was the original progenitor and source of prosperity and life who sent rain or drought, plenty or famine, health or disease, peace or war. In this sense, *Engoro* was all-powerful and ever present everywhere, but they also attributed to him purity, impartiality, love and generosity. The people believed that the ever-present and mysterious sun, mediated between the people and *Engoro.* When a child was born, they beseeched the sun to take care of it saying *rioba nderere,* and directed prayers to *Engoro* through the sun (cf. Were and Nyamwaya, 1986).

Another aspect of Abagusii religion related to supernatural spirits, regarded as immortal beings that were always in touch with the living. They were agents of *Engoro* who acted on behalf of the Supreme Being. There were also *ababania* (prophets), *abanyibi* (rainmakers), *abanyamesira* (medicine men) and *abaragori* (diviners) who mediated in less subtle ways with *Engoro* (cf. Were and Nyamwaya, 1986). The notion of ancestoral spirits has remained strong in Gusii discourse to the present day. During fieldwork, it was observed that whenever people were drinking local beer they started by deliberately pouring a portion on the floor and pronouncing, *chisokoro tonywesia, nainwe nyora,* meaning they sought the blessings of their ancestors. Whenever beer poured accidentally, they happily said *ay'echisokoro*, meaning that was meant for the ancestors.

Abagusii carefully intertwined their religion with their livelihoods. Gusii religion easily accommodated the acquisition of wealth arguing that that an individual's animals and crops increased because *Engoro* willed it (Were and Nyamwaya, 1986). Thus a rich person, essentially a person with many heads of good cattle and goats, usually sacrificed many animals to please *Engoro* and thank him for the riches. Abagusii also enjoined their religion with labour organisation such as *egesangio* and *risaga* (cf. Philip Mayer, 1951). They offered sacrifices before land preparation, planting and harvesting. Labour cooperation was viewed as part of true religion and thus a person's wealth was shared with relatives and friends, who may as well have been part of the production process in *egesangio* and *ekerisio* (cf. Levine and Levine, 1966). Locally produced beer was central to organising labour as patriarchs whose wives or sons participated in work parties had a right to the beer and thus encouraged such labour organisation (Philip Mayer, 1951). Mayer adds that in general a beneficiary of a work party tried to give more and better beer, in order to attract labour, *abanyaisaga*. As part of good religion, fair play was expected between fellow Abagusii, but stealing from other ethnic groups was considered a legitimate way of acquiring wealth (Were and Nyamwaya, 1986). While this type of religion does not capture the inter-clan or even inter-household feuds and thefts in pre-colonial times, it appears to be the genesis of theft and general insecurity in contemporary Gusii society. Individualism has apparently created 'the other' closer to home and provided for internal (intra-Gusii) sites for theft to earn a living.

A major continuity in terms of religion in contemporary times is the notion of a single entity of God, which fits well with Christianity. The idea of *Engoro* residing in or radiating from the direction of the sun also ties in very well with the concept of Christianity's heavenly (skyward) God. Many Abagusii people embraced Christianity when it arrived at the beginning of the twentieth century, although not without contextualising it within their traditions such as retention of some of the rites of passage such as circumcision of boys and girls alongside conversion. Bride price has also persisted through the ages in spite of Christian churches preaching against it. Although Christian churches have preached against believing in ancestral spirit powers and witchcraft, it has only managed to drive those aspects of the religion underground and has not extinguished them. Jealousy and witchcraft dominate village discourse on failure and success in life in Sengeta, albeit in guarded tones due to the dominance of Christianity. Silberschmidt (2001) reported that in Kisii District most people said they were Christians (60 per cent Catholic and 40 per cent Protestants mainly Seventh Day Adventists) suggesting that Christianity has been embraced in place of pre-colonial religions. Labour organisation has also changed over time and, just like religion, it remains a mixture of the past and the present. Changes in labour organisation occurred alongside those in religion, for example Adventist Christians who abjured beer tended to withdraw from beer-based *risaga* and organise around 'sweet gruel' (cf. Philip Mayer, 1951).

This discussion on the Abagusii origins, religion and labour organisation brings out the people's life experiences and views about living in the way that they preferred. Their political organisation reflects a lack of centralised authority, and is characterised by inter-clan conflicts and cooperation. As shown in chapter one, marriage is a major avenue for collaboration and gift exchange between families in otherwise often feuding clans. Therefore, amidst inter-clan tensions social ties were organised in terms of labour sharing in *ekerisio* and *risaga,* through marriage and local brew. These are the socially embedded and pluriactivity based livelihoods of the Abagusii that the colonial and post-colonial state has reduced to partial agricultural reports laden with discourses about poverty. Over time, the state has created centralised authority and administrative units, new ways of doing things and viewing life that provides only a narrow picture of rural realities. This process of imposing a narrow view has been ongoing since colonisation.

Colonisation

The onset of colonialism in the Gusii country occurred by default rather than by design. Maxon (nd) has shown that the transfer of Uganda's Eastern Province, of which Gusiiland was a part, to the East Africa Protectorate (which eventually became Kenya) in 1902 did not result in any immediate steps by the British to bring the Abagusii under effective control. Gusii's neighbours, the Kipsigis to the East andthe Luo to the West were effectively colonized when administrative stations were established in those areas in 1902 and 1903 respectively. However, Maxon (nd) also argues that the British were able to make contact with the Abagusii from these two stations. The first attempt to enter Gusiiland and make contacts with the people met with varying responses.

H.B. Partington, the officer in charge of Kericho, visited North Mogirango in late 1904. The local people received him in a friendly manner owing to the fact that the wealthiest person from the area Mr. Ndubi had visited Kericho a number of times already (Maxon, nd). Compared to that, when another Officer F.W. Isaac attempted to enter Kitutu in early 1905 it was impossible due to the people's attitude. The Imperial British East African Company (IBEAC), which the British Government had appointed to take care of her interests in East Africa had no contact with the Abagusii; having concentrated their work in Buganda (Maxon, 2002).

In general, the Gusii response to the arrival of the colonialists was not unified mainly because the Abagusii did not have a centralised government. But attracted by reports of inter-clan hostilities involving the Kitutu, Mogusero and Bonchari, the British military arrived to punish them in September 1905 (Maxon, nd). The People of Bonchari and Kitutu fiercely resisted the British expedition, losing sixty-seven and sixty of their warriors respectively, with no death on the British side due to their superior weaponry. On October 5, 1905, there was a cease-fire agreement with the dominant Kitutu clan and the patrol ended, but it was not until May 1907 that the colonial state constructed an administrative station at Getembe, now Kisii town (Maxon, nd). With this, colonial rule had effectively descended on the Gusii country. Northcote, who remained in Kisii as Assistant District Commissioner, directed the construction of the administrative station (Maxon, 1989). He remained in-charge of the Gusii country appointing influential individuals as chiefs[14] of the various Abagusii groups and headmen for the various clans who would act as agents of the colonial state in the Gusii country (Maxon, 1989). The chiefs and headmen appointed were to collect hut tax for the government. Maxon has argued that the first chiefs that Northcote appointed were men of considerable wealth and influence (cf. Glickman, 1974). The colonial power and economy thus entered the lifeworlds of the people diversely but also apparently based on their social standing at the time.

Even as Northcote laid ground for effective control of the Gusii people and country by the British, the Abagusii had not forgotten the punishment inflicted on them by the British raid of 1904, they kept a 'memory of resistance' arising from the previous British military operation (cf. Lonsdale, 1967). A local influential woman, also a prophetess, called Moraa hated the alien invasion of the Gusii country (Maxon, 1989). On January 12, 1908, she agitated for the

[14] Appointment of chiefs and headmen as well as the commencement of construction of the administrative station did not mean that the Abagusii fully accepted colonial rule. There were open revolts against the British especially from the Kitutu who were closest to the station partly because of their pride as the largest sub-tribe (see Ochieng', 1974) and also to safeguard their land. This way the Abagusii were the last Bantustan to be subjugated (see Maxon, R. KNA RW 967.629 Max. The Gusii and the British 1907 – 1963.)

intervention of young people to recover cattle that Northcote had forcibly taken away and in response, one warrior ambushed Northcote and speared him in the back, sparking off open armed resistance especially in Kitutu areas (Maxon, 1989). In the resistance two police officers, a trader and two porters were killed and several cattle raids organised against the Luo areas. In retaliation, an expedition was organised by the colonial government to punish the Abagusii. In the ensuing punishment cattle were captured, huts and granaries burnt and people killed (Maxon, 1989). The colonial state destroyed resources and livelihoods to weaken the people. Therefore, in both British and Gusii thought, the homesteads represented home, identity and meaning. The homestead was not just a piece of land with some huts and other structures on it, but rather a cultural artefact laid out according to rules, some of them subtle but well understood and applied. Each aspect of the land had meaning and was put to use in ways that expressed the people's identity.

Gusii resistance to colonial rule did produce one positive effect in that it dissuaded the planned white settlement of their land and meant that the Abagusii kept their ancestral lands (Maxon, 1976; 1989). This is mainly because after the peace agreement between the Abagusii and the British on February 12, 1908, the latter did not pursue the fertile Gusii land for white settler farming (Maxon, 1989). The Abagusii also defended their autonomy on September 12, 1914 when following a clash between the British forces and German invaders both groups retreated and the Abagusii moved into town and destroyed property in the colonial post (cf. Maxon, 1976: 77-78). During the rest of the colonial period the British remained brutal to the Abagusii, without demeaning them by taking over their land. February 12, 1908 then is the day when the respect for the land of the Abagusii was achieved. In more than one respect the Abagusii secured their land rights and thenceforth the British never violated those rights. In this sense, the Abagusii had permanently shattered a major colonial vision and have a legitimate reason to mark February 12, as the day their fallen heros and heroines stamped their authority and control over their fatherland. It is on this achievement of stopping Great Britain's ambition dead on the tracks that modern Gusii pride and independent streak for ever rests.

While the road to establishing British administration had been bumpy and met with much resistance from the Abagusii, in terms of economic development progress was encouraging (cf. Ochieng', 1974: 242). Maxon (1989) has shown that by 1914, a covered market had been put up in Kisii town and roads constructed to the ports of Homa Bay and Kendu Bay. Chiefs constructed and maintained many bridle paths to link the various locations of the Gusii country. These facilitated trade in the highlands and especially the movement of produce to the large market at Kisii. Several markets[15] had been

[15] The British established market centres with 12 shops each together with an open air market space. In the study area of Sengeta Village, Nyamira District villagers said

founded, economic crops encouraged and the cash economy introduced. As colonisation gained momentum, the poll and hut taxes were imposed mainly to force men to leave for the White Highlands to work and raise money with which to pay the taxes (cf. Maxon, 1992: 65-8). This process was recounted by respondents during fieldwork in Sengeta Village in 2004/5. The migration to the White Highlands, coupled with the recruitment of some Abagusii men into British military service for the two world wars denied many households both men's traditional leadership and their labour. Some migrant labourers who went to work in the White Highlands especially in the tea estates brought back home with them a knowledge and interest in tea growing and were some of the first to take up tea growing in the villages (Field Discussions, 2004/5). After the establishement of Kisii as a business centre and its security guaranteed, labour agents for the tea estates in Kericho came to the town and started recruiting labour for the tea industry (cf. Silberschmidt, 1999). This opened up opportunities for local people to go out and work to earn *chirobia* (money) that was now necessary for life (Field Discussions, 2004/5). With the establishment of Kisii town as a major business centre and other markets, the Abagusii started to produce surplus food such as sweet potatoes, bananas and vegetables, which mainly the Asians in the town bought (cf. Maxon, 1989).

The colonial administration generally encouraged the Gusii people to produce for the market and distributed seeds of new crops such as maize, sim-sim, groundnuts and wheat and by 1913; posted an Agricultural Instructor to Kisii (Maxon, 1989). The instructor was instrumental in the introduction of ox-drawn ploughs and oxen training. As a result, of these innovations, the acreage under crops grew rapidly during the colonial period. Africans were first allowed to plant coffee in 1933 and by 1951 there were 370 acres (150 hectares) in the region under coffee and this increased considerably to 21,165 acres (8569 hectares[16]) at the end of 1956[17] (see Heyer and Waweru, 1976: 193). The state also allowed the production of tea on a limited scale in one area of the Kisii Division that was too high for growing coffee; hence, a trial plot was planted at Kebirigo[18]. There were differences in the ways in which different peoples accepted and adapted to these changes. The Luo for example generally "remained unwilling to modify their traditional land tenure which made enclosure by some of the more progressive minded individuals

---

Manga market was established earliest around 1915 and Tombe which is nearer to Sengeta was established in 1935, but picked up business after 1945, when local people had more income to spend.

[16] This area under coffee included some in the Luo and Kuria areas in South Nyanza (present-day Migori, Suba, Rachuonyo, Kuria and Homa Bay Districts) which formed the greater South Nyanza District up to 1961 when the Gusii people were left with their own Kisii District (see KNA - Kisii District Annual Report 1961)

[17] See KNA, South Nyanza District Annual Report for 1956

[18] KNA, South Nyanza District Annual Report for 1956, Page, 17.

exceedingly difficult"[19]. While their Luo neighbours appear to have been cautious with innovations and considered them at group level, the Abagusii seem to have embraced innovations, and especially cash crops, in a more individualistic and competitive way.

Colonisation led to several innovations which changed the landscape in significant ways. The introduction of tea, coffee, pyrethrum, dairy cattle and hybrid maize changed not only the physical space but also interpersonal relationships. By the end of colonisation an economy that was previously livestock-based had largely become agricultural and the cash economy had become significantly entrenched. People started mobilising resources to try to gain a lasting foothold on the cash economy. Leonard (1991) provides an account on how a colonial chief in Gusiiland mobilised societal resources through the Native Council to send his son to Britain to study, ostensibly to come back and serve the Abagusii. When the chief's son returned he got a posting that he did not like and quit the public service for the private sector against his father's will. In response, the chief mobilised local leaders, went with them to Nairobi and pressured the colonial government to re-hire his son and post him to a place of his liking, an endeavour in which surprisingly he was successful. This account demonstrates that colonisation placed demands on individuals that set them off on a perpetual pendulum swinging from individualism to altruism and back.

The downside of embracing the innovations soon became apparent. In 1961, it was reported, "the enormous increases in pyrethrum planting in higher Kisii (Gusiiland) led to a reduction in the maize acreages and either because of this or because people sold too much maize, it was necessary for the Nyanza Province Marketing Board to sell back about 5,000 bags of maize in the second quarter of the year"[20]. Thus, the idea of balancing food and cash crop production was already an issue even while world market prices for pyrethrum were good. When the world pyrethrum market collapsed in the beginning of the 1980s, the Abagusii protested by uprooting the crop (Field Discussions, 2004/5).

Physical Features

Gusiiland is mostly hilly with several ridges, mostly in the eastern parts, which generally rise to over 1,800 metres above sea level. It includes the Kisii highlands that lie between 2,000 and 2,350 metres (Were and Nyamwaya, 1986: 3). These hills are undulating and there is much local discourse on population pressure on the highlands. Local people argue: *onye Gusii n'ebirubo yare anga ase tari tokomenya, ebitunwa n'ebigoro nabio orogongo* – that if their country was made up of plains rather than rolling hills, land would have

[19] KNA, South Nyanza District Annual Report for 1956, Page, 35.

[20] See KNA Kisii District Annual Report, 1961 P. 18.

become scarce much earlier (Field Discussions, 2004/5). Maxon (1989) argued that Gusiiland is an area of high agricultural potential with good soils, and adequate and well distributed rainfall. The vegetation of the Gusii Highlands is woodland-Savannah, characterised by low trees and high grasses, although there were less trees at the time of colonisation and the vegetation at the time was predominantly highland grass.

The geological base of Gusiiland consists of Bukoban, Granitic, Nyanzian and Kavirondian rocks with Bukoban as the dominant type (Were and Nyamwaya, 1986). Villagers dig out some rocks for construction. Murram is also extracted in some parts of the district for road construction. Stones and murram are harvested from private land and the owners of the land are paid for the products. Some villagers increase the value of the rocks by crushing them by hand to make ballast and sell them at higher prices than solid rocks. In general the villagers struggle to get the best from their physical environment in order to make a living (Field Discussions, 2004/5).

Several permanent rivers and streams run through the area and drain into Lake Victoria, the main ones being the *Gucha* (Kuja), *Risonto* (Sondu) and *Omogonga* (Mogonga) (Were and Nyamwaya 1986). There are many valley bottoms and depressions, most of which are marshy. The marshy areas have been key sources of clay soils that widely used for plastering house walls and floors. Clay soil was harvested from the valley bottoms and plains for free by everybody who needed it until the end of the 1980s[21]. Since the beginning of the 1990s, most valley bottoms and plains (*amaranya n'ebirubo*) have fallen into private hands, and since then (or earlier in some parts of Gusiiland) clay has become a saleable commodity. Those who control the land on which it is found sell it to merchants who transport it on their heads or on donkeys' backs to whoever can buy it. Many water points for livestock and for domestic use are also located in the valleys and depressions. These water points have been for common use since time immemorial, hence the Gusii people's rationalisation: '*amache nonya n'enyang'au ekonyua anyakorinwa monto* – water is free for all' (Field Discussions, 2004/5).

Water courses, whether rivers or streams have also been the bases for land claims. In the past people[22] owned strips of land[23] stretching from the hilltops

[21] In Sengeta the study village, it was reported that people had generally started claiming private control of river valleys and plains in the late 1980s and the process was largely complete by the beginning of the 1990s. There were no CPRs in the village except drinking water points. Clay soil was routinely purchased from land owners, although villagers argued that the colonial government had set aside *ebirubo, amaranya n'ebigoro* (plains, valley bottoms and hilltops) for common use but that successive independence governments had watched helplessly as these CPRs fell into private hands.

[22] By people we mean family heads of the 1930s and 1940s and earlier who had shared the abundant land according to tradition enabling everyone to own land running from

to river valleys and traditionally did not claim ownership of land across the water course. Other people also owned land from that point to the top of the hill on their side, but always shared the water across valleys and hills. At the homestead water was also a basis of claims over land. Co-wives or brothers claim and share ancestral land in ways that ensure that rainwater from the roofs does not fall onto each other's land. Co-wives lay claims more bluntly and forcefully as they pose: *'baba noire baka isiara mache riane'* ('you dare claim my backyard?')

Grass for thatching houses has traditionally been sourced from *ebigoro* (specific hilltops with the appropriate grass called *ekenyoru*) or *chitente* (marshy points with a broad grass called *esasati*). *Ekenyoru* has historically been used by the better off in society to thatch their houses as it is longer lasting but more time-consuming to harvest and thatch as it is very fine. Its use has always been expensive, requiring more people for longer and implying the need to brew more beer for the *risaga* (work party). This has largely restricted its use to the well to do who could mobilise sufficient resources –ingredients, whether bought or in the form of *obori* in a grainhouse, – and women's labour to brew enough beer (cf. Mayer, 1951). Also because *ekenyoru* is a fine grass, the thatching process takes many more days and requires more compensation, whether in food and beer (as in the past) or in cash.. *Ebigoro* (grassy hilltops) have also fallen firmly into private control since the beginning of the 1970s[24] and *ekenyoru* has become a commodity for sale and its price has risen year after year.

Esasati has historically been easier to harvest from the marshy areas using tiny traditional machetes and is also easier to use in thatching as it is broader and requires less time to complete the work. As such the poor could more readily access and use *esasati*. However, the marshy areas have also fallen into private hands, and *esasati* has also become commoditised, albeit at lower prices because of its association with poverty. It is common to hear villagers referring indirectly to the poor by the nature of the thatch on their houses as '*abamenyete chinyomba chiesasati' i.e.* the poor live in *esasati* thatched houses.

---

the hills to the river valleys.

[23] According to fieldwork discussions (2004/5), up to the early 1970s family strips of land stretched from the hilltops to the river valleys. However, since then land has been shared out between the generations and families now barely own an acre each, whether on ahill, in a valley or in between.

[24] Information from a respondent who has been thatching houses since the late 1950s, saying that at least up to 1968, as far as he could remember *ekenyoru* was free as all people avoided grazing their cattle on it. All that was required was labour to harvest and deliver it to the construction site.

Eucalyptus

In the days prior to the 1990s, the marshy areas were difficult to use for agricultural or any other economic purposes (cf. Were and Nyamwaya, 1986: 3). However, since then, they have become sites of fruitful livelihoods. Brick-making kilns are part of the landscape and many of the marshy areas have been drained for horticultural production, pasture and even tea growing (cf. Mironga, 2005). During fieldwork in 2004/5 elders indicated that apart from pressure on land sharpening the people's skills for land reclamation, the *Eucalyptus* tree plays a central role in the drainage of marshy areas. They said that before the tree had been planted along the water courses, plains and marshy areas, floods were common and one could see the flow of River *Gucha* for kilometres. However, since the *eucalyptus* trees have started to take over water courses, water flows in the streams and rivers have significantly reduced and the courses rarely overflow their banks. The elders cited a number of water falls in the village and beyond that were noisy with large amounts of water in the past, which had "gone quiet due to the *eucalyptus* trees".

The *eucalyptus* has put pressure not only on the river valleys and plains, but also on the hilltops where people are growing them as a way of laying claim to the land on the hills in the process displacing the *ekenyoru* that is used for thatching houses. However, in both the hills and the river valleys *eucalyptus* has become a key source of energy in the brick making kilns that dot the landscape and in the tea factories which process the tea that dominates the Gusii terrain. In 2000 a local factory opened up, purchasing fuel wood from villagers to reduce electricity costs, and since then new livelihood avenues have been devised and organised around the *eucalyptus*. Chain saws have been purchased and local people trained to use them, trucks are used to transport wood to the factory, labour hired to cut and split the wood and ferry it from the valleys and hills to the roadsides for transportation to the factory. Brick-making is also dependent on the *eucalyptus* tree and has also given rise to many livelihood opportunities that include cutting the trees, preparing the soil for brick-making, building the kilns, firing the bricks and transporting the finished bricks.

Population

Given the hilly terrain and because of the rapid growth in the population, cultivation on steep slopes is necessary and soil erosion has become an increasing problem (Were and Nyamwaya, 1986; cf. Garst, 1974). In 1979, the district which covers about 844 square kilometres had 300,956 people and that population rose to 498,102 in 1999 (Kenya, 1999a - National Population Census). By 2002 the district had a total population of 535,288 and an average population density of 609 people per square kilometre (Kenya, District Dev. Plan, 2002 – 2008). The district has no major urban centres or industries to absorb the high population growth. Agriculture or working the land is the key avenue to livelihoods in the district as it is in Gusiiland, and soil erosion is becoming a pressing problem. The problem has been handled differently at different times of Gusii history. At the onset of colonialism the colonial government initiated livestock culling as it had noticed that livestock numbers exceeded carrying capacity (cf. Hall, 1936). In the 1970s and 1980s when cultivation was pushed into hills due to population pressure, the government responded with nationwide community-based soil conservation efforts (cf. Kenya, National Dev. Plans, 1979 - 1983; 1984 - 1988 & 1989 - 1993). Population pressure and the reluctance of the Abagusii to migrate demand that agricultural production be expanded and intensified to provide adequate employment (Garst, 1974). In Nyamira land sizes per household declined to an average 0.45 hectare by 2002 (Kenya, 2002 – Nyamira Dist. Dev. Plan, 2002 – 8). However, the tendency to stay home and not migrate may have changed over time and the Abagusii are now more involved in businesses and employment in major towns across the country (cf. Hakansson, 1994).

Population pressure on the land is handled in a variety of ways in the village and in the wider Nyamira District. Those villagers who are well off due to embracing employment or cash cropping in the late 1960s and early 1970s and who identified the problem of land scarcity bought land in the former 'White Highlands' in the eastern parts of the district now known as Borabu Division or in settlement schemes in other districts where land previously occupied by white settlers was sold to Africans soon after independence in 1963. People from Nyamira District are reported to have settled in Trans-Nzoia, Uasin Gishu, Nakuru, Trans-Mara and Narok. As the pressure on the land continued other villagers have migrated from mainly to the Molo areas of Nakuru District, Borabu Division of Nyamira District, Uasin Gishu District and Trans-Nzoia District and bought land from the first post-independence settlers in the various settlement schemes. These areas together with major urban areas where Abagusii people have migrated to for work, business and education such as Nairobi, Mombasa, Kisumu, Eldoret, Nakuru, Migori and Homa-Bay constitute their major diaspora. Today, villagers also report links with their sons and daughters in the diaspora in America and Europe.

The efforts made in the 1960s and 70s to purchase land in the emerging settlement schemes eased population pressure in the district for a while. However, population growth coupled with economic difficulties put pressure on the land and is reflected in high unemployment (cf. Silberschmidt, 2001). Figure 2.1 shows the projected population growth in the district up to 2010.

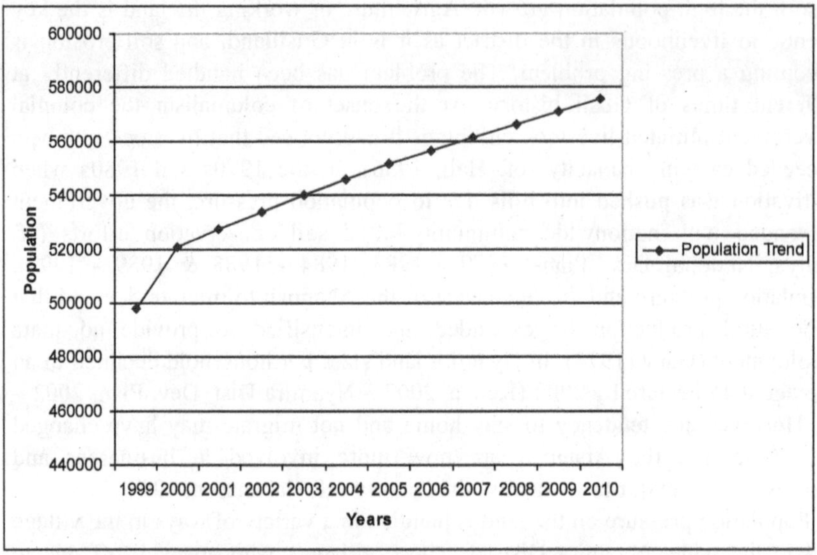

Figure 2.1 Population Projections for Nyamira District, 1999 - 2010
Source: Central Bureau of Statistics (CBS), Kenya

The projected growth of the population in the district up to 2010, unless accompanied by extra-ordinary and equitable development is likely to be a major test for local social organisation. During the time of fieldwork, it was evident that crime rates were high and soaring and these are likely to increase in the future unless local initiatives to improve opportunities are supported and encouraged by the central government.

Education, Communication and Employment

According to official reports (Kenya 2002 - Nyamira District Development Plan, 2002 – 8) primary school enrolment is 93 percent for boys and 92 percent for girls while secondary school enrolment stands at 46 and 42 percent for boys and girls respectively. The adult literacy rate is about 70 per cent for females and 81 per cent for males. There are 53 trading centres in the district which are crucial for leisure and information exchange activities. These trading centres are very important for information exchange because it is business people (mainly local restaurant owners) who have radios and occasionally televisions for their customers to access news and information. The decline of agriculture as a source of livelihood due to land scarcity has forced many parents to invest heavily in their children's education, hoping that they will obtain salaried work and support them later in life (Hakansson, 1994). In Nyamira District only 30.7 percent of the households own a radio set. Of the 107,000 households in the district only 388 or 0.3 per cent have telephone connections; while the mobile phone service coverage is just 0.2 per cent (see Kenya, District Dev. Plan, 2002). During fieldwork it was noticeable that youth unemployment was a worrying problem. Many trained school teachers and university graduates in various disciplines were without jobs. Silberschmidt (2001) sums up the situation in Gusii as follows; 'population density, land pressure, unemployment, criminality, violence and alcohol abuse mainly by men are among the highest in the country'. Levine (1980) also claims that crime and violence especially against women in Gusii is the highest in British Sub-Saharan Africa. The extent to which criminality and violence may emanate from conflict over resources or struggles to make a living in difficult circumstances has been a thread in research on the Abagusii.

Trade

In pre-colonial Gusii society, most trade was conducted internally within the ethnic group. Because of hostilities with neighbouring peoples on the frontiers, trade with other ethnic groups was limited. It was almost non-existent with the Masai and Kipsigis (Were and Nyamwaya, 1986) but there was some trade with the Luo. Ochieng' (1974) argues that trade between the Luo and the Abagusii continued during peace and war[25] times, as it was mainly carried out by women and children from both sides, who were usually not harmed even during hostilities[26]. The trade involved cattle, goats, pottery, baskets, salt for livestock and mats from the Luo side and *obori*, iron products, soap stone dust, carvings and vessels from the Gusii side (cf. Levine and Levine, 1966; Ochieng', 1974). During the fieldwork it emerged that the Luo remained the most visible import/export trading partners of the Abagusii. They still deliver lick-salt, sisal ropes and baskets on donkey back to the Gusii villages, exchanging them for grain or selling them for cash. Villagers from Sengeta travel to Daraja Mbili Market in Kisii, and Oyugis and Nyamiobo Markets on the border with Luoland where they sell green vegetables like kale, *obori*, bananas and tobacco to Luo traders and consumers. In return they buy baskets, mats, pottery and fish.

---

[25] It should be noted that in general there were no wars between the Luo and the Abagusii, only skirmishes involving intermittent cattle raids perhaps (see Levine and Levine, 1966, page 3, for example). The real wars were with the Kipsigis, the Masai and the Kuria and are clearly and unequivocally indicated in oral history and Gusii initiation songs that prepared warriors for the wars with identifiable enemies, which do not include the Luo.

[26] Traditional conventions on both sides may have prohibited the harassment or killing of women and children from the enemy side during war or peace time. The traditions were internal to each group and were not the result of any negotiations, nor were they exclusively aimed at the interaction between the two ethnic groups.

Apart from *obori* production and livestock keeping, key industries in Gusiiland during the pre-colonial period were iron smelting and soap stone carving. The Luo were at that time the key consumers of iron products including hoes, axes, spears, razors, arrows, *ebitinge* (leg rings), *emeotoro* (arm rings) and earrings as well as soap stone vessels (cf. Ochieng', 1974). Iron working which had commenced around the sixteenth century, (Ochieng', 1974: 213) declined and collapsed on colonisation and the arrival of Asian traders who sold their iron products cheaply, pushing Gusii producers out of business. The soapstone industry on the other hand survived colonisation and globalisation and remains the key field of Gusii creativity and agility in the local and global markets. The variety of carvings such as chess boards and pieces are sold both locally and internationally, especially to tourists who visit Kenya. While the soapstone works have been located in South Mogirango since pre-colonial times the products are sold in almost every major town in Kenya.

Craft Making and Sales

Other specialised skills which the Abagusii people have passed on from generation to generation include a wide range of craftsmanship specialised in thatching houses, *abasereti;* making chairs – *amarindi n'ebirogo;* granaries; musical instruments; traditional clothes out of animal skin; metal crafts, *abaturi;* pottery; mats; traditional house doors, *ebige;* bowls, *ebiee;* and baskets, *ebibari n'ebitonga* (cf. Were and Nyamwaya, 1986). During the pre-colonial period these crafts were the life-line of the Gusii as there were minimal import opportunities. During and after the colonial period some industries such as traditional cloth-making was quickly overrun with cheap imports, while mat-making and basket-making have survived into the twenty first century amidst stiff competition from synthetic products. Basket-making has survived largely by adapting to supplying local small scale tea farmers.

Agricultural and Livestock Development

As already indicated the Abagusii were mainly herders and had picked up *obori* growing on their way to their present settlements. Once they settled on the fertile highlands and new crops arrived with colonisation, the Abagusii turned more attention to cropping than herding (cf. Levine and Levine, 1966). They also took up exotic dairy cattle with a keen interest (Garst, 1972; 1974). In terms of cash crops coffee growing took hold in Nyamira District by 1935, while the 1950s saw not only the spread of pyrethrum, local maize and tea, but also of hybrid maize, peaking at about 100 percent adoption in some areas (Garst, 1972; Uchendu & Anthony, 1969).

After independence in 1963, the agricultural and livestock innovations that had commenced during the colonial period gained momentum alongside other infrastructural developments in the education, transport, health and telecommunications sectors. The area under coffee rose from 150 hectares in 1951 for the whole of South Nyanza District, to 6,785.5 hectares in Kisii District alone by 1974[27] and subsequently to its peak of 7,100 hectares in 1987-8. Coffee yields reached 24,906,247 Kgs in 1974 and a high of 37,574,167 Kgs in 1985, before declining to 30,441,735 Kgs and 27,521,353 Kgs in 1987 and 1988 respectively[28]. Coffee expansion in the Gusii Region was linked to the General Agreement on Tariffs and Trade (GATT) mechanism and the shifting International Coffee Agreements (ICA) contained therein. For instance, there was a ban on coffee planting during 1964 as a result of a new ICA (Freeman, 1985).

The recent decline in coffee production is the result of falling coffee prices on the world market since the 1980s, which discouraged farmers and sent them in the direction of other crops such as tea whose market was more stable. This is clearly reflected in the Nyamira District coffee statistics[29] which indicate that hectares under coffee increased slowly while output has fluctuated significantly as shown in table 2.1.

Table 2.1 Area under coffee and yields in the period 1988 – 1995 in Nyamira District

Year	Hectares Under Coffee	Yields in Kilograms
1988	2020	7055586
1989	2300	5936798
1990	2350	4962844
1991	2350	4560000
1992	2359	4110000
1993	2359	5610000
1994	2364	4090000
1995	2365	7510000

Source: Ministry of Agriculture Annual Report, Nyamira District, 1991 and Nyamira District Development Plans, 1994 – 1996 and 1997 – 2001.

Field discussions in Nyamira District in 2004/5 indicated that the coffee industry in the district was more or less on its knees with farmers going for years in the late 1990s and early 2000s without any payment for the coffee delivered. In recent years the coffee industry in Gusiiland in general and Nyamira District in particular has been battered by the knocks and shocks of the global market and individual farmers have had to find alternative avenues and sites to make a living.

[27] See KNA Kisii District Annual Report, 1974.

[28] See, KNA Ministry of Agriculture Annual Report, Kisii District, 1988, p. 50.

[29] See KNA Ministry of Agriculture Annual Report, Nyamira District, 1991, p. 14.

The Abagusii continued to rely on maize and *obori* as the most important grains. Gross food production has generally increased in the post-independence period in attempts to satisfy the requirements of a rising population and a national economy that was in decline throughout the 1980s and 1990s[30]. According to Garst (1972: 183-89) hybrid maize was introduced into Gusiiland in 1959 and by 1970/71, there were clusters of about 100 percent adoption. By 1985, about 50,300 hectares of land in Gusiiland was under maize production rising to 53,858 hectares in 1988[31].

Land

Even as the Abagusii took a keen interest in agriculture, land scarcity has been their main problem ever since settling on the highlands of south-western Kenya between 1786 and 1809[32]. This was part of the reason for the constant fighting with their neighbours the Luo, Masai and Kipsigis, to defend their land and livestock. Colonisation significantly curtailed, war as a means of territorial expansion[33] and the practice was discontinued after independence in 1963 as the new government established clearer land tenure laws and an elaborate local administration (provincial) system. The area has some of the fastest population growth rates in the country as indicated in Kenya National population Census (Kenya, 1999a), showing inter-censual population growth rate at 4.0 percent per annum between 1969 and 1979, 2.7 percent per annum between 1979 and 1989 and 3.1 percent per annum during 1989 to 1999. As a result the pressure on the land is overwhelming. But even at the onset of colonisation, competition over land was considerable. Glickman (1974) argued that control over land was a major consideration in the selection of the first chiefs by the colonisers.

After independence there were land market opportunities in the former White Highlands which were also accessed on the bases of political patronage and considerations (cf. Bates, 1989). In the process of the ensuing resettlement some of the Abagusii from Nyamira District were able to resettle in various parts of the country mainly in Borabu Division of the same district which became a settlement scheme after the colonial settlers left in 1963. Those who bought land in the settlement schemes were fairly well off and were close to the chiefs who selected people from each location for resettlement. All the same, the venture provided an outlet for land hungry people from Gusiiland. Other people managed to buy land in the Rift Valley Province but not in significant numbers. Among the Abagusii, land is inherited along male lines. At marriage, each group of uterine brothers is allocated parcels of land originally farmed by

---

[30] UNICEF Kenya Statistics (http://www.unicef.org/infobycountry/kenya_statistics.html downloaded July 18, 2006) indicates that Kenya's Gross Domestic Product (GDP) per capita average annual growth rate (%), 1970 – 90 was 1.3 and -0.6 during 1990-2004.

[31] See KNA Ministry of Agriculture Annual Report for Kisii District, 1988, p. 40.

[32] See Ochieng' (1974), p. 108.

[33] See KNA South Nyanza District Annual Report, 1956, p. 4 for instance.

their mother (Hakansson, 1994). The District Development Plan, 2002-8 (Kenya, 2002) indicates that average farm size in Nyamira District is less than an acre and most farmers plant a mix of cash crop(s), staple food crops (mainly maize, millet and beans) and vegetables including kales, *rinagu* (night shade, *solonum nigram*), *chinsaga* (spider weed) and *ototo* (*amaranthus hybridus*). It is against this background that 62.3 percent of the population in the district lives in absolute poverty (Kenya, 2002 - Nyamira Dist. Dev. Plan, 2002-8).

Livestock

Livestock have been kept by the Abagusii throughout their history. One reason for their frequent migration was the constant raids on their cattle which they valued as the basis for marriage in terms of bride price. According to Levine (1963 cited in Garst 1972: 93) traditional Gusii life centred on herding of cattle and cultivation was relegated to a secondary position. The social worth of men was determined by how many head of cattle they accumulated through breeding, rustling and marrying their daughters. Mayer (1965) argues that the main corpus of law dealing with marriage, patrimony, and compensation, has bride price as its central institution. It regulates claims between affines, but also between agnates competing for shares of their patrimonial cattle. Patriarchs are important interpreters and enforcers of this law. In marriage, both husband and wife are elevated to a new status, and bring two clans and families together in exchanging gifts and visits (Philip Mayer, 1950). Polygamy and large numbers of children were greatly valued perhaps because of high child mortality rates and the generally labour intensive nature of the economy. In any event the style of earning a living through cultivation had emerged around 1650 AD when the Abagusii arrived in Kano and started growing *obori*. Prior to that the Abagusii had relied on livestock herding, hunting and gathering for their living (Levine and Levine, 1966).

With colonisation, (Levine and Levine, 1966) the importance of cattle, sheep and goats in the Gusii prestige system and diet diminished over the years especially because of a growing cash economy and of the reduction of herds initially occasioned by cattle epidemics and government restrictions on cattle villages, *ebisarate*[34] as well as pasture shortages. Pastureland was particularly under pressure from population growth and competition from newly introduced crops such as corn, sweet potatoes, bananas, legumes, tea, coffee and pyrethrum. Moreover, the establishment of the colonial administration ceased the expansionist tendencies of the Gusii nation, and the traditional war economy which was the third most important source of additional cattle to households after breeding and bride price exchange during the pre-colonial era. Since pre-colonial times men had private land, *emonga* cultivated for their own profit. The produce from *emonga* does not swell the ordinary household

---

[34] See Maxon (1989: 50-1).

resources, but remains at the disposal of the male owner, to be exchanged for money, goats or cattle (Philip Mayer, 1951).

The government restricted cattle villages, *ebisarate* mainly because they thought that the middle aged men who manned the villages were cattle rustlers. In attempting to deal with inter-tribal cattle raids they discouraged *ebisarate* and required people to keep their livestock in their homesteads over night. In addition the Zebu cattle, which the Abagusii people kept, were declared an ecological hazard and a barrier to food security (cf. Hall, 1936). The establishment of settler areas for whites only, and 'native reserves' for Africans, (see Okoth-Ogendo, 1976:55; Brown, 1968) also severely reduced the amount of land at the disposal of Africans, including the Abagusii. This further reduced grazing land and either shrank livestock keeping or pushed some people out of herding all together. The final blow to the traditional Gusii economy came with the incorporation of the Abagusii into global conflict on the side of Britain and the allies. Zeleza (1989a, b) shows that African farmers in Kenya were required to plant new crops, particularly maize, which was required in surplus by Europeans especially during the two world wars, leading to the relative displacement of herding and other traditional activities such as *obori* production.

However, even as the traditional livestock economy came increasingly under pressure and significantly lost its mainstay the zebu cattle, graded dairy cattle were introduced in Gusiiland in 1961 (cf. Garst, 1972: 178). The number of grade cattle in Gusiiland expanded from 89 in 1962 to 10,207 in 1967. The more prosperous farmers took loans from the German Agricultural Team operating in Gusiiland in the 1960s and early 1970s to acquire grade cattle (Garst, 1972). This changed the way cattle were viewed, prestige shifted from numbers to the income from milk yields. The exotic dairy cattle were quickly transformed to serve as bride price as they became available in large numbers. During fieldwork it was noticeable that they were preferred to the zebu for bride price payment because of their higher milk yields.

Tea

Tea was first planted in Nyamira District on an experimental basis at Kebirigo in 1956[35]. Thereafter it continued to capture the imagination of the Abagusii farmers and according to the Kisii District Annual Report[36] (1961:2) all the stumps planted in 1961 were from the district's own nurseries, increasing the acreage under tea from 224 to 374 acres (90 to 151 hectares) during the year. The report points out that Locational Tea Committees and a District Tea Committee were formed to enhance acceptance of the Special Crops Development Authority (SCDA) extension and marketing activities in the district. The committees were perhaps meant to ease the tension between

[35] KNA, South Nyanza District Annual Report for 1956, Page, 17.

[36] see KNA - Kisii District Annual Report 1961

farmers and the colonial extension officials who were notorious in coercing farmers, especially in soil conservation efforts. As one villager put it during my fieldwork, "they whipped us with hippo whips". The report further indicates that in the same year a site for the first tea factory was chosen at Nyankoba on the Rigoma Road. The report concluded that there was a great demand and interest in tea and that the tea planting area should be extended into the lower country.

The Special Crops Development Authority (SCDA) was formed under the Agriculture Act in 1960 to promote cultivation of cash crops especially tea and was replaced by the Kenya Tea Development Authority (KTDA) following the Kenya Tea Development Order 1964 (Kenya, Sessional Paper No. 2, 1999b). These two bodies steered smallholder tea production in Kenya while it was in its infancy.

The area under tea in Kisii District (Gusiiland at the time) rose from just 151 hectares in 1961[37] to 13,172 hectares in 1985 and to 14,556.5 hectares in 1988. Expansion of tea growing in Nyamira District, which was carved from Kisii District in 1990, continued into the 2000s as shown in figure 2.2 below.

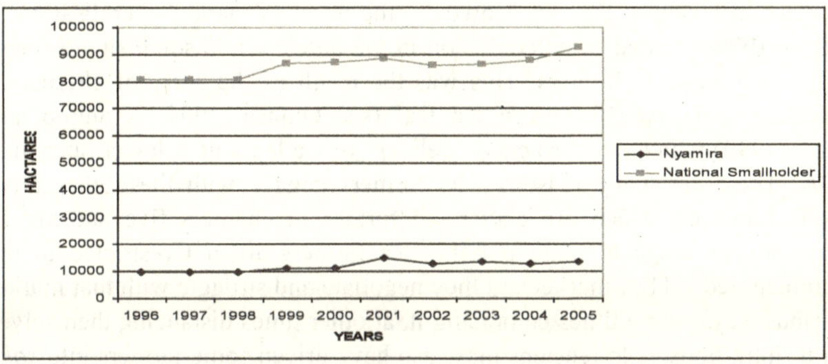

Figure 2.2 Area (Ha) under Tea 1996–2005:
Nyamira District and National Smallholder Compared
Source: Tea Board of Kenya

The area under tea is rising faster nationally than it is in Nyamira district. This is most likely due to land scarcity curtailing significant expansion in Nyamira District. In terms of tea yields Kisii District (of which Nyamira was a part) produced 13,458,143.50 kilogrammes of green leaf in 1973 which rose to 63,284,877 kilogrammes in 1987[38]. Tea yields in Nyamira District fluctuated between 24 million kilograms and just below 28 million kilograms between 2001 – 2005. Figure 2.3 compares the national smallholder tea production with the district's production.

---

[37] See KNA, Kisii District Annual Report, 1961, p. 22.

[38] See KNA Ministry of Agriculture Annual Report for Kisii District, 1974, p. 27.

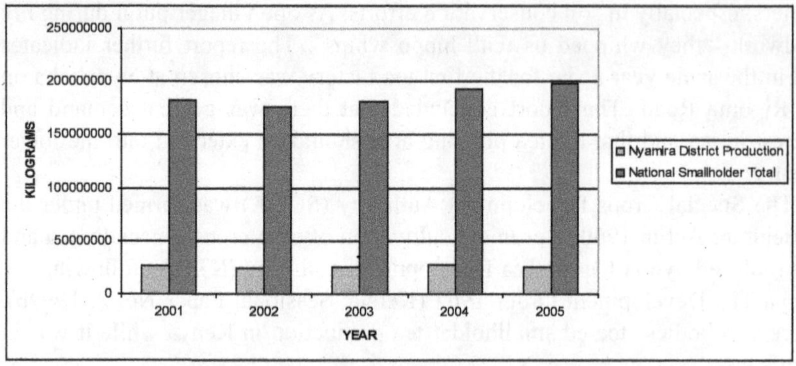

Figure 2.3 Tea Leaf Production (KGs) 2001 – 2005:
Nyamira District and National Smallholder Total Compared
Source: Tea Board of Kenya

Since independence there has been general growth in the smallholder tea sub-sector in Nyamira District. However, the onset of market liberalisation in the early 1990s created some confusion in the industry and some sluggishness in payments made to farmers. This was the result of the entry of alternative markets or *soko huru* for green tea leaf (see Omosa, 2004; Nyangito and Kimura, 1999) which pay farmers on delivery of tea leaf but at lower rates than KTDA. There are many reasons why farmers engage with these alternative markets however, which are elaborated further in chapters five and six. It suffices at this stage to point out that tea farmers are not restricted to the government led KTDA market and they negotiate and struggle with that market in various ways, some times embracing it, at other times distancing themselves from it. Intra-household tensions may also have driven some farmers into *soko huru*. For instance, Silberschmidt (2001) reveals that many of her female respondents had special arrangements with local dealers so that they could sell some of their cash crops without their husbands' knowledge. Figure 2.4 below shows that most payments to farmers are made during the second round of payments, as opposed to first and implies that the KTDA keeps farmers' money for long periods without paying any interest on it (cf. Tallontire, 2001).

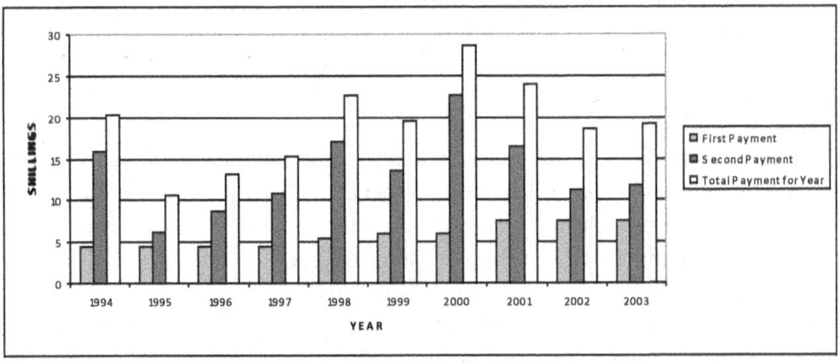

Figure 2.4 Smallholder Tea Leaf Payment Trend in Kenya, 1994 - 2003
Source: Kenya Tea Development Agency.

Delayed and late payments by the KTDA and its failure to make monthly or on-delivery payments KTDA may be one of the factors driving farmers with a desire for a quick and regular income into the *soko huru* market.

Maize

The origin of maize in Nyamira District and Gusiiland in general is not clear. However, maize seed was introduced around 1913 when an agricultural instructor was posted to Kisii (Maxon, 1989). Thereafter production grew steadily, largely due to the introduction of a tax that forced people to produce surpluses for the market to raise cash for taxes (cf. Maxon, 1989). Land under maize in the district was 19,487 hectares in 1989, rising to 24,820 hectares in 1992 and about 23,700 hectares in 1995[39]. In terms of maize yields Nyamira recorded 779,480 bags of 90 kilograms in 1989, which rose to 1,021,500 bags by 1995[40]. The government emphasised cereal production particularly during the Second World War when the allied forces required surpluses for the war effort (Freeman, 1985). The introduction of maize as a staple food was one of the major outcomes of colonisation. Figures 2.5 and 2.6 below show that the area under maize and maize production in Nyamira District rose steadily between 2001 and 2005. It is however unlikely that new land was being opened up for maize and that the main explanation for the rise in the area under maize is due to intensification of maize growing by increasingly planting in two seasons per year.

Villagers in Sengeta said that maize has replaced *obori* as their staple food. The main reason for this is that the labour requirements for maize production from land preparation through weeding, harvesting and winnowing are lower than for *obori* production; (Field Discussions, 2004/5). Most people do

[39] See KNA Ministry of Agriculture Annual Reports for Nyamira District, 1991 & 1995

[40] KNA Ministry of Agriculture Annual Reports for Nyamira District, 1991 & 1995

continue to grow *obori* in small acreages especially for sales and consumption on special occasions.

Finger Millet

Obori, the traditional staple food of the Abagusii people has remained the most important cereal after maize. It is popular because of its traditional role mainly during ceremonies such as circumcision and weddings[41]. Old women in Sengeta village said that finger millet porridge served to a prospective bride groom on his maiden visit to a suitor's home indicated to him that the lady's family was ready to transact the marriage with his family (see chapter one for a detailed discussion) and during weddings nowadays finger millet *ugali* is the special dish for the bridegroom's party visiting the bride's home prior to the wedding ceremony (Field Discussions and Observations, 2004/5). Table 2.2 provides a picture of acreages, output and market value of *obori* in the mid 1970s, late 1980s and early 1990s.

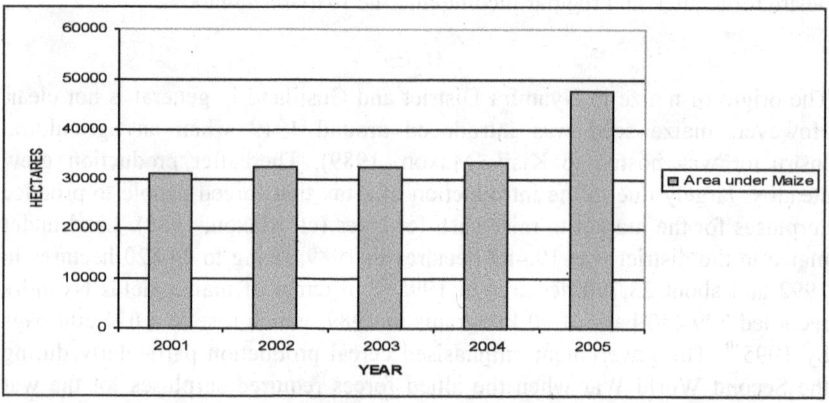

Figure 2.5: Area (Ha) under Maize in Nyamira District, 2001 - 2005
Source: Ministry of Agriculture, Nyamira District Annual Reports

[41] See KNA Ministry of Agriculture Annual Report for Nyamira District, 1995, p. 22

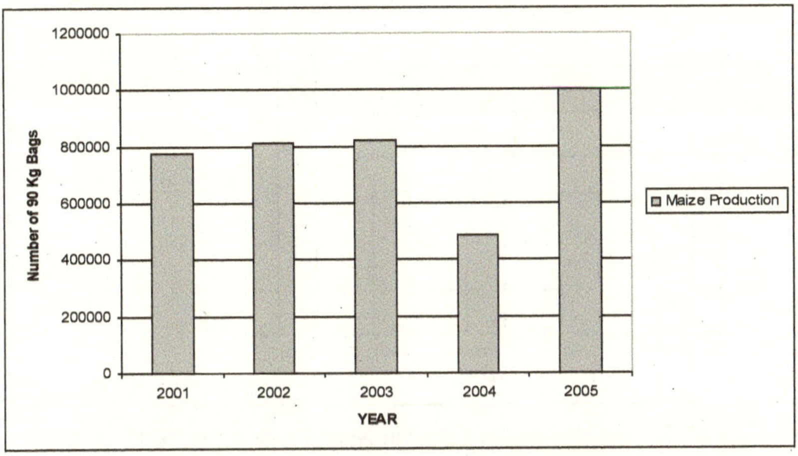

Figure 2.6: Maize Production in Nyamira District, 2001 - 2005
Source: Ministry of Agriculture, Nyamira District Annual Reports

Table 2.2 Nyamira District finger millet output and value in KES

Year	Hectares	Output (90kg) Bags	Value (KES)
1974	1,058	8,464	719,440
1989	1,360	12,250	7,350,000
1990	1,454	13,086	8,833,050
1991	1,767	17,670	11,928,600
1992	2,450	22,050	14,883,750
1993	2,757	29,155	20,143,507
1994	2,727	28,114	20,067,773
1995	1,400	14,400	23,212,800

Source: Ministry of Agriculture Annual Reports for Kisii District 1974 and for Nyamira District, 1988, 1991 and 1995.

While the area under *obori* appears to fluctuate with time due to competition with other crops, the importance of the crop remains fairly stable. The value of produce seems to rise every year and the produce dominates food markets in Gusiiland. Between 2001 – 2005, the area under *obori* increased, as shown in figure 2.7. However as with maize this expansion mainly involved embracing a two season cropping pattern. Production of *obori* increased proportionately to the expansion in acreage, as shown in figure 2.8.

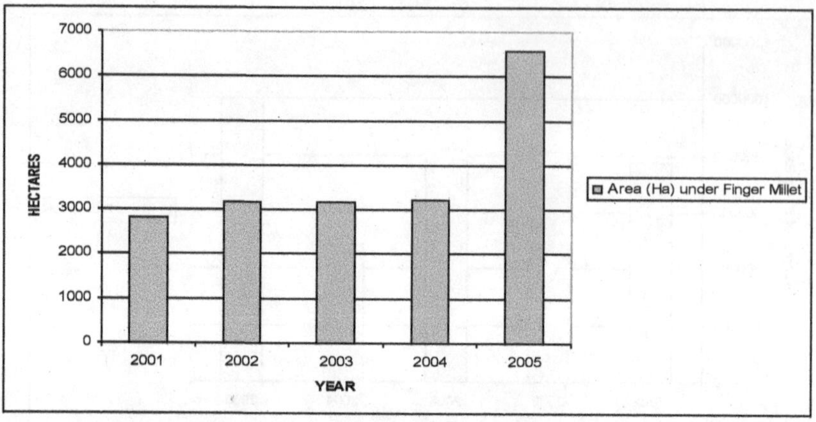

Figure 2.7: Area (Ha) under *Obori* in Nyamira District, 2001 - 2005
Source: Ministry of Agriculture, Nyamira District Annual Reports

The continued expansion of the area under *obori* emphasises the important place of the cereal in ceremonies. Finger millet has also historically been a significant basis of trade between the Abagusii people and their Luo neighbours (cf. Levine and Levine, 1966: 15-6) and remains important today (Field Discussions, 2004/5).

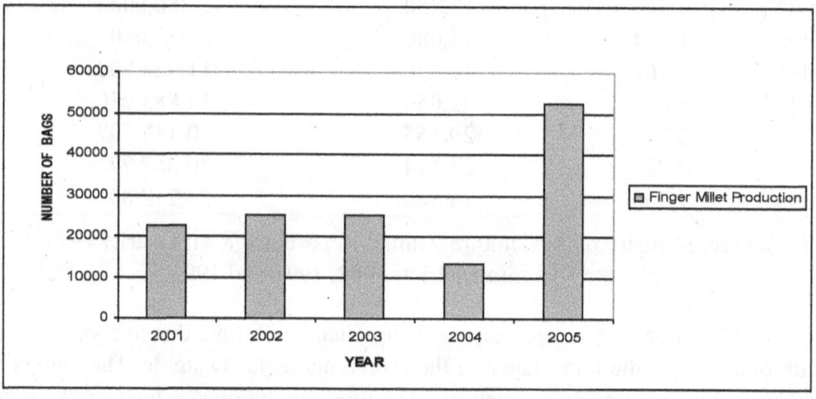

Figure 2.8: *Obori* Production (90 Kg Bags) in Nyamira District, 2001 - 2005
Source: Ministry of Agriculture, Nyamira District Annual Reports

Besides being an item of trade and having an important role in local brew production and consumption on special occasions such as weddings, *obori* is also important in gift giving especially between affines, and in rural – urban exchanges. Some Abagusii in the diaspora purchase finger millet grain from Gusiiland that is delivered to food markets in the various urban areas in Kenya. A villager with children in America said that she occasionally sends five to ten kilogrammes of finger millet flour to her children in America.

Conclusion

This chapter has shown that the Abagusii were herders when they migrated from their original country of 'Misiri'. They embraced *obori* growing in the course of their migration and expanded its production upon settling on the fertile Gusii Highlands. In general the people were creative in terms of iron works, crafts, trade, livestock and agricultural production during the pre-colonial period. They resisted colonisation fiercely, successfully securing their land against appropriation from settlers. As Maxon (1976; 1989) puts it, 'Gusii resistance to colonial rule did produce what must be seen as the positive effect of saving the Gusii from losing land to the whites (British)'. In that sense, the peace deal between the British and the Gusii on February 12, 1908, marked their autonomy, as the British remained confined to Kisii town which was more of a diplomatic post throughout the 'colonial' period.

In the following years, the Abagusii embraced new crops, dairy cattle and education. Their creativity in everyday practice has however not been documented and explained as reflected by the somewhat truncated data in this chapter. This chapter has alluded in general terms to how livelihoods were constructed, but the real picture including the place of villagers in everyday life lacks a detailed and clear perspective on their creation of resources amidst land scarcity and poverty. This is why government statistics and reports provide such a partial picture of rural life that focus on depicting the people as poor due to their low monetary incomes, estimated at 1,239 shillings per capita per month - about 57 US cents per day (Kenya, 2005 – Geographic Dimensions of Well-being). This study goes beyond these government statistics to focus on and view the Nyamira landscape as co-produced through the interaction of the natural environment and social action. It shows a broader picture of the landscape that relates to the people's identity and space as an integrated whole. The social ties involved in the resource creation; sharing and use processes are brought to the fore and discussed. The rest of this book describes and explains this creativity in everyday practice, focusing on villagers' efforts at creating and co-creating resources and constructing livelihoods. The next chapter provides a theoretical mapping of the study.

CHAPTER 3

Resources and Livelihood: A Theoretical Mapping

Introduction

This chapter explores several key areas of literature that have relevance to the study question set out in chapter one, that of how rural villagers create and use resources to make a living and with what results? The issue of how villagers link up with resources is certainly not a neglected one. Research in these issues has been carried out in disciplines focused on natural resources, poverty, food production, social security, the landscape and livelihoods. Few of these approaches however focus on villagers' capacities to create resources and how they use these to make a living. This chapter uses the actor-oriented, livelihood and landscape perspectives as entry points to the study question. It searches among these perspectives for useful insights on this question, identifies the gaps that exist in these approaches and, on this basis, elaborates some of the key concepts that feature in the rest of the book. The chapter ends with a discussion of the unit of analysis for the study followed by concluding remarks.

An Actor-Oriented Perspective

How does an actor-oriented perspective explain the possibility of villagers creating resources for use in making a living? The perspective provides a cognitive framework to this question since it recognises that people individually or in groups (hereafter actors), including the poor, have agency, the knowledge and capability to act meaningfully and strategically. It recognises that villagers have the capacity to interact with their environments[42] and to work and re-work them in their interests. Even poor people have power because power and knowledge are relational and, however poor, people never cede all of their knowledge (cf. Long 1992, 2001; Scott, 1985). In this sense then actors are not just gliding down life's avenue, but are part of the process of life as conscious agents interacting actively, meaningfully and strategically with their environments (cf. Long, 1992).

---

[42] The word environments, is used in plural here to include its many facets such as the physical, the socio-cultural and thus the economic and institutional.

As conscious agents, social actors act to create social space and strategically make claims on resources and relationships in the social landscape. They construct their social worlds on the basis of these relationships and resources, both material and non-material. However, these processes of social life are not linear and preordained by structural forces and arenas, but are variable, composite and provisional (Long, 1992; 2001). In other words, the process of social life is never complete, but is constantly being reworked and recreated as circumstances shift, interests coalesce or diverge and life objectives change. These dynamic actions by social actors are part of the process of resource creation and application to make a living. Essentially villagers' everyday lives are about making their living. Entering into strategic relationships with other actors or networks, negotiating and defending certain occupied positions and claiming certain resources and relationships that convey specific 'value' or endow certain perceptions internally and externally are all strategies through which actors further their objectives. Actors realise their agency in these complex ways because their environment is composed of social relations and can only be altered through these avenues (cf. ibid).

In understanding these complex and dynamic relationships and actions, the actor-oriented approach places the actors centre stage, rejects linear, deterministic thinking and recognises the multiple realities that actors create (Long, 1992). The basic idea is that it is not tenable to approach everyday life as being driven by structural forces such as the state or the market. On the contrary, everyday life and the way in which actors make their living should be understood as a product of the interpenetration and intermediation of the internal and the external. From this perspective, resources are co-produced with the environment and with other actors. These resources can be located either locally or in distant areas, provided that the actors have the knowledge and capability to affect local decisions and actions.

Resources are used in a dynamic fashion, in the same manner as they are created. This dynamism depends on the diversity of actor preferences and choices and on the ways that different actors or groups encounter multiple realities. The idea of choice and preference is not absolute but arises from the view that, even within highly restricting circumstances, actors can explain their actions and have some room for manoeuvre, which provides a basis on which choices and alternatives may be pursued (Long, 1992, 2001; Jones, 1999). The notion of choice is particularly relevant to this study because it helps us grapple with and explain the diverse outcomes of resource use such as tea as a cash crop in relatively homogenous circumstances. It helps us to explain the emerging heterogeneities without attributing them to conventional conceptualisations of rational choice that would obscure dissimilar actor evaluations and explanations of outcomes. Therefore, the differential patterns of outcomes that emerge are the creation of actors. This provides an interesting focus of analysis because throughout the body of this book the actors discuss their livelihood outcomes, attributing them to certain choices they made or battles they lost in their relationships with others. This type of analysis privileges the social embeddedness of resources creation and livelihood construction. This stance is expounded by Joas and Klipinen (2006) in their discussion of creativity of action, which they argue is 'situated', meaning that social actors sometimes operate in circumstances beyond their choice and control. For this reason discussions about creativity should be contextualised. 'Situated creativity' can be explained further through Bourdieu's concept of *habitus*, as an infinite capacity for generating products including actions whose limits are set by historically and socially situated conditions (1990: 55). Actor's experiences and historical embodiment are thus prime movers in their creativity and its extent. The tension between unrestricted choice and creativity on the one hand and 'situated or restricted' agency should not be lost.

Socio-cultural reasons can help explain issues where determinist planes of analysis such as rational choice construe irrationality (Jones, 1999). It is therefore important to cast the net wider in order to capture deeper explanations and descriptions of resource creation and application. Apart from gaining deeper insights and understanding, it is methodologically crucial to view everyday life in rural areas as socially embedded because that is what it is. Ignoring the context-specific nature of rural everyday life provides a superficial analysis as it overlooks the actual nature of reality. Additionally the realities surrounding everyday practice are multiple and diverse and their analysis must be equally dynamic to locate and explain relevant nodal points of social action.

From another angle this issue of social embeddedness of everyday rural life enables us to recognise that attributes such as knowledge, power and prestige are attached differently to the concept of person (Long, 1992). Long further argues that knowledge emerges out of processes of social interaction and is essentially a joint product of the encounter and a fusion of horizons. This means that knowledge, like power and prestige, is socially constructed and emerges and is wielded differently in different societies. Even then there are no specific normative attributes of knowledge that apply uniformly across any one society. Knowledge like power and prestige, are dynamic social forces that must be analysed and understood within specific time-space contexts. This is crucial for this study when locating what actors define as knowledge and power at any one time and how they utilise it to further their interests. Creation of resources may also involve giving meaning to phenomena: a process that is inevitably contested because of the variety of meanings that may emerge

As much as actors work and rework their social realities by way of creating resources and even contest some of their tenets in order to position themselves strategically in their search for opportunities for making a living, the way that perceptions and definitions of resources are pursued is socially constructed. The social construction of resources brings us to the idea of livelihood as being socially embedded, a conceptualisation which is much broader takes the view of livelihood beyond that of the economic undertakings of putting food on the table, increasing income and sustaining the environment (as implied in DFID,

1999; 2000; Carswell, 2000 and Carney, 1998, for example). Rather it places the concept of livelihood within a bigger picture of life. That is to say, livelihood encompasses ways and styles of life/living, choice, status, and a sense of identity vis-à-vis other persons (Long, 2001; cf. Wallman, 1984). Everyday endeavours to earn a living therefore hinge upon and are largely framed by the lifestyles that actors choose.

The view that lifestyles are central in constructing livelihoods gives rise to a broad consideration of actor preferences including identification, primary resource creation and use processes, social networks and time use as well as information sources. Resource creation processes are thus shaped and themselves shape actor lifestyles. But lifestyle formation is a contested process straddling local, macro and global terrains. As new ideas emerge existing lifestyles are put to the test locally at the household and village level with a shifting equilibrium resulting from continuous negotiation and uncertain accommodation. The scenario is replicated, albeit in subtle ways, with macro and global level exposure to 'globalising' processes and their ramifications in the emerging global village (cf. Long, 2000). The idea of change and adjustment of lifestyle requires further elaboration here. Most analyses of changing lifestyles use 'replacement' as a fundamental process of change, arguing that 'over time new forms of family and lifestyles replace the old' (Sussman, 1975: 568). However, this study assumes that lifestyle change defies and transcends 'replacement', which is an overly determinist evolutionary framework for analysis. Rather, change is negotiated and slow; accommodating conservative and pragmatic aspects of livelihood coalitions, yet also responding in strategic ways to the avant-garde attributes of coalitions and interests wherever they are located. It is such subtle aspects of resource creation and livelihood construction in the everyday lives of villagers that this study aims at illuminating and explaining.

From an actor oriented perspective it is sensible to conclude that villagers create resources because they have agency, which they realise through social relationships as they negotiate their actions. Therefore as social actors their actions are creative, but 'situated'. This perspective also highlights that livelihood is socially constructed and related to villagers' resource creation and livelihood construction on the bases of their human agency, power, knowledge and creativity. The actual processes of resource creation in everyday life are not conceptually or empirically clear. There is need to seek further clarification on these issues in the livelihood approaches.

Livelihood Approaches

The discussion above about villagers creating resources and using them to make a living in a socially constructed process, raises one main issue, namely; how this occurs in practice? Livelihood approaches recognise that resources are at the centre of livelihood construction. The approaches view resources in terms of 'capitals' which are perceived as accessible or inaccessible to people mainly on the basis of structural factors. These approaches generally define resources narrowly and from a materialistic viewpoint. Such approaches focus on sustainable livelihoods and were largely developed by DFID, ODA and allied institutions in the 1990s (Carney, 1998; DFID, 1999; 2000; Shankland, 2000; Toufique, 2001).

Livelihood studies has come to the fore in recent years in response to the limited success of poverty studies and other types of studies in informing policy and practice in poverty alleviation and development (Nooteboom, 2003; Kaag, *et al.*, 2004; de Haan and Zoomers, 2003; 2005). Proponents of livelihood studies view poverty studies as overly focused on the weaknesses and helplessness of poor people, to the extent of being paternalistic. According to Nooteboom (2003), livelihood approaches improved on poverty studies by starting its analysis with the strategies and creative choices of people in making a living. The approach shifts from a focus on what poor people lack to analyse how they manage to survive and thus emphasise the strengths of the poor rather than their weaknesses and provide a message of hope rather than of despair. Perhaps because of these early promises the livelihoods approach attracted many users from different fields including academia, policy-making and development practice (Murray, 2002).

As these approaches glued varied interests together, they initially coalesced around the approach advanced by the Department for International Development (DFID) of Great Britain. This approach elaborated in guidance sheets 1 – 5 issued by DFID (see DFID, 1999 & 2000) has become the starting point of most livelihood studies ever since. Borrowing from Chambers and Conway (1992), DFID (2000) views a livelihood as *comprising the capabilities, assets (including both material and social resources) and activities required for a means of a living. A livelihood is sustainable when it can cope with and recover from stresses and shocks and maintain or enhance its capabilities and assets, both now and in the future.*

Many subsequent livelihood studies have followed DFID's conceptualisation and are based on identifying and analysing four main social domains. These are the assets [described as a pentagon][43] on which livelihood is based, the contextual/institutional setting that frames access to and utilisation of the assets; the emergent livelihood strategies; and the particular livelihood outcomes of this process (Francis, 2000; Swift and Hamilton, 2001; Carney, 1998 and Scoones, 1998). These analyses appear to be underpinned by an assumption, largely derived from neo-classical economics, that attributes an economic vecúe to individuals (cf. Arce, 2003) that on balance people should pursue economic and environmental goals. Furthermore, the livelihood approaches as described above also assume a linear process through these four

[43] In the DFID Livelihoods Framework, assets are presented in a pentagon format as physical, social, financial, human and natural.

domains. In a sense then they reduce social actors to different types of capital (the asset pentagon) continually being constrained or facilitated by the contextual/institutional settings in their everyday lives (Arce, 2003).

Thus livelihood approaches throw up a number of contestable issues, which this book seeks to address in order to develop a sound theoretical orientation. The main one, the lack of consensus over what assets or capital really entail (Whitehead, 2002; Arce, 2003). Whitehead argues that from sociological /anthropological and political economy perspectives assets are relational and that inclusion / exclusion debates need to be intrinsic to the idea. This brings the debate about assets/capital to the point of recognising that social actors are 'knowledgeable' and 'capable', that they have agency and are active in struggles to claim and access assets. This however, does not deconstruct the assets pentagon beyond the descriptions provided by proponents of livelihood approaches, which only explain why the pentagons shrink or expand (with fluctuating access to assets) in relation to the determinist notions of the institutional /contextual setting.

Arce (2003) pinpoints the existence of crucial differences between asset and capital and appears to advocate discarding 'capital' because of its neo-classical economics derivation and material connotations. This does not however help in highlighting the linkages inside the pentagon and the apparent blurred boundaries within it. For instance, how is time to be treated? Is labour time a human or a financial resource? How about time spent visiting a neighbour or chatting at a roadside kiosk? Arce's important contribution to the debate, which is crucial to this work; is his conclusion that the starting point of sustainable livelihood approaches should be the actor's reality (Arce, 2003: 6). This opens up analysis of livelihoods and brings out the possibility of taking actors' choices, culture and lifestyles into account. In the same vein that Hebinck and Bourdillon (2001) earlier argued that creativity, experience and drive towards experimentation are all a part of actors' resource base. They, like Arce, were concerned about the neglect of social actors' multiple realities and the social embeddedness of everyday life. Pursuing his point further, Arce (2003: 6) argues:

> '...a more dynamic approach to the understanding of local livelihoods, which stresses the interplay and mutual determination of the contestations of values and relationships and which recognises the central place played by human action and identity rather than capital is needed'.

This argument not only moves the livelihood debate to the actor-oriented arena for further deconstruction and refinement but also challenges the 'livelihood system' connotation implied by proponents of the approach (see for example Carney 1998:2; Toner et al., 2004 and Kamuzora, 2004). The assumed coherence within the system, which mostly hinges on the alleged economic rationality of actors, is thrown off balance once issues such as identity and social action, which are not always based on rationality, come into play. The 'permissiveness' of livelihood pursuits is thus underscored as it logically flows from the realities and lifestyles of actors. The notion of 'permissiveness' in everyday life is borne out by realities such as 'everyday forms of peasant resistance' (Scott, 1985), Gaffey's 'second economy in Zaire' and 'women smugglers in Cameroon' (Niger-Thomas, 2001). The key argument here is that actors' realities interpenetrate with other local and macro domains of a diverse nature to produce livelihoods that defy rational systems. These types of livelihoods are critical to this study and are approached in ways that sought to discover rather than pre-ordain forms of everyday life.

Another contestable issue in livelihood approaches relates to access modalities and power relations related to institutions (de Haan and Zoomers, 2005; Watson, 2003). It is claimed that livelihood approaches take too narrow a view of power and institutions in influencing livelihood processes. Haan and Zoomers (2005) propose that power never completely belongs to one party due to constant processes of interaction. They do not accept that the poor are powerless as other studies have done and devise the concept of 'wielding and yielding' power as an important handle for analysing power equations within institutional analysis. In a similar vein, Long and Villareal (1994) argue that possession of power or knowledge does not necessarily entail that others are without them. Watson (2003) argues for a broader definition of institutions that includes sets of enduring ideas, rules – formal and informal – and practices – *de jure* and *de facto* – as well as organisations and decision-making groups. Such institutions are also structures of power. She maintains that these institutions are socially embedded and should be viewed as part of power struggles that take place in different social situations. She recognises that there are problems in attempting to use these institutions in promoting development because they are embedded in other matters, but concludes that this attribute can also make them a more powerful resource for development precisely because the challenges of development are socially embedded. These arguments tie in well with the conception in this study of institutions as sites of struggle and negotiation for actors and actor groups in resource creation and livelihood construction.

The issue of institutions as structures of power may be elaborated further to explore the notions of cooperation and accommodation within and between them. Besides being sites for struggles and bargaining, institutions (as broadly defined by Watson, 2003) provide the basis for organised exchanges (both formal and informal) of material and non-material forms, including knowledge, that are critical for resource creation and livelihood construction. However, these interactions are not inherent and predetermined results of institutions, but evolve over time and are outcomes of continuous adjustments by actors, according to their preferences, lifestyles and realities that are also equally fluid. This study draws on this additional perspective of institutions, power and knowledge.

Leach *et al* (1999) draw attention to the simplistic manner in which power and agency have been handled in livelihood approaches. Following the same lines as the proponents of the approaches, Leach *et al* regard institutions as shaping access to and use of resources, but go beyond this to argue that they are also the results of contests and negotiations between different social actors. However, this only partially brings out actor responses to disadvantageous power structures and continues to explain access to resources from an institutional perspective (cf. Swift and Hamilton, 2001: 91). This raises the issue of the extent to which institutional meanings of resources, at say, the village or household level, coincides with individuals' conceptualisations. If these conceptualisations do not coincide, then institutional lines[44] can only tell part of the story of how resources are defined and accessed. The rest of the story must be sought elsewhere including within the creativity employed by individuals and groups in improvising resources and activities, and the way in which these actors seek to define or defend their identities.

Leach's contribution moves the discourse from one focused around assets/capital to one focused around resources. It is useful to explain this transition in more detail at this juncture. The issue of whether or not to stick with the concepts assets/capital, as represented on the pentagon in livelihood approaches, has not been fully resolved and since it was raised by Whitehead (2002) and Arce (2003) has proved a contentious one. The issue at stake is to determine whether and how we can accommodate the material and non-material aspects in new conceptualisations that strengthen the approaches. It is clear from the review so far, that livelihood approaches conceive assets or capitals as material entities and for largely material ends in terms of income, food security, wellbeing and environmental sustainability (DFID, 1999; 2000; Carney, 1998). To go beyond this materialist stance and goal, we need to subsume the pentagon and other non-material forms of capital/assets under a broader term that captures its multi-dimensionality and the conception of livelihood as transcending the material. In this context the term resources seems the most appropriate, firstly because it has been axiomatically used by some writers in livelihood approaches and secondly because, it has been applied beyond the disciplinary confines of economics to capture non-material aspects (cf. Berry, 1989a, b; 1993; and Lubeck, 1992; Francis, 2000).

This broader conceptualisation of resources goes beyond the pentagon in that it also encompasses non-material aspects, providing a crucial link between this study and livelihoods approaches. In other respects livelihood approaches have much relevance, especially for the prominence they give to the issue of

[44] The boundaries between institutions and individual actors are theoretically blurred, because people are born into institutions such as families or households with their own rules. But conceptualisations such as "unruly practices" (Gore 1993 cited in Leach 1999: 238) and "passive resistance in everyday life" (Scott, 1985) explain how action outside institutions occurs.

resources, as represented by the various assets in the framework, for making a living. As already pointed out resources are the building blocks of livelihoods and constitute arenas of contestation and negotiation. In stretching the concept of resources beyond material aspects, many other aspects can be encompassed, including knowledge, power, time, identity and information (cf. Wallman, 1984). Such a broad conceptualisation clearly challenges the fallacious assumptions that people are always striving to maximize their gain and that they continually calculate which move has the highest returns (cf. Alumira, 2002: 5). It also captures the issue of social capital perceived to hinge on "trust relationships that facilitate economic exchange" (Bryceson, 2000: 5) and symbolic exchanges (Bourdieu, 1990: 114 – 117). Such exchanges often transcend economic rationality and have distinctive non-material aspects including gift giving, rituals and religious sacrifices (cf. Adato and Meinzen-Dick, 2002). Recognition of this permits a more realistic analysis of the true diversity and complexity of rural livelihoods.

To extend the leeway further, one needs to look more critically at how the nexus between livelihood and resources is presented in livelihood approaches. Again resources are defined narrowly in terms of assets or capitals, hence, anything useful but which may not fit into the categories may not be considered a resource. Livelihood pursuits are presented as largely being aimed at increasing income, food security, sustainable resource utilisation and well-being. Income and food security have been elaborated on and there has been significant exploration of the meaning of the sustainable use of resources; but the issue of well-being has been less explored and remains relatively obscured. It is not clear just what it entails and even less clear is how it relates to the other outcomes. The notion of well-being requires more creativity so that it represents the more qualitative aspects of livelihood outcomes. For instance self-esteem, sense of belonging, leisure, peace with the supernatural and with diverse definitions and meanings that exist within and between social groups and social actors are all aspects of well-being.

Some of the literature also refers to "outcomes that people consider important" (DFID, 1999) and "successful or less successful livelihood strategies" (Carswell, 2000: 3). While it is not clear what these entail, the livelihoods approach does not address the issue of how and why in relatively homogeneous circumstances some actors have more successful livelihoods than others. Overall livelihood approaches appear to overstate quantifiable or more obvious livelihood outcomes such as income, food security and natural resources. In turn they downplay more qualitative or symbolic and subtle outcomes such as self-esteem, identity and lifestyle which may be equally important in people's lives.

Resource – Livelihood Nexus

Livelihood approaches provide a good point of departure for understanding how rural actors in Nyamira give meaning to resources, mobilise and apply them to make their living. However, because of its very broad coverage of issues and the shortcomings outlined above, I attempt in this sub-section, to re-orientate the approach by re-defining, re-emphasising or extending some of its key concepts in order to provide a firmer theoretical anchorage for this study.

This study extends the notion of *resources* as building blocks for livelihoods by taking the view that resources can be both material and nonmaterial. In taking this stance this study goes beyond the view that resources are made up solely of five types of assets or capitals – human, social, physical, financial and natural. Rather it takes the position that a livelihood resource is wider than all the five capitals collectively or individually. Resources are not fixed, they evolve; attributes that were less useful in the past may later become more useful as people's knowledge and meanings of reality shift. Therefore, over time the meanings given to resources by villagers vary as does their use of them. In this sense then, villagers create resources through *giving meaning* to phenomena in dynamic ways. Creating resources is a social process done in league with experience and history, values, norms and identity, in cooperation with other individuals and groups and with the natural environment (cf. Scoones, 1999). But villagers may also create resources through improvisation (Scoones, 1998: 8), which may be legitimate within existing norms; values or social identity or 'unruly', contradicting social norms and practices. If it is 'unruly', and the practice enlists followers it becomes the genesis of new identities, resources, rules and practices (Holland *et al.*, 1998). These processes of creating resources are complex and dynamic and are by no means smooth. They involve contests and struggles with the established rules and practices.

Livelihoods approaches maintain that access to resources determines how a living is earned (Ellis, 2000: 9-10) and that access to resources is mediated through social relations, institutions, social organisations, trends and shocks (Ellis, 2000; DFID 1999, 2000). Given the arguments developed so far that villagers continually create and re-create resources, the issue of 'access to resources' is contested. However this does mean to say that by creating resources villagers become self-sufficient and isolated from the rest of society. Villagers interpenetrate other spheres of society in the course of their everyday life: through markets, personal networks and other social organisations. These diverse spheres of society have their own rules, but these rules do not circumscribe human behaviour, otherwise social life would be rather predictable. Therefore, this study proceeds on the premise that villagers *create and re-create resources through naming and re-naming them, but also struggle to extend resource meanings while defending existing ones and hence, embrace new opportunities thus getting involved in more complex relationships, identifications and lifestyles.* This is not a phased process but often a contemporaneous one. This brings us to the theoretical position that accessing resources is more dynamic and at times more subtle than implied in livelihood approaches. This study therefore, embraces institutions as central in understanding resources, but rather than see them as 'determinants'[45], they are considered protagonists in the struggles to extend meaning and embrace new opportunities and consequently rework institutions (cf. Berry, 1989b). Once resources are understood as opportunities, the imagery of creating them through naming and re-naming makes sense. Likewise the view that opportunities are taken rather than accessed emphasises the issue of struggles and protection of opportunity in the course of pursuing livelihoods. By reframing resources and institutions in these ways it becomes easier to explain how by giving meaning people, create and recreate opportunities (cf. Wallman, 1984) and defend them often in subtle ways (cf. Scott, 1985).

The view taken in this study, that social actors create resources and that this process evolves and unfolds in different directions in the course of which new opportunities are embraced, fundamentally challenges the concept of livelihoods strategies/activities as presently constituted in livelihood approaches. These approaches take the position that villagers pursue livelihoods through any aggregation or disaggregation of three given strategies: agricultural intensification/extensification, diversification or migration (Ellis, 2000; Swift and Hamilton, 2001 and DFID, 2000). They present these strategies as hierarchical and linear with returns and security rising with movement from agriculture to migration. Evidently, this linear-hierarchical conception of livelihood is strongly related to concepts of 'de-agrarianisation', the process of movement away from agriculturally based livelihoods in rural Africa (cf. Meagher, 1999). Such a shift ties in with the linear-hierarchical livelihood dynamic, and can be presented as either (or both) driven by short-to-medium term rural livelihood strategies or is part of a longer-term historical process of migration and industrialisation (cf. Bryceson, 1996). This study re-examines the process of de-agrarianisation, with a view to questioning its claimed processual and permanent characteristics and reviewing its interaction with macro-level processes. This is because the movement away from agriculturally based livelihoods is not a matter of course, based on economic rationality, but one that is socially embedded and of necessity pegged on complex non-economic factors that contradict its assumed linear character.

Furthermore, this approach challenges the assumed linearity of the livelihood dynamic, as there are situations where the logical option (from the perspective of livelihood approaches) in a villager's livelihood trajectory is migration, but social ties deny this choice and the villager instead hangs in, surviving in some inconceivable manner (cf. Bryceson, 2000: 6). Such scenarios challenge the logics of livelihood strategies, as conceived in the livelihood approaches, and call for a closer look at what rural people really seek

[45] Ellis (2000: 39) for example argues that land tenure institutions determine access to land. However in reality institutional positions are often contested and negotiated upon by individuals and households, and the outcomes of such struggles do not always echo institutional stances (cf. Leach et al. 1999).

in life: the sorts of identity, values, statuses and self-actualisation that they seek and the tasks they devise to arrive at these. To capture these complex dynamics this study employs the concept of identity to attempt to understand where rural dwellers are headed and the tasks devised (lifestyles) to see them through. Identity may order tasks, guiding actors to the interpersonal networks that they embrace and distancing them from others, thus influenced the lifestyle followed (Andersson, 2002). For livelihood approaches to be valuable they need be actor-focused and recognise the tactical and strategic behaviour of poor people as being as, if not more, important than the institutional environment within which livelihoods construction takes place (cf. Whitehead, 2002: 576).

Elaborating livelihood approaches in this way allows for an extended and re-oriented approach, which is less contestable in providing a framework for investigating and analysing how villagers create resources, use them to make their living and with what results. One aspect however remains outstanding. How does one conceptualise and explain the interaction between human action and 'nature' in the course of creating resources and making a living? This question is taken up in the next section where the actor-oriented, livelihood and landscape approaches are brought together with a view to developing a common approach to the study.

Landscape, Actor and Livelihood: Co-production of Resources

This sub-section brings together the landscape, livelihood and actor-oriented approach to show how together they explain aspects of co-production of resources. To take an illustration: the alternative tea market, *soko huru* for smallholder farmers does not enforce tea leaf quality and enables farmers to sell poor quality leaf resulting from hailstones or drought (see Chapter 6). This brings out the interaction between the natural environments, the actor and livelihood pursuits in resource creation processes. The actor-oriented perspective emphasises the centrality of actors in the creation of resources and the construction of livelihoods. The thrust of the argument so far is that resources and livelihoods are socially constructed. This line has not been without caution, as it has also been argued that resources are co-produced in league with 'nature' and often in collaboration, competition or conflict with other actors. The point made in deploying such concepts as conflict, struggles and negotiation is that social constructionist perspectives should not deflect attention from nuanced counter processes of 'nature', local and extra-local forces.

The argument that 'nature' determines livelihoods is not tenable as actors are endowed with agency, yet at the same time the neglect of the relationship between the external forces of 'nature' and social action in human-agency sociology is also not tenable (Murphy, 1995: 700). This is because social actors continually and dynamically encounter 'nature' as an ally or foe, depending on their circumstances, strategies and objectives. As Murphy (1995) argues, the natural world not only provides external limits, but also external possibilities for human activity. While natural conditions can present shocks such as droughts, pests and diseases, they also give forth opportunities such as good soils, medicinal products and other resources. As Murphy (1995) shows sociology should also take account of social actors' adaptation to 'nature' rather than their 'production' and 'construction' of it. He concludes that 'humans are shaping the world more than any other species, and are being shaped by 'nature' in ways never before experienced'. This clearly acknowledges the dialectical interaction between 'nature' and social action in the production of reality (cf. Scoones, 1999; Marsden, et al. 2001). In the same vein van der Ploeg, et al (2000) argue that the pluriactivity resulting from grappling with the emerging rural development problematique involves reconfiguring rural resources, through creating new resource bases and new linkages between rural areas and society at large.

The notion of adaptation to 'nature' also relates to the tensions between endogenous and exogenous development in rural areas. Exogenous development is interventionist and external, attempting to drive change from without and to define externally the utility of resources for locals (Long and van der Ploeg, 1994). These top-down development attempts are frequently negotiated, transformed and adapted by social actors (*ibid.* see also Ray, 1999: 259). The exogenous perspective lacks much resonance with local social action that encompasses dialectical interaction with 'nature' through which landscape is historically constructed. This is the theoretical stance taken by this study, which resonates more with the endogenous approach.

Endogenous development is locally constructed through locally defined styles aimed at discovering, recovering or inventing local identities and resources to drive largely idiosyncratic forms of development (Long and van der Ploeg, 1994; Slee, 1994; Picchi, 1994; Ray, 1999). This perspective privileges place or territory as the arena for resource creation and use in livelihood construction and identifies the sources of the requisite territorial identity as cultural, historical or physical: e.g. landscape/architecture (Ray, 1999). Landscape is particularly important because logically it embodies the territorial identity (see Saugeres, 2002) on which actors have defined themselves and their resources, stamped their art, knowledge and architecture; in which they intercepted, transformed and adapted external influences and located themselves in ways that reflect their lifestyles and livelihoods. Thus landscape anchors actors' diverse projects, mediated external forces and understandings of the world – its material organisation and the meanings and values attributed by people (Panelli et al., 2003).

The analytical power of interweaving the landscape perspective together with livelihood and actor-oriented approaches lies in its ability to bring together heterogeneities in livelihoods. These can be found in diverse actor projects, identities and lifestyles, and ways in which resources are constructed and used amidst endogenous and exogenous factors. These forces can exert influence over different sites and levels, from the local to the regional and international. Their influence is played in arenas where the struggles over meanings and creation of resources and endeavours to make a living manifest themselves. This reaffirms Tuan's (1990) concept of 'topophilia' which suggests that humans either have, or need to have, a love of a particular place (cited in Ray, 1999:261). It is around this loved place, this landscape, that everyday life revolves, even if it is shaped from multiple sites. But the love of a place is not for nothing, as Saugeres (2002) points out, the meanings that landscapes take on over time come to define how people think about the place, how they behave and how they expect others to behave. Therefore people defend meanings of things, such as resources, as they understand them in their landscape which leads to instances of contestations and collaboration. Panelli et al. (2003) underscore this when they argue that, as products of socially embedded and culturally significant constructions of the countryside and specific, individual rural settlements, landscapes contribute to local identities, cultural values and social power relations. The power relations structure the pecking order and the contours of struggles and negotiation in everyday life within landscapes. Power relations also reflect the institutional map of a landscape and the resources that flow through it.

Landscape also serves as a record of the changes that occur in place and with people (Panelli *et al.* 1999) and therefore can be seen as the arena for everyday life, through giving and contesting the meaning of phenomena as resources, enrolment and distanciation from social institutions and deployments that lay claims on resources and defend certain styles and identities. Landscape is an interaction of people and place and thus the people's source of identity and meaning (Groth, 1997). As such it is the arena where reality is created. It is the theatre of life and making a living is therefore better understood on the basis of reading the 'text' of a people's landscape, providing a record of life as played out. The painter Pieter Brueghel vividly expresses this, presenting the world's landscape as a 'stage' upon which human life is acted out (Cosgrove, 1997: 101). Similarly, Egoz *et al.* (2006) indicate the creation of rural landscapes and people's responses to them as expressions of their social beliefs and practices.

In a nutshell, landscape defines people and people define landscape. To read the landscape is to read the dialectical relationship between the two. In addition the landscape also reflects people's fears and aspirations and, thus on the basis of their history, they depict their strategic directions on their landscape. The landscape can also reveal 'how the dominant meanings given to phenomena are reproduced and contested in everyday discourse and practice' (Saugeres, 2002).

The relevance of landscape (as co-produced) to this study lies in its role as the arena for everyday life and discourse, resource creation and livelihood construction. Additionally it helps us to fine tune livelihood and actor-oriented approaches by privileging the dialectical relationship between nature and social action. The landscape perspective thus reflects local/extra-local relations and tensions, lifestyles and rural change more robustly when deployed together with the actor-oriented approach and livelihood perspectives, than any of the approaches do by individually. None of the three approaches discussed can individually fully account for the scheme of things in the processes of villagers' creation and use of resources to make a living. The common approach presented in this sub-section provides an important theoretical and methodological handle on the research question. It points out the centrality of social actors, endowed with agency and of social action as both creative and socially constructed and embedded, and hence a historical phenomenon. Human agency also implies social relationships and action, and the dialectical relationship between social action and nature, upon which livelihoods and landscapes are contemporaneously constructed. These all provide important nodal points of inquiry and analysis that inform this study. With these nodal points in mind the study shifted to the field to capture and explain the actual scheme of things in resource creation and use to make a living. In the remainder of this chapter key concepts including resources, agrarian change, institutions, identity and lifestyle are elaborated, the unit of analysis presented and concluding remarks made.

Conceptualising Resources

Livelihood approaches view resources as assets and categorise them into five sorts: physical, human, social, natural and financial (DFID, 1999, 2000; Carney, 1998; Toner, *et al,* 2004 and Scoones, 1998). This narrow conceptualisation of assets, which views them solely as material items, has already been critiqued earlier in this chapter, together with a proposal for adopting this concept so as to transcend this problem. This expanded conceptualisation is further elaborated here to explain what it means in, and for this particular study.

The hyper dictionary[46] defines a resource as (i) a source of aid or support that may be drawn upon when needed; (ii) the ability to deal resourcefully with usual problems; and, (iii) available source of wealth; a new or reserve supply that can be drawn upon when needed. The main theme that runs through all the three definitions is 'need' and by extension 'problem', because meeting a need implies solving a problem or overcoming a problematic situation. In this sense, resources are related to the 'security' of a person or people as much as to the resource in question. The third definition brings out a new element; of wealth or reserve and implies another dimension of resources, in not just providing bare security, but also demonstrating affluence or prosperity. This is in line with Peach and Constantin's (1972) assertion that 'resources are the basis of both security and opulence; they are the foundations of power and wealth.' This

[46] From: http://www.hyperdictionary.com/search.aspx? define=resources, downloaded August 7, 2006.

exposes the complexities surrounding not just the definition of resources but also their use or misuse.

Peach and Constantin (1972) argue that the term resources presupposes a person or groups of persons as resources are expressions or reflections of human appraisal. This means that something is not a resource until and unless it is appraised as such by a person or a group. This converges in some way with Wallman (1984: 28) when she advises that 'we need to ask for whom and in what way an item has economic potential and whether its owners recognise that potential'. Following this line of thought but eschewing economic essentialism, Peach and Constantin (1972) conclude that 'the word resource is an abstraction reflecting human appraisal and relating to a function or operation in which it may take part'. Human appraisal is crucial here and following the actor-oriented approach this implies that resources are not obvious to every eye and are never the same before every eye, even in relatively homogeneous conditions, places or groups. It also implies that resources are not constant; they change in line with actor preferences, lifestyles, commitments and other repertoires. Peach and Constantin (1972: 11) support the notion of fluidity of resources, albeit from a rather deterministic point of view, arguing that, 'resources change with each change in human civilisation.'

Moving to another level of specificity, Wallman (1984: 28) interrogates the conception further arguing that:

> Since it is fundamentally an economic concept, a resource tends to be visualised as a material item. But this usage is based on a misunderstanding of economic notions, and more important, conceals too many of the realities of livelihood. Even those who limit the resource concept to material items will recognise that resource management involves organisation and some number of layers of social and cultural embroidery.

The notion of resources should thus be carried beyond economic realms to capture the realities that surround livelihood construction in everyday life. As a socially embedded process, livelihood construction transcends the material to embrace the non-material spheres that may include 'perceptions, skills, symbolic structures, organisational strategies, and any sense of commitment to those structures or strategies' (ibid: 28). Such non-material aspects frees our view of social actors from a perception that they solely are driven by economic rationality to seek the highest gain or profit in their livelihood pursuits and recognises their 'cycles of reciprocity' and 'non-economic interests' in life, that is they enable us to capture the social representation of production and exchange (Bourdieu, 1990). This follows from the fact that the material and non-material aspects of reality are seamlessly interlocked and often mutually and subtly influence each other. Bourdieau views an actor's *habitus* as an active residue or sediment of his history and experience functioning within his or her present, shaping perception, thought, and action, and thereby moulding social practice in a regular way (Crossley, 2001: 83). The idea of reciprocity as a resource and a basis of gift giving and exchange is a social and historical phenomenon that cannot be viewed as a 'passing cloud'. As Peach and Constantin (1972: 10) indicate, resources are socially embedded so that the "bulk of man's resources are the result of human ingenuity aided by slowly, patiently, painfully acquired knowledge and experience".

Human ingenuity gives rise to experimentation and skills, and this reinforces that view that resources are created and evolve over time and space, already taken in this study (cf. Hebinck and Bourdillon, 2001). This is a socially constructed process, shaped by and shaping actor preferences, lifestyles and other specificities. As Peach and Constantin (1972) argue, the concept of resources is functional and inseparable from human wants and human capabilities. Thus as these human wants and capabilities change, resources also change. Capability is also informed by knowledge, which according to Peach and Constantin (1972) is truly the mother of all other resources as it is the means through which resources are identified and created. Following this line and taking into account both material and non-material aspects, Berry (1989a) argues that productive resources should be broadly defined to include not only material and financial means of production – land, labour, fixed and working capital – but also social relations and knowledge that are employed in the processes of production.

Knowledge here is conceptualised broadly to include the shifting bodies of knowledge, local/indigenous, expert and global, that inform and produce everyday life. Confrontations between these bodies of knowledge are continuous and not necessarily disruptive; sometimes they are smooth and subtle, other times they are overt and truncated, often leading to visible 'counter-tendencies' or local actors 'becoming independent' (cf. Arce and Long, 2000a, b). The main point here, which informs this study, is that there is no dominant knowledge in rural societies nor is there any static, 'repugnant' knowledge; the available bodies of knowledge are in a continual contest for space and applicability.

Berry's (1989a, b) notion of social relations and identity as resources (actual or potential) resonates with this study. She argues that social identity can be a basis for access and control over resources and that kinship and community relationships are important, not just in acquiring rural resources, but also in rising to political office or accessing employment opportunities. This is particularly important in agriculture because of the importance of kinship relationships in land inheritance and the 'market'. Haugerud (1989) emphasises the centrality of kinship relationships in land borrowing and lending in Kenya. She points out that kinship relationships are a site of interpersonal conflict over resource ownership, particularly land. This study therefore approaches social relationships with an open mind and views them both as arenas of contests over resources and their utilisation, and of cooperation and exchange of knowledge, information and other resources. This perspective sharply brings to focus

Haugerud's (1995) notion of 'moral economy' and Hyden's (1980) of 'economy of affection', as sites of contradictions, contestations and negotiation, rather than of predictable patronage and even 'egalitarianism', as the concepts imply at face value.

Finally, this study holds that material resources only have meaning for livelihoods when combined with non-material resources (cf. Wallman, 1984). Through making such combinations, which involves giving meaning to phenomena as resources, interactions between actors begin and in the ensuing process, resources evolve and unfold in their meaning and usage. In their interaction with phenomena, actors mould and re-direct resources to their economic and 'non-economic' (Bourdieu 1990: 113) interests. This contrasts with the purely economic dimension, which Bourdieu conceived as 'relations of war', that pertain between strangers in bigger markets where people do not know each other (2000: 19). Bourdieu shows that in many purely economic relationships the notions of buyer and seller dissolve into genealogically based and guaranteed relationships (ibid: 115). He is arguing in other words about the strength of non-economic interests in life. Schrauwers (1999: 118-9) reinforces the centrality of non-economic interest in his discussion of petty traders and their customers in Indonesia. Both largely disregard price and profit in their transactions, the former viewing their trade as part of their household budgets and enterprise and the latter avoiding large 'alien' stores and seeking credit facilities from their kin, petty traders. Through such processes actors co-produce resources with others in their networks, this involves contestation and collaboration with the wider environment including polity, markets and 'nature'. These processes of production and co-production of resources imply that livelihood opportunities are seized as they unfold. This brings us back to the argument that livelihood objectives and outcomes include both the material to non-material, and that the production and co-production of resources is simultaneously or sequentially both a livelihood aim and an outcome. In view of this, evaluation of livelihood outcomes is an intricate and subtle process, which requires careful analysis of livelihoods and resources over time and space.

This research commenced by focusing on specific resource domains around which livelihoods appeared to be mostly organised in Nyamira. These are land including crops and livestock, labour, income, time and social relationships. This is not a watertight list of resources framing the study. Rather it is an entry point to the discussions that flowed in the directions that social actors follow in creating and availing themselves of resources needed to construct their livelihoods. This notion of villagers creating resources links well with Rodney's (1973) notion of development as meaning increased skills, creativity and capacity of individuals, including an improved capacity to deal with the environment at the societal level. Rodney argues that this last element depends on people's understanding of nature (science) and and ability to devise tools (technology) with which to deal with the environments. This implies that science and technology are cultural attributes and that each culture will have its own. The concept of agency is very applicable in the context of villagers' capacity to deal with their environment, and to produce and co-produce resources. The resource domains identified as entry points for this study imply a rural study site in which livelihoods were organised around agriculture. Nevertheless, agriculture's importance as the main basis of livelihoods in rural Sub-Saharan Africa is changing (cf. Bryceson, 1996). Different researchers have conceived these changes differently and there is no consensus on the nature of this change. We now turn to review the changes that are attributed to agriculture, which appear to run deeper and span entire rural sectors.

Agrarian Change: shifts of emphasis in rural livelihoods

Agriculture has been the mainstay of Sub-Saharan African (SSA) economies for centuries. Kofi (1977) shows that more than two thirds of the economically active African population lives in rural areas and earns their livelihood from rural activities. In most African countries, the agricultural share of GDP is over 50 percent. At some points in time, the agricultural outlook in Kenya has been good. For example, Leys (1971) reported that the Kenyan economy expanded at an average annual rate of 6.3 percent in real terms from 1963 to 1969, with smallholder incomes increasing at an average rate of 2 per cent per capita per annum in the same period. Kitching (1980) similarly wrote about startling growth in gross farm output and income on Kenya's African smallholdings between 1952 and 1958, with their gross farm revenue increasing by 425 percent between 1958 and 1968. This background led Carlsen (1980) and Heyer (1981) to describe Kenya's small-scale agricultural sector as a 'successful exception' and 'showcase' in Africa, respectively.

Cracks started showing in the agricultural sector in Africa during the recession of 1974 and 1975, when export prices peaked (Kofi, 1977). Kofi argues that the world recession (wrought mainly by the 1973-74 oil crises) reduced export volumes from Africa by 4.1 percent in 1975. The countries hardest hit by the fall in volumes and export prices, and a simultaneous rise in import prices, included Zaire, Zambia and Kenya, all non-oil producing countries, relying on depreciating exports to secure badly needed foreign exchange for oil imports. These countries experienced very low growth rates in GDP and a mounting trade deficit. This led to heavy borrowing, most of it internal and subsequently to significant indebtedness on the part of African governments. At the same time, 'derived urbanisation' linked to 'parastatalisation' of national economies was under way, although the new jobs later ran out (cf. Bryceson, 1996). The straw that broke the camel's back was the 1985 drought that devastated Africa and created a serious food insecurity crisis with far-reaching economic implications (cf. Timberlake, 1985). Under these scenarios, world optimism about African development gave way to an onslaught of criticism about African governments' economic policies and more latterly their civil rights and governance record (Bryceson, 1996). International Financial Institutions (IFIs) started to prescribe structural adjustment programmes (SAPs) for SSA. The implications of all these influences on the role and centrality of agriculture to rural livelihoods in SSA have been the subject of much debate by scholars in different disciplines.

Most writers on rural Africa are of the view that the nature and role of agriculture in those economies is changing and that this change is greatly influenced by changes wrought by the SAPs, accompanying neo-liberal policies and globalisation. The changes, they argue, are deep and far-reaching. Agricultural stagnation has harmed the rural poor by creating food shortages and higher prices that have reduced their ability to buy food (Khan 2001: 8). Two main arguments are advanced: that agriculture's role as the main source of livelihood is being diluted through livelihood diversification and/or is slowly being replaced through de-agrarianisation. This means that food production for self-provisioning and for the market as well as regular cash cropping like tea, cocoa and coffee production are all on the wane in rural Africa.

The reasons underlying diversification are variously explained by market penetration since colonial times throwing agricultural systems off balance and the effects of SAPs in the 1990s in compounding an already precarious agricultural sector by withdrawing agricultural subsidies and introducing user fees for health and educational services (cf. Lubeck, 1992; Haugerud, 1989). The rural small-scale African farmer has been exposed to the unfamiliar 'invisible hand' of the market and is scampering around in the dark. As Francis (2000: 55) puts it 'making a living in Africa today involves improvising responses to disappearing job prospects, falling agricultural output, collapsing infrastructure and the withdrawal of public services'. African rural dwellers are also faced with increasing input prices and poor market opportunities (Bryceson, 2000: 2). This makes life difficult as farming becomes tricky and markets frosty to the farmers and their needs. The result has been diversified livelihoods that involve combining farming with wage labour, trading, selling services or producing commodities for sale (Francis, 2000).

Livelihood approaches generally distinguish three broad categories of strategies for making a living: agricultural intensification/extensification, livelihood diversification and migration (see Scoones, 1998; Swift and Hamilton, 2001; Ellis, 2000 and Shankland, 2000). Scoones (1998: 9) points out that the three core strategies are often presented as static and need unpacking to distinguish different dynamics and outcomes. For example, agricultural intensification/extensification may be capital-led or labour-led, livelihood diversification may be a coping mechanism for shocks or stress or may involve more a permanent adaptation of livelihood activities. Equally, migration may be voluntary or involuntary and its implications for agriculture are diverse. In general, people pursue different strategies at different times and for different reasons. Shackleton *et al.* (2000: 1) aver that strategies may depend on the assets available and the livelihood outcomes being sought. Thus, as Scoones (1998: 10) points out, the degree of specialisation or diversification relates to the availability of resources and the risks accompanying various options. Actors are therefore, viewed as often weighing options and drawing on experience to make the best of their situations. In this sense, the benefits accruing from particular strategies at different levels will depend on broad social norms and on internal management within the household (Scoones, 1998).

Francis (2000) has shown that the help, transfers, exchanges and information that people have access to through their social networks shape diversified livelihoods. Some of these sources of income and livelihood may be more dependable than others and sometimes these social networks may be fallbacks rather than adequate substitutes for other forms of resources. Therefore, besides spreading a livelihood through agricultural and non-agricultural activities, social actors also rely on social relationships of friendship, kinship, community or neighbourhood for support. Francis (2000) identifies at least four reasons for livelihood diversification. First, it may be a response to seasonalities in agricultural production. This implies that actors diversify during lean times such as drought seasons. Second, it may be a means for spreading risks, as when someone has multiple livelihood sources, the consequences of any one failing will be less severe. Third, diversification may be part of a strategy of accumulation. Fourth, diversification strategies may be associated with subcultures of social actors as well as location-specific factors.

Orvis (1993) for his part argues that 'population pressure on land and the risks inherent in rain-fed, market-oriented smallholder agriculture mean that the great majority of rural Kenyan households sooner or later must combine agricultural and non-agricultural activities to survive and attempt accumulation'. This implies that diversification is inevitable among smallholders across Africa under prevailing structural circumstances. However, its nature and direction will not be uniform and the micro-macro factors at play should be investigated, as poor rural farmers are not homogenous anywhere (cf. Ellis, 2000; Khan, 2001 and Chambers, 1990). As Khan (2001: 2) has pointed out, the differences among the poor reflect highly complex interactions of social constructions, markets and public policies. Investigating the interactions of these structural factors with livelihood diversification might explain the heterogeneity that exists in rural areas.

What seems to emerge from this discussion is that livelihood diversification is not an inevitable and linearly determined stage in the process of social change processes. Rather, social actors combine farming with a variety of other activities and relationships in order to resolve immediate survival problems or to position themselves in good stead for the future through a complex process. Such complex processes and the emergence of multiple livelihood strategies are likely to lead social actors to follow a range of trajectories and these will give rise to inevitable conflict and negotiations. The outcomes for actors of such processes will also vary, for a variety of reasons.

Deagrarianisation is a related change that is taking place in rural Africa. Bryceson (1996: 99) has defined it as a process of livelihood reorientation, occupational adjustment and spatial realignment of human settlement away from agrarian patterns. She argues that deagrarianisation has proceeded in SSA through two main processes. The first is the 'derived urbanisation' of the post-independence period fuelled by rural people's perception that urban areas offered superior economic opportunities. This belief was underpinned by the urban jobs, which became available because of emerging parastatals and the Africanisation of public services and commerce. These changes have transplanted some people from agriculture to urban areas.

The second process has to do with economic diversification and population settlement dispersal under structural adjustment. The results of the SAPs in many countries have been civil service retrenchment and the withdrawal of subsidies for the agricultural and other sectors such as health and education. This has led to food and general price increases (cf. Razavi, 2003: 3). With such uncertainty, urban and rural dwellers alike pursued household livelihood strategies that mixed subsistence activities, market oriented production, and trading in order to spread risks of failure (Bryceson, 1996).

Bryceson (1996) argues there is inadequate theoretical understanding into the process of deagrarianisation and suggests that 'an understanding of deagrarianisation could be pursued at two levels: as a long-term historical process and as an integral part of rural households' short-to-medium term livelihood strategies'. At the macro level, it is possible to capture some of the overt and measurable manifestations of the process, such as shrinking proportion of the population residing in rural areas and a decrease in agricultural output per capita in the national economy relative to non-agricultural output, but such aggregate statistics mask huge variations, patterns and tendencies (*ibid.*). This then calls for observations and conceptualisations of deagrarianisation at the micro-level in order to capture local variations and process these in the context of existing macro and global trends. This study therefore follows Meagher (1999) in conceiving deagrarianisation as simply a movement away from agriculturally based livelihoods and an embracing of non-farm activities. Non-farm activities include agricultural wage labour, other forms of wage labour and other non-agricultural activities. Agricultural processing activities for sale beyond the household, such as beer brewing and trade in crops/livestock produced by others, like butchery are categorised as non-farm activities, as these lie outside agricultural self-provisioning activities organised around the household farm (Meagher, 1999).

Deagrarianisation is a slow process and is the result of many subtle interactions and considerations in households, locally, and at the macro arena. As Lubeck (1992) points out 'neither state intervention nor market forces have transformed African agriculture into a green revolution miracle, nor have they forced proletarianisation by blocking the reproduction of the African peasant household'. The analysis of deagrarianisation should be able to show how and why this process is taking place.

In the midst of livelihood diversification and deagrarianisation, cash crop production especially for export has remained significant in SSA. From the fourteenth to about the eighteenth centuries, external trade in Africa revolved around the exchange of mostly luxury items such as ivory, gold, alcohol, textiles and tobacco (Kofi, 1977). The slave trade was of a different category, its end coincided with the industrial revolution, which ushered in a new form of international trade and foreign influence in which foreign economic agents such as missionaries, sailors, colonial administrators, and European settlers joined indigenous peasants in organising production and trade. In some countries 'enclave sectors' emerged that were dominated by white settlers and these led the way in export production (Kofi, 1977). Cash crops and other new crops were introduced to African peasants during the colonial period, mainly to generate a cash income for the African so he might pay his taxes (cf. Kitching, 1980). In Kenya and Uganda, it was necessary to spur production of new crops to justify the construction of the Uganda Railway, entrench the cash economy and to end the payment of taxes in livestock (Kitching, 1980).

Haugerud (1989) explains that cash crops were intended to stimulate rural economic growth and demand for agricultural wage labour so that the landless and the near landless might be employed. The thrust of this argument is that cash crops would be the basis for a landed capitalist peasantry that would drive both economic and proletarianisation processes in the rural areas. This linear relationship could not take hold in many African countries, such as Kenya, because as Leys (1971) pointed out, large-scale dispossession of the type in eighteenth century England was not possible in country that was not ruled by a committee of property owners, as peasant interests managed to some consideration at the centre. Under these circumstances, Leys argued that development might still come to the poorest peasants through improved techniques and seeds which enable them to eat better and slightly improve their cash incomes. Cash crop income and general agricultural income in rural areas is also crucial for investment in non-farm activities, employment and as a source of rural accumulation and a ladder out of poverty (Leys, 1971; Orvis, 1993; Razavi, 2003 and Sachs, 2005). This means that cash cropping was seen as the launching pad for successful rural livelihoods. However, this view also needs to be considered along side the preferences of social actors, their identities and lifestyles. In other words, cash cropping cannot be explained without taking heterogeneity in terms of objectives and outcomes into consideration.

Struggles with and within institutions

The notion of institutions has often been used both by politicians and by 'experts 'to explain the marginalisation of people in 'developing countries' and particularly those in rural areas The main line of argument is that people are trapped in institutions and practices that reduce their competitiveness or alienate them from markets and mainstream development. This section looks at arguments such as the 'moral economy' (Scott, 1976; Haugerud, 1995) and the 'economy of affection' (Hyden, 1980) from an actor-oriented perspective, in order to show that actors are not merely passive victims of institutions, even if they are often quite entrenched in those institutions and practices because of state actions and interests (Schrauwers, 1999). Instead, the processes of resource creation and livelihood construction are negotiated with and within institutions. Schrauwers for instance argues that farmers in Indonesia make closely-calculated choices based on resource organisation in commodified markets which often leads them to make conscious decisions to invest in a non-market moral economy (1999, p. 126). Others institutional analysts have seen it differently.

Early institutional analysts attempted to understand the behaviour of African producers in terms of their moral economies and group rationalities (Lubeck, 1992: 525). He argues that African producers operate in risky and uncertain conditions, which is why their responses to material incentives and market forces often contradict the expectations of state planners and rational choice assumptions. Pursuing a similar line of argument, Hyden (1980: 18-19) posits that the peasant mode presents an economy in which affective ties based on common descent and residence prevail – an 'economy of affection'. In such an economy, economic behaviour is not solely motivated by individual profit but is embedded in a range of social considerations that allow access to opportunities and benefits in ways that can not occur in modern capitalist or socialist formations. This corresponds to the 'moral economy' (Haugerud, 1984: 11; 1995; Scott, 1976) where the neo-classical emphasis on individual rationality and market criterion of profit maximisation are irrelevant, and production, consumption, distribution and exchange are socially organised. Hyden's and Haugerud's caricatures of 'affection' and 'morality' as the dominant bases of economic behaviour in Africa have been criticised as empirically flawed.

In her later work, Haugerud (1995: 134-6) delves into cliental relations that occur in interpenetrating domains of kinship and politics. She shows that "material flows in Kenya's patron-client pyramids reproduce in part familiar cultural patterns in which a few individuals become prosperous and maintain material exchanges with subordinates". In this, Haugerud presents institutions as powerful mediators in actors' struggles to access resources. From this perspective, institutions are understood as; "regularised patterns of behaviour that emerge from underlying structures or sets of rules in use" (Leach *et al.*, 1999: 237). Such rules are made and remade through people's practices (ibid) and therefore, as the rules change so do the regularized patterns of behaviour and practices.

As Berry (1989b: 41) indicates, people's ability to generate livelihoods depends on their access to productive resources and their ability to control and use resources effectively. This occurs against the backcloth of institutions. Berry maintains that access to resources hinges on participation in a variety of social institutions, on material wealth and market transactions. Thus, institutions are structures of power (Watson 2003: 291). They constitute arenas of contest over resources. According to Berry (1991, p. 11 cited in Lubeck 1992: 527) "to cope with increasing economic instability and decline ... people pursue influence and opportunity through shifting alliances or by contesting the boundaries or structures of the networks themselves". Institutions then do not confer resources and opportunity on a silver platter, but people struggle and negotiate with each other, sometimes seeking to reinterpret institutional positions. Success in this creates changes, new opportunities for winners and, perhaps, constraints for losers. The losers in these processes, however, are left weaker, not down and out, and so re-position themselves to face the future. Such processes imply that the need for a broader conceptualisation of institutions to cover not just access to and utilisation of resources but also the dynamics and complexities involved in processes of contestation and negotiation. This broader view can be found in Watson's statement (2003: 291) that "institutions encompass sets of enduring ideas, rules (formal and informal) and practices (*de jure and de facto*), as well as organisations and decision-making groups".

Within this broader conceptualisation, the institutionalists' view on resource allocation is captured by Lubeck (1992: 526) thus:

> 'Producers often choose to allocate resources – land, labour and credit – for the reproduction of groups (i.e. households, lineages, Islamic brotherhoods, or cultural associations) precisely because these diversified investments guard against environmental risk, market uncertainties, and the political instability associated with planning in a way that assures that they recover a small surplus at the very least. These behaviours reproduce an insurance-like network of moral obligation at the expense of greater surpluses earned through specialised, profit-making strategies'.

Social relations therefore, come into play at different times and for different reasons, and with a range of implications. By attempting to take care of risks, uncertainties and instability, actors end up with productivity levels below the 'optimum'. Their intention however, is not accumulation but generating a minimum surplus to re-invest in production and reproduction of interpersonal networks.

Berry (1989b) provides at least four elements of the institutional approach to resource studies in Africa. First, that perpetuation of access to resources via social identity leads to further investment in institutions as potential channels of access. For instance, labour-exporting areas use farm resources to educate their children and to control migrant ones, all in anticipation of remittances. Migration itself depends largely on the use of interpersonal networks such as of kin to find work, land or establish businesses in a new area (Berry, 1989b: 46). Such actions are assumed to lead to below optimum productivity at both ends of the migration phenomenon.

A second element is that if investment in social groups rises faster than production capacity, the 'returns' to such investment will tend to decline. With such institutional devaluation, the incentive to invest in them declines, but the proliferation of access channels makes it difficult for people to withdraw from them (Berry, 1989b: 51). However, recent field evidence (e.g. Francis 2002: 7) indicates that divestiture in social relations does occurs, for example because of "(unemployed) young people find(ing) it difficult to acquire the resources needed to form or sustain households". This view contradicts those that see interpersonal networks as crucial in accessing 'soft' resources such as information and logistical support, securing the basis of social action and 'springboards' and a way in which individuals initiate new branches of activity (see Francis, 2002; Berry, 1993: 169-179; Harris, 2002; Uphoff and Wijayaratna, 2000; Long, 2001). These conflicting views call for a study on the place of these networks in people's struggles to mould and improvise resources and livelihood opportunities in everyday life.

A third element is that the inclusive mode of labour management and recruitment associated with investment in institutions as channels of access may promote unproductive patterns of resource use. Berry (1989b: 48) argues that this presents certain dilemmas. First, if resources are fixed, an inclusive approach to recruitment based on social identity implies less for each and reduced fortunes for all. Second, labour is not effectively supervised, so productivity is low and the workers often cause environmental degradation.

The fourth element relates to the state, and Berry (1989b: 44-45) shows that state power can be used to manipulate rules of access to land, labour and capital. As a result, ability to influence the state becomes a pre-condition for doing business successfully. However, as Francis (2002: 31) argues, formal institutions are also shaped by informal practices governing resource access and use through such discriminatory practices governed by patronage relations and other power inequalities. Hence, the state presents uneven avenues to a myriad other resources such as credit, formal employment, information, education and security[47]. As Korf (2004) argues institutions such as markets and legal restrictions, define the value of resources and influence the extent to which one

---

[47] Security is a major influence in the manner in which resources evolve and are used in constructing livelihoods, Ellis and Kutengule (2003: 1502) for example found that in some villages in Malawi, civil insecurity had deteriorated and livestock theft was so rife that villagers no longer kept them. In most African countries security in rural areas is ignored and priority given to urban areas, especially those with foreign installations or those frequented by tourists.

resource can be transformed into other types of resources. In particular, markets have to be conceived broadly in order to include the whole range of resources and the constraining factors and processes that come with them in order to bring out the ensuing negotiations and struggles in the construction and use of markets (cf. Dorward et al., 2003).

'Such an institutional approach aims to show how integration into an external network of institutions, 'develops its own coordinated rationality, undermines independent forms of production and decision-making' (Long, 2001: 42). This approach is criticised for a number of reasons. First, it presents rural populations as passive and faced by overwhelming external forces. Equally, it understates the inter-agency conflicts and struggles that take place between farmers' organisations and governments or private institutions. Another criticism is that the approach eschews power structures at regional or national levels (ibid p.43). This study deals with these shortcomings by dealing with institutions both as arenas for contests and as objects and outcomes of struggles and negotiations over resources and opportunity.

One of the outcomes of actors' struggles with and within institutions and with other endogenous and exogenous forces is a possible shift in the levels of vulnerability of their livelihoods. Vulnerability however, is not wholly and exclusively a result of institutional contradictions, but of complex interactions of many factors, some beyond the control of actors. Vulnerability has been defined as 'a high degree of exposure to risk, shocks and stress; and proneness to food insecurity' (Chambers, 1989; Davies, 1996; both cited in Ellis, 2000: 62). Chambers sought to distinguish poverty, which he defined as 'deprivation, lack or want', from vulnerability, described as 'defencelessness, insecurity, and exposure to risk, shocks and stress (Yamin et al. 2005). Yamin et al. further argue that vulnerability is not poverty, but that the concept depicts the factors that drive people into poverty, keep them in poverty and block their exit routes from poverty. This is an important insight because it takes the development debate beyond the poverty reduction rhetoric organised around definitions of based in terms of monetary metrics and policy interventions aimed at improving incomes, to capture the triggering and trap factors that genuine development interventions should be seeking to address (cf. Yamin et al. 2005).

In refining the concept of vulnerability, Ellis deploys two other concepts, resilience and sensitivity (Ellis, 2000). Resilience refers to the ability of an ecological or livelihood system to bounce back from stress or shocks while sensitivity denotes the magnitude of a system's response to an external event such as a shock. He concludes that the most robust livelihood system is one displaying high resilience and low sensitivity, while the most vulnerable displays low resilience and high sensitivity. Livelihood adaptation may increase resilience even in a highly sensitive system (Ellis, 2000). This brings us to the Economic Commission for Africa's (ECA) definition of vulnerability, which does make the link with resources.

The ECA (2002) defines human vulnerability as the lack of key assets, which exposes societies to increased risk of poverty. Poor people tend to have not only low incomes, but also low and unstable natural resource bases. Because of this, their livelihoods are more likely to be disrupted by prolonged drought, major crop failures, or devastating human and livestock diseases. Ellis (2000) classifies these disruptive factors, which he describes as 'livelihood mediating processes' into two; endogenous factors that include social relations, institutions and organisations and exogenous factors such as economic trends and policies, and unforeseen shocks like floods, pests and diseases. He concludes that endogenous factors modify access to resources, while exogenous factors provide the context within which actors devise livelihood strategies. Moreover, these mediating processes evolve over time, often with ruptures or stresses and strains. However, such a conceptualisation of vulnerability begins from the premise of the inadequacies of actors and obscures how they rise from the abyss. Because actors do attempt to climb out of the abysses of inadequacy, greater focus should be placed on their creativity and struggles.

In order to position this analysis within the dynamism and creativity of rural life, this study views vulnerability as a dynamic process. Actors juggle resources and opportunities in a variety of ways in an attempt to come out stronger and to survive the worst conditions. The challenge for them is to avoid sliding into irreversible responses to crisis, such as selling off their production assets or dissolving the family unit (Kabeer, 2002). Actors face trade-offs between their search for security and the value they give to the dignity and self respect of members, which sometimes involve choices between different kinds of 'ill-being' rather than different kinds of well-being (Kabeer, 2002). This perspective denotes the concept and state of vulnerability more clearly as 'actors in search of social security'.

Social security and its analytical relevance

Social security programmes were originally designed essentially for the purposes of poverty alleviation. This meant bridging the gap between a socially dysfunctional life and what society considered a socially functional life. The aim therefore was to enhance social functioning where it was under threat (cf. Siporin, 1993). As part of public policy, social security programmes originated in Renaissance England through the Tudor and Elizabethan Poor Laws, which aimed at regulating labour and controlling vagrancy by using public revenues to alleviate poverty (Midgley, 1993; cf. Macarov, 1993). Midgley (1993) adds that the link between social security and poverty has been explicit as shown in Britain's Beveridge Report of 1942 and in the United States through the Social Security Act of 1935, which embodied the New Dealers' belief that social security would play a vital role in preventing poverty in the future.

Social security can be thought of as the product of centuries of effort to provide people with a means of support in times of individual, social or economic distress (Dixon and Scheurell, 1993; Adams, 2010:3). The social norms that mould and infiltrate society's perceptions of social security are the result of an accumulation of preferences generated by a people as they shape their specific society. The institution of social security is thus part of a society's heritage, an indelible mark of her history and aspirations. This is why the British Poor Laws, which facilitated assistance for the poor in church vicinities, were essentially an acknowledgement of the Judeo-Christian traditions. The social security programs resulting from the Poor Laws of 1601 were organised around church parishes (see Persky, 1997: 179). From these early beginnings, social security has evolved considerably, first on both sides of the Atlantic and to other regions thereafter. According to Dixon and Scheurell (1993), this evolution has led to the development of traditions that promote and enforce patterns of beliefs, prejudices and preconceptions about social security, about its gainers and losers. Over time, this has shaped the way societies view social security.

The direct or indirect diffusion of the notion and institution of social security from the British Isles into Continental Europe and the English diaspora of North America, Australia and New Zealand was smooth. The institution has also been perfected in the Scandinavian countries especially since the Second World War. According to Dixon (2000), Australia has the best-designed social security system in the world followed by Sweden, France, Denmark and New Zealand in that order. In German Chancellor Otto Von Bismarck for political rather than humanitarian reasons, introduced a formal social security system in 1889, and as of 2000 it was the tenth best designed in the world (Macarov, 1993; Borsch-Supan and Schnabel, 1998; Dixon, 2000). In ranking formal social security systems around the world Dixon (2000) indicates that the institution has been transplanted into Africa, although the only country mentioned in the work is Tunisia. The transplantation of social security to Africa largely took place during the colonial period to cater for the European settler communities and the independence governments inherited them.

According to Midgley (1993), social security programmes in the developing countries do not reach the vast majority of the population who live in conditions of poverty and deprivation. This is because formal employer-based programmes do not reach most of the population in the peasant and urban informal sectors who often subsist on the margins of survival. Besides their limited reach, social security programmes in the Third World are sometimes poorly administered and ineffective (ibid.) and have been victims of state corruption over the years.

In Kenya, the formal social security system is almost entirely employer-based and does not include those in the peasant and informal sectors, except in the health sector where some benefits are open to anyone who can pay an insurance premium to the National Hospital Insurance Fund (NHIF). The minimum premium is 160 Kenya shillings (about two US dollars) per month, which is too high for most peasants and the unemployed. Dixon and Scheurell's

(1993) contend that there are village, tribal or family level informal social protection mechanisms in the Third World that interface with formal social security measures. However, in many countries, such as Kenya, the informal and formal social security institutions hardly interface in any meaningful way. Equally, in Tanzania, where the majority of the population do not work in formal employment, their security is mainly created outside of formal systems (Steinwachs 2002). In this sense, as Nooteboom (2003) indicates, social policies in developing countries leave the poorest segment of the population (often the great majority) relying on 'self-help', or self-organised social security arrangements. The key question then is how villagers organise themselves individually or in league with others to confront their vulnerability and attain a status of security in everyday life. In responding to this question, the study adopts the definition of social security proposed by Nooteboom (2003: 33) as 'all ways in which individual people, households, and communities protect their livelihood and are protected socially against the shocks and stresses that threaten its continuity and stability'. Following this operational definition and Steinwachs' (2002: 4), social security can be understood as including efforts to first, protect against sudden loss of incomes and livelihoods; second, protect against the reduction of means of existence, and third, to enhance people's capability to cope with uncertainties.

This book explores the various ways by which social actors protect their livelihoods i.e. try to increase their means of existence and overcome any crises. The main aim is to bring out the ways through which villagers maintain their preferred lifestyles. Pursuit of this line of analysis means that actors' identity and lifestyles can be captured.

Identity and Lifestyle

This book shares the argument made by Holland *et al.* (1998: 5) that "identities are lived in and through activity and so must be conceptualised as they develop in social practice and also as psycho-historical formations that develop over a person's lifetime and motivating social life". Holland *et al.* (1998) add that identities are important bases from which people create new activities, new worlds, and new ways of being. This relates to the perspective developed so far of resources as unfolding and being moulded in village everyday life and means that the social processes that constitute knowledge clash in labelling, and consequently utilising, resources. These processes are dynamic and complex leading to clashes between individual and group identities, and negotiations or redefinitions of group identities often to rationalise deviating individual identity. One implication of this is that an actor's social identity may be different from the actual lived identity of that subject (Kearney, 1996: 146-47).

An individual usually has a social identity, for example as a teacher, peasant, commercial farmer or businessman, but what are their actual lived identities? A teacher may have several other identities such as a petty trader, peasant, drug dealer, or brewer and distributor of local brew, and may hold these identities either simultaneously or sequentially. These identities may translate to the moulding and utilisation of resources in a manner that is completely different from official assumptions concerning the main identity of, for example, a teacher. Hence, as Bryceson (2010: 4) has indicated social identity represents an individual's or group's claim to rights in social space. It is the basis for social negotiations and manoeuvres to make a living and to self-fulfilment. Therefore, 'occupational identity' (Bryceson, 2010: 3); is critical to the analysis of resource and livelihood constructions. Additionally, Bryceson (2000: 5) shows that for many people in rural Africa, "non-agricultural activities have imperceptibly snowballed from 'filler' cash-earning tasks, to year-round activities providing ready cash". Nevertheless, these individual identities that are often contradictory, produce tensions that have to be dealt with on a daily basis. They have implications for the interpersonal networks that evolve around individuals, the resources co-produced and the livelihood outcomes sought. This book therefore, delves into villagers' actual lived identities in order to describe and explain how these 'composite and often contradictory identities' (Holland *et al.*, 1998: 8) relate to the resources that unfold in the process and to the pursuit of livelihoods.

Composite identities result from contests with social identity and its constraining character in everyday practice. Some of these contests may lead to 'improvisations' (Holland *et al.*, (1998: 15-18) which are expected outcomes "when people are simultaneously engaged with or pushed by contradictory discourses" (Holland et al., 1998: 17). This occurs for example when rural people are confronted and negotiate with external forces such as modern technology, state policy or markets. Holland *et al.* (1998) add that improvisations start as impromptu actions, but when they become systematised, conventionalised and taken up as symbols; they become potential beginnings of altered identity. An altered identity in turn, leads to new waves of resource evolution and moulding, utilisation and activities, and lifestyles. As these improvisations occur, 'social legitimacy' (Bryceson, 2000: 5), based on agrarian values, is of concern. Thus agrarian values, such as food self-sufficiency and livestock keeping for symbolic purposes, are points of intergenerational contestation that play an important role in the processes of labelling, moulding and mobilising resources for livelihood construction.

Another relevant dimension of identity is the place of clan, kinship and religious affiliation in the creation and application of resources (Seur, 1992). Religion in particular, provides acceptable reasons for behaviour changes in rural areas, such as abandoning certain traditional rituals, distancing from certain local and kinship networks or embracing new networks (cf. Long, 1968). Religious affiliation also leads towards particular lifestyles and away from others and ultimately to an embracing or repudiation of resources, practices and networks.

The idea of lifestyles is closely related to that of identity, because the former is largely constructed based on the latter (Arce and Hebinck, 2002). Following the theoretical orientation developed so far, which focuses on resources as unfolding and being moulded by actors, a lifestyle is understood as the process of moulding opportunities into some coherent everyday life practices that are satisfying, continuous and promising in terms of identity affirmation, resource flows, relative consistency with prevailing institutional regimes and self-esteem. According to Hebinck and Bourdillon (2001: 7) the notion of lifestyles helps us take the issue of "livelihoods beyond the confines of economic activities only, to incorporate issues pertaining to people's socio-cultural repertoires such as value choices, status, senses of identity vis-à-vis other types of actors and local forms of organisation". Wartena (2006: 76) discards the term lifestyles for what she calls 'styles of making a living' arguing that the latter enables her to avoid the popular association of the former with consumption. However, I take the view that livelihoods include consumption and sociability, and the concept of 'lifestyle' that I use in this book helps pull the analysis beyond the materialist connotations of livelihood.

Stretching livelihood beyond the confines of economic activities, implies that symbolic resources and tasks are also incorporated. This helps livelihood studies to capture certain aspects of peoples' lives such as cultural attributes like beliefs, identity, festivals and sacred sites, which are important for explaining people's decisions and choices (Adato and Meinzen-Dick, 2002). These cultural repertoires are important components of lifestyles because they form bases for ordering life in a given way and hence, producing a style. According to Nooteboom (2003: 218), "a style is both an institutionalised pattern and a construction of an individual through negotiations within the household, neighbourhood and family". Such a conceptualisation, acknowledges individual strategic behaviour that is embedded in available cultural repertoires, rather than merely bounded by structural constraints imposed by geography or demography (Haan and Zoomers, 2005). In line with that Nooteboom (2003) notes that styles may be inherited, but are also being constantly reproduced and 'restyled' by the changing needs and orientations of villagers. The point here, therefore, is that a lifestyle is a result of a villager's history; present opportunities and predicaments, as well as their aspirations vis-à-vis the cultural repertoires that they confront. The key point is that lifestyles are not founded solely on economic rationality but are embedded in cultural processes that relate to both material and non-material outcomes.

As Wedel (1969: 45 cited in Wallman, 1984: 219) indicated "the focus of economic activity at any point is not solely determined by what brings in the largest amount of income, but also by its interrelations or linkages to other activities, and by factors such as tradition, place of residence, or by what (one) would prefer to be doing". It is a matter of styles of resource management that are drawn from one's historical experiences, present dilemmas and opportunities. People handle resources in diverse ways, even when in similar circumstances and the resultant diverse lifestyles lead to heterogeneous social forms and livelihood outcomes. In such cases, livelihoods may be better evaluated in terms of their being sensible rather than viable (cf. Wallman, 1984: 219).

Different lifestyles rely on different elements of local socio-cultural repertoires (cf. van der Ploeg, 1994: 19) to flourish. In drawing on diverse cultural repertoires, actors mould and re-mould resources in diverse ways in order to service their lifestyles. Because lifestyles hinge on values, it follows that what may be considered a resource in one lifestyle may not be in another, even in the same locality. Hence, there is need as Long (2001: 54) points out "to explore the issue of lifestyles and the factors that shape them". Links between lifestyles and resources are perhaps be best explained by exploring case studies and inter-personal networks to locate the lifestyle typologies that relate to particular levels of both material and non-material resources. This is because villagers are not just drifting through life eking out a living however they can, they have value orientations that 'style' their responses to 'opportunities'. Indeed, their ability to recognise a situation as presenting an opportunity is also a negotiated issue.

Negotiations are not always overt; they are often covert and draw on resources in very subtle ways. While material resources may be crucial in these processes, other elements such as time, information and identity (Long, 2001: 55, following Wallman, 1984) may be critical also. These crucial processes and their implications for livelihoods are pursued through analysis of the bases of the various lifestyles with regard to support networks as they shift over time. The key markers of lifestyles reflect the theoretical perspective developed so far and include social relationships, labour processes, interactions with technology and markets and allied institutions such as formal education (cf. van der Ploeg, 2003).

Unit of analysis: the elusive household

This study takes the household as the unit of analysis, even though this is an empirically problematic grouping. A household is traditionally defined as constituting a consumption group, that is composed of relations essentially organised around a family who eat from the same kitchen. In line with this Guyer (1981: 89) has argued that 'household implies a domestic unit with decision-making autonomy about (re-production), production and consumption'. Guyer also shows that recent scholarship has shown that the concept disguises variability in the ways things are done within households, but there has been reluctance by researchers to distance themselves from the concept because of the practical need for a simple unit of analysis. According to Guyer (1981: 98), the concept household in Africa is a fluid one and almost every survey that takes it as a unit of analysis has indicated a problem with defining its membership and in maintaining continuous records highly mobile people[48]. Such mobility implies fluidity in the household as a unitary decision-making unit with members able to exercise rights and subject to obligations beyond the household where they presently live (Guyer, 1981: 98).

Membership of households is particularly complex because a household may include a group of brothers, their families and parents living in a common compound, with varying levels of economic and social integration (cf. Poate and Daplyn, 1993). This is common in Gusiiland, Kenya where the compound constitutes a homestead (Omosa, 1998). This does not however imply membership or internal relationships can be taken as given (Guyer, 1981: 98). Rather they are negotiated and contested upon on a continuous basis. During fieldwork, it was observed that a homestead was usually home to a man and his wife or wives, married sons, their wives and children. It occasionally included married sons and their wives, unmarried sons and daughters and divorced or separated daughters, often with their children. In such scenarios, the man and his wife may have aged and may have subdivided their land for their sons for inheritance. However, for as long as they lived, they remained the unifying force and *de facto* head of the homestead. When these matriarchs and patriarchs passed on, the complex homesteads gave way to simple and smaller ones started by their sons much on similar patterns. The conventional concept of a household as constituting a married man and his wife or wives and direct children is not very common in Sengeta Village (cf. Whitehead, 2002: 582). After the demise of the patriarchs and matriarchs, the newly emerging homesteads continue to closely cooperate and interact, especially during funeral ceremonies maintaining a unified face to other parties despite any conflicts that may exist between them.

Harris (1981: 6 cited in Guyer, 1981: 100) best captures this diversity when pointing out that "segments of households operate semi-autonomously at some levels but coalesce at others". Even within households, the 'heads' do not fully control labour or all the resources. Assumptions to the contrary only conveniently simplify a complex situation (Guyer, 1981: 100). One aspect of this semi-autonomy is the varying levels of economic independency/integration of unmarried sons and daughters of different generations who reside in the homestead. While this does not necessarily confuse the definition of a household, it does blur attempts to identify a single unit of action in livelihood construction. The household model assumes that families have resources, and make joint decisions about allocating them. However, in practice resources are not just commodities and people have to continually invest in assuring their continued access to them: because social and political resources are required to access material ones (Guyer, 1981: 102). This means that inter-household coalitions of diverse strengths can develop in the short-term and for strategic

---

[48] See also Francis (2002) who brings out issues of labour migration and household dissolution due to resource constraints, arguing that households vary considerably in terms of both their composition and their stability over time.

reasons. Therefore, this study is flexible in regarding the household as the main unit of analysis and takes cognisance of issues about resources that transcend allocation, in terms of what the resources are, and how people get and keep them, before, during and after allocation (Guyer, 1981: 102). This calls for an understanding of interpersonal, intra- and inter-household networks and resource flows. Information, visits and friendship webs are important indicators of directions in which resources flow between and within households.

This study uses the group organised around a common kitchen as an entry point and constructs the actual composition of households or 'confederations' (Alderson-Smith, 1984) of them, over time in terms of the observed flows of information and resources. In tracing these confederations, significance is given to the connections that exist and are developed within and between households (Murray, 1998: 22) which is a useful way of estimating resource sharing or co-production. These confederations of households turn out to be 'clusters of households' related to one another in a variety of ways (kinship, working contracts, and mutual help) often transcending village, location, district or even national boundaries (cf. Murray 1998: 24). Some of the relationships are based on labour organisation, kinship, trade or mutual help transactions. Thus, social networks take precedence over discrete geographical or political areas. The livelihood activities take place within and between households via social networks. The units of observation, that is to say the actors studied directly, are the individual adults in the households. As expected, some adults related to the study households live miles away in other countries or in cities, but have an influence in decision-making and provision of information and/or resources. Their contributions and exchanges with the selected households are pursued through interviews with various adults within the households. Children and youth also initiate connections and ultimately resource flows within and between households and link up with their grandparents and other relations for assistance, sometimes without the knowledge of their parents. While the units of observation sometimes overflowed from the local setting, the local setting remained the research level.

This methodological approach of focusing on linkages between individuals in households and networks of them as constructed locally, regionally and globally fits well with the chosen theoretical orientation in which resource creation and livelihood construction are viewed as unfolding and negotiated amongst different interests and preferences. The focus on linkages emphasises the flow of resources and support between people wherever they are located, rather than focusing on geographically united households within which decision-making and resources sharing may be uncoordinated and disjointed (cf. de Haan and Zoomers, 2003; Kaag, et al., 2004 and Wartena, 2006: 73-74). The focus on linkages between people involved in resource creation and sharing processes is particularly important since fundamental connections between people do not depend on institutions and often outlive them (Rocheleau, 2001: 85). The interpretive framework in the study followed emergent social networks that span local and global levels. This applies in terms of not only the location of network members, but also in terms of global influences on local activities and processes and the ensuing negotiation and intermediation of the same. In spite of recognised partial cooperation and sharing within households, the unit remains a good basis for investigation, if the inherent weaknesses of relying on it too strictly are borne in mind.

Conclusion

This chapter has developed a theoretical perspective for the book. It has reviewed the actor-oriented perspective, which explains the notion of resource creation in terms of social actors having agency, power and knowledge and therefore, the capacity to act meaningfully and strategically. This perspective does not however fully explain the actual scheme of things in villagers' resource creation and use to make a living. To remedy this I turned to livelihood approaches, which have been widely explored especially with regard to resource studies. I show that livelihood approaches privilege a materialist view of resources by analysing them in terms of a pentagon of assets that determines economic activity and hence, livelihood outcomes. These outcomes are generally conceived in specific measures of food security, sustainable natural resource use, increased income and improved well-being. This determinist view of reality notwithstanding, the approach represents a bold move in centralising resources in poverty and rural development debates and thus presents a useful framework and starting point of analysis in this book. The determinist element of livelihood approaches, does not however provide a complete picture on how villagers link with resources as it addresses this question through structural analysis of accessibility and inaccessibility, availability and unavailability, and ignores the creativity of villagers in practice. To address this shortcoming and sharpen the analytical power of livelihoods approaches, they are interwoven with concepts from the actor-oriented and landscape perspectives. This enables recognition of the dialectic interactions between 'nature' and humans, the struggles between endogenous and exogenous initiatives, and the place of identity and lifestyle in resource creation and livelihood construction processes.

This approach recognises that, actors' resource creation processes are central to making a living. Resources are viewed as fluid and transcend local and national boundaries. They include, for example, decisions, influence and remittances from the diaspora. This spatial boundary transcendence of resources enables the analysis to follow linkages between individuals within and between institutions such as households. It also brings out the complexities of resource creation processes and casts them as largely collaborative and contested responding to interplays between endogenous and exogenous relationships and initiatives. These complex resource creation processes entail the production, co-production and use of both material and non-material resources. The issue of resource creation is cast as hinging on people's exercise of agency, which leads to creativity. Creativity has been described as an essential element of all activity that should be placed at the centre of theorising about human agency (Dalton, 2004: 605). However, it is also restricted by *habitus,* which is the immanent law inscribed in people by identical histories that precondition not only the coordination of practices but also the practices of coordination (Bourdieu, 1990: 59). This does not negate the notion and importance of creativity of action, but emphasises that 'creativity is often a restricted set of strategies embedded in bodily hexis and the logic of a particular social milieu' (Bourdieu and Passeron, 1977 cited in Dalton, 2004: 613) and historically constructed dispositions (Bourdieu, 1990: 62). Rocheleau (2001: 78) similarly argues that social networks can be envisioned as patterns of habit-forming connections between people (individuals and groups), other beings, physical surroundings and artefacts. This underscores that landscape and livelihoods are co-produced through actor experience and learning in historically constructed processes. Therefore, I agree to the fact of creativity as 'situated' within the socio-cultural circumstances of the 'nature'- human nexus. With this theoretical path developed and key concepts elaborated, the study attempts through fieldwork to address the study question of how villagers create resources, use them to make their living and with what results more completely.

In the field, the households and homesteads that are referred to as entry points for the study were viewed as mini-theatres of human life, situated in a distinct local landscape. Space, place and identity are important in the definition of household and homestead in the study area. Kinship and friendship networks evolve and extend the landscape beyond the household and homestead as well as blowing them up into virtual entities, which continue to remain true to 'home' and local landscape. Exogenous initiatives such as the nation-state and globalisation throw up 'imagined communities' (see Crehan, 1997) that offer their own challenges to the local landscape without overcoming it. The next chapter deals with the study methodology

CHAPTER 4

Methodological Approach

Introduction

The study reported in this book examined how rural villagers in Nyamira District, mid Southwestern Kenya created and used resources to make their living. The study analysed the diverse ways in which villagers struggled to redefine and reorient phenomena to serve their purposes as resources over time and space. It was an exploratory study focusing on how ordinary villagers created resources through imaginative everyday practices by redefining phenomena and giving them new meanings that led to new or additional uses. The goal is to generate some generalisations, description and explanation (Stebbins, 2001: 6-7) of the turning points and processes involved in resource creation and use.

A first attempt to grapple with the main central question in the book was made through a relevant theoretical review. This subjected the problem to the actor-oriented, livelihood and landscape approaches for explaining the resource creation and use processes. The first of these enhanced appreciation of the fact that villagers are endowed with agency and have the capacity to strategise and act in ways that make the creation of resources possible. However, it did not cast much light on the scheme of things in this process: how this process actually works. The livelihood approaches posit five types of assets that are at the centre of people's endeavours to make their living. Unlike the actor-oriented perspective these approaches do not allow the possibility of villagers creating their own resources but emphasise issues of availability and accessibility to resources. The landscape approach has a powerful explanatory power through the notion of the dialectical relationship between humans and 'nature'. Combining actor-oriented concepts such as agency, power and knowledge with livelihood and landscape as co-produced moved the study closer to appreciating the idea of villagers' resource creation. In themselves, the three approaches provide only a partial account of the process of resource creation. Only through shifting, the exploration to the field was it possible to capture, describe and explain the process as it unfolded.

Fieldwork was carried out in Sengeta Village, Nyamira District in 2004-2005. Sengeta Village is at the centre of a convergence of three important agro-ecological zones: the lower highland tea-dairy zone, the lower highland maize-wheat/pyrethrum zone and the upper midland coffee-tea zone (Kenya, 1994 – Nyamira District Development Plan). My masters' thesis research ten years earlier was the springboard to the present study and had included the village in a one-off survey although that study concentrated in villages further to the East in the higher areas. The purpose of picking Sengeta village for this study was to follow up on some of those earlier contacts and work in an area with the broadest agricultural production possibilities, provided by the villages' varied agro-ecological conditions. The range of choices available provided a chance to examine how resources are created and livelihoods made without reference to obvious constraining ecological conditions and to analyse the emergence of heterogeneous forms.

Data Collection

Data were collected during two years of fieldwork in 2004 and 5. The field work process was largely iterative, seeking as much qualitative data as possible on how people created and used resources to make a living. The main research strategy employed was case studies, focusing mainly on individual villagers within their household, local and macro contexts to capture contemporary and historical moments of household resource creation and use to make a living (cf. Yin, 1981; 1994; Burawoy, 1998; Stake, 2003). This approach is in line with Bagchi et al. (1998) who argue that livelihoods can only be fully understood in a specified personal and cultural context. The main aim of the exercise was to attempt to reconstruct a full picture of how people in the village commenced their lives, the resources they needed and how they created, organised and deployed them to support their lives. This was intended to provide as comprehensive an answer as possible to the research question. In doing this the fieldwork proceeded as follows.

Secondary Data

The study proceeded to build on the partial account on the research question already provided by the theoretical approaches by looking up more information in the Nyamira District Archives. But these only contained truncated reports, mainly comprising routine administrative reports of farm output, marketed farm produce and prices and on-going agricultural extension activities. The search for descriptions and explanations of how villagers may even have contributed to resource creation and use at household level were frustrated on at least two accounts. Firstly, reporting is premised on the assumption that farm output was the result of agricultural extension efforts and focused on crop, livestock and business activities. Local services and craftwork for instance, were missing. Two, reports for many periods of time were missing. Given this I decided to move the exploration between the district archives (specific Government Department document stores) and the National Archives in

Nairobi, with a view to constructing the historical development of the Nyamira landscape. That, I thought would help explain what went on in the past and situate the villagers in the story. Most of this attempt is reported in Chapter 2. The material in that chapter provides an important context for the analysis in subsequent chapters by clarifying the cultural and livelihood pursuits of people in Gusiiland.

Music – a search was mounted in the village and in neighbouring ones, for local popular vernacular secular music which might have recorded the processes of resource creation and use at household level. I collected more than fifty items of music estimated to have been produced between the late 1960s and the early 1990s. I was able to locate and purchase a turn-table in Sengeta Village to play and transcribe the music, and transcribed about thirty relevant items of music. This focus on music was motivated by the argument that it is a powerful symbol of cultural identity and aspirations and evokes a wealth of associations of an emotional and social kind (Long, 2001b: 4). Music constitutes popular commentaries on a range of issues from a variety of angles, and constitutes an accurate social record of local thoughts, meanings, aspirations and strategies. In a sense music is an incredibly rich source of ethnographic material. In line with this, Hyslop (1972: 55) maintained that traditional instrumentalists should be recognised as embodying a significant part of the cultural heritage, and belonging to a category of professionals. Popular music may thus be seen as a reflection of peoples' lived experiences. Roberts (1965) pointed out that Kenya's popular music reflect the life of the ordinary person in the street, arguing that whatever the subject of the music it provides a pretty accurate guide to the attitudes of the average Kenyan over politics, work, education or social stresses (cf. Wekesa, 2004; Tsuruta, 2003; Street, 2003). In line with this Nyairo and Ogude (2005), point out that popular music documents a people's history, and the history of a community can be told through that community's collection of popular songs. Using popular music, this study attempted to capture the Gusii people's struggles to create resources and livelihoods over time.

Extended Case Studies

Engagement with theoretical approaches clarified the issue of the capacity of actors (villagers) individually or in groups to create resources, and that social action is created at the same time as it creates livelihood and landscape. The secondary data throws some light on these processes and the historical resource creation practices of which they are a part in Nyamira District and at a higher level of generality. They revealed some aspects of the shared meanings of these processes; but did not clarify how actors experienced and actually contributed to or engaged in these processes in their varied ways of seeking survival and satisfaction (cf. Levine, 1979: 3). This shifted my attention to the village and household, to find diverse ways of engaging local inhabitants in order to gain understanding of their everyday undertakings of resource creation and making a living. Following Eriksen, (2004:48) the aim of the fieldwork was to understand local practices and notions in their full context.

I used my experience and knowledge of Nyamira District from previous studies and visits, as well as secondary data to purposively select a research site, Sengeta Village which presented a wide range of agro-ecological opportunities. I chose to work in one village as opposed to the whole district on the basis that the village was still connected to the district, country and the world, and as van Velsen (1967) pointed out, isolating one village for analytical purposes should not be confused with *de facto* isolation. The villages' links to the wider society are still crucial to the choices villagers make and are recognised as such. The collection of case material started at the village headman's home. However, I had to quickly move out into the village after my courtesy call which lasted about three days. This was also necessary in order to keep my work separate from the local bureaucracy that he partly represents. The actual work began with a search for three Sengetans identified in my master's study questionnaires that provided useful and insightful responses and comments. One of these three people had since passed away, another was sickly and old, and in and out of hospital, and only the third was available. When I initially tried to meet the man I found him enmeshed in a tight schedule of farm work and church meetings, but as I got to know him better I learned how to 'catch him'. Eventually, this man Petro became a dependable respondent, friend and second entry point to the village. I visited him many times and interviewed him about his early life aspirations, how he had lived up to them or failed; the resources in his life and how they had become at different times and the problems he had encountered over time. Sometimes I came round to his home and we walked to the village shops where he liked taking tea at a restaurant and I could observe his interactions with other people. Through my discussions with him, the village headman and other villagers I grasped an idea about the main livelihood domains in Sengeta village. After about two months of iterations between the village headman and Petro, my research colleague and I got some references from Petro and started contacting other individuals for case studies a process which continued through snowball sampling (cf. Murray, 1998; 2002).

Throughout our focus was on subjects who could remember much about their past and what they did at different times to 'earn' what they considered a living and to resolve problems. Thus, we sought subjects who were available to discuss and interact with us, and articulate about their lives and circumstances over time (cf. Wallman, 1984: 48-9). Over time we interacted with people in their homes, fields, churches, school meetings, restaurants, tea buying centres, water points, posho mills, village headman's court and burial ceremonies. Participant observation was thus inbuilt into the research process by our temporary immersion into village life in its many facets (cf. Yin, 1994; Emerson, Fretz and Shaw, 1995). We listened to conversations and discussions in local brew drinking places, in restaurants and on the road sides, and wrote up interesting and illuminating issues later. In all twenty one usable case studies were developed, with some following the patterns of everyday life by flowing out beyond the boundaries of Sengeta village. These case studies are hereafter referred to as case material or case records (cf. Stake, 2003). In constructing explanations, I am not completely removed from the process as my own lifeworld as a member of and raised in the Gusii society overlaps somewhat with those of the subjects and implicates me in the research process. However my prejudices about 'our way of life' are also enabling, leading me to seek explanations and justifications and developing a form of critical hermeneutics, in some instances attempting to understand the subjects through my own experience as a member of this ethnic group(cf. Drinkwater, 1994: 38-9; Peacock, 1986: 70 - 2).

Survey data – in October 2005 towards the end of the fieldwork a short questionnaire survey was carried out focus mainly on tea issues. This played a part in another study but also played a role in this one, which had identified the importance of tea as resource in Sengeta. The issues around tea that had emerged by this point included 'theft' at tea buying centres and marketing problems. It became necessary to triangulate some of the issues through a brief survey. A systematic sample of 50 individuals was obtained from the village headman's list of 210 households by sampling every fourth household on the list progressively. The sampled person or their spouse (or in the absence of both, a neighbour on any side who was not on the sample list) was interviewed using a standard interview schedule. The data obtained were run on the SPSS computer programme and I used some of the descriptive statistics generated in Chapters 5 and 6.

Extended Case Studies in Context

This section briefly outlines the case material collected, which provides a central element of the story line and analysis in this book. Of the twenty-one case studies collected, eight are presented in this section. These are largely typical of the corpus of data and are selected for their historical richness, and their capacity to take the analysis through issues of resource creation and use from the 1940s or earlier through to the 2000s. The selected cases include people who were young during different decades between the 1940s and the 2000s. This relates to the selection criterion of people's ability to remember and articulate issues in a historical perspective, and ties in with an integral aim of the study, namely to capture changes over time in the way that resources have been encountered. Analysis of the extended case study data focuses on the agency of rural villagers, their lifestyles, identity and embedded practices with regard to resources and livelihood construction, and especially how they negotiate meanings over phenomena as resources. This hinges on the view that objects and events such as resources have no single absolute meaning, but that they are interpreted as they evolve and meanings coined around actor's experiences, evolved beliefs and preferences (cf. Hannafin, et al. 1997). The selected cases are central to providing explanations for issues emerging in the study and excerpts from these studies, together with at least four others, are used in the subsequent chapters to illustrate specific themes and sub-themes, which emerged from insights garnered during data collection and through reading and re-reading the corpus of data (cf. Mason, 1996; O'Leary, 2004). In the course of analysis, the same cases are looked at from different perspectives, as there are no right or wrong views, only differing views or multiple truths representing differing interests (cf. van Velsen, 1967: 147; Emerson, Fretz and Shaw, 1995: 3). This is theoretically interesting as it helps the book to show that a villager may not follow a single livelihood trajectory but often follows multiple trajectories simultaneously. This section provides the contextual settings of the excerpts used later to ground the analysis in subsequent chapters. By setting out the individual case studies here they retain a level of wholeness which may be drawn later to premise certain study themes. In all the cases the terms actors, individuals, people and villagers are used interchangeably.

Petro

Petro was born in 1927 in a polygamous family. He has three brothers, three sisters, and a number of stepbrothers and sisters. His father was a herder, but the family was generally poor. As a boy, he was involved in herding and clearing bushes to open new millet fields. Petro was circumcised at the age of 15. Like other young men in his village, he toyed with the idea of raising his own resources to commence life. At that time, many young men were being recruited to work in the then White Highlands. In 1942, his neighbour and uncle who already had work in the plantations assisted him with in finding a job and temporary accommodation there. After a while, he bought some household items and was provided with a small round hut by the plantation management and he moved out of his uncle's house. Petro worked plucking tea in the Kericho tea estates between 1942 and 1947. His salary then was three shillings per month and he hardly saved any money for future use. While working in the tea plantations he came to appreciate how easy it was to tender the tea crop and developed an interest and aspiration to own his own tea crop in the future.

After working in Kericho for six years, he came back home and started school at the age of 21 in 1948. He supplemented his plantation work earnings with maize and pyrethrum growing to raise his school fees of nine shillings per year as his parents did not value education at the time. Petro got his first pyrethrum seedlings from neighbours. He used to sell the produce through a cooperative Society. He said that tea became a more important cash crop after pyrethrum farming collapsed when world market prices tumbled in the late 1970's and early 1980's, leading farmers to uproot the crop and start doing other things to gain money. He sat Common Entrance Examination (CEE) in 1954 and passed. After primary school, he was employed on probation as a teacher in Kitutu Chache. He worked as a teacher for two years (1956-1958) but left because his salary of a hundred shillings per month was too low. In 1960, he joined a pyrethrum cooperative society as a treasurer and later as a storekeeper. Here the salary was 170 shillings per month. During that time, he saved five hundred shillings with which he bought an exotic dairy cow. The cow used to produce eight litres of milk per day, but it died after only two years. He has however, kept a cow ever since.

Petro became a Seventh Day Adventist in 1950, was baptised and wedded in the church the same year. The bride price for his wife was six heads of cattle, a bull and a goat, which he obtained from his sister's bride price. The wedding expenses were low because they walked to the bride's home to church and back to his home. In 1951, they got their first-born child, a son; who dropped out of school in form four and is now married with a number of children. Formerly he used to do lumbering for a living but nowadays is a farmer. Petro occasionally assists him by paying school fees for his children. Petro has three other sons and seven daughters. One of his sons died in 2002 after a long illness that drained the family's resources. Petro is still an active member of the Adventist church, has been an elder and is a choir member. The church members assisted him during his children's weddings, and with his late son's burial, praying with his sick wife and providing finger millet for his wife's meals. Church members regularly give offerings in the church drawing mainly from their tea earnings. Through such offerings and under his leadership as head elder of the church in the 1990s they managed to build a permanent church in the village.

In 1961, he planted tea after soil from his father's farm was examined and permission to plant granted by Kericho's Tea Research Foundation. After paying a deposit, he was provided tea stumps for planting on credit from Kericho, which he paid off after harvesting and selling the tea leaf. He started by planting a thousand stumps and gradually increased to three thousand bushes. Through his parents he mobilised family, kin and neighbourhood labour (*amasaga*) to prepare a seed bed and to plant the stumps early the same morning that they were delivered. Through this work group many people in the village and beyond, especially his relatives, learnt of and took up tea growing with his assistance. His father was helpful in prevailing on his mother, younger brothers and sisters to help him on the farm. At the Iranya Tea Buying Centre, which served the villagers in the 1960s and 1970s, I found out that seven out of its first ten registered tea growers had worked in the Kericho tea plantations in the 1950s and 1960s[49]. After Petro was registered as a grower, he developed his own '*egesa*' (shade) and started to grow his own seedlings from mature tea as he had learned in the tea plantations. He did this initially for infilling dried

---

[49] Personal discussions (February 2004 and November 2005) with the founder chairman of the tea buying centre Mzee Jonathan who served from 1964 – 1984 and with the current chairman Mr Maguara and committee member Mr Ongaga.

stumps on the farm and later as a business. In 2004 and 2005, his farm had a tea seed bed, napier grass, tea, maize, beans, sugar cane and kale.

Petro has a semi-permanent house and a grass-thatched hut that serves as a kitchen and sleeping place for his daughters when they visit. The living room is well furnished and he has a transistor radio. He does not have a cell phone and does not intend to purchase one saying, "it is for young people". I observed that Petro was an influential person in the village and at church. When he speaks in village meetings or in church, people listen keenly and often support his ideas. Some of his peers referred to him as *mwalimu* (teacher) from his stint in teaching in the late 1950s. He is known to be generous in buying tea for his peers at the village centre and for helping during burials and other community activities.

In 1968, the family divided their father's farm. In the sub-division, his younger brother got 900 bushes, his father 400 bushes and Petro retained 1800 bushes. The division of his father's land effectively provided for the inheritance of the land and Petro focused his farming and other development activities on his own land. Having given some of his tea to his brother and his father, he started looking inwards to his family and personal development. His wife focused more on their farm plucking and wedding tea, planting finger millet, maize and bananas, and less on her parents-in-law's fields. In 1969, Petro bought land at Irandi about two kilometres from his home for one thousand six hundred shillings and planted tea there. This money came from his tea and pyrethrum earnings and a bank loan. He planted one thousand six hundred tea bushes on the land and later increased this to three thousand tea bushes. His tea leaf yield averaged seven hundred kilograms per month. This earned him an average of three hundred shillings in the 1970s, one thousand five hundred in the 1980s and about three thousand in the 1990s. Petro has educated all his children mainly using tea earnings.

Petro's wife is bed ridden with diabetes. He said that his own health was failing and he only weeds his tea especially in the mornings before it gets hot but rarely plucks it. He has employed reliable people including his daughter in-law and his neighbour's two daughters-in-law, whom he pays four shillings per kilogram of tea leaf plucked and delivered to the tea buying centre. He describes these three women as trustworthy to pluck his tea, control the quality of tea leaf and ensure that his crop is not stolen on the way to or at the buying centre. He explained that these workers treated his farm as their own, counting the days and going to pluck when the time came without him having to prompt them.

One of his sons is a school teacher in Rift Valley Province and had bought a farm there. He regularly visits his parents and assists them whenever there is material or financial need. In particular, he assisted with school fees for his younger brothers and sisters, when they were in school. Petro's daughters (one of whom is a teacher) and their husbands also assist with hospital bills and drugs occasionally. Another son, Simon, married through a church wedding in

1991. The family assisted him to pay bride price. He had one cow, which he bought from his earnings as a photographer. His father gave him one cow, his brother the teacher gave him another and his paternal uncles provided one. The church assisted with transport costs. Petro's two daughters also married through church weddings recently. The bride price paid for them was used to cover wedding expenses and to settle their eldest brother's bride price. His son the teacher provided money for feeding visitors during the bride price negotiations.

Petro has subdivided the tea on the land at Irandi for his sons' inheritance. Each has been given seven hundred bushes. The tea at home belongs solely to him and is part of his '*emonga*'. He harvests about three hundred kilograms per month earning him about three thousand shillings per month in 2004/5. The tea leaf earnings have risen steadily from 25 cents per kilogram in the 1960s to 50 cents in the 1970s, three shillings in the 1980s, seven shillings in the 1990s and nine shillings in 2004/5. These earnings enabled him to acquire a cow from time to time as need arose. He feeds it on the napier grass from his land, which he says, is more than enough; and they graze on the pasture paddocks he has established. He has shown his married sons the portions of land on which they plant their food crops like maize, finger millet, sugar cane and kales. His first-born son grows napier grass at the edges of his portion. He sells the grass to neighbours and other villagers, and sometimes gives it free of charge to his father for his cow when he has not enough from his fields. Members of Petro's family, including his wife and his sons' wives, take turns in milking[50] the cow. At the lower edge of his land by the river, he has planted trees, mostly Eucalyptus that provides him with firewood. He occasionally sells some of the trees to get money for his day-to-day needs.

Petro has also ventured into business in the past using tea earnings. In 1970, he joined a group of six people, each contributing five hundred shillings, to start a business of buying and selling timber. "The business collapsed due to mistrust, the chairman ran it down but explained it as arising from sales on credit and defaulting customers". Petro used to be a member of several self-help groups. In particular, the Sengeta II Group assisted him with money, helping him to pay hospital bills. He also used to be a member of Sengeta One Group although he never benefited from it. He quit the group earlier and it is collapsing steadily. The group started in the late 1970s pooling resources from about fifty villagers to buy *matatu* (taxi) vehicles. This was achieved without a hitch and with the profits a posho mill was purchased in the early 1980s and another in the early 1990s. Recently they sold the vehicles and there were rumours in the village of plans to sell the posho mills.

Petro said that in the community, they have initiated several projects such as Sengeta Primary School, a dispensary and a tea buying centre. Originally, their children used to walk to school about three kilometres away, but now it is in

[50] Petro's wife being sick, a daughter-in-law milked for her during her turns.

the village. He has also worked with other villagers to improve their water point (*ensoko*) with support from the Ministry of Water. The village has impromptu organisations to oversee funeral arrangements. When death occurs, villagers usually sit down, set up an organising committee and agree on certain issues pertaining to the burial. They then contribute according to need, for example, they may agree to contribute five hundred shillings per family, if the body has to be brought in from Mombasa or Nairobi but if the body is at Kisii or Nyamira, they contribute a hundred shillings per household. It also depends on the amount of money owed in hospital bills at the time of death. Similar arrangements are set up when there are weddings and parties for children (*ekerero*).

Petro considers his life as successful and that he has achieved what he aspired for by the grace of God. He advises his sons how to save and invest for the future needs of their children. He regularly returns his tithes and offerings to the local church. He explained that he had brought up his children as Christians and given them a formal education. The education has enabled some of them to gain formal employment and they support the family. Mzee Petro could be one of the richest people in Sengeta. However, because of the ill health of some of his family members his resources had dwindled. One of his sons was sick for a long time and later died and since then his wife had been sick for a long time, spending long periods of time in the hospital. This has drained him financially. His last-born son who is a trader usually takes his mother to hospital and buys fruits for her as recommended by doctors.

Saulo

Saulo was born in 1928 at Karantini about ten kilometres to the east of Sengeta. They moved to their present settlement in 1929 or 1930 after their father died. After their father's burial at Karantini, their mother felt that the place was not good anymore, and she moved with a group of other people to join others from their clan who had earlier moved to Sengeta. Saulo attended school up to standard one. He quit schooling because his mother feared that he could be taken away by the white people (British) as many had been taken away for wars when she was young and they never returned (referring to participation in World War I). So he stayed at home to look after their cattle. The cattle were originally his elder sister's bride price and in later years came from his three other sisters. Saulo has two brothers, one older and the other younger.

He was circumcised in 1945, and employed picking pyrethrum on settler farms the same year. Later his maternal uncle took him and his elder brother to Dobi farm to work as pyrethrum pickers. Saulo's salary was one shilling and fifty cents per month at the first farm and at Dobi farm it was three shillings and thirty cents per month. After some time at Dobi, Saulo moved to Nyaronde where he earned six shillings per month, still doing pyrethrum work. From Nyaronde, Saulo went to Kimari where he was employed as a turn boy on trucks carrying green tea leaf to Shauji factory. Here he earned twelve shillings per month and was taught how to drive by his driver, a friendly Kuria man. He was employed as a driver in the same company in 1951 and worked there until 1959 on a salary of fifteen shillings per month. While working with Shauji tea factory he developed interest in tea growing. From 1952 he took tea stumps home from Shauji every time he went back and planted them on his farm. He showed his mother how to weed and to harvest when the crop was ready.

By 1955, when his tea crop was mature, he in collaboration with his mother harvested tea leaf and produced home-made tea for domestic use. They fermented the tea leaves for a day or two and used wooden pestles and mortars to pound it. They then sun dried it and it was ready for use and for sale around the village. In 1959, he retired and returned home, planted coffee and pyrethrum. Due to declining coffee prices, he later uprooted the coffee. In 1963 he added some more bushes in his already mature tea farm so he would be recognised as a tea grower by the KTDA. Savings from his work across the country enabled him establish his cash cropping ventures from 1959 to 1963. By 1963 he had already inherited land from his mother who held what had now become their ancestral land.

Saulo married his first wife from Bosinge in 1963 paying thirteen heads of cattle and a goat as bride price. He raised the bride price from his sister's bride price of thirteen cattle and five goats. The intermediary in the marriage was a friend Maturi, whom he had worked with in the tea plantations in the 1950s. He married his second wife in 1966 after his first wife had given birth to three daughters. This made him lose hope of ever having sons with her but they were born later. He paid bride price of six heads of cattle and one goat for his second wife, all of it accrued through his tea earnings. He has three sons and two daughters by this marriage. He built semi-permanent houses for his wives and two grass thatched huts, one for the daughters and another for the sons, next to their respective mothers.

Saulo gets some additional income from thatching houses, an occupation he has been in since 1959. Thatching houses is taboo for women in Gusiiland and is purely a male occupation, although since 2000 thatching contracts have become rare. Times have changed and the price for thatching a house nowadays ranges from three hundred shillings for the smallest house to six hundred shillings for a big one, unlike in the 1960's when they were paid between twenty five and thirty shillings. Saulo also weaves baskets for sale. He specialises in baskets used for chicken rearing and those for carrying green tea leaves to the buying centres. Because there are no forests nowadays to provide sticks for weaving baskets, he splits mature napier grass canes and weaves with them. He uses the extra income from thatching houses and selling baskets to supplement his tea earnings for use to pay school fees (for a grandchild), buy food and largely for entertainment with the local brew *chang'aa* and *busaa* in the company of friends. He also used the savings to buy iron sheets to roof his house. Saulo is a member of Onchera Group based in Sengeta village which he joined in 1995 with a membership fee of fifty shillings and has been paying a monthly subscription of thirty shillings ever since.

Saulo had cattle and was generally a prosperous man until 1980 when his second wife was arrested for planting marijuana with the aim of selling it to educate her children. The marijuana case led him to sell most of his cattle to travel to court over a long time and eventually pay a court fine. "So that was the start of poverty in this homestead". Eventually none of his sons and daughters went beyond primary school and none joined formal employment. Saulo has used some of his tea earnings to build houses for some of his sons, but he spends more money handling their village headman's court cases when they had stolen, accumulated debts in drinking places or destroyed property while fighting in drinking places. This is partly why he has not trained any of the sons to thatch houses, as they might fall off the roofs when drunk. Four of his daughters are married and bride price has been paid for two of them. Both of Saulo's wives used to brew *busaa* for sale to supplement their tea incomes. They have since stopped because of aging and harassment from the administration and the police. Since they stopped brewing Saulo's wives became Adventists attending Sengeta Church with some of their unmarried daughters.

In 2000 Saulo sold one of the cows paid to him as his daughter's bride price for 5050 shillings to buy dry maize for his two wives and roofing iron sheets for his youngest son. Saulo said his son needed a house and iron sheets were easier because grass was rare and expensive. In 1999 Saulo's sons started agitating for part of their father's tea farm for their maintenance, as they had no income sources. In 2001 he wanted to be baptised into the Adventist Church to avoid his sons who came to his house when drunk and made a lot of noise. He figured that if he was baptised they would fear to visit him while drunk as he would be Christian. When he asked for baptism, the church leadership demanded that Saulo should first settle struggles over land and tea by his wives and his sons. So he divided it up between his two wives and subsequently their several sons. This left him with very few tea bushes (*emonga*) which he shares with his first wife.

Since dividing up his land his life has changed. His tea earnings have dropped from about two thousand shillings per month to a mere four to five hundred shillings. His first wife plucks her own tea as well as Saulo's by herself while he goes thatching houses or drinking. When she has no work on their farm she goes to pluck tea at neighbours' farms and is paid four shillings per kilogram of tea leaf. She uses the money to buy necessities for the home. Saulo occasionally gets contracts to thatch houses. His second wife and her sons have abandoned him. They do not assist him with anything and she never gives him the customary food rations. Saulo has retreated to his first wife's house, although previously when he had all the tea money he was welcome in his second wife's house and spent much time there. When his sons are drunk, they threaten that they will take away his *emonga*, but he tells them: "you know my last weapon; I will curse you, *inkobarama*". Even so Saulo tries to improve his relationship with them by assisting as much as he can in paying bride price.

Saulo has a cow, which is with his first wife, and he sometimes takes time to take it for grazing on the portions of his land with pasture. Recently he bought a goat that has now given birth to triplets, making Saulo very happy about his new investment. His first wife's house where he lives has a spacious living room. There is a big dining table and six chairs and in one corner there is a wooden cupboard and a 100 litre plastic water container. On the open ceiling structure Saulo keeps bundles of split napier grass canes ready for making baskets. Some newly made baskets ready for the market, are also stored in the ceiling structure.

Saulo had some carpentry tools that he bought with earnings from tea and thatching houses. He used to make simple furniture for his household. His sons were interested in carpentry and he gave them a complete carpentry kit. His brother also assisted him with some tools to complete the kit. But the influence of alcohol led them to start selling the tools. Their father salvaged a few, which he hires out to carpenters who needed them. With the earnings he has purchased a table and soon the people he hires the tools to will make for him a bed as in-kind payment. Saulo's sons give him problems as they did not succeed in school, get jobs or learn any skills. The sons drink a lot of alcohol but do not have income to finance the drinking and often turn to theft.

Saulo's daughters are good to him and on their visits they usually leave him with twenty to fifty shillings for his *busaa* drink. Recently his sons-in-law came and gave him three thousand shillings to assist him to take his wife to hospital when she had sprained her leg, but she was healed using traditional herbs. The money will assist him in buying basic items at home and for his entertainment with *busaa.*

Saulo lives with two of his grandchildren, one girl and one boy. His first wife wanted the girl so that she could help her in the house and fetch water. The boy was born before her mother married. Saulo paid for their school requirements and food. Sometimes Saulo sells his tea to s*oko huru* (the middlemen who buy tea leaves in cash and sell it on to the private tea factories in the former White Highlands in the neighbouring Kericho District). In December 2005 Saulo sold a small portion of his land to the local dispensary for 50,000 shillings at the request of the dispensary management committee that needed land to expand the facility. He gave some of the money to each of his two wives and used the balance to buy a cow, which he gave to a friend of his for *sagare*, tenant keeping.

Saulo participates and contributes whenever there is a problem in Sengeta village or in his clan. He has lived peacefully with his neighbours and fellow clansmen. Sometimes there were suspicions and allegations of witchcraft, which create animosity among the people. He said "some families do not share anything". Mzee Saulo believes that his life has not been successful because his children especially the sons have serious problems: some of them drink too much and turn to theft. None of the sons paid bride price on their own initiative without his insistence and assistance. They hardly ever assist him especially since he divided up the land for them and their mothers. His perception is that the division of the land caused him to lose power over his second wife and her children and he feels that he no longer has any control over his land and tea.

Nyandika

Nyandika was born in 1933 and has two elder brothers and five sisters, all his juniors. He received some formal education up to standard one, which at the time took three years to complete. He stopped schooling due to a misunderstanding between him and his class teacher. When Nyandika was young they were poor, his mother did not have much property, but his dad had cattle, which he used to graze in his first wife's *bweri*. His father had gone to his maternal uncle and brought a cow in *omosuto* – a brother's gift to his sister's son to appreciate use of that sister's bride price in his marriage. Nyandika said his father may have collected *omosuto* in the late 1930s. This cow stayed at his first wife's place. Nyandika's step sister got married and the bride price of five heads of cattle and six goats added to the stock of his step mother. Nyandika's father bought two cows from selling *wimbi* (finger millet) that they planted at his *emonga.* Each wife used to milk the cows in turn.

Nyandika joined an '*egesarate'*, a cattle camp where old men lived with young men educating them as they took care of cattle. He was circumcised in 1947. All the boys circumcised at the same time in any village had a leader called "*omosegi*". The leader guided and taught them while in seclusion. At the end of the seclusion period, their faces were painted with clay soil and after some partying in the village their grandfathers and/or peers spurted '*busaa*' and sour milk on the boys to bless them. The boys were then released to take care of cattle. They spent the first night after seclusion at their leader's home and later returned to their respective homes. Those who could raise bride price could marry after eight months of leaving seclusion.

Nyandika went to work at the Kericho tea plantations plucking tea leaf in 1950 and was promoted to tea pruning in 1952. In 1953 he became a tractor driver in Cherimo Tea Factory and worked there up to 1960 when he retired and came back home. His salary averaged fifteen shillings per month while working in the plantations. He went there as a result of hearing stories from other young men in his village and was taken by one of the men from the village. He needed to earn money to improve his family and be able to marry and commence his own life. From the earnings he bought goats, which he later exchanged for cows. Through this process he managed to acquire four cows and two goats, which he paid as bride price for his first wife and the ten goats for the second wife. When asked why he retired early, at the age of only twenty seven; he said, "I had learned many things already by that time, from driving to pruning tea. I knew that I would not fail to do my own work without being supervised brutally by white people. When I came home I continued making money from pruning people's tea locally here in the village".

Nyandika married his first wife from Bosinge clan in 1951. He paid a bride price of thirteen heads of cattle for her. Nine of them came from the bride price paid for one of his sisters. He already had the four other cows and two goats from his savings from working in the plantations, so easily completed paying the bride price. Nyandika had two daughters by this marriage. Both were married but no bride price had been paid for them. He married his second wife in 1952, paying a bride price of twelve heads of cattle and twelve goats most of which he got from another sister's bride price. The remaining ten goats he raised from his own sources including the offspring of the goats he had bought with savings from his job as a tractor driver. Nyandika had eight children by this marriage, five daughters and three sons. Two of the daughters were married and a bride price of three heads of cattle had been paid for each. Two other daughters were married but bride price had not been paid for either of them.

Their eldest son, whom Nyandika named after his late father, completed secondary school and went on to train as a carpenter and is now self-employed in town. He assists his father with money for *busaa* from time to time. He is married but has not paid bride price. The second son also completed secondary education, is married, and engages in farming and pruning tea for other farmers in the village. The last born son and a daughter are secondary school students. Nyandika has built a house for his second wife and another for his two younger sons to share, both with iron sheet roofs. He has two grass thatched huts one for himself and the other for his daughters. His first born son has a house of his own with an iron sheet roof. Nyandika now has a cow and two goats.

Nyandika planted coffee in 1955 and tea in 1962, in both cases using earnings from his employment at tea plantations to pay for the planting material. After he had paid for the plantings they were delivered after the extension officer ensured that the field was ready. He mobilised *risaga* to prepare the field and to plant the tea on the day planting materials were delivered. Asked if it was expensive to pay for the tea plantings, he said that it cost him about five hundred shillings to plant two thousand bushes and that was too much for most villagers who had not worked outside the village or inherited many heads of cattle to sell. He said many people desired to plant tea but could not afford it. "Teachers and those of us who worked in the plantations planted tea and coffee as we were easily able to afford it because we had an income".

At the tea plantations Nyandika learnt tea pruning skills and he has offered pruning services in the village ever since returning from Kericho in 1960. His second born son had picked up the skill and was making money in the village. Nyandika started the work in 1962; he used to be paid five cents per bush pruned, which rose to ten cents in 1970 and fifteen by 1980. After tea leaf price increases in the early 1980s they were being paid fifty cents in 1986 and by

1990 it ranged from eighty cents to one shilling. He said that the highest he had ever been paid per bush was two shillings in 2003, when he last pruned. His son charges according to the thickness of the branches being pruned, if they are very thick close to an inch and a half in diameter he charges three shillings and for younger braches he accepted as low as two shillings.

Because she did not have a son, Nyandika's first wife '*married*' Dinah (a woman) in 1977 and she bore two daughters and four sons (see Dinah's case study below). The bride price for her was six heads of cattle, which she and Nyandika raised together. Dinah grows tobacco and sells the leaves to Batigo, Nyandika's second wife. Dinah also grows coffee, tea, maize, beans and kale. Nyandika and his wives treat Dinah as their eldest '*son*'. They chose a man to take care of her needs and to sire children. He was a widower and had three children from this relationship. He bought her a cow for milk but they later quarrelled over school fees, which he was not paying for her children, and they separated. As a result he took his cow together with a calf with him. In December 2003 Dinah's half-year tea earnings enabled her to buy a cow that recently calved, so she had milk again in 2004.

In 1979, Nyandika's first wife moved to Rift Valley Province, where she bought a parcel of land. Her four brothers assisted her in raising money for the purchase. They gave her some money and she sold seven cows given to her by Nyandika for the rest. Nyandika usually visits her there. Recently she came home to attend a burial for one of her brothers.

Dinah insulted Nyandika and his first wife for not helping her and being good for nothings. These differences led Nyandika and his first wife to hit back by adopting three children in 2000. These children currently stay with Nyandika's first wife in Rift Valley. The land previously given to Dinah was divided up between her and the adopted children. This further diminished Dinah's land and made life difficult for her. Nyandika has a strained relationship with Dinah, although he usually goes to her house to buy busaa like any other customer. His position is that he does not get any preferential treatment there. I observed though, that occasionally Dinah gave him *busaa* for free but that he kept a distance from her lest he annoys his first wife. Nyandika and his first wife were on good terms, although he only occasionally visited her; spending more time with his second wife.

Nyandika's second wife Batigo was born in 1938 in the Bonyangoge area about seven kilometres from her marital home. She had a year's schooling. Her father never wanted to send girls to school because they would eventually get married away from home and never be of any help to him in old age, unlike sons who would remain in the home even after marriage. She has three brothers. The one who used her bride price for his marriage, a retired schoolteacher was a drinking friend of her husband Nyandika. He visits her regularly and supported her whenever she was in need. Her other brothers did not visit her as often, although her relationship with them was good.

Batigo is a trader. She buys tobacco leaves locally in the villages and sells them at Daraja Mbili Market just outside Kisii Town every Monday and Thursday. She is well known for buying tobacco and people bring it to her in small quantities until she filled a gunny bag or two for sale at the market. After selling the tobacco in the market she buys earthen pots, mats, baskets and fish to resell by the roadside at the village business centre. She said of her trade, "it keeps me busy and I make profits here and there to buy things for the house like utensils, cooking oil, salt and sometimes tea. It also enables me to get out of my home and meet other people and talk. You know men have no problem, they can go to the market and just sit there, but as a woman I need something to do, sometimes to enable me be free from idling in the house. In the market I get to know how other people live and I relax away from plucking tea and other farm work". She started trading in 1978 but stops the trade during millet weeding and harvesting time, about five weeks each year.

Nyandika relates well with all his sisters and they often visit him. He also occasionally visits them in their various homes. He treats all his sisters equally – and makes no distinction between those whose bride price supported his marriage and those whose bride price supported the marriages of his brothers. He said they were all useful members in the family tree. He likes Helen most though, because she visits him more often than her other sisters do, sometimes sends her children to visit him and supports him financially from time to time. Nyandika and his second wife attend Sengeta Catholic Church. He drinks and uses snuff. He drinks in the company of his nephew and his second wife's brother.

His sister Helen has two children who are athletes in America. They came to visit Nyandika in March 2004. They brought clothes, shoes, and a cap for him and gave him some money to purchase fertiliser and to repay a debt of one thousand shillings that he incurred on maize seed. They also left him with some money to buy some *busaa* and enjoy a drink with his friends. During the visit in March 2004 they promised that would visit him from America again within six months.

Nyandika has shared out his parcel of land equally between his two wives. This was overseen by the neighbours and all his brothers. He also kept a parcel a parcel of land for himself: his *emonga* – "cutting across the wives' parcels from one end to the other for my upkeep". In 2005 Nyandika's two daughters who had been married returned home, each with two children. They help their father with plucking tea and he occasionally gives them some pocket money. They also routinely brew *busaa* and distil *chang'aa* for sale locally, to make money for their upkeep.

Dinah

Dinah was born in 1962. She has one brother and four sisters as well as a stepbrother and step-sisters. She attended primary school up to standard three. Her father did not want his daughters to continue in school. Her brother completed seven years in primary school. Her father was willing to pay for him but he did not continue with school.

Dinah got 'married' to Nyandika's first wife in 1977. Her uncle was the intermediary. He approached her brothers and mother and they discussed the bride price. Her brothers wanted eight heads of cattle as the bride price but the intermediary informed them that Nyandika was willing to pay six heads of cattle, which they accepted. Her brothers went with the intermediary to Nyandika's place to collect the bride price in December 1977 and she moved to Nyandika's home in January 1978.

Dinah said she married Nyandika's first wife because she had experienced problems in her first marriage. This marriage failed because her mother-in-law was allegedly involved in witchcraft and Dinah could not cope with the situation. After the break-up of that marriage the intermediary was the first to approach her on behalf of the Nyandikas and after he assured her that the Nyandika family was morally upright, she accepted the proposal.

Her parents-in-law had chosen a man, Nyakeenga, 'to assist her'. With him she bore seven children. Her mother-in-law bought a piece of land in Rift Valley, where she now lives. She last came to visit them in June 2003 and stayed for one week. One of Dinah's sons stayed in Rift Valley with her. When she refused to send him to school they fell out and he came back home. After that he got married and he now works as a posho mill operator near Sengeta village. Dinah's mother-in-law has not assisted her financially in paying school fees for her children. Dinah fell out with the man chosen for her after he failed to pay the school fees that he promised for her daughter Sabina. "He later came and took away his cow which he had left with us", Dina said.

Dinah has always grown tobacco, which she sells at Daraja Mbili market in Kisii town. She started selling the dry tobacco leaves at seven hundred shillings for half a gunny bag. From this she had to pay seventy shillings on transportation and a further ten shillings to municipality officials at the market gate. She used the money she earned to pay school fees for her daughter Sabina and to make contributions to Nyarirorera self-help group of which she was a member.

Lately Dinah does not grow much tobacco due to ill health. The little she grows she sells at the local market or to her step-mother-in-law, Batigo who sells it at Daraja Mbili market in Kisii Town. She now concentrates on brewing *busaa*. Dinah only sells beer to adults, if she sells to children or to students their parents usually come to quarrel with her. Most of her customers are men, even though there are a few women who drink. Most young women who come to drink, do so behind the house to avoid being seen drinking in public. Dinah gets into trouble with the local chief and his assistant and when they pass nearby, the customers run away for fear of arrest, often without paying for their drinks. So she closes her house if she learns that they are around. She found brewing better than tea as its returns are more immediate. She relies on the *busaa* business to pay school fees for her son who is in secondary school. In

2005 he was not awarded a government bursary and she spent earnings from tea and *busaa* to pay his school fees.

Dinah's sister, married nearby, is not in a position to assist her financially because she has three children in secondary school. Dinah's daughter Sabina is now married and came to see her mother in 2004. She stays with her husband in Nairobi, which makes it difficult for Dinah to contact her to ask for her assistance in paying her brother's school fees.

Her stepbrother visited her regularly. He last visited in April 2004 to inform her that his wife was sick. Dinah later sent her son to find out whether his aunt had recovered. She also went to her brother's home in February 2004 to attend the burial of one of his grandsons who had passed away. Her own brother and her sisters had never visited her except one who visited her in May 2003. Her father passed away in 1975 and the mother in 2002.

When I visited Dinah in September 2005 she looked sickly but went about her business as usual brewing her *busaa* every Friday to sell the following Sunday and plucking her tea leaf. She told me that her daughter Sabina in Nairobi had now started assisting her with money and that she soon hoped to give up brewing *busaa* because government officials were harassing her. She fell sick at the beginning of March 2006 and was admitted to the District Hospital with a malaria attack. She died in the early morning of March 6, 2006. At the burial a week later she was described by mourners as an industrious woman who worked hard to provide for her children.

Nyarwaru

Nyarwaru is representative of young people in rural life; ambitious, on the move, unattached to the land and shy of family responsibilities. Upon leaving high school he tried his hand in various jobs, all of them non-farm. While in high school he had helped his parents with herding and farming to pay for his keep and his way through school. The demise of his parents meant all family responsibility was thrown upon him, together with a serious scarcity of resources. This scarcity sent him thinking and soon he was using purchased grain, most of it rotten, to make local brew and generate income. With this income, he got married, purchased a cow and precariously returned to agriculture. Recognising the precarious nature of his agriculture on limited land he invested in a sewing machine for his wife, as a fall-back plan.

Nyarwaru's father had two wives. Nyarwaru is the first born son of the first wife and has three brothers and two sisters. He has several step brothers and step sisters. He was born in 1969 and started school at Sengeta primary in 1976. He completed primary education in 1987 and went to secondary school in 1988 from which he finished in 1991. His parents were farmers growing maize, beans and some bananas and rearing cattle and goats. His father occasionally sold goats or cattle to raise his school fees, and his mother worked on other people's farms especially plucking tea to earn some income whenever she was not working on her own farm. Nyarwaru has an iron sheet roofed house and a grass thatched hut for a kitchen. He plants kale, maize, beans some napier grass and indigenous vegetables. He has not shared the one and half acre land they inherited from his mother with his brothers. His youngest brother lives in his house, while his middle brother has a house of his own and tries to cultivate his own food crops; often borrowing from Nyarwaru to make ends meet.

Nyarwaru worked as a *matatu* (matchbox-like public service vehicles) tout from 1992 to 1994, earning a salary of seven hundred shillings per month. In 1995, prompted by a friend, he left this for Tilweti Tea Estates in Kericho because of poor pay. At Tilweti he was plucking tea and earned sixty six shillings per day. While he was there his mother passed away, so he came back home for the burial. He never returned to the estate, remaining at home to take care of his younger siblings, and assist his father in running the family. He remained at home throughout 1995 and 1996.

In 1997, he went to Suneka town and was employed as a salesman dealing in eggs and kale for a salary of a thousand shillings per month. He worked there for two years and left in 1999 for another job in Kisii town, which he got through a cousin. He changed jobs because of late payments and not receiving any salary increments despite growing the sales during his tenure there. In Kisii town, he became a bus-park based tout, booking people into the *matatus* on the Magonga route and earning twenty shillings per vehicle per trip. In 2000, he left the job due to a government order that only local government personnel could manage *matatu* termini.

That year he married Susana and they have since had two children. In 2001, he went to Magonga and was again employed as a *matatu* tout on a route where there was no traffic police harassment. However the vehicle he was working with had to be scrapped and he returned home in 2002. His father passed away the same year leaving him completely responsible for his younger siblings. He went back to the Kisii Bus terminus as a tout but worked for only three months before "Michuki drove us out in February 2003" – referring to then Minister for Transport who spearheaded a campaign that streamlined public transport across the country.

Nyarwaru started distilling local beer '*chang'aa*' in October 2003 to raise some money to support his siblings, wife and children as his late parents did not leave any wealth behind for them to meet their needs. Nyarwaru prefers to sell his beer wholesale because it is quicker and paid for upfront in cash, which enables him to purchase more supplies to maintain continuity in his business. According to Nyarwaru his competitors who deal in all phases of the business from selling jaggery (unrefined whole cake) sugar, making the beer, to selling it wholesale and retail, have affected the price leading to lower profits. Recently he took a loss when the local assistant chief and his police officers raided his house, taking away beer worth one thousand shillings and arresting him. He bribed them with five hundred shillings to be released but lost ten litres of alcohol. This was a major setback to his business.

Nyarwaru said he uses money from the business to pay debts, school fees for his children and family upkeep. He has also bought a cow and a sewing machine for his wife. He bought hens to get eggs for his family and repaired his house. Because he does not have enough land, the cow grazes by the road side and he buys napier grass for it from other villagers who have a surplus. His follower brother borrowed five hundred shillings to buy maize. His two sisters are married and they often came to visit him at his home. No bride price has been paid for either of them. Nyarwaru and his brothers also visit their sisters. His maternal uncles and cousins came during his father's funeral but have not come to visit again since. Nyarwaru has also not gone to visit them, because he had much work to do at home. Nyarwaru's wife is a member of Sengeta Adventist Church, but Nyarwaru does not belong to any church denomination. His wife is also a member of Serianya Self Help Group.

Angima

In April 2004 I had interviewed Nyarwaru who operated a *chang'aa* distillery near the village business centre. Nyarwaru sold the brew to both retail and wholesale customers. He had explained that he valued his wholesale customers who bought twenty to fifty litres from him every two to three days depending on turnover at their end of the business chain. One of his trusted wholesale customers that Nyarwaru identified was Angima in a neighbouring village across the valley west of the village business centre. I decided to link up with Angima to explore the role of the local brew business in his life and establish the extent to which he, like Nyarwaru, had played around with agriculture in his livelihood.

Angima's homestead is unlike most in Sengeta. He built his house very close to an unmade road, hardly five metres away. The three roomed house is built like a roadside kiosk. It has an iron sheet roof. The floor and walls are earthen and plastered with clay soil. The house is L-shaped, with the base making up one big room facing the road complete with a wide door while the rear tail had two rooms, each with a door leading to a bare garden. Next to the main house is a two-roomed grass thatched hut, which served as a kitchen and his daughters' bedroom. Some fifteen metres away from this small compound is his brother Ombongi's main house, built in the same manner as Angima's. His brother does not have a grass-thatched hut and the family cooks in the main house.

Angima was born in 1959 to Onsinyo and Kebungo. Besides his younger brother Ombongi, he had a sister who died in 1989. Angima attended primary school up to standard four in 1970 when he quit for lack of school fees. His parents separated in 1969 and they never came back together again after that, so Angima and his sister grew up in their paternal grandmother's house mostly helping her in the fields. Their grandmother was a peasant, growing bananas, maize, beans and kales. She had occasional monetary support from her first born son who worked away in town as a mechanic and received maize and beans from her two other sons in the village. Their grandmother organised Angima's circumcision rites in 1970 and his sister's in 1974, in both cases using her earnings from bananas and kale sales as she did not have any high value cash crop.

Her son Onsinyo owned coffee on about one and half acres but did not share his earnings from the crop with them and did not support them in any way with earnings from his herbal practice or his other income generating activities including leasing sections of his land to tenants. Angima explained that his most trying time in life occurred in 1972, (two maize seasons after he was circumcised) when there was a serious drought and the maize crop failed. He used to collect wild fruits from the nearby Geita forest, which was rocky but had a thick natural forest and wattle trees on the edges. As the hunger intensified his father got food from a widow he had inherited (married temporarily) and was able to support his mother and the children.

In 1976 Angima went to live with his paternal uncle Nyagwencha who was an accomplished motor vehicle mechanic in Longisa town. Angima became an apprentice and assisted him in the workshop where he learned motor vehicle mechanics and driving. He learnt informally through observation and doing. After some time he could repair small faults on motor vehicles and make some money for himself. When he became good at motor vehicle repairs, his uncle started collecting payments centrally in the workshop and paying him and two other workers at the end of each working day. The work was very good and Angima bought himself a pair of shoes for the first time in 1978. Soon however, his uncle started paying after two or three days, he failed to bring in spare parts and by mid-1979, the business collapsed and he moved to another town. Around this time Angima's grandmother died and her hut went to his youngest uncle, as it was on his land.

Angima did not return to Longisa after his grandmother's burial but started to farm on his father's land, growing bananas, maize, cabbages and kale. He built a grass thatched hut and married Pauline from Mokorongosi that year. The marriage however only lasted to late 1980, because she was not hard working on the farm. Neighbours scorned her for sitting at home when Angima worked hard in the fields. She eventually left and went back to her parents. By late 1981 Angima was making good money from working the land. His father realised this and asked him to pay rent for the land he was using and when Angima resisted he was evicted in September 1982. Angima started working for Jonathan a local farmer as a farm hand at three hundred shillings per month. With this income he repaired and improved the thatch on his hut. The rest of the money he used on local brew drinking each day after work.

Around 1985 while still working as a farm hand for Jonathan, he married Stella a *chang'aa* dealer from Moromba. Around this time his father died followed shortly thereafter by his sister. Angima's younger brother Ombongi came from Rift Valley where their mother had been remarried for the burials and stayed on. After their father's burial, Angima was assisted by his uncles and other village elders to divide their father's land equally between his brother and himself. He said "now I had my own land and was comfortable, I worked for Jonathan up to 1987 and left to farm my own land". However he did not start farming at that point but instead renewed a few of the land leases his late father had set up. Following on from their late father, Angima and his brother frequently leased out their land whenever they needed money rather than work it.

Since she was married, Stella has been selling *chang'aa,* the local brew with an alcohol content of about seventy five per cent. She initially started by buying it from wholesalers in Kerira areas and retailing it from her house to local consumers. With the profits they were able to build their corrugated iron sheet roofed main house. After marrying Stella, Angima worked as a farm hand for about two years and then quit to start the *chang'aa* business with his wife. Angima sources his *chang'aa* supplies from Sengeta village across the valley. One of his major suppliers is Nyarwaru whom he said distilled very likeable *chang'aa* that his customers liked.

Besides the *chang'aa* business Angima deals in quarry stones for construction. He buys the stones from nearby Geita hill and makes ballast for sale. The hill, which was previously for the villagers' common use, is now a commercial source of quarry stone for house construction. Each family that owns a portion of land there quarries the stones and sells them as they are or makes ballast. Angima's ballast customers include teachers who have built their houses around the village and neighbouring ones. Other customers have come from the market centres to buy materials to construct shop buildings. In addition since 1988, Angima has been slaughtering cattle and goats around Christmas and New Year's days, selling the meat through the front door of his main house to supplement his chang'aa and ballast income. He sometimes relies on Oremo, a livestock trader from a neighbouring village, to get livestock for slaughter if he has not commenced his yearly livestock trade.

Angima's children are struggling with school and some of them had already dropped out. The first born son, Morinwa, went up to standard eight but his follower Moraa quit at standard six. Since the commencement of the Free Primary Education Programme in Kenya in 2003, the last three children have been attending school. Mirera, Bago and Kerubo are in primary school. They are older than most of their classmates because they joined school late. Angima does not value his children's education much, which is why he did not send them to school earlier. They only went to school on the insistence of neighbours who argued that education was free and he should send them. The children are usually at home during school time, mostly helping with the *chang'aa* sales.

Angima's first born son Morinwa built a grass thatched hut in 2001. He married in 2003 and his wife started cooking from their hut in the middle of 2004. Neither of them drink and his wife usually attends the local Adventist church. He planted tea bushes on half an acre of land in 2000 and became registered with the Kenya Tea Development Agency (KTDA) as a tea farmer in 2003.

In an apparent twist of the custom whereby son learns from father, Angima has taken the cue from his son Morinwa and planted tea bushes on half an acre of land in 2005. He also pruned and weeded his late father's coffee that was on his parcel of land in 2004 and earned six hundred shillings from it that year. He was tired of police harassment due to dealing in *chang'aa* and wanted to slowly shift into farming to make a living. He is getting old and does not want to continue running up and down to bribe the chief or police officers. Angima said; "my age does not allow me to be chased around by police officers, *nabeire ekorera'* – I am senior – and should settle into farming".

Onsinyo's family appear to have had a strong relationship with the Jonathan family over four generations. My discussions with Jonathan, a stocky elderly man aged about 84 years, revealed the complexities of the relationships between the two families, which revolved around land leasing, labour processes, and concoctions to deter the theft of livestock, which Onsinyo's father used to provide in the village.

Morinwa, Angima's son has also developed a good relationship with the Jonathan's. He is hired by them by the day to pluck their tea, buys milk from them often on credit and occasionally runs errands for Jonathan's son who is a teacher in the village. He was happy with the pay that he received, so always checks in on the teacher early in the morning before going to the fields in case of any work that day. Angima's brother Ombongi also occasionally works for Jonathan or one of his sons plucking tea, weeding it or spraying acaricide on their cattle. His wife, a distant relative of Jonathan's wife, often visited her to help with house work as she was aged. Whenever Ombongi's wife visits the Jonathans she is given tokens such as vegetables and milk.

Angima said his life has been successful as he has an income to buy food and has made friends who drink with him. He said people look at him as the one ruining their children with local brew. He finds that annoying "some people whose children are ruined with brew do not greet me; I did not go calling them from their homes to come and drink. I will stop this business and live like anybody else without people pointing fingers at me some day, people should respect me".

Isena

Isena was born in 1952 and is Petro's youngest brother. He has three brothers and three sisters. He is a member of the Adventist Church. He lives in a permanent, fully furnished house that he put up using a loan from a teachers' cooperative society. He has three other semi-permanent iron sheet roofed houses; one for his daughters, another for his married son and another for his unmarried sons. He also has a zero-grazing stall with two exotic dairy cattle.

Isena went to school early and sat for his Kenya Junior Secondary Examination (KJSE) in 1974. From 1975 to 1978 he worked in various casual jobs. He started as a van salesman in Eldoret in 1975 where he sold biscuits. When the business went down he moved to Kericho, where with the help of his cousin he took a job plucking tea in one of the tea plantations. In 1978 he came home and started planting his own tea in addition to the bushes he got from his brother, Petro. By that time he was frustrated with poorly-paid short term work contracts and was keen on working in his own farm to make the money he needed. Over his working years he had saved only four hundred shillings, which he used to purchase tea seedlings. He also planted pyrethrum, which matured fast and used the earnings from this to buy more tea seedlings, eventually planting about two thousand tea bushes. He used money that he earned from his farm to purchase a plot in Sengeta village from his cousin. He planted tea on this plot and has already given the tea to his first born son. He started rearing dairy cattle in 1979 and has never stopped, so has a plentiful supply of manure from the zero grazing stall. The cattle are mostly fed on napier grass from his fields. Just beyond the cattle stall there is a fine kale crop raised on the manure.

Isena married in 1974 but did not pay the bride price until about 1980. He raised the bride price of five cattle and a goat from his savings as a teacher and his earnings from tea. He had to raise the funds himself as his sisters were much older and, by the time he was ready to marry, all their bride price cattle had been used up by his elder brothers.

> "In 1979, when I was still a farmer, there was an advertisement in the newspapers and over the radio that teachers were being recruited. I applied and was lucky to be selected. I was posted to South Nyanza District where I worked for five years before transferring to Nyamira District. My health was not good in South Nyanza. I used to have recurrent malaria and was transferred on health grounds to my current station". Once he started working as a teacher the farming activities reverted to his wife who took care of the fields.

In 1990 Isena was recruited for an in-service teacher training course at a teachers' college. He qualified as a trained teacher and was posted to Mogweko Primary in 1993. He was transferred from Mogweko in 2000 to Sengeta Primary School where he teaches to date. At Mogweko, which is in the former White Settler Farms, he was able to hire land plant maize. He said he liked the place and made many friends who usually help him to get good dairy cattle to rear whenever the need arises.

Isena has three sons and three daughters. One daughter completed secondary education and is married. The first born son dropped out of school early and is married with two children. Sometimes he is a taxi driver but mostly works at home with his wife on the tea that his father gave them. When he has no work in the fields or with the commercial taxis, he sometimes takes his father's old car to a nearby town and transports people to the main road to make a little money. The car however has no papers for the road. When law enforcement officers appear he retreats home with the car. Isena explained,

> "I usually buy my grandchildren clothes and even loaves of bread. I have given their father tea bushes. He uses the tea earnings to support his family. I have planted tea and some food crops on my land. I use earnings from teaching and tea to raise fees for the children in school".

Upon marriage Isena had kept chicken and had pyrethrum, which supported him in starting life as he was not yet employed. He recalled that life was very difficult then. His parents were old and expected support from him. With those pressures he could not manage much and lived in a grass thatched house. Isena built his permanent house with a loan from a cooperative society a few years ago. He was inspired to build by other teachers who had done the same. However, he lamented that the house is not complete because of competing pressures, like paying school fees, and supporting his family and relatives. Isena supports several nephews with school fees and some of them stay with him because they are orphans.

Of his Christian life he said, "I am a church elder at Sengeta Adventist Church. Conflicts do rise and due to my position, I am involved in solving these conflicts by advising parties involved appropriately. People around here come for my advice. They consider me a resourceful person because I am a teacher and a church elder. Whenever we have problems I attend and get involved until the problem is solved. In funerals, I give a hundred shillings and my wife also takes flour, vegetables and fetches water to support the bereaved. I spend most of my time in school. After school I come home to look after my goats and cattle. In the late evening I join other people in the church for choir practice".

Due to a decline in earnings and the rising cost of living, Isena said he had started a tea nursery, leaving his mature blue gum trees for future use. "Soon I am retiring and my children are still in school, so I will start taking timber to meet the future school fees requirements. Life is very difficult. I have come a long way. Although I am employed, when I compare myself with those who are not employed, the difference is very small". His wife said that the major problem she faced in her farming activities is being cheated on tea leaf weight at the tea buying centre. She explained that there were people with little or no tea on their land who colluded with the buying centre clerk to embezzle their tea and record it in their names. She said they had raised the issue in many meetings but it still persisted.

Isena's early ambition in life was to buy enough land for his family, even now he hopes to get more land and plant tea in a nursery. Scarcity of land is the major challenge to Isena's plans of rearing cattle and feeding them with napier grass as well as producing enough food for his family. Isena said that because he is a teacher, his brothers and sisters feel that he should help them and that they heap all their problems on him. "My brothers-in-laws (husbands to my sisters) rarely come to visit me but my sisters do visit. We usually talk about development matters, especially on the need to educate children".

Isena was previously an official of Sengeta I Group but he was not keen to talk about the problems bedevilling the organisation. This may have been because his church position made him unwilling to discuss matters that appeared to divide the community. He said that the group was strong when he left his leadership position in it.

Ogwagwa

Ogwagwa was born in 1963. He is the last born in a family of eight, three brothers and four sisters. All his three brothers are school teachers, as are two of his sisters, the other two are housewives. His father and mother are peasants, but are aging and ailing. Ogwagwa attended Sengeta Primary School before joining a local secondary school which he completed in 1981.

Ogwagwa married in 1992 and has four children aged between four and twelve years. Three of the children are in a private primary school and the youngest in a public nursery school. Ogwagwa inherited two acres of land from his father in 1997, with just under one acre of that land planted with about a thousand bushes of tea. His small compound is just next to his fathers' and not far away from his two other brothers' compounds. He has a three roomed house roofed with corrugated iron. Next to which is a grass-thatched hut that serves as the family kitchen. He keeps tens of chickens and five goats. His wife has a turn at milking his father's cattle at least once a day so they do not own any cattle. The Ogwagwas plant maize, beans, kale, some bananas, sweet potatoes and millet on their land at home and on a half an acre plot he has bought at nearby which is not yet developed. They also grow millet on a quarter an acre plot which he has borrowed from his brother-in-law (his sister's husband). His brother-in-law lives in town and not yet put together the resources to develop the plot and so Ogwagwa has grown two seasons of millet on it each year since it was bought in 1999.

Ogwagwa and his wife farm full time. They spend most of their time on the tea that they inherited. In 1997-8 they used to harvest 200-250 kilograms of green tea every month. This earned them about one thousand shillings every month, besides a second payment of a ten thousand per year. As his children attend a private school requiring fees on a monthly basis, they have to plan for an income that will cover this and see them through. His wife sells sugar cane, peanuts and fish at the village Centre in the evenings after working in the fields and profits from this enable her to purchase household items such as sugar, kerosene and salt, leaving the tea earnings mainly for school fees.

In 1999, following some discussions with friends on the financial problems they faced one of the friends approached Ogwagwa with an idea. He explained to Ogwagwa that ten people had come together to work with the tea buying centre clerk to help him handle the tea leaf once it had been delivered it to the centre. They had negotiated with the clerk to sell to each of them 30 kilograms of tea leaf every working day at 100 shillings. Ogwagwa said that when he looked at the deal closely he noticed that if he joined he was going to put in his time and 100 shillings every day and earn at least 210 shilling per day in addition to the second payment which could be higher. He agreed to become a *shabiki (pl. mashabiki)* – the group that hangs around the tea buying Centre clerk mostly comprised of 'ghost farmers' registered irregularly who buy stolen tea from the clerk. He was introduced to the other members of the group and to the tea buying Centre clerk. They bonded well because he knew most of the members of the group personally as the majority were from Sengeta, so he started buying the leaf in August 1999. "Previously my total leaf weight averaged 230 Kilograms but that month my accumulated weight on factory records increased to 550 kilograms and earnings to about four thousand shillings. This encouraged me a lot and I became more dedicated to the work as a *shabiki* of the clerk in order to buy tea more consistently".

Mashabiki directly help the clerk in cheating farmers on their weight so that the difference in weight will be sold back to them. One *shabiki* usually stands near the scale and holds up the bag in which tea leaf is weighed to make it lighter on the scale. When farmers complain about *mashabiki* intervening, the clerk does it himself. The idea is to intimidate, confuse and cheat farmers on the weight of their leaf. Discussions with various mashabiki and with Ogwagwa revealed that the clerk can loot between 250 and 600 kilograms per working day depending on the season, with the higher figure being obtained during the rainy season when farmers deliver maximum yields. These fluctuations mean that individual *mashabiki* have to negotiate with the clerk for the amount they wish to buy. The clerk has his preferred *mashabiki* who get their full order and others who get what remains. These preferences are based on how closely the *mashabiki* are individually related to the clerk.

The *mashabiki* group fluctuates in number from time to time depending on how members raise money for 'purchasing the stolen leaf. The clerk usually insists that the leaf must be paid for upfront. This is because the whole process is about stealing and if he lets any group member accumulate debts it may be "difficult to collect them as he cannot sue for stolen tea that he irregularly sold". The other complicating factor is that some of the *mashabiki* are known to have no tea bushes and if a dispute arose, the whole scam would be revealed.

Ogwagwa said that the clerk sometimes offers the *mashabiki* three to four kilograms free of charge for their work in the tea buying Centre including protecting him from rowdy farmers and turning the leaf on the floor for good aeration to keep it fresh. This however, depends on how hard a *shabiki* works. Those who work hard are rewarded, especially if they show commitment by reporting even when they have no money to purchase tea. These are the kind of *mashabiki* that the clerk trusts and deals with more frequently as opposed to those with a purely business relationship with him who only come in when they have money to put in.

All *mashabiki* have to be registered farmers, although not all have tea bushes. However, some are irregularly registered and pose as tea farmers who have hired tea bushes from others, but in actual fact they are 'ghost farmers'. Some *mashabiki* also use genuine farmers' registrations to record their stolen tea leaf, but keep records which they compare with the owner who pays them the difference, with the 'ghost farmer' paying the genuine farmer some money in appreciation. In 2005, the Sengeta tea buying Centre committee started insisting that the clerk sits down and records kilograms as each farmer weighed his or her own tea. They also suggested that people who would work with the clerk to turn tea leaf during peak seasons be paid by members and that they rotate every week so that as many villagers as possible are able to work at the centre. I observed that the question of *mashabiki* is a thorny one at the tea buying centre general meetings with farmers always insisting that the committee should rid the *mashabiki* from the buying Centre.

Ogwagwa said that he had earned significant amounts of money as a *shabiki,* which enabled him to purchase five heads of cattle for his wife's bride price, to purchase a plot at a nearby market centre and to build a residential house. He said that having done the business for several years he finally stopped in mid-2005 to concentrate on his farm. He stopped because it involved a lot of work at the buying Centre and he thought it was a bad business given that many people were hiring tea bushes only to be cheated on weight when they bought tea to the Centre. He had hired some 500 tea bushes in 2003 for five years and wanted to concentrate on them.

I observed that the *mashabiki* are serious about their business and many of them have very little land and families to support. They are not drunkards trying to get quick money and they work very carefully at the buying centres, always keen not to antagonize farmers, and presenting themselves as employees of the clerk rather than volunteers. Ogwagwa said that: "*mashabiki* will not allow a drunkard in their group; they want disciplined people who will not expose their secrets and who want to develop themselves". They always reach out to farmers most critical of them insisting that they are employed by the clerk and should be left alone. They also work behind the scenes during tea buying centre elections to ensure that committee members sympathetic to them are elected. They talk nicely to farmers and are generous in buying tea for farmers in the restaurant outside the tea buying Centre.

A tea buying Centre clerk I talked to about the issue of cheating farmers over their tea denied that the practice existed. He said: "Because people know we are poorly paid they think we steal from farmers. Even when I go for a cup of tea at the kiosk people think I have just received payment for tea I sold. We are treated very unfairly by the factory management and farmers. You were there in the buying centre. How could I steal from all these young people who have gone to school? They look at the scale and I tell them what I am recording and they agree. I only deduct two kilograms for the weight of the bag".

Many tea farmers I talked to were of the view that they were being cheated over their weight. An elderly farmer was emphatic about this in Sengeta TBC general meeting in 2005, he posed: "in the 1960s and 70s, our records used to show weights in half kilogram. Since the 1980s when they started cheating us, only whole numbers are recorded, where do the halves go? There were never many people hovering around the buying centres like nowadays. Something is very wrong in that tea buying centre". Farmers were of the view that if the tea extension service and the factory leaf officers wanted to end the cheating they would have done it long ago. They said officials are aware of the problem, but that they are benefiting from it and thus side with the clerks, "who are poorly paid but get rich on our toil".

Ogwagwa said he does not regret having involved himself as a *shabiki* as it was the buying Centre clerk who was in business. One of his brothers has since assisted him with money to start building a small house at the market for business people to rent and this will help him raise the school fees for his children. He was also optimistic that the payments per kilogram of green tea by the factory would increase in the future and so he would earn more from his own bushes and those he has hired in. Ogwagwa has two heads of cattle on *sagare* (with a tenant) which he said will help him when his first born child goes to secondary school.

Concluding Remarks

In this chapter I have sought to show the process through which answers to the research question were sought. The extended case study approach brought me face to face with issues I had known about as I grew up in Nyamira or visited it later in life, but which I took for granted. The approach enabled me to look at the issues afresh, to ask questions that revealed new dimensions about how people encountered resources in everyday life. I started to become distrustful of official positions over many issues on rural life and to dig deeper for explanations. These included the views that rural life is about farming or that the poor are lazy. I started to see rural people as tough negotiators in their everyday life, capable of handling their problems even in apparently difficult circumstances. My handling of the data is done from two perspectives, both as an insider (having been born and raised in Nyamira) and as an outsider (a trained researcher). The outsider position was reinforced by my long absences from the district, by the changes that have taken place over time and the social distance that 'western' education and urban life creates from the 'rural'. From the insider's perspective, I was part of the subject of study and perhaps unconsciously and inherently sought explanations in league with the subjects. In this sense, I may have become involved in the co-construction of explanations at irresistible and subconscious instances as a result of my insider's empathy with the subject. This is a common occurrence in such circumstances because "qualitative research" is in " itself social action" (see

Holliday, 2002: 145). I recognise that, to some extent, however limited, my field notes reflected my a priori understandings of actors' concerns and doings (cf. Emerson, Fretz and Shaw, 1995: 12-3). My outsider stance and training, however, helped me distance myself from the subjects and to retain 'neutrality' or 'objectivity' that enabled me to seek interesting and illuminating explanations on issues, sometimes from a critical hermeneutics perspective. In this respect the process reflects what Peacock (1986: 86) described as the 'impossibility of making a carbon copy of reality and therefore the necessity of interpreting even as one describes is true in all sciences'. In such circumstances the researcher necessarily proceeds within a framework of his or her own perceptions.

CHAPTER 5

Smallholder Tea Farming and Livelihood

Introduction

This chapter addresses the question of how villagers have embraced and moulded smallholder tea farming as a livelihood opportunity. The chapter commences with a brief discussion about the place of tea in the Kenyan economy and the history of smallholder tea growing in Kenya. This is followed by an elaboration of themes that emerge from the corpus of data, which is structured so as to build an argument that responds to the central study question of how rural villagers create and use resources to make a living and with what results. The first theme relates to the genesis of tea growing in Sengeta village. Here I show that the practice of tea growing originated and grew when migrant labour to the Kericho tea plantations in the 1940s through 1960s returned to the village with knowledge to make tea a new resource for making a living. The second theme explores how labour as a resource for tea farming has been cultivated differently at different historical moments but has always focused on buttressing the tea resource for making a living. The third theme concerns the various ways in which 'tea' has been reworked in order to make a living in Sengeta village. This has a sub-theme: about making a living in communion with others, which highlights how livelihoods are embedded in community life. The fourth theme explores the tea-based livelihood outcomes and attempts to bring out villagers' explanations of their failure or success in making a living from tea. I conclude that making a living on tea is a socially constructed process and success or failure is a result of resource creation processes at the household level.

The Place of Tea in the Kenyan Economy

Tea is an important cash crop in Kenya's economy. Kenya is the third largest tea producer globally after India and Sri Lanka and the second largest tea exporter after Sri Lanka (Nyangito, 2000) with sixty per cent of that produce coming from smallholder farmers (Odhiambo, Nyangito and Nzuma, 2004). The centrality of tea in Kenya's economy hinges not only on its value as an export crop but also the ease with which it has been adopted by smallholder farmers. This has led to the penetration of the crop deep into rural areas where land is scarce and continually subject to subdivision. The government has supported the establishment of tea factories to support smallholder tea production through a statutory body, the Kenya Tea Development Agency (KTDA). KTDA installs and manages tea factories on behalf of smallholder tea farmers who are registered with each factory. The agency also provides extension services and fertiliser to farmers, collects green leaf that it processes and markets (Gitu, 2004). Farmers on their part manage their tea farms and deliver green leaf to specific tea buying centres, which they build and manage collectively. The tea buying centres form the basis electing factory directors who collaborate with the KTDA in managing the tea factories. The KTDA is also a symbol of the Kenyan state's struggle with multi-national companies that Kenya's tea sector throughout the colonial period. In the 1990s the government took the struggle one stage further by starting the Nyayo Tea Zones Corporation (NTZC), which develops and manages state tea plantations around major forests in suitable areas to prevent encroachment on the forests by squatters. However, large-scale multi-national tea estates remain important in Kenya's tea sector and by 2004, they produced about 40 per cent of Kenyan tea while smallholders [under KTDA] produced 60 per cent (TBK, 2004 – Fact Sheet on Kenya Tea).

Tea is the single most important crop in Nyamira District and in many ways defines the Nyamira landscape. People in Sengeta village describe it as the main source of income to buy food, clothing, educate their children and improve their housing. Its importance is evident when looking at housing, as a villager pointed out, "*you see the corrugated iron sheet roofed houses that dominate our village, they are from tea income; tea has housed us decently and we also get clean rain water from the good roofs. None of these were here when we were starting to plant tea in the mid 1960s but now most households have a good house*". In effect agriculture is the mainstay of this rural economy and tea is the core of that sector. While most land in the district is considered to be of medium to high potential, it is growing increasingly scarce as subdivision occurs for the purposes of inheritance. Even as land sizes per family decline towards uneconomic holdings, tea growing is common amongst most landholders in the district.

The main reason for tea growing advanced by people in Sengeta village is that it fetches income monthly and perennially. In addition other historically important cash crops, such as coffee and pyrethrum, have suffered marketing problems over the years to the extent that the latter was abandoned and uprooted in the early 1980s and the former is increasingly shunned by most farmers in the district (Fieldwork, 2004-5). The importance of tea in the local economy can therefore not be gainsaid and Kenyan smallholder tea growing is often described as a success story (see Swynnerton, 1966; Due, 1969; Heyer, 1981 and Gitu, 2004).

Smallholder Tea Growing in Rural Kenya

According to Mandi (1971) and Otieno (2002) tea is believed to have originated in South East Asia where it has been cultivated for many centuries. From there it was dispersed to other continents. Mandi (1971) claims that tea was first introduced to African soil at Durban, South Africa in the 1850s but has survived longest in Malawi where it was first introduced with some problems in 1878 and finally with success in 1891.

There is a general consensus that tea was first planted in Kenya at Limuru, Kiambu District, about forty kilometres east of the capital city Nairobi, in 1903 (see Mandi, 1971; Kenyanchui, 1992; Kenya, 1999b – Sess. Paper no. 2; Otieno, 2002 and Omosa, 2003; 2004). The planter was a British settler G.W.L. Cane who had previously planted it in Manipur, India (Kenyanchui, 1992: 120). From here it spread to other climatically suitable districts on a commercial basis during the 1920s. This dispersal of the crop was essentially driven by plantation production by the colonial settler farmers.

In 1952 tea was introduced to African areas of Kenya in Kirinyaga and Kericho Districts on an experimental basis and in 1957 a tea factory was constructed in Kirinyaga District to process green leaf from African smallholder farmers. By 1959, African smallholder tea production was under the statutory management of the Special Crops Development Authority, which was transformed into Kenya Tea Development Authority (KTDA) in 1964 (Mandi, 1971; Due, 1969; Kenya, 1999b – Sess. Paper no. 2). These developments followed closely from the promulgation in 1955 of the Swynnerton Plan (Swynnerton, 1954) on the Intensification of African Agriculture that recommended organised state support and investment in African agriculture (Talbott, 1992: 86).

Although the Troup Report (1953) and the Swynnerton Plan (1955) encouraged agricultural extension in African areas across the country, relations between African farmers and extension officers were severely strained during the period after World War Two due to brutally enforced soil conservation ventures and merciless livestock culling (see Brown, 1968: 80). Brown (ibid: 37) has further shown that despite increased technical support to African farmers, high value cash cropping was not allowed to spread all over the country in the 1955 – 1960 period. Surprisingly, and in spite of a chequered extension service in African areas new crops such as maize, tea, coffee and pyrethrum and others had been widely adopted in Gusiiland of which, Nyamira District was a part by the 1950s (Uchendu and Anthony 1969; Garst 1972).

Conventional explanations for the widespread uptake of new high value cash crops, particularly tea, in Gusiiland centre on aggressive extension work by the Special Crops Development Authority and its 1964 successor, the KTDA (Due, 1969; Nyangito 2000: 13-4; Gitu, 2004). Zeleza (1989 a, b) reinforces this argument indicating that African farmers were required to plant new crops, particularly maize, a surplus of which was required by Europeans, especially during the two world wars. Tea growing in African areas was spurred further by economic conditions during the depression in the 1930s and the collapse of international tea production quota agreements after World War Two (Talbott, 2002). Levine and Levine (1966) argue that a rapidly increasing population, the introduction of new crops and the possibility of obtaining cash through agriculture turned the primary economic attention of the Abagusii away from cattle to their extremely fertile soil.

Such explanations are structural and based on outsiders' or experts' knowledge and assumptions and ignore the capacity of actors' appropriation through struggles or negotiation with and around external forces. In seeking a more balanced explanation for the relatively quick uptake of tea by the Abagusii, I propose to apply an actor-oriented perspective in order to locate the socio-culturally embedded genesis and growth of smallholder tea production and its place in their livelihoods over time (cf. Long, 2001).

Tea: Locating a Resource in the Hands of Villagers

This section examines how villagers started to grow tea and to hold it in their own hands as a resource. It also discusses how they have moulded the resource in different ways to earn a living. In doing this, it is imperative to examine how labour has been handled historically and how tea earnings are encountered and translated into a livelihood.

Genesis of Village Tea Growing: the Kericho Connection

The origins of tea growing beyond Kenya's former 'White Highlands' where colonial settlers developed the crop on a large scale is hardly debated. As indicated above it is assumed rather axiomatically that after the colonial government allowed African smallholders to cultivate the crop, and especially after the Swynnerton Plan on African Agriculture was promulgated in 1955, the national extension service spread tea growing to smallholders in all suitable districts. This interventionist approach to tea studies ignores local actor experiences, ingenuities and knowledge that in some instances placed them well ahead of the extension service. Evidence from fieldwork in Sengeta Village, Nyamira contradicts the attribution of the beginnings of tea growing in the district to the extension service. It is evident that some tea growing, at least on a trial basis, preceded tea extension in the district. Even after colonial restrictions on African tea growing were lifted the unidirectional and central influence attributed to the extension services is doubtful.

Figure 5.1 shows that tea growing in Sengeta village was established in the 1960s when 27 percent of the respondents first planted tea on their farms. In the 1970s a further 32 percent of the farmers interviewed planted their tea. In the 1980s and 1990s, 19 percent and 14 percent of the farmers respectively planted their tea, while only 8 percent of the respondents planted their tea between 2000 and 2005. Thus 59% of respondents planted their tea in the twenty years to 1979 and only 41% in the twenty-five years between 1980 and 2005. Part of the explanation for this is that land acreage per family has been declining steadily over the years. Most of the tea was planted in the 1960s and '70s when land was first consolidated and registered. This was a prerequisite for approval by KTDA for a farmer to plant tea (Due, 1969). Because this process started in Gusiiland as early as the beginning of 1960s the planting was smooth. The first tea growing therefore coincided with the commencement of land titling in Gusiiland, so as people became landowners they also planted tea. Since then whenever land is subdivided for inheritance the tea on it is also inherited. New tea planting is mostly done by those do not inherit tea, for a variety of reasons including sibling numbers, household land sizes and the geography of family landholdings that make it difficult for each son to inherit tea bushes. This largely explains why new tea planting has been declining since the end of the 1970s.

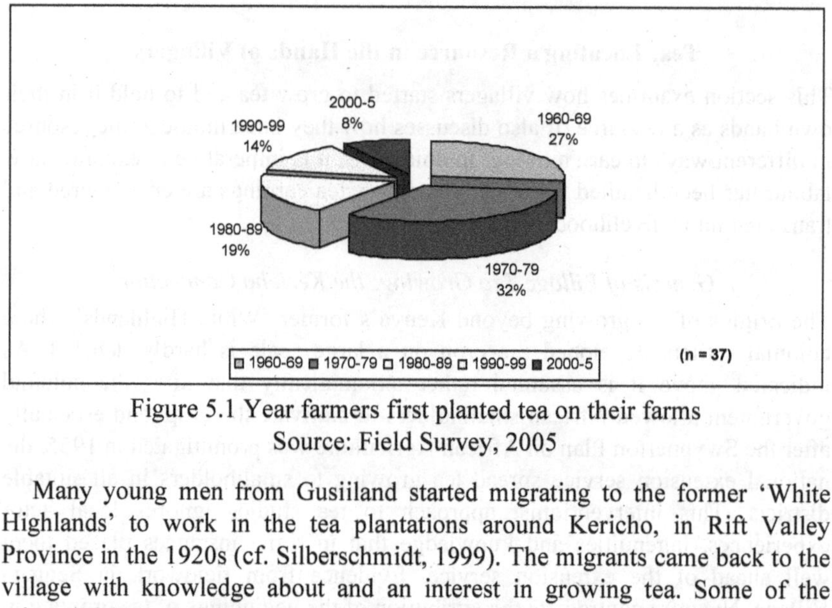

Figure 5.1 Year farmers first planted tea on their farms
Source: Field Survey, 2005

Many young men from Gusiiland started migrating to the former 'White Highlands' to work in the tea plantations around Kericho, in Rift Valley Province in the 1920s (cf. Silberschmidt, 1999). The migrants came back to the village with knowledge about and an interest in growing tea. Some of the migrant labourers began to grow tea even before it was allowed in African areas, and without the authority of the colonial government. An extract from case material on Saulo provides a picture of this.

> While working at the Shauji tea factory Saulo developed interest in tea growing. In 1952 he carried tea stumps from Shauji every time he went home and planted them on his farm. He showed his mother how to weed and to harvest when the crop was ready. By 1955 when his tea crop was mature he and his mother harvested the tea leaf and produced home made tea for domestic use. They fermented the green leaves for a day or two then used wooden pestles and mortars to pound it and after sundrying, it was ready for use and for sale around the village.

The extract shows that tea growing and processing in Sengeta Village predates any government efforts. It is also clear from the extract that the home made tea was sold around Sengeta and that the Saulo family made an income from it. The knowledge that Saulo applied in growing and processing the tea for domestic use originated in his work and experience with tea in the Kericho tea plantations. Therefore, with knowledge and experience from the tea plantations Saulo was able to create a resource for his family without any support from the government, contrary to conventional wisdom that credits the extension services with introducing tea growing to Gusiiland and other smallholder areas in Kenya. This interest in tea and its actualisation shows the strong desire of migrants to grow tea, which is confirmed by the fact that the migrants where the first people to plant tea when tea growing was eventually allowed in African areas. In Iranya Tea Buying Centre, which served the villagers in the 1960s and 1970s, I found out that seven out of the earliest ten registered tea growers had worked in the Kericho tea plantations in the 1950s and 1960s.

Tea planting is a labour intensive exercise and it was necessary to organise labour to cover the necessary stages. When the stumps were delivered early in the morning they all had to be planted the same day to ensure the highest survival rates. Group labour (*risaga*), which was based around kinship and neighbourhood, was usually organised for the purpose. An excerpt from Petro's case record illustrates this point.

> Through his parents Petro mobilised family, kin and neighbourhood labour (risaga) to prepare a seed bed and to plant the stumps early in the morning after their delivery from Kericho. Through this work group many people in the village and beyond, especially his relatives, learnt of and took up tea growing with his assistance. His father was helpful in prevailing on his mother, younger brothers and sisters to help him continually on the farm.

This excerpt shows that labour for planting tea was organised in a particular way, based on existing cultural repertoires. Local labour organisation was thus used to anchor this new crop, which requires intensive labour to establish. This labour process was also significant in other ways in helping the spread of tea growing in Sengeta. Kin and neighbours learned about tea growing as they worked in these pioneers' farms. What needs to be made clear here, is that members learnt about tea in the work groups. They may then have approached extension officers for further assistance or, as the excerpt shows, worked with a pioneer such as Petro to establish tea.

It is common in the village for an elder brother to plant tea across their parents' land and for it to end up shared with their younger brothers when land is eventually shared out for inheritance. Benefits from the 'big brother' essentially originated in their migration to the Kericho tea plantations and the experience and skills that they gained there. An excerpt from Nyagwanga's case record, presented below, shows how elder brothers pass tea on to younger brothers.

> Nyagwanga pointed out, "My brother had planted tea on our mother's land in 1960. When we shared the farm in 1965, some of the tea was on my part of the farm and it became mine. I did not pay him for it; he left the tea for me as a younger brother. I had also bought land at Kepkelion, but we were evicted and lost the money to the government in the early 1960s. I planted more tea in 1969 using my earnings from the tea plantations. There is a lot of work plucking this tea and the work is often especially interrupted by my work as village headman. My wife and our daughter-in-law are very helpful in the work, but it is overwhelming when I am not in to assist because we pluck every eleven days as we used to do in Kericho. This is how we are able to leave the young shoots to grow again and end up with higher yields". Nyagwanga explained that after pruning he leaves the branches to rot there in the farm to fertilise the soil unlike other farmers who use them as firewood leaving the soil bare and weedy. Nyagwanga did not intercrop his tea with any other crop, as this would lower yields.

While this case record shows how tea planted by an elder brother ends up with a younger brother, Petro's indicates the tea that he had planted on his father's land ended up with two of his brothers. His work and experience with tea in the plantations as well as his ability to raise money to establish tea had trickled down to his younger brothers who may not have been able or predisposed to plant tea at the time. The spread of this experience and skills in tea farming was supported by the strong extended family networks common among the Abagusii people. In such kinship arrangements an elder brother carries himself as an elder in his father's company or in his place if the latter died early, and in the process seeks develop the land, which will be eventually shared with younger brothers.

> In 1968, Petro's father divided up his land for him and his brothers. In the division, Petro's younger brother got 900 bushes and his father 400 bushes, which ended up with his youngest brother when his father passed on, while Petro remained with 1800 bushes. This division of his father's land effectively provided inheritance of the land and focused Petro's farming and other development activities on his own land. Having given some of his tea to his brother and some to his father, he started looking inwards to his family and personal development. After he was registered as a grower he developed his own 'egesa' (shade) and started to grow his own stumps from mature tea as he had learned in the tea plantations, initially for infilling dried stumps on the farm. In later years especially after 1972, when polythene sachets were introduced for tea seedling development, he went fully into tea seedling production for sale. He waters the seedlings from his well and sells them to other farmers who collect them from his home. In the early years most of his customers wanted to expand their tea farms but KTDA was taking too long to allow them and to supply seedlings. Others

were those who planted without registration and sold leaf to KTDA through registered relatives while awaiting registration. In 1969 Petro bought land at Irandi about two kilometres from his home for 1600 shillings. This money was from his tea and pyrethrum earnings and from a bank loan. He planted 1600 tea bushes on the land and later increased this to 3000 tea bushes. In 1999 the bushes started drying up. He decided to uproot all of them and replant a better variety. He used seedlings from his own tea nursery and has planted 2500 seedlings from it. He also sold 300 seedlings at five shillings each to raise school fees for his last born child. Petro has largely paid for educated all his children with tea earnings. On his farm in 2004 and 2005 he had a tea seed bed, napier grass, maize, beans, sugar cane and kales.

Petro planted tea before sharing his parents' land with his brothers, eventually inheriting about five acres of land from his father. The inheritance arrangements among the Abagusii, where uterine brothers inherited the land their mother cultivated or that owned by their father in monogamous marriages, enabled Petro's brothers to inherit the tea that he had planted on their father's land. Using his 1940 tea plantation experience Petro raised his own stumps to circumvent KTDA's stringent requirements for acquiring a minimum of one thousand stumps for infilling when the original plantings had withered (cf. Due, 1969). This also enabled him to extend his tea farm without KTDA's approval and gave him stumps to plant. His earnings as a teacher and as a cooperative society worker allowed Petro to invest in tea growing. People without a regular income found it harder to acquire the resources initially required for land preparation and purchasing tea stumps for planting. This is underscored by Saulo's case (see Chapter 4). Savings from his work in the plantations across the country enabled Saulo to establish his cash cropping ventures from 1959 to 1963.

Petro and his contemporaries such as Nyagwanga (above) who worked in the tea plantations were some of the first people to plant tea in their village. Part of the reason for being first is that they had gainful employment, which provided the requisite capital for the tea venture. As Due (1969) and Orvis (1993) have shown tea establishment required substantial capital outlays that were not easy to muster from the farm for many people. In fact Steeves (1978) shows that KTDA insisted on a minimum purchase of one acre of tea at 264 shillings, a huge amount of money in those days. Besides providing the requisite capital with which to finance the establishment of tea, the pioneers' connection with Kericho helped demystify the view that tea growing was a European plantation affair and sharpened their appetite for income. Unlike other villagers, migrant labour came to appreciate that Africans could successfully grow tea. When other villagers may have been worried about the procurement of stumps for planting and the possibilities of learning to pluck tea, they "had seen it all at Kericho". These explanations differ from those of Donovan (2001) who asserts that the near universal acceptance of smallholder tea among the Ndaraweta farmers of Kericho District was the result of several interventions, including an energetic extension programme that was both enthusiastic and often high-handed.

In Sengeta Village, the extension service was reportedly high-handed and was hated by the farmers. This raises deeper questions into the apparent contradiction between the extension service being hated but their messages apparently being implemented. An excerpt from Saulo's case record explains local farmers' relationship with extension officers in Sengeta.

Saulo said that the colonial extension officers were rude and the white ones used *ekeboko kiengubo*, the 'hippo whip' on African farmers in the course of farm inspection or instruction. He grieved that: "extension officers and local chiefs were the face of colonial brutality and we hated them". Beyond the hippo whip, which was used by the highhanded extension service, there were a number of farmers already planting tea on their own initiative as Saulo's case record demonstrates; and who later illegally planted stumps from their on-farm nurseries, without KTDA approval. The migrant labour commenced both tea growing and nursery establishment, which enabled them to flout KTDA rules on acreage allowed per grower. The rules were also challenged from another angle, when people inherited tea before gaining registration as farmers. These findings agree with Steeves (1978) who reports that up to 20 percent of the farmers in Kisii District, which included present-day Nyamira District, had illegally acquired planting materials by 1970.

Migration to the Kericho tea plantations appears to have provided a critical mass of knowledge about and an aptitude for tea growing long before the tea extension service arrived in Sengeta village, as Saulo's efforts at planting and processing tea shows. At another level it is plausible to argue that tea extension work, when it did eventually arrive in the village although highhanded, was easier because of the skills and experience accumulated by the migrant labour and their families. While the two domains, migrant labour skills and extension service may have complemented and reinforced each other in spreading tea growing in the village, migrant labour clearly originated the idea and practice.

Migration to tea plantations thus provided the focal point for tea growing in the early years of crop acceptance in the 1960s and early 1970s. The striking thing about the role of migrant labour in the spread of tea growing in Nyamira District is that it was voluntary and informal to the extent that it has hardly been documented or debated. This reality challenges the common view that tea growing was a result of external interventions by the KTDA (see Nyangito, 2000: 14 for instance) and questions the assumptions about the non-physical conditions that may have contributed to the relative smoothness of external intervention. The existing physical factors that supported KTDA extension include adequate climate, topography and soil types. Beyond these physical factors there was a positively predisposed population that had some of the required knowledge, capital and confidence in tea, all a result of the work and presence of migrant labour. This evidence further challenges views that privilege planned intervention in promoting smallholder tea development, such as those of Talbott (2002: 152) who attributes the rise of African tea growing in Kenya after the Second World War to government efforts. The evidence also demystifies commonly held assumptions about the spread of tea growing in Nyamira.

The people currently working in the tea plantations constitute a third or fourth generation of migrants from Sengeta. Although tea growing is widespread in Sengeta and the sizes of tea gardens per family are steadily declining due to land sub-division, the nature of tea husbandry in migrants' farms can be traced to their migration to the tea plantations. The tea farms of current migrants and some former plantation workers stand out as they are plucked more neatly, weeded in time and the tea bushes levelled out better than in the rest of the village where the bushes are largely rugged. These findings support those by Donovan (2001) in Kericho where he observed that some farmers who had worked in the tea plantations organised their own tea farms and production along the lines of plantation management such as plucking tea like "those people from the African Highlands". In some non-migrant farms tea is also inter-cropped with passion fruit trees or with maize, whereas migrants keep it in pure stands. Migration thus continues to influence tea management in the village.

The period 1960 – 79 may be described as one of tea establishment and expansion. This is when Petro first planted tea on his farm and went on to purchase additional land for tea expansion. Other respondents such as Nyagwanga and Saulo also planted tea during the same period and had worked in the tea plantations in the 1950s and 1960s. From 1980 onwards establishment of new tea farms declined significantly (Figure 5.1). Although records in Sengeta tea buying centre indicate that the number of growers was growing much faster after 1980 than before, a majority of those newly registered growers inherited tea rather than establish new tea farms. The real innovative work in establishing tea in Sengeta was carried out by the first generation of growers and was anchored in connections with the Kericho tea plantations.

The genesis of tea growing in Nyamira district was a contested process. KTDA stood their ground with stringent regulations about acreage and soil tests prior to approval while illegal prospective farmers used ingenuous methods to acquire planting materials. Farmers such as Petro, who set up their own tea nurseries, especially after 1972 when vegetative propagation took root, fuelled this struggle further by making planting material available to farmers outside KTDA's controlled system. As Petro's case shows this led to unauthorised expansion of tea acreage among registered farmers and illegal planting by others. The villagers reworked KTDA interventions in ways that meant that they could end up with tea farms without the Authority's approval and thus began a silent resistance to the KTDA that has dominated but not interrupted operations of the smallholder tea sub-sector. These initial struggles to gain a foothold in tea growing relied on the Kericho plantation connection to source plantings and local KTDA frontline staff who were more sympathetic to farmers (cf. Steeves, 1978).

Cultivating Labour for Tea Farming

After the tea crop is established, labour is required regularly. While weeding may be fairly irregular especially for a mature crop, plucking is done repeatedly every eleven to twelve days and can be demanding on labour (cf. Due, 1969). Tea plucking is also a significantly skilled activity because of the high quality tea leaves demanded by tea factories. For this reason labour for tea production must be carefully organised with a view to obtaining the best possible quality and quantity of tea leaf to obtain the highest returns. Small holder producers rely as much as possible on family labour to carry out all related tasks.

In planting the tea, communal labour in form of work parties were crucial. While family labour was also crucial, it was not sufficient and was more important for mobilising and catering for the community labour that was urgently required as plantings were delivered in one go and had to be planted the same day. Styling labour for purposes of establishing oneself in tea production was therefore a relational issue in the extended family and neighbourhood. This is particularly important because the mere provision of food to the work party in this agriculturally high potential area would be enough not pull labour to one's farm. Trust and reciprocity were more important, that is why Petro although an adult at the time still relied on his aged father to summon work parties. The centrality of community labour in food production and later in the transition to cash crops in Sengeta village agrees with Tosh's (1980) discussions of the agricultural history of tropical Africa showing that locally organised collaborative initiatives were central to peasants' strategies.

Over time labour has increasingly been transformed into a source of income and this has weakened *amasaga* arrangements. In its place, a mixture of hired and family labour has become the centrepiece of tea production. This is captured by the extract below from Petro's case.

> Petro's wife used to help in tending the tea crop and growing food crops before she fell sick. Petro said that his children were very helpful in the farm when they were young and lived with him. Now that most of them have their own homes, he does most of the work on his own and uses hired labour to pluck tea. His own health was failing and he does not pluck regularly. He has employed some people like his daughter in-law and his neighbour's two daughters-in-law, whom he pays four shillings per kilogramme of tea leaf plucked and delivered to the tea buying centre. He weeds his tea on his own, especially in the mornings before it gets hot. He has selected the three ladies as he sees them as trustworthy to pluck his tea well, controlling the quality of tea leaf plucked and to be sure that his crop is not stolen on the way to the buying centre. They treat his farm as their own, counting the days and starting to pluck on their own when the time came without

> prompting from him.. He provides them with breakfast every day they work for him and lunch if they returned to find his family having it. The workers told me that some of Petro's children usually visit them in their homes with gifts such as sugar or cooking oil to thank them for supporting their father on the farm. They said they like a part of the Petro family because of his generosity and that of his children.

Petro hired specific people to pluck his tea regularly to hold them responsible for the quality and quantity of tea plucked. Because they plucked the tea regularly, it would make it easier to recognise and discuss any crop deterioration with them. Equally it ensured a consistent quality of tea delivered to the buying centre, which avoided complaints by the buying centre clerk over varying quality which might occur if workers were hired randomly, changing from time to time. Petro has developed trust in his workers and is confident to let them deliver the tea leaf to the buying centre in his absence not expecting them not to cheat on weight. Age and ailment compels Petro to a style of labour organisation that differs from other farmers who are younger and stronger or who can rely on family labour to run the tea enterprise. Petro's style centres on labour hired to pluck the tea and deliver it to the tea buying centre. This requires careful selection of workers to ensure that family interests are not threatened with theft or poor quality leaf that could lead to rejection by KTDA and wastage. This is why he picked trusted workers from the extended family and the neighbourhood. Tea quality is zealously maintained by KTDA and is a major benchmark of its success (cf. Due, 1969; Steeves, 1978).

The idea and practice of employing labour to pluck one's tea has a broader connotation of making a contribution to the wellbeing of the worker. This is part of the reason for retaining trusted relatives, neighbours or friends in the work so that they can draw other benefits from the work relationship. Yet, as Donovan (2001) found in his study of smallholder tea farmers in Kericho District, the relationships between farmers and workers are rather fragile. It was observed that the Sengeta farmers covertly attempted to influence those who work for them to follow certain practices such as Christianity or certain forms of farming in their homes. One elderly farmer told me: "Matara was my worker for about fifteen years and I helped him plant tea on his farm because he was a loyal worker, now he is a prominent tea farmer in the village". Farmers who hire labour in Sengeta strive for what one villager called '*obwaamate obuya*' – responsibility on both sides of the relationship that benefits both parties without counting work hours in a materialist manner (cf. Donovan, 2001).

Thus labour is not just acquired in the market on a first come first served basis. Rather trust plays a crucial role in labour management, because the bushes are fragile and if plucked roughly, carelessly or maliciously yields will drop. Supervision is not sufficient to ensure careful plucking, trust on the part of the employer and faithfulness on the part of employees is required. Trusted workers consider the tea their life line and pluck carefully to ensure their work is continuous and their employer is happy with their work and will continue to rely on them. As Petro put it, his workers treated his tea as their own and knew when it was ready for them to start plucking.

Other villagers said they had specific people who regularly work for them in the tea farms. It was also observed that not all relatives who sought work are recruited, only trusted ones. Fear of witchcraft is another criterion for the selection of workers although this is not discussed openly. Trusted workers are treated well by their employers. Besides paying them, most employers provide them with breakfast and, to a lesser extent lunch, for free. The employees usually commute from their nearby homes to work on working days. After work employees would often get vegetables or firewood from the employers' homes for their own use. Some workers who had worked for many years in one farm often enjoyed intermittent financial support from employers' children who worked away from home, as in Petro's case.

In particular, it was observable in the village that tea farmers and their trusted workers who were more often than not trusted members of the farmers' extended family, lineage or neighbourhood formed recognisable moral communities; based on trust, loyalty and solidarity (cf. Sztompka, 1999: 4-5). The farmers trust the workers and leave them to work without supervision and to deliver and weigh tea leaf at the buying centres on their own. This trust is not based entirely on the money paid to the workers but also on the fact that they have accepted the employer's trust and could not break it. Apart from being based on their pay and continued retention at work their loyalty and solidarity stem more from their sense of belonging to a moral community with the farmer as exemplified in their communion over meals and other gifts including milk and vegetables, and other social security relations, in the extended family and lineage. One should not romanticise such forms of collaboration; there were also incidences of distrust where workers siphoned tea from employers, weighed and recorded it in their own names.

While the labour arrangement is indicative of growing social differentiation around the basis of the cash crop, it does not even begin to approximate the sharpened class division between owners and labourers that Clayton (1961) and Steeves (1978) pointed out as emerging in the smallholder tea areas of rural Kenya nor is it like Hyden's (1980) economy of affection. As Petro's case indicates, his workers are not fully dispossessed or landless. These farm labourers are also part-time farmers and do not (as yet) constitute a rural proletariat. Both the owner of tea and the labourer, struggle in different ways to earn a living from the tea. The labourers are usually engaged because of the failing health or the advancing age of the tea owners than because of rational economic criteria such as affordability, higher accumulation or profit.

Earning a Living through Tea: Resource Moulding in different ways

Petro has relied largely on tea earnings to organise his life as shown in the excerpt below.

> Petro has educated all his children mainly using tea earnings. One of his sons is a school teacher in the Rift Valley Province and has bought a farm there. He regularly visits his parents and assists them whenever there is a financial need. He assisted with paying school fees for his younger brothers and sisters. Petro's daughters (one of whom is a teacher) and their husbands occasionally assist with hospital bills and drugs. Another of Petro's sons married through a church wedding in 1991 and the family assisted him to pay the bride price. He had one cow, which he bought using earnings from his informal business. Petro gave him one cow, his brother the teacher gave him another and his paternal uncles provided one. The church assisted with transport costs. Recently Petro's two daughters also married through church weddings. The bride price paid for them was used for their wedding expenses and to settle their elder brother's bride price. Their brother who is a teacher provided money for feeding visitors during the bride price negotiations.

In moulding his tea earnings into the education of his children, Petro has specifically secured his livelihood in old age, as evidenced by the support his employed son and daughters give to him and his ailing wife. Additionally, the employed son has been a pillar in his siblings' lives, assisting them to meet their bride price requirements and paying school fees for some of them. Thus, the level of social stability that Petro enjoys in his household hinges on his investment of tea earnings in his children's education, even though not all of them gained formal employment. The fact that his children support each other when in difficulties and that their father is able to chip in using his tea earnings underscores the important place of tea in Sengetan life. This reflects a high level of intergenerational respectability and support, which Petro has worked for and values.

Using tea and other sources income, Petro purchased land near his village and planted more tea on this land to increase his tea earnings. This way he used his tea earnings to extend his tea farming and to raise more income. This land has turned out to be useful in old age when he divided it up for his sons, leaving the tea on his original farm for his own use. Unlike other people of his age in the village, his sons' inheritance of tea has not disempowered him. The land he purchased has cushioned him sufficiently. This is one reason why intergenerational conflicts over resources are not pronounced in his household.

Petro's case demonstrates how the understanding of tea growing that he gained while working in the Kericho plantations, eventually led him to start a tea nursery business. This business has provided an extra income stream intermittently since the 1960s. He stops the business for a year or two when he runs out of money to buy inputs. Others who had worked in the Kericho plantations during the colonial period had also picked up one or more tea skills, which they moulded into a saleable service in the villages. Some, like Petro, run tea nurseries, others provide tea pruning services to tea farmers as indicated in the excerpt from Nyandika's case below.

> Asked why he retired from the tea plantation so early at the age of only twenty seven, Nyandika said, "I had learned many things already by that time, from driving, to pruning tea and knew that I would not fail to do my own work without being supervised brutally by white people. When I came home I continued making money from pruning people's tea here in the village".

In this way, agile farmers went beyond tea growing to create and recreate further resources from the skills they acquired as they interacted with the tea plants on their farms and elsewhere.

The tea nursery business is a good indication of Petro's go-getter lifestyle. It further illustrates the extended meaning of tea as a resource, which also provided an opportunity to create a tea nursery business. When Petro commenced his tea nursery in the 1960s, farmers used to purchase tea seedlings directly from the KTDA nurseries or from the Kericho tea plantations, run by White Settler farmers. His experience in the Kericho tea plantations is arguably part of the reason for customers' confidence in his tea seedlings, as he had worked at the known credible source of knowledge in tea husbandry.

Overall Petro has moulded his tea earnings into a significant accumulation in terms of cattle, land and his children's education. This accumulation has been crucial in buttressing intergenerational stability because the land he bought eased pressure on ancestral land when he shared it out to his sons. This reduced the chances of outright intergenerational conflict and has enabled the patriarch Petro, to continue commanding respect from his children, as he still has some form of economic power to wield. This sets him and others like him, apart from other villagers such as Saulo who tried but did not meet these goals as shown in the extract below.

> Eventually none of Saulo's sons and daughters went beyond primary school and none is in formal employment. (Sometimes) Saulo has used his tea earnings to build houses for some of his sons.

Netting (1993) argues that it is rural elites who succeed in accumulation because they are favoured clients of the state. These findings, however, do not support Netting's assertion, because the state in this case appears to constrain the livelihoods discussed. For instance, villagers struggle to plant tea all at the same time and the apparent differentiation among them has less to do with the state than with differential moulding of tea earnings. Embracing accumulation in land and in children's education is a choice made by some actors and not by others for apparently idiosyncratic rather than state instigated reasons. A political economy perspective to these scenarios such as that advocated by Netting, credits the state with too much influence in rural life and downplays local initiatives and peculiarities (cf. Tosh, 1980).

Tea Earnings and Making a Living through Sharing with others: 'Feeling Alive'

Village life is organised around tea. It is therefore expected that tea earnings would be a meaningful resource in mobilising villagers around village wide activities. Although community life is itself a resource in the sense of providing networks for accessing other resources, latching into such networks requires some basic and tangible resources. The notion of community life is deeply entrenched in Sengeta Village and encompasses people's participation in social life beyond the household or family. This is largely, but not exclusively for the benefit of others. Arenas for participation include taking tea in the village kiosk in the company of others, taking *busaa* with other people in the village drinking houses, linking up with other villagers to negotiate the bride price for a neighbour's daughter, getting involved in the construction of a church, school, tea buying centre or even protecting a village water point. One villager explained the importance of doing things in communion with others, saying, "In working with other people for the benefit of all of us, I feel alive". In a sense, villagers assess the success or otherwise of their lives partly based on their abilities to participate in sharing resources with others, including greeting the newborn and bidding bye to the dead. The extract below from Petro's case brings out the complexities of community life in Sengeta.

> Petro is a strong Adventist who pays ten percent of all his income including tea earnings as a tithe to the church. He is also a member of the local church choir. He said God had blessed him with a united and supportive family in spite of Satan's attacks through disease. Occasionally he goes to the village shopping centre to have tea and have a chat with his friends and age mates. The money he spends is from tea earnings. Church members visit his home especially to pray with his sick wife. Friends and relatives also assist him with finger millet for his wife's consumption, as doctors have discouraged her from consuming maize meal (ugali). In the community, he has initiated several projects such as Sengeta Primary School, a dispensary and the tea buying centre. Originally, their children used to walk to school about three kilometres away, now there is a school in the village. He has also worked with other villagers to improve their water point (ensoko) with support from the Ministry of Water. They are impromptu organisations that oversee funeral arrangements in Sengeta. When a death occurs, villagers sit down together, set up an organising committee and agree on certain issues pertaining to the burial. They then contribute depending on the degree of the problem, for example, they may agree to contribute five hundred shillings per family, if the body has to be brought in from Mombasa or Nairobi but if the body is at Kisii or Nyamira they contribute a hundred shillings per household. The amount also depends on the amount of money owed in hospital bills at the time of death. The same process occurs when there are weddings and parties for children when maternal grandmothers visit to see them for the first time since birth (ekerero).

Petro like most other villagers turns his tea earnings into entertainment and leisure. He occasionally uses his money to drink tea in local kiosks. He spends time in the church and believes in regularly paying tithes and offerings to his local church. Petro is comfortable with his God's blessings for being a staunch Christian. He sees the blessings in terms of his children's unity and assistance to each other, his relatively good health and attributes his wife's ill health to Satan's tribulations of God's elect. In taking such a stance, Petro draws energy for his life from the realms of the supernatural and thus potentially carries the power of his tea earnings via church to the mystic. In a sense, he moulds his tea earnings into mystic resources that add value to his life, which in his mind ultimately explains his success in life.

Petro comes across as a formidable community leader who has used his wealth, created through tea growing as well as his church network, to rise to an informal leadership position. Petro's seems to be taken seriously as a local leader. Many people who have been teachers for decades, but no Sengetan seemed to remember anyone else being referred to as *mwalimu* (teacher) as Petro often was, after having been a teacher for just two years, and that at the end of the 1950s. He put his resources where he put his mouth, and because of that people respected him for carrying through his promises, especially of resource contributions. This is perhaps why Sengetans listened to him keenly and recognised his leadership.

Villagers such as Petro who did not drink beer shared tea together with their friends in the local kiosks. By contrast, those who drank said they 'felt alive' in the drinking places. Two forms of local brew are commonly consumed in Sengeta village, *chang'aa* and *busaa*. Local brew drinking places are good venues for communing with others, as this extract from Nyandika's case record indicates.

> Nyandika has been taking busaa since his childhood. His parents used to brew and as a child, he used to be given some with his brothers. He mostly gets money to buy busaa from his tea earnings. He takes it in the company of his friends as part of socialising. He says, "sharing the little I have with others is a blessing". While drinking they discuss and exchange ideas. They cost share by buying the drink in bulk and thus reducing their individual contributions. He buys the drink for those he most frequently meets in the drinking places, who also buy drinks for him when he has no money.

This demonstrates that Sengetan men buy beer for one another and share it in a form of benevolence that characterises village everyday life. This benevolence however is based on existing friendship and kinship networks and do not indicate a free for all Sengeta. This form of beer consumption is embedded in Gusii customs, where beer is taken in groups such as in work parties or during ceremonies. Drinking together in groups is a demonstration of belonging to Sengeta and a source of self-esteem. This is why people like Nyandika used their tea earnings in this way. Birundu's case, reproduced below, brings out yet another dimension of resource sharing in village life where a neighbour borrows napier grass.

> Birundu is an Adventist and a founder member of Sengeta SDA Church. He donated a piece of land free of charge for building the church. In the course of a discussion with him in his house one day, he was called outside by his wife to see a visitor. He excused himself and left me in the house. He came back after a short while and informed me that he had gone to show a neighbour where to cut napier grass, because his cow had calved the previous day and he needed to feed it well, but did not have ready napier grass. His sons in formal employment have employed two workers for him to take care of the tea and livestock. Before he and his wife had to work on their own, struggling to raise their children's school fees.

This extract from Birundu's case record indicates that villagers provide support to community causes from time to time. However, the understanding demonstrated in offering land free of charge to the church or even napier grass to a neighbour represents a network transaction rather than a random occurrence. Resources regularly change hands within established networks in Sengeta Village, where it is seen as a virtue to share resources with other Sengetans but a disgrace to depend on others. This explains the various layers of support networks created in the village to cater for various interests, groups and needs. The extract from case material on Festus, presented below, underscores this point. It shows how every Sengetan strives to locate his/her bearing in the existing networks depending on their kin, friendship and even occupational ties. Festus lamented:

> "I am telling you, life is not easy the way it looks. I greeted them because I know they are from the neighbouring village. You have to know somebody in a special way before he can help you. You do not easily get anybody to lend money to you even if he has plenty of it. You have to go to somebody you know very well to be helped".

In general, villagers venture into community activities in proportion to their personal wealth or success in their lives. Villagers' propensity to provide leadership and offer resources to establish or improve village facilities such as schools or dispensaries is dictated by the level of success in one's life. I observed that less successful or relatively poorer villagers are often shy in taking part in community life, including even facilitating funeral ceremony meetings in the village, and that they are less likely to attend other meetings to discuss village-wide problems. These findings confirm Omoka's observation (1991) in Kakamega District, Kenya that actors with economic power are more likely to use it to assume leadership positions and conversely that those in leadership positions are likely to use these to gain economic power.

In Sengeta, inter-household assistance in monetary terms or in kind is derived directly or indirectly from tea. Inputs for food production are acquired through tea income or tea-related sources such as remittances from adult children outside the village who were educated using incomes from tea. Church offerings and gifts for parties to welcome the newborn or to bid bye to the dead have a direct or indirect link to tea. In this sense, most village life is tightly bound up with tea and participation in village life is a function of involvement in the tea economy. Those at the periphery of the tea economy are also peripheral actors in village community life.

Making a living in communion with others in Sengeta village is a desire that many Sengetans display in such venues as church, drinking place, tea kiosk, and *ekerero* or at a burial ceremony. The essence of village life in Sengeta is to belong and to commune with others. To do this Sengetans deploy their tea earnings. These earnings constitute villagers' basis for belonging, and thus their being human. Besides seeking an income through tea with which to pay school fees, buy food and other necessities, Sengetans evidently also need the income to demonstrate their belonging to Sengeta and to wider communities, which appears to be a paramount definer of their wellbeing. These findings support Deneulin's (2006) assertion that 'the good of each community member can not be separated from the good of the community as a whole.' Deneulin adds that 'common good' (*bonum commune*) does not dwell in an individual life, but in the life of interaction among individuals.

Villagers' Assessment of their own Livelihood Outcomes

Having examined in some detail how tea originated in Sengeta and how it has been moulded in a variety of ways to make a living, this section interrogates the villagers' extent of success in tea based livelihoods in Sengeta. This is done through the eyes of villagers with a view to capturing what a livelihood really is to them and the bases for their evaluation of it as successful or less successful.

Deploying the tea resource with limited success: Saulo's story

Saulo's life history is inter-twined with the history of tea in Sengeta village, as he was among the pioneer registered tea growers in the early 1960s. In fact Saulo tried out tea planting on his own farm in the early 1950s long before tea growing was allowed in their area and long before processing and marketing channels were established locally. In so doing Saulo was able to set up one of the earliest income generating activities in his village; that of home made tea for sale to villagers. In later years Saulo was hardly involved in any community projects although he continued to assist fellow clansmen when problems such as death arose, doing so primarily as he drank his local brew *busaa*.

> In 1959, he retired from the tea plantations and returned home, planted coffee and pyrethrum. To be recognised as a tea farmer with KTDA in 1963 he added some more bushes to his already mature tea farm and was registered as a tea grower. He

> married his first wife from Bosiango in 1963 and the second one in 1966. Saulo gets some additional income from thatching houses for people, an occupation he has been in since 1959. Saulo also weaves baskets for sale. He specialises on baskets for chicken rearing and for carrying green tea leaves to the buying centres. He uses the extra income from these activities to supplement his tea earnings for buying food and more for entertainment with the local brew chang'aa and busaa in the company of his friends. Sometimes he sells his tea to soko huru for quick money to drink. Saulo also bought some carpentry tools with his earnings. He used to make simple furniture for home use. His sons were interested in carpentry and he gave them a full carpentry kit. His brother also assisted him with some tools to complete the kit. The influence of alcohol led them to start selling the tools. Their father salvaged a few, which he leases to carpenters who need them. With the fees he gets from hiring the tools out he has been able to purchase a table and soon the people using the tools will make for him a bed as payment in kind for using the tools. Saulo's sons were giving him problems as they did not succeed in school, have not got jobs or learned any economically useful skills. Since dividing up his land for his wives and sons for inheritance, his life has changed. His tea earnings have dropped from about two thousand shillings per month to a mere four to five hundred shillings. His second wife and her sons have abandoned him. They do not assist him with anything and she does not give him food, even though this is customary. Saulo has retreated to his first wife's house. She plucks their tea by herself while he goes thatching houses or drinking. She also goes out to pluck tea at neighbours' farms, where she is paid four shillings per kilogramme of tea leaf. She uses the money to buy necessities for the home.

Saulo is involved in consumption without replenishment, which has undermined his livelihood and turned it quickly into a precarious undertaking. Saulo had married two wives and spread his resources too thinly ending up with poor quality in the children's education and other forms of investment and accumulation. As his resources were being depleted he turned to local brew consumption early in life and compounded this by taking up a career in thatching and basketry, which pushed him deeper into a vicious cycle of low earnings. In indulging in the local brew, Saulo enjoys the company of his age mates but at the cost of his own welfare as his scarce resources are wiped out.

Saulo also relies on his first wife to pluck the tea and to work the land for their survival. He did not apply himself in the tea farm with the same energy as he had done when he introduced the crop and when he stood out in the village as a leading innovator. It was observed that his first wife was occasionally assisted by her last born son when he had no casual work outside the home. Saulo's labour for tea production is organised around his family excluding himself. He spends most of his time thatching houses and drinking. He does however share in the tea earnings and his first wife also occasionally shares in his earnings from thatching houses.

Apart from using tea earnings to educate his children (and with little success), Saulo's case can be seen as one of a "clogged" tea resource moulding process. His children did not succeed in school and thus have not been helpful to him in his old age. The household has slid from a position of relative affluence when he worked in the tea plantations in Kericho, to one of need in recent years. Part of the reason for this change of fortunes is that his children spent money in school but did not succeed and have fallen back on Saulo's shrinking tea farm to survive. Additionally, because of or in spite of the foregoing, Saulo did not use any of his tea earnings to extend his land or venture into business to cushion himself from pressure on his ancestral land. These changing fortunes have led to intergenerational conflicts over tea and land, with his sons taking most of it and leaving him in need. As his agility to thatch houses declines with age, Saulo's avenues of resource creation are likely to be diminish.

Saulo tried his hand in business by hiring out carpentry tools to carpenters and has been making some income. He also weaves baskets for sale. His wives had also relied on *busaa* brewing and sales to earn some income over the years. but the business failed due to raids by the local administration and police. Saulo has therefore not ventured into business partnerships or business oriented self help groups like Petro and others had. In a sense Saulo was shy of taking risks in group business activities. Most of his time is spent thatching houses and drinking *busaa*. It is perhaps, in order to service his *busaa* adventures that Saulo delivers some of his tea to *soko huru* (middlemen) who pay for it in cash rather than to the factory that pays more, but on a monthly basis.

These outcomes of Saulo's resource creation and moulding processes agree with Silberschmidt's (1999: 121) findings that if a father drinks excessively, the repercussions on the family's welfare are considerable and more severe than if the mother drinks. In Saulo's case his drinking hampered accumulation and his children's education, the family inheritance arrangements were a disaster for him and his old age will almost certainly be spent in poverty. His children had spent his money in school but did not succeed and his second wife left him after he had shared out his land and tea with her and her sons. Saulo's is an example of clogged resource moulding processes influenced by negative social ties.

Varied Socio-cultural Dispositions and Livelihood Outcomes

Although both Saulo and Petro commenced their lives by working in the tea plantations and later planting much the same acreage of tea, their own verdicts on their livelihood varied; Saulo saying he was unsuccessful and Petro that he was successful. These varying livelihood outcomes support the argument that widespread adoption of cash crops such as tea in rural areas does not necessarily imply prosperity, educated children and success in rural life as argued in some of the literature (such as Bates 1989: 55). Bates takes the view that cash crops have brought prosperity to the Highlands of Kenya, and argues that those who had planted cash crops enjoy higher incomes and better lives. In the same vein Sachs (2005: 52-55) argues that cash cropping is one important pathway to higher family incomes and thus a useful ladder out of poverty. He implies that cash crop production lifts subsistence farmers into the market and subsequently instils disciplined specialisation that brings about successful livelihoods. Swynnerton (1962) had – while justifying the enormous efforts and expenditure on African smallholder development in Kenya – argued that the costs were high but that the smallholders could expect to derive substantial benefits compared with their former standards of living. Expectations of significant change in the outlook of smallholders upon adopting cash crops, was thus entrenched in colonial and post-colonial policy circles alike. The reality in Sengeta does not fully tally with these arguments. Rather the outcomes of tea growing are mixed, and for different reasons. Petro's verdict about his success, shown in the extract from his case record below is only one side of the story.

> Petro summed up his life as follows: "I have tried to have a good life and I have given education to my children. I used to get enough money to cater for daily needs easily. It is not like today. I got the employment I wanted after pursuing education. In those days, parents never bothered to take their children to school. I struggled all by myself, first by going to Kericho looking for money that assisted me through the first few years of my schooling. I bought land to expand on what I had inherited from my father. I am in good health and I can do tedious work unlike other men of my age (78) who wasted themselves drinking (beer). If you see them they look older than me. I have grandchildren who will pass on my line. God has blessed me with a united and supportive family. Diseases are just the traps the devil's places in the way of God's people".

This case stands in sharp contrast to Saulo's case, which shows that cash crop adoption does not always lead up successful rural life.

> Mzee Saulo believed that his life had not been successful because his children, especially the sons, were in serious problems. Some drank too much and others were thieves. None of the sons had paid bride price on their own initiative without being pestered and assisted by him. They have hardly assisted him, especially since he divided up the land for them and their mothers. His perception is that the division of the land caused his younger wife and her children to disown him. He felt that he no longer had any control over them.

The two verdicts on livelihood outcomes of people who arguably started off on the same footing tests the arguments (such as by Swynnerton, 1962; Bates, 1989; Sachs, 2005) that cash cropping constitutes a ladder to successful livelihoods. Both men owned much the same acreage of tea bushes, but the outcomes of their lives are markedly different; Saulo turning in a verdict of failure and Petro one of success. For his success Petro had pursued frugality and accumulation in terms of children's education, land and tea expansion while Saulo's limited success is explained by his spendthrift tendencies, evidenced in his regular consumption of *busaa* and *changaa*. Despite this Saulo does not go hungry, he is not isolated from village social life and participates in the market in significant ways. His discussion of failure in life refers more to the lives of his adult children, his relations with them and his spouses, and his shrinking control over productive resources.

Saulo's description of limited success brings to light a locally embedded view of life lived through the extended family. The success of a patriarch's livelihood depends on his adult children's success in life and their ability to support each other and their parents. If the larger family is in need, then so too is the individual member. For instance, Saulo ably pursued his daily life through income from tea, basket sales and thatching services. With three streams of income, Saulo was certainly a well to do person at individual level. However, in evaluating his life, he looked at livelihood in totality to include his children and wives, and the existing intra-family relationships. This view implies a notion of livelihood that extends beyond individual welfare and comfort and includes the quality of social relationships, power and control over other people, respect from others and the welfare of one's larger family and close relations. This explains the important place of intergenerational relationships in peoples' minds when assessing the success or failure of livelihoods.

In ordinary village discourse it is common for people to talk of their adult children as if they were toddlers. Parents never get out of parenting; they care and attempt to provide for their adult children, even when they are better off. This explains why Petro paid school fees and often bought clothing for his grand children. This reciprocal, even symbiotic relationship between parents and their adult children's families is common in daily village life. The relationships are not just based on resource sharing or exchange, but much more on intergenerational respect and service. The older generation like to be consulted for advice and direction on major decisions, even those such as purchasing a personal car or land that should not ordinarily concern them. It satisfies older people if their offspring, of whatever age and education, show that they value their views and support. This evidence supports Sachs' argument (cited in Stewart 2004: 536) of the need for a holistic view of social change when he argued that 'development economics cornered itself by looking at too limited a range of issues'. Additionally the emphasis of the extended family as a basis of success or failure relates to the social embeddedness of rural livelihood in Nyamira. This embeddedness pushes individuals to pursue 'bonum commune' or common good in and for the larger family (cf. Deneulin, 2006). If some of the extended family are unsuccessful and lack support, the entire extended family sees itself and is seen as unsuccessful.

Tea, as a resource at the disposal of villagers, is moulded differently by different actors. To some, like Saulo, it presented opportunities for entertainment with *busaa and chang'aa,* while others latch on it to accumulate and invest in land purchases, livestock, their children's education and businesses. Those who treat tea earnings as a vehicle for entertainment with *busaa* are observed to keep their options open. They rarely work on the tea unless pay day was nigh – their spouses and children routinely work on the tea but hardly share in the income. In this type of lifestyle, tea is a contested resource. The 'big man' such as Saulo routinely reaps the benefits and decides where the tea will be sold depending on his immediate needs for cash to finance entertainment. When in need of quick cash, the green tea leaf is sold at a low price to *soko huru* middlemen who pay on delivery. When relatively liquid financially for entertainment, the green leaf is sold to the KTDA at higher prices that are paid at the end of each month. These scenarios lead to hidden resistance from the less powerful, to the extent that some women are reported to have secret KTDA registration to enable them siphon their husband's tea and cushion themselves from their economic high-handedness. Jason's case illustrates the intra-household struggles over tea earnings in Nyamira.

> Jason spoke to me a day after his brother was allegedly offered tea his wife had contaminated with poison and reported the matter to the village headman. Jason said: "Before my children went to school, we used to have many conflicts with my wife over tea earnings. She wanted to poison me just like my sister-in-law has done to my brother, everybody knows my brother escaped narrowly, he could now be dead just because of tea that he planted. In my absence my wife used to record some of the tea in other people's accounts to earn money secretly. I sensed trouble and left all the tea to her. I still rely on casual work in other people's farms to be self reliant. I just tell her that whatever she earns be put into proper use, it is all up to her".

In other lifestyle, tea is a resource that unifies households. For instance, in Petro's case, the tea was sold exclusively to KTDA, which offered the highest possible returns. Petro's children's education and their marriage were organised around the tea earnings either directly or indirectly via intra-household support among siblings, who in economic terms are products of the tea. In this life style initial trust breeds more consistent intergenerational trust, valuation and respect, creating a symbiotic relationship within and between generations. This essentially points to a successful livelihood.

Most tea from the village is sold to the KTDA for processing and export. The KTDA pays for the tea on a monthly basis. The final payment made to farmers for the tea delivered during any one year to the KTDA depends on political and economic conditions in Pakistan, Britain and Egypt, three of the most important export markets of Kenyan tea. Thus, life in Sengeta Village is closely linked or at least affected by such global issues as the war on terrorism, security and stability in the Middle East. Tea production and marketing involves local efforts at the village and factory level, and international conditions in the export market. This is one of the reasons why there is tension and suspicion between farmers' groups and the KTDA, especially over tea and fertiliser prices. Tallontire (2001) found that the deductions made by the KTDA from payments to farmers are arbitrary and lack transparency, and concludes that if the ineffective representative structures and control of the (KTDA) board can reduce the incentives to maximise the price received by the farmer. Such tensions between the KTDA and farmers are likely to continue until further restructuring compels transparency and financial disclosures, and the privileging of farmers' objectives in KTDA practices. One of the consequences of this tension is the practice of tea farmers selling their leaf to *soko huru* rather than KTDA, which is taken up in Chapter 6.

Concluding Remarks

This chapter has shown that tea growing in Sengeta originated with labour migration to the former 'White Highlands' of Kericho District. The migrants learnt tea husbandry there, developed an interest and raised the requisite resources, including knowledge, to set up a tea enterprise on their farms. Thus, the KTDA extension service complemented the process of tea development in the area rather than originated it.

As a resource in the hands of villagers, tea has been moulded differently by different actors to make a living with equally varied outcomes. Some actors have used tea earnings to educate their children, provide for their family and household, and partake in community life. Some have done this successfully, to the extent that they entered into the sphere of accumulation in land, tea and livestock. Their success hinged on a disciplined lifestyle that emphasised children's education, adherence to Christianity and accumulation. This will be referred to as the accumulators' lifestyle in Chapter 9.

Yet, tea has also failed other actors who followed other lifestyles. A common lifestyle that leads to limited success in life encompasses polygamy combined with excessive consumption of local brew and weak involvement in community life. Tea earnings are quickly consumed through food purchases and local brew, and this pattern permeates from parents to children, disorganising the next generation. In Chapter 9 [figure 9.1], this disorganisation is one of the reasons for movement of villagers in lifestyles on the left to those in the right – a largely undesirable movement.

As a resource tea is socially constructed and deployed. Inside the household tea earnings are used for school fees, food and other life requirements. As the character of rural life in Nyamira dictates, tea earnings are deployed with equal zeal in communion with other villagers in arenas including the local brew drinking place, tea kiosk, *ekerero*, burial ceremony and church. This communion constitutes the main bases of village social life and is thus a part of livelihood in Nyamira. A further factor is the symbiotic relationship between patriarchs and matriarchs on the one hand and their grown up and independent children on the other. This relationship is largely shaped by the historical moulding of the tea resource, which can either anchor or destabilise intergenerational respect. Sengetans with a successful livelihood appear to have stronger intergenerational relationships than their less successful colleagues. Villagers themselves tend to evaluate the success or failure of their livelihoods in terms of the quality of their intergenerational relations and the wellbeing of their adult children, especially sons. If the patriarchs and matriarchs are losing power over their children and control over resources, then they feel their livelihoods are unsuccessful. In Chapter 6, I focus on the marketing problems that tea farmers face, how they respond to them, and the resource and opportunity creation processes that ensue.

CHAPTER 6

Everyday Dealings in Smallholder Tea Markets: *Soko Huru*, *Mashabiki* and 'Ghost Farmers'

Introduction

This chapter continues the discussion about tea farming and livelihood commenced in Chapter 5, which presented tea as a resource that farmers mould differently to make a living. In this chapter the focus shifts from the farm to the tea buying centre where tea is reworked as a resource by some who grow it marginally and others who do not grow it at all. In locating this important process the chapter looks first at two other issues. First, the key marketing problems faced by tea farmers in Nyamira, and how they respond to those problems to continue making a living through tea. These responses include turning to the alternative market *soko huru* to sell green tea leaf. The second issue is emergence of 'ghost farmers' and the creative livelihood activities that they carry out at the tea buying centres. It is argued that activities resulting from the two issues lead to livelihoods on the margins of smallholder tea farms i.e. tea-based livelihoods beyond regular tea farming. I conclude that tea leaf theft at the tea buying centre constitutes a creative way of resource moulding and livelihood construction, which may theoretically be looked at as an example of a counter-tendency at the local level. These creative countertendencies point to problems in governance in the smallholder tea industry in Kenya. From a governance perspective, the Kenyan tea industry has loopholes and a lack of checks and balances that provide opportunities for some people to construct their livelihoods at the expense of others. In this respect tea markets are socially constructed and constitute arenas of power imbalances which lead to negotiations and struggles over resources and their creation.

Overview of Smallholder Tea Organisation in Kenya

Smallholder tea farming in Kenya is under the macro-management of the Kenya Tea Development Agency (KTDA), which manages all 54 tea processing factories that process smallholder tea leaf in Kenya. This management function involves the recruitment and supervision of factory management staff. The management staff report to KTDA but work in continuous consultation with respective factory boards of directors.

Prior to the privatisation of KTDA in 2000, the government guaranteed loans to construct tea factories and KTDA repaid these through deductions from farmers' tea earnings (Kenya 1999b, Sessional Paper No. 2). Since privatisation the KTDA guarantees loans, provides the minimum 30 per cent equity required from smallholders in advance through temporary acquisition of the equity and mortgage assets of the new factory to cover its construction costs (ibid: 15). KTDA thus continues to play a pivotal role in smallholder tea development under liberalisation.

In terms of management of the smallholder tea sub-sector, KTDA has a complex web of relationships with tea factories, the Tea Board of Kenya (TBK) and the Kenya Union of Small Scale Tea Owners (KUSSTO). TBK is the national regulator of the tea industry in Kenya and KUSSTO represents the interests of smallholder tea farmers in the country. TBK licenses tea growers and factories, regulates tea cultivation and processing, controls tea research and marketing and maintains a data base on the industry (ibid: 4-5; Nyangito, 2000: 6). An organisational chart of the smallholder tea sub-sector is presented in Figure 6.1.

The Kenya Tea Development Agency (KTDA) Board runs the agency on behalf of the farmers who actually 'own' it. Below the KTDA Board are twelve zones, each containing between two and ten tea processing factories. Each zone is represented on the KTDA Board by one director, elected by all the factory directors in the zone. Zones with six or more factories are represented by two directors (Kenya, 1999b, Sessional Paper no. 2). These directors are farmers' elected representatives. The Board also includes KTDA's Managing Director, Operations Director and Finance Director, and the Permanent Secretary for Treasury. KTDA posts a manager to each of the twelve zones to provide policy and managerial oversight to the factories in each zone. Each tea processing factory has a Factory Board of Directors, with each of the directors representing a growers' zone of several tea buying centres (TBCs). Farmers from each buying centre directly elect their zone director for the factory. These directors converge at the factories' zone to elect one among them to the KTDA Board. The Factory Board essentially runs the factory via the factory management and is involved in hiring junior staff and in procurement. Each tea buying centre has a committee elected directly by the farmers who deliver their tea leaf there. The committee maintains the tea buying centre and admits new growers in consultation with the Factory Extension Manager. Each buying centre has a clerk who represents the factory and purchases green leaf from farmers on the factory's behalf. Once the tea leaf is transported from the TBC, at the factory it is received by a senior clerk working in conjunction with a Leaf Base Officer. The two officers ensure that the TBC clerks maintain the required quality of tea leaf purchased from farmers. Each grower manages his/her tea farm and delivers green tea leaf to the tea buying centre. There are over 424,000 such smallholder tea growers in Kenya[51]. The upper echelons of the KTDA's management, including senior clerks, leaf base officers and factory managers include many Abagusii, largely from other districts. The TBC clerks are also Abagusii, but mostly work in TBCs away from their home villages, apparently to avoid conflict of interest, ie their having to deal with farmers who are close relatives, a situation that may compromise quality control.

Figure 6.1 Schematic representation of the KTDA management func tion in the smallholder tea sub-sector in Kenya

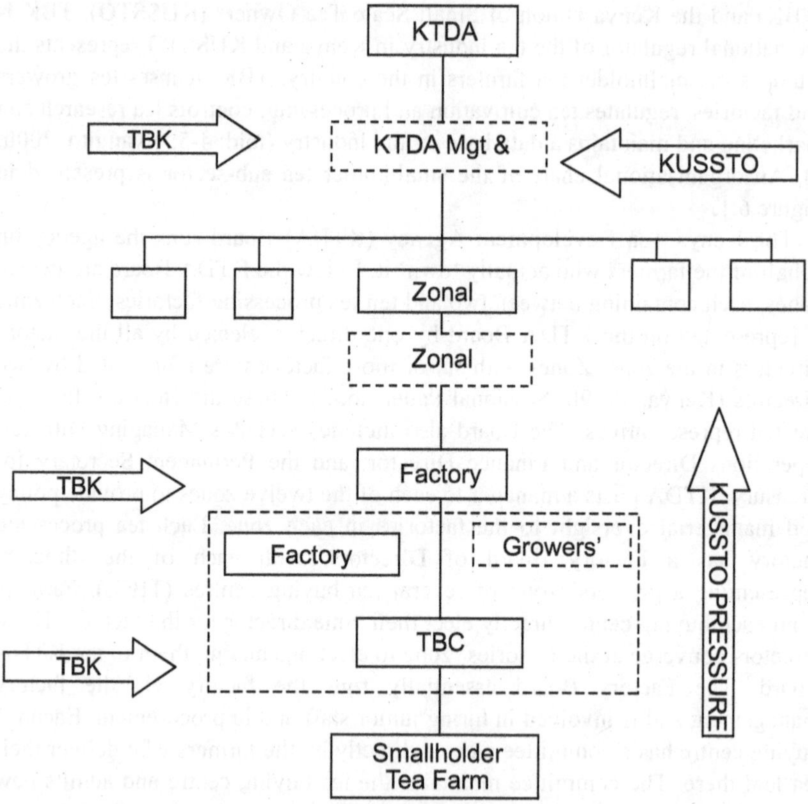

Once the tea leaf has been delivered to the tea buying centre and accepted by the clerk, factory trucks transport it in specially made gunny bags to the factory for processing. After it is processed into made tea, of various grades,

51 Figure from www.ktdateas.com/newsarticle.asp?newsid=15 downloaded November 1, 2006.

each factory labels its teas and the KTDA arranges for transportation of the same to its warehouses, mainly in the port city of Mombasa. Tea from each factory is auctioned separately and fetches different prices, allegedly due to quality variations. Some teas of particular grades are transported for packaging and branding at the Kenya Tea Packers (KETEPA) premises in Kericho, destined for the domestic and Eastern African market. KETEPA has had a long association with KTDA in servicing the domestic and regional markets. KTDA uses tea brokers to auction made teas. The brokers are paid one percent of the gross sales they make for KTDA (Kenya, 1999; Sessional Paper no. 2). Overall KTDA retains 31 per cent of gross tea sales value to cover brokerage, selling and distribution, agricultural services, government taxes and factory expenses. Factory expenses are the highest single item cost in the process (Nyangito, 2000). KTDA then pays the balance of 69 per cent of the gross tea sales value to farmers in three installments – monthly at nine shillings per kilogramme of green tea leaf (as of 2005) delivered, then half-yearly and annually for the tea delivered during the year. According to Bates (1989: 6-7) the first payment is based on quantity of production in kilograms of green tea leaf delivered and the subsequent payments are on the basis of earnings realised from the sale of the crop and reflect the quality of the product. Because each factory's tea is auctioned separately, the prices vary from factory to factory and this is reflected in the second and third payments to farmers.

The basis of price variations and the reasons for delays in payments of the second and third instalments have never been fully explained to farmers (Nyangito, 2000). This despite claims that the KTDA has a management structure that allows for farmer participation (Baumann, 2000). This provides an arena for contests between farmers and KTDA. Mistrust over variations in payments between factories leads farmers to sell some of their green tea leaf to the parallel market, *soko huru.* Besides, enforcement of quality of tea leaf that farmers deliver to the tea buying centres is critical to the quality of made tea and ultimately to the price tea fetches at the auctions (Nyangito, 2000; Cowen, 1984; Due, 1969). However, enforcement of tea leaf quality at the tea buying centres is not a straight forward matter and is often meant to create opportunities for theft by the clerk and for the emergence of 'ghost farmers'.

Stolen tea is often channelled through 'ghost farmers' local people registered with a smallholders' tea buying centre as tea farmers but having few or no tea bushes on their farms. They 'buy kilograms' of tea leaf that the clerk 'steals' from other farmers at the tea buying centre. Some 'ghost farmers' are not registered themselves, but use their friends' accounts to carry on the practice of 'buying kilograms'. Some 'ghost farmers' also 'work' as *mashabiki,* hired to help the clerk with work at the tea buying centre. Some *mashabiki* are 'ghost farmers' and others are genuine farmers hanging around the tea buying centres 'to buy kilograms'. The rest of this chapter illustrates how these two phenomena of *soko huru a*nd 'ghost farmers' are constructed and how new or additional livelihoods are organised around them.

Tea farmers and KTDA agents: a fluid intersection of lifeworlds

The actual link between KTDA and smallholder tea farmers occurs at the tea buying centres in villages in tea growing areas such as Nyamira District. There were two such tea buying centres serving Sengeta Village. Contrary to Due's (1969) assertion that KTDA operated tea buying centres these were built and equipped by local farmers. At no time in the history of tea growing in Sengeta did KTDA even subsidise tea buying centre construction and furnishing. A tea buying centre is a big hall, which in the case of Sengeta is approximately 100 by 40 feet with brick walls, iron sheets roof and a screed floor. Wooden tables about a metre high and a metre and a half wide are mounted along the walls and a small table and chair provided for the centre clerk. Farmers display their tea leaf on the wooden tables for inspection by the clerk. If the clerk is satisfied with the quality, the leaf is put in a bag and weighed; the clerk records the weight in the farmer's account in triplicate, retaining two copies while the farmer takes a third. It is at the point of tea leaf inspection and weighing that major problems can emerge between farmers and tea buying centre clerks. The farmers want to weigh in all the leaf that they bring, but sometimes the clerk insists that some mature and hard leaves be sorted and thrown away. The clerk is under pressure not to deliver poor quality leaf to the factory and to be as accurate as possible on weighing. This can sometimes frustrate the farmer. In general, smallholder tea marketing problems begin at the tea buying centre and eventually reflect in their earnings.

Smallholder tea leaf marketing problems

Smallholder tea farmers face many problems in marketing their tea leaf. These problems limit their income and may hinder their capacity to make a living. As shown in Figure 6.2, the tea marketing problems that affect most farmers interviewed include poor prices, being cheated on green leaf weight at the buying centres and rejection of tea leaf by KTDA agents, allegedly on account of poor quality. These findings tally with Tallontire's finding (2001) that, in spite of a KTDA guideline, that in the dry season only 1.5 kilograms be deducted on account of weighing bags, some factories deduct a minimum of 2 kilograms during the dry season, and up to 6 kilograms in the wet season on account of the bag being wet.

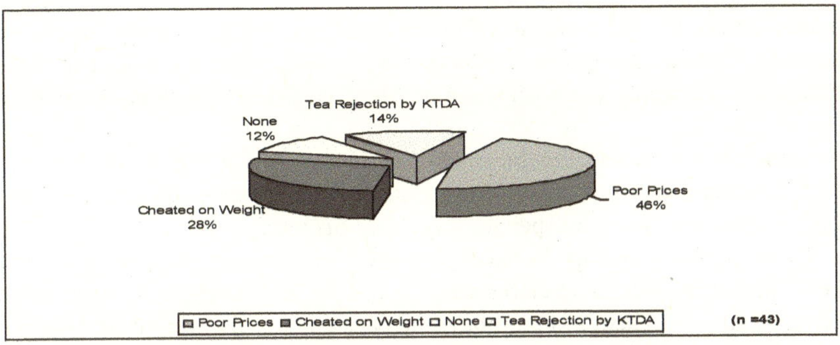

Figure 6.2 Main tea marketing problems faced by farmers in 2005
Source: Field Survey, 2005

The issue of the quality of tea leaf delivered to the buying centres by farmers is a highly contested one. Farmers always insist their tea is of high quality while the KTDA clerks often question the quality, and at times reject the tea. A survey of farmers carried out in parallel with this research indicated that farmers suffered from at least one of three tea marketing problems; tea rejection by KTDA clerks (14 percent), poor prices (46 percent) and cheating on weight by KTDA clerks (28 percent). In identifying these problems the actors were contesting their relationship with KTDA, the main tea buyer and processor. This challenges the conventional view that as tea farmers receive monthly payments they are happier and more contented than others, such as coffee farmers who go for years without pay. The much celebrated high quality of smallholder tea that KTDA is praised for (Due, 1969) is in fact the result of much pain, loss and resistance from the farmers, as elaborated below.

Beneath the Quest for Quality

High quality tea leaf determines the quality of made tea and the prices the tea fetches at the international market (Nyangito, 2000). Many farmers know and have internalised what constitutes quality tea leaf. I asked many farmers what kind of leaf the clerk expects them to deliver at the buying centre and all responded usually in a split second "the top two leaves and a bud". Many farmers aim at delivering just that; high quality tea leaf. This excerpt from Petro's case illustrates the point.

> Petro said that he had selected the three ladies whom he described as trustworthy to pluck his tea in order to control quality of tea leaf plucked and to be sure that his crop is not stolen on the way to the buying centre. He explained that these workers treated his farm as their own, counting days and starting to pluck on their own accord when the time comes without him having to prompt them.

Petro is keen to deliver the right quality of tea to the buying centre and he prepared for this through carefully selecting his workers. Many farmers made similar efforts but the problem of rejection of tea leaf on account of quality persisted. One farmer told me: "I have worked in Kericho, plucking tea in the plantations for twenty years without a problem, but when I pluck my tea here in Sengeta, the buying centre clerk rejects it saying it is not good enough. With my experience how can this be true"? Sometimes it is thought that the clerk goes overboard just to punish farmers and to subdue them by making them think that selling their tea depended largely on his mercy.

There quest for quality in tea leaf is used by clerks in pursuit of another partly hidden agenda. The clerks can use quality as a strategy to wear down farmers and make them more prone to be cheated over the weight of their tea. Sometimes the quality issue allows 'ghost farmers' or *mashabiki* get some tea leaf for free by collecting rejected leaf lying around the buying centre. This excerpt from Ogwagwa's case explains this more.

> Sometimes the clerk asks farmers to sort their tea and only weigh the good quality leaf and if they did not carry away the rejected poor quality leaf the mashabiki weigh it and mix with the good quality tea that the clerk has purchased on behalf of the factory. Being asked to sort tea leaf before weighing usually annoys farmers and by the time they get to weighing they never even look at the scale and the clerk cheats them on the weight easily. So sometimes the clerk has to just get mad with the farmers asking everybody to sort their leaf and in the process causing confusion and anger so he can cheat them easily. Some farmers talk to the clerk and persuade him to accept their tea leaf even of poor quality by offering a service such as helping the clerk with repacking the tea leaf into bags for dispatch to the factory. These farmers often end up as mashabiki after helping for some time and know the inside operations of the tea buying centre. The clerk can also reject tea leaf completely on account of quality and the owners carry it away often to sell in soko huru the following day.

This excerpt shows the tea buying centre clerk as a master of deceit, who understands his victims well and knows which buttons to press to get the results s/he seeks. In other words beneath the high quality tea leaf that the clerk seeks lies an opportunity to cheat farmers on the weight of their tea leaf, in order to obtain 'kilograms to sell to 'ghost farmers' and *mashabiki*. Thus the clerk turns KTDA regulations to his advantage and that of 'ghost farmers', by using regulations against the farmers who are meant to benefit. They lose both ways; by throwing away some of their leaf in the course of sorting and by being cheated on weight when they were too tired and disappointed to look at the scale. These strategies create streams of income for the *mashabiki*, 'ghost farmers', *soko huru*, village scouts and the clerk, thus opening up additional or new livelihood opportunities for some people. They also raise ethical questions as these practices contravene trust, and violate fair trading practices (Blowfield, 2003). Their continuation is a reflection of the poor quality of governance in the smallholder tea sector and the lack of mechanisms for handling smallholder farmers' concerns.

Farmer's responses to tea marketing problems

The ways in which tea farmers are cheated of their tea at the point of weighing may imply that farmers are overpowered by KTDA and that they have limited room for maneuver. This however is not the case. The farmers set out to resist KTDA and her tea buying clerk in a variety of ways, including physical fights with them and their henchmen, the *mashabiki*. The most important form of resistance however, which brings out new or additional resources and forms of livelihood is to sell tea leaf to *soko huru* buyers. Another response to the marketing problems is, as shown in Figure 6.3, complaining to factory directors, who are farmers' representatives. The directors are the actual employers of the tea buying centre clerks, the clerks report to the factory management which is more answerable to KTDA headquarters rather than the factory boards.

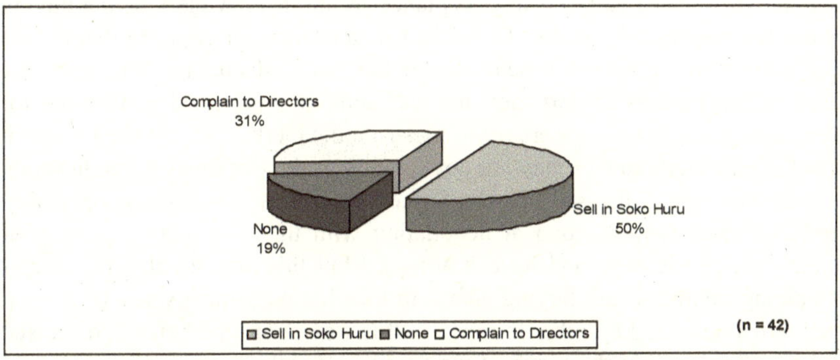

Figure 6.3 Farmers' responses to tea marketing problems in 2005
Source: Field Survey, 2005

Figure 6.3 indicates that actors do respond way to tea marketing problems. The majority of farmers interviewed (50 percent) do so by selling their tea leaf in *soko huru* (middlemen's markets) from where it is sold on to private tea factories in the neighbouring Bomet and Kericho districts. Selling in the *soko huru* market is considered act of protest against the KTDA and a painful step toward freeing themselves from a single marketing channel. It is a painful step because the *soko huru* middlemen pay ten shillings per kilogramme of green leaf on a one-off basis on delivery. This is in comparison to the KTDA, which pays nine shillings per kilogramme at the end of the month of delivery and two bonuses, one every June for the green tea delivered over the previous six months and another every December for the green tea delivered during the year. Thus, overall the payments from KTDA for green tea leaf are far more than the ten shillings per kilogramme paid by the *soko huru* dealers. Yet farmers embrace the *soko huru* because they feel alienated by KTDA. Similarly, in Malawi, when the parastatal Smallholder Tea Authority (STA) got into problems and failed to satisfy farmers in the 1990s, they started to sell their tea leaf to adjacent plantation factories (Chirwa et al. 2005: 4).

Many farmers contest their skewed relationship with KTDA by taking a more painful road to make a point about their relative suffering. Other farmers respond to their marketing problems by complaining to the tea factory directors who represent them. This indicates a higher level of awareness of their problems and a different form of resistance to KTDA hegemony in tea processing and marketing. According to Omosa (2004) the *soko huru* route has many problems; sometimes dealers buy tea on credit and fail to pay up. All the same, the *soko huru* market creates livelihood opportunities in Sengeta for village *soko huru* scouts and to farmers alike.

Soko huru livelihood opportunities

The delivery of tea leaf and its acceptance by the KTDA clerk at the buying centre is a negotiated process. The clerk is responsible for ensuring that the tea leaf purchased on KTDA's behalf is of the required quality. Whenever the clerk orders farmers to sort their tea leaf and set aside good quality tea for weighing, the affected farmers try to persuade the clerk to accept their tea as it is, which the clerk may or may not do. Sometimes the clerk may agree instantly or sometime she will insist that the farmers remove some of the poor quality leaf. A farmer who is good at negotiating with the clerk may deliver poor quality tea consistently and have it accepted but this may involve the farmer remaining behind at the buying centre to mix his poor quality tea with good quality tea delivered by other farmers. In this way poor quality tea is disguised and the clerk escapes the wrath of the factory officials. Farmers who negotiate delivering poor quality tea also remain behind in the centre to help the clerk load the tea onto a truck for transportation. This smoothens their negotiations with the clerk, who might overlook their poor quality tea. If the clerk rejects the tea leaf outright or makes overwhelming demands on the farmers to sort tea leaf at the buying centre the farmers will resist and complain to factory directors. If no action is taken against the clerks, some farmers will resort to selling their tea leaf cheaply to *soko huru* dealers to distance themselves from the KTDA.

The *soko huru* market arrangement in Nyamira District is complex and involves many actors. They include smallholder tea farmers, brokers, their drivers and loaders, local and multi-national private tea factories and their contracted out-growers (Omosa, 2004). Contact between smallholder farmers and the *soko huru* market occurs at the points where agents, out-growers or brokers buy tea leaf from the farmers and transport it away. These three categories of actors frequently make forays into the villages to purchase the tea. In the course of time, another category of actors has emerged in the *soko huru* market: local young men who operate in their villages or hang around the *soko huru* pick-up points. When the vehicles arrive they 'herd the farmers' together to sell their tea and then demand commission from the buyers. I call this category of actors, *soko huru* village scouts, hereafter village scouts.

This section focuses on two main types of actors in the *soko huru* market, the smallholder farmers who sell their tea leaf and the village scouts who mobilise them. This focus is due to these categories of actors being locally based in Sengeta who have creatively positioned themselves to benefit from *soko huru* as an emerging livelihood opportunity. The excerpt below from Saulo's case brings out the unfolding livelihood resources and opportunities for smallholder farmers and village scouts in the *soko huru* sphere.

> One day while in the village I found Saulo seated on the roadside just near the entrance to Sengeta Dispensary. After discussing with him, I found out that he had brought tea leaf to sell to soko huru buyers. Saulo, like some other villagers, mostly sells poor quality tea leaf, that is unacceptable to the local tea factory, to soko huru dealers. He also sells good quality tea leaf to them when he needs quick money, because they pay on delivery rather than once a month. Some of the farmers who sell their tea leaf in soko huru do so because their tea leaf has been rejected at the buying centre, they keep it overnight in a cool place outdoors and sell it in soko huru the following day. Occasionally bad weather such as hailstones and drought means the tea bushes fail to bring out the soft two leaves and a bud required by KTDA. Farmers will then sell their tea leaf to soko huru people who do not mind about quality. The choice of soko huru is also a result of immediate individual cash needs by farmers. Some farmers need quick money to meet daily requirements such as buying maize, sugar or soap. Others need immediate cash for local brew consumption. Soko huru is a good source of such quick cash.

Saulo sometimes sells both poor and good quality tea leaf to *soko huru* to raise money for local brew. *Soko huru* gives him an opportunity to raise quick money for his drink and to socialise with his friends and age mates. This means that his everyday livelihood activities are not disrupted for lack of money; he runs his life according to his preferences. I interpret Saulo's and other farmers' advances to the *soko huru* market as creative undertakings to service their livelihood, and *soko huru* as a resource that they have embraced. This resource creation aspect in the *soko huru* arena becomes more profound when taking into account that hailstones and drought reduce the quantity and quality of tea that farmers have available, denying them incomes. The KTDA insists on good quality tea regardless of the weather. *Soko huru* then presents an opportunity for farmers to turn poor quality tea into income in unexpected ways. *Soko huru* markets allow farmers to successfully fight back at 'nature' in new ways by turning hailstone and drought destruction on their farms into some income and at least salvage a bad situation.

> There are about five different soko huru vehicles that collect tea leaf from Sengeta and neighbouring villages at two points, the dispensary gate and the junction of the main road and the main village track. There are two young men from the

> village, one at each of the pick-up points, who organise farmers to sell their tea. After the tea is weighed and the farmers paid the young men negotiate for a commission. Depending on the purchases made each buyer offers ten to twenty five shillings. Some buyers refuse to pay and subsequently the young men discourage farmers from selling tea leaf to them. Sometimes a vehicle could arrive at the pick-up point and no farmer moved to sell his or her tea leaf. When the young men see their friendlier buyers, they whistle to alert farmers of the approaching vehicle and the farmers respond by jostling for positions to sell their leaf. The young men attempt to mobilise farmers to sell to particular buyers and help them to weigh the tea leaf when the vehicle arrives. I observed that they weighed the tea leaf in the baskets and farmers had little opportunity to look at the scale. It appeared to me as one of the briefs of the village scouts to shout the weight to a farmer as soon as the basket touched the scale, so that it would appear that their son had witnessed properly. Tom, one of the village scouts, is aged twenty-five and completed secondary education in 2000 but has not secured any job. He slid into soko huru work in 2003 by "trying to act as the matatu touts do on the bus stops, where once passengers get into the vehicles, the operators give them some commission. The soko huru people were initially unwilling to give us money but we talked to farmers and they sided with us. Those who did not give us money for mobilising farmers did not get any tea leaf. These days they pay us fifteen to twenty five shillings depending on how much tea they get". Tom said that he had saved some money and planned to go to college to study accounting and would leave the soko huru work for his younger brother who completed secondary school in 2004.

The village scouts who mobilise farmers to sell tea leaf in the soko huru markets have created livelihood opportunities for themselves. They make an income from commissions or kickbacks. This enables them to pursue their aspirations in life, whether planning for further education (as in Tom's case) or just to get by. The tea buyers embrace village scouts as the scouts have local knowledge and networks and mobilise farmers to sell their tea leaf to them. The scouts are likely to know which farmers are more likely to sell their tea leaf to *soko huru* and will target them. The village scouts also represent a local stake in the *soko huru* business because the *soko huru* dealers are seen as their employers. The entrenchment of the village scouts in *soko huru* has been slow and negotiated. They have pulled farmers to their side and forced buyers to pay them a commission for an intangible, possibly even non-existent, service. Perhaps this is creativity at its best. The village scouts have successfully managed to create a service, set its delivery standards and impose it on tea leaf buyers in *soko huru* markets.

Farmers' engagement with *soko huru* is usually temporary and when circumstances change, for example when clerks reassess their strategies for self preservation on their job and in life, the farmers link up again with KTDA. Clerks continually reassess their situation and do damage control by becoming more lenient on quality enforcement to win back disgruntled farmers, lest they be seen as undermining KTDA by pushing away farmers to the *soko huru* dealers. No smallholder farmer in Sengeta sells tea leaf exclusively in the *soko huru* market, they all strive to sell at least some tea leaf to the KTDA. This is perhaps explains why clerks who attempt to shut farmers' doors to the KTDA tea buying centres through cheating on weight or overzealous enforcement of leaf quality are physically resisted. Ogwagwa's case illustrates how tea buying centre clerks must arrange for protection from physical assault.

> Ogwagwa said that the clerk sometimes offered the mashabiki three to four kilograms free of charge for their work in the tea buying centre, including protecting him from rowdy farmers and turning the tea leaf heaps on the floor and tables for good aeration before transportation to the factory. This however, depended on how hard a shabiki worked.

Younger and more militant farmers resort to violence against tea buying clerks who are notorious in cheating on weight or ambitiously enforcing quality requirements. If the clerk in question is widely disapproved of by farmers, this violence may be during the day, otherwise most assaults on clerks occur at night when they are late in the buying centre. In anticipation of such violence, clerks often surround themselves with *mashabiki*, some of whom are 'ghost farmers' to provide security at the buying centres, especially at night. Farmers also target and ostracise 'ghost farmers' and others known to benefit from tea leaf theft at tea buying centres. These findings illustrate farmers' resistance to government institutional arrangements, such as KTDA and the rules it seeks to enforce. This resistance represents a form of countervailing power, which is meant to remind the KTDA that it is not indispensable and should be more responsive to farmers' problems. This form of countervailing power is not collective and political but a sign of farmers' power to stand up to KTDA (cf. Leeuwis, 1989: 120-1). The excerpt below from a national newspaper in Kenya indicates that the government and KTDA have felt the heat as farmers engage with *soko huru* more consistently.

> Smallholder tea farmers yesterday[52] blamed hawking of green leaf on frustration towards the Kenya Tea Development Agency. They told the Nyanza provincial director of Agriculture that the KTDA buying centres were controlled by arrogant clerks who falsified weights and rejected their tea, claiming it was of poor quality. Agents of multi-national companies buy the same tea at a lower price but pay cash.
>
> The farmers also complained that most of the so-called bonus was lost through deductions by the KTDA and the factories. The provincial director of agriculture said tea hawking was threatening the survival of six tea factories in Nyamira District. Addressing the farmers at Nyangoge, the officer promised to present the farmers' grievances to the Kenya Tea Board and KTDA. He told the farmers that hawking of leaf is affecting the quality of tea because those who bought it did not

[52] Story by a DAILY NATION Correspondent; Publication Date: 11/17/2006

provide loans to buy farm inputs like fertiliser. The director explained that if hawking continued and the factories, which are owned by the farmers, closed, they would be bought out by the same people who are encouraging hawking. "We want to pre-empt a situation where farmers will lose their factories, in which they have heavily invested", he said.

The countervailing power of farmers is beginning to be felt and the government is listening to their problems more keenly because the farmers are distancing themselves from KTDA and challenging its tea marketing hegemony. While the future of *soko huru* may not yet be under threat in a liberalised economy, farmers' problems may be addressed in time to save the tea factories from collapse. The farmers' actions show the power of the weak even in positions of disadvantage and the response from the state vindicates peasant resistance to powerful state agencies.

'Ghost farmers' in invisible livelihood

The clerk negotiates his way when cheating farmers on their weights of tea leaf. He first links up with some 'ghost farmers' i.e. those farmers mischievously registered with KTDA but with few or no tea bushes on their land. The 'ghost farmers' pay the clerk to record an agreed number of kilograms in their accounts which the clerk acquires by cheating other farmers on the weight of their tea leaf. The 'ghost farmers' and other *mashabiki* who agree to the clerk's tricks pay in cash for the 'stolen tea' to be recorded on their accounts at the end of each day. To cheat farmers on the weight of their tea, the clerk tampers with the weighing machine so it under-weighs and also deducts more than the one kilogramme allowed for the bag in which tea leaf is weighed (Tallontire, 2001). Additionally, clerks also work slowly to create artificial congestion in the buying centres so that when farmers are tired and eager to leave, the *mashabiki* offer to assist farmers to weigh their tea. In the process the *mashabiki* partly hold the bag of tea on the weighing machine thus under-weighing it.

How do 'ghost farmers' emerge and how do they recruit each other? One way, already shown above is through joining the buying centres as *mashabiki* by negotiating with the clerk for favours in return for some help from them. As they help out they learn the inside happenings in the buying centre and join the fray for 'buying kilograms or weight'. The 'ghost farmers' and *mashabiki,* can also be recruited by those already involved in the practices. The extract below from Ogwagwa's case provides insights about recruitment.

> In 1999, after discussions with friends about financial problems one friend approached Ogwagwa with an idea. He explained that ten people had come together to work with the tea buying centre clerk to help him handle the tea leaf once the farmers have delivered it to the centre. In turn they had negotiated with the clerk to sell to each of them 30 kilograms of tea leaf at 100 shillings per working day. When Ogwagwa looked at the deal closely he noticed that if he

> joined he was going to put in his time and 100 shillings every day and earn at least 210 shillings per day and still expect a second payment which could be higher. He agreed to become a shabiki and was introduced to the other members of the group, and to the tea buying centre clerk. He said they bonded very well because he knew most of the members of the group personally as the majority of them were from Sengeta. He started buying the leaf in August 1999. "At the end of that month my accumulated leaf weight on the factory records rose from 230 to 550 kilograms and my earnings to about four thousand shillings. This encouraged me a lot and I became more dedicated to the work as a shabiki of the clerk to get to buy leaf for my account more consistently". When the tea buying centre clerk was transferred, it was always a moment of anxiety. Usually the mashabiki knew before hand about transfers and worked on getting themselves introduced to the incoming one. When this did not work one of the group members had to be bold and introduce the new clerk to the idea that there was a group of mashabiki ready to help turn the tea leaf on the floor and convince the new clerk that they would pay for their kilograms in a timely manner. Once the new clerk is in the loop, it is back to business as usual.

The key to being recruited into the ring of 'ghost farmers' and *mashabiki* that engage in buying stolen tea at the buying centres is to be identified as trustworthy. Ogwagwa was trusted by his friend who recruited him. Perhaps he anticipated that because he had expressed financial difficulty he would not reveal the deals that they made and the origins of the 'kilograms that they bought'. The ring is also apparently kept top secret and presents itself as existing to help the clerk turn the tea leaf and pack it in bags for transportation to the factory. The word *shabiki,* which the 'ghost farmers' hide behind, means supporter, and in the tea buying centre jargon it stands for a helper or sympathiser. This implies the clerk is weak, overwhelmed with work and in need of assistance. This masks the real business behind the name *shabiki* that of . 'stealing, buying and selling kilograms'. Shrouding this reality from the other farmers and their common interest in delivering fresh tea to the factory requires a close knit team, hence recruitment is restricted to close and trusted friends and relatives.

In recruiting the 'ghost farmers' another major consideration is their secure registration as tea farmers with a tea buying centre. Some 'ghost farmers' are registered fraudulently, as they do not possess any tea bushes, others are properly registered and others are not registered at all, but have secured the cooperation of *bona fide* farmers. Ogwagwa's case throws some light into the various ways by which the 'ghost farmers' infiltrate the smallholder tea industry in Nyamira.

> All mashabiki have to be registered farmers, although not all have tea on their farms. Some are irregularly registered and pose as tea farmers who have hired tea bushes from others, although they are really 'ghost farmers'. Some mashabiki use genuine farmers' registration numbers to record their stolen tea leaf, and keep records which they compare with the owner so they can be paid for their deliveries. The 'ghost farmer' pays the genuine farmer some money in

appreciation. The mashabiki always reach out to farmers who are most critical of them, insisting that they are employed by the clerk and should be left alone.

Most 'ghost farmers' make sure their presence at the tea centre is legitimate by being registered tea farmers with a stake in the centre. Those who cannot do this feign unemployment and present themselves as the clerk's employees or *mashabiki.* In reality they use their friends' accounts to siphon off other farmers' tea leaf, through 'buying kilograms' from the clerk. As 'ghost farmers' they can be seen as creative entrepreneurs, anchoring their exploits in their friends who are genuine farmers. The tragedy of this relationship is that a genuine farmer who agrees to assist a 'ghost farmer' by using his account to 'buy kilograms' from the clerk; is in effect offering their own tea leaf for theft, because what is sold to the "ghost farmers" is stolen from genuine farmers by the clerk. This contradiction becomes more complicated as the 'ghost farmer' only compensates the genuine farmer for his stolen tea through a token payment as appreciation of use of their account through.

'Selling kilograms' to 'ghost farmers' is big business and the tea buying centre clerk tries every trick to get 'kilograms to sell'. The practice is called 'selling kilograms' because while the 'ghost farmers' and *mashabiki* pay for tea leaf, they never actually handle the tea leaf as such, all they get in return for their money is a record of the 'kilograms' entered in their accounts. Ogwagwa's case shows how the clerk obtains the kilograms in collaboration with his *mashabiki* and 'ghost farmers'.

> Mashabiki assist the clerk directly in cheating farmers on their weight so that they can receive the stolen tea leaf. One shabiki usually stands up by the scale and holds the bag in which tea leaf is weighed to make it lighter on the scale. When farmers complain the clerk does the same himself. The idea is to intimidate, confuse and cheat farmers on the weight of their leaf. The actual amount of leaf stolen is known at the end of the day as the clerk and mashabiki weigh all the tea for transportation to the factory. The difference between the total kilograms recorded for farmers during the day and the actual weight ready for dispatch to the factory constitutes the clerks' loot for the day. Discussions with various mashabiki and with Ogwagwa revealed that the loot ranges from 250 to 600 kilograms per working day depending on the season. The higher figure is achieved during the rainy season when farmers deliver maximum yields. These fluctuations mean that individual mashabiki have to negotiate with the clerk for the amount they wish to buy. The clerk has his preferred mashabiki who get their full allocation and others who get less than the orders they placed. These preferences are based on quality of friendship, trust or blood relationships. The clerk usually sells a batch of several kilograms for one hundred shillings, although the precise size varies over time. Between 1995 and 1997 the batch was thirty kilograms; between 1998 and 2000 it fell to 16 kilograms and further to twelve kilograms in 2001 – 2005.
>
> Sometimes farmers are very vigilant and the clerk cannot cheat them much because they insist on having a second look at the scale. When farmers insist like this consistently the clerks try out many tricks on them. Sometimes they tamper

> with the scale to under weigh and know how to make it accurate again at the end of the day to ascertain their loot and dispatch tea leaf accurately to the factory. In 2002, one clerk had two scales, one tampered with to under weigh by as many as six kilograms, which he used directly to weigh farmers' tea leaf and the other accurate for use to weight tea leaf for dispatch to the factory. Farmers got to know this and they tipped officers from the government's Department of Weights and Measures who arrived abruptly in the tea buying centre one afternoon and arrested him with the two scales. The clerk was later sacked and since then the trick of tampering with scales is a bit more controlled as government officials conduct spot checks. The other trick that clerks use to cheat farmers is to report to work late and rush farmers through the weighing process so that they are not able to see the actual weight.

The *mashabiki* help the clerk to steal and in the process of cheating they may even buy their own tea, if they had any, or even that of their parents. The same applies to the 'ghost farmers', who though they have no tea of their own may be paying for tea stolen from their parents and other relatives in the village.

The price of the 'stolen kilograms' has risen steeply over the years. This may be because of the rising payments per kilogram to farmers for green tea leaf, but it may also be a reflection of the higher risks associated with cheating farmers, including facing the sack. Despite the high price the 'ghost farmers' and *mashabiki* sometimes do not get their full order, especially during the dry season when tea production and deliveries are also low. They have to negotiate for allocations with the clerk, who will have his special friends and relatives whom he gives priority to. Thus social relationships also underlies these transactions. Without the protection of loyal *mashabiki* at the buying centre and their smoothing of the buy-out of, and negotiations with, those critical of their practices, it is unlikely that clerks would be able to sustain the practice of 'stealing of kilograms'. Thus the network of deception, which sustains these thefts runs deep in the local community. The *mashabiki* and 'ghost farmers' deflect their critics and bribe them with tea in the restaurant; which creates a subsidiary livelihood for some people in Sengeta.

The clerk puts the *mashabiki* and 'ghost farmers' under pressure to pay for their 'kilograms' upfront. This means that they have to plough their earnings back into the business regularly. When this is not possible, especially because of the rising price of the kilograms; some 'ghost farmers' and *mashabiki* fall out of the ring. Ogwagwa's case shows this.

> The mashabiki group fluctuates in number from time to time depending on how members manage to raise money for purchasing kilograms. The clerk mostly insists that the leaf is be paid for upfront. This is because the whole process is about stealing and if he lets any group member accumulate debts it may be "difficult to collect them as he can not sue for stolen tea that he irregularly sold". The other complicating thing is that some of the mashabiki are known to have no tea and if a dispute arose, much more would be known. Ogwagwa said that the clerk sometimes offers the mashabiki three to four kilograms free of charge for

their work in the tea buying centre including protecting him from rowdy farmers and turning the tea leaf. This however, depends on how hard a shabiki works. Those who work hard are rewarded especially if they show commitment by reporting in even when they have no money to purchase tea leaf. These are the kind of mashabiki that the clerk ends up trusting and dealing with more frequently, as opposed to those with a purely business relationship with him reporting only when they have money to put in.

The clerk guards his risks by requiring payment for the 'kilograms' upfront. This enables him to pre-empt any disputes that may lead to 'spilling of the beans'. The clerk only embraces the *mashabiki* and 'ghost farmers' when they meet their part of the bargain, if the fail to do so he sends them packing from the practice. He maintains a bait of a few free kilograms for the trustworthy and hardworking among them, perhaps to retain a team of core 'customers' and 'protectors'. Therefore although 'stealing and selling kilograms' appears to be mostly based on the cash nexus, the clerk often repackages it as a social process in which those with purely business objectives are discarded while those who put a social touch on it are embraced and retained. This brings the clerk's interests in the practice quite clearly to the fore as he shows he is willing to sacrifice some earnings to perpetuate the practice. This shows that distrust and theft are lonely adventures, and the perpetrator seeks the loyal friends around him for physical security and, perhaps, for social assurance that he has not gone overboard in wronging society.

The process of cheating farmers on tea leaf weight through theft at the tea buying centres benefits and enhances the livelihoods of 'ghost farmers', *mashabiki* and the centre clerk at the expense of *bona fide* farmers. By way of reiteration, the 'ghost farmers' usually have little or no tea to warrant their being referred to as tea farmers. The *mashabiki* may have some tea but spend their time in the buying centre and their tea left in the hands of their spouses. The clerk never poses as a tea farmer, at least in the tea buying centre where he works. The extract below from Ogwagwa's case shows that each of these actors defend themselves from a different moral point of view, and that there is no doubt that the practice has improved their livelihoods. µ

Ogwagwa said that he has earned significant amounts of money as shabiki that enabled him to purchase five head of cattle for his wife's bride price, a plot at a nearby market centre and to build a house for himself. Having done the business for several years he finally stopped in mid 2005 to concentrate on his farm. He stopped because it involved a lot of work at the buying centre and he came to see it was a wrong business given how much people struggle to hire tea bushes to bring tea leaf to the buying centre only to be cheated on weight. He had hired some 500 tea bushes in 2003 for five years and wanted to concentrate on them. Ogwagwa said he does not regret having involved himself as a shabiki, because it was the buying centre clerk who was in business. With help from one of his brothers he had started to build a small house for business people to rent at the market centre and this would help him pay school fees for his children. He is also

> optimistic that the payments per kilogram of tea leaf by the factory will increase in the future and so he will earn more from his own bushes and those he has hired. He has two heads of cattle on sagare (with a tenant) which will help him when his first born child goes to secondary school.

> I observed that the mashabiki are people who treat their business seriously. Many of them have very little land and have families to support. They are not drunkards trying to get quick money, but enterprising people who work very carefully at the buying centres, always keen not to antagonize farmers, and carrying themselves as employees of the clerk rather than as volunteers. The mashabiki will not allow a drunkard in their group; they want disciplined people who will not expose their secrets and who want to develop themselves. They always reach out to the most critical farmers insisting that they are employed by the clerk and should be left alone. They work behind the scenes during tea buying centre elections to ensure that committee members sympathetic to them are elected and they talk nicely to farmers and are fairly generous with buying tea for farmers in the restaurant outside the tea buying centre. A tea buying centre clerk I talked to about the issue of cheating farmers of their tea denied that the practice existed. He said, "Because people know we are poorly paid they think we steal from farmers. Even when I go for a cup of tea at the kiosk people think I have just received payment for tea I sold. We are treated very unfairly by factory management and farmers. You were there in the buying centre. How could I steal from all these young people who have gone to school, they always look at the scale and I tell them what am recording and they agree. I only deduct two kilograms for the weight of the bag in which they weigh".

Ogwagwa's future plans show that being a *shabiki* has acted as a springboard for his other activities at the local market centre. It is possible that his brother's assistance is based on the seriousness that he has displayed in meeting his livelihood objectives such as purchasing a plot at the market. Therefore, through his creativity at the tea buying centre he has attracted his brother's involvement in his livelihood activities. The clerk, as the fulcrum of the entire process, feigns powerlessness and low pay, and plays up his victims' awareness of their rights, to camouflage his role in inflicting piercing pain on smallholder tea farmers in Sengeta. If the practice has worked for Ogwagwa, then there it surely works for the clerk and for the 'ghost farmers' who surround him. All these actors are united in defending their livelihood by making themselves out to be weak. The *mashabiki* and 'ghost farmers' further even attempt to defend their turf by infiltrating the tea buying centre committee elections and get their sympathisers elected. This is a strategic move because the committee registers tea farmers and is a gate keeper to the general membership meetings. If the *mashabiki* control the committee they will further entrench their practices. Thus they have identified the tea buying centre as a resource which needs to be retained and defended and by working to control the buying centre they are attempting to perpetuate their livelihoods.

The depth of theft at the tea buying centres has placed the issue of *mashabiki* and 'ghost farmers' on the agenda of smallholder tea farmers' discussions in various forums, including the tea buying centre's general meetings. This extract from Ogwagwa's case is illustrative of this.

> Many tea farmers I talked to are of the view that they are being cheated of their tea weight. An elderly farmer was emphatic about this in a Sengeta tea buying centre general meeting in 2005, he asked, "in the 1960s and 70s, our records used to show weights in half a kilogram. Since the 1980s when they started stealing from us, only whole numbers are recorded, where do the halves go? There never used to be as many people hovering around buying centres as we see nowadays. Something is very wrong in this tea buying centre". Farmers thought that if the tea extension and the factory leaf base officers wanted to end the cheating, they would done it long ago. They said the officials are aware of the problem but are benefiting, so they side with the clerks, "who are poorly paid but grow rich on our toil".
>
> In 2005, the Sengeta tea buying centre committee started insisting that the clerk sits down and records each farmer weigh their tea. They also suggested that people who work with the clerk to turning tea leaf during peak seasons be paid by members and that they change every week, so as many villagers as possible can get work at the centre. The question of mashabiki is a thorny one at the tea buying centre general meetings. Farmers are always insisting that the committee should get rid the centre of the mashabiki. But this does not happen and is always resisted by hecklers during general meetings. I found out that these hecklers are sympathisers of 'ghost farmers' who are organised to disrupt meetings of the buying centre members

The reality of cheating and theft in the buying centres has been taken for granted for a long time but is now beginning to be questioned and deconstructed by smallholder farmers. The farmers questioning where the halves go is telling. It shows that there is critical awareness of the practices at the buying centres and a serious desire to correct things has been born. This is not without counter-resistance from the 'ghost farmers' and *mashabiki* through their henchmen who pose as drunks to disrupt meetings whenever cheating on tea leaf weight is being discussed. Discussions at the general meetings have brought out signs of a general ostracisation of these 'ghost farmers'. The farmers are beginning to discuss the clerk's schemes and what needs to be done to correct matters. Aware that even genuine farmers employed at the tea buying centre would be compromised with 'free kilograms' the farmers are already talking about paying members to work in the buying centre on a rotational basis to help the clerk and thus get rid of the *mashabiki*. With this, the contest over tea as a livelihood resource in Nyamira District has come full cycle. Those who are harvesting where they have not sown are now being challenged to stop it. The smallholder farmers are beginning to take control of their lives and to defend their resources and livelihoods.

Cheating and theft at tea buying centres is socially and historically constructed and largely results from the nature of the smallholder tea industry and its historical development in Nyamira. As indicated earlier, smallholder tea establishment coincided with land adjudication and registration mainly from the mid 1960s into the early 1970s. This gave registered landowners a first opportunity to plan their farms and plant as much tea as possible. With the population in the larger Gusii areas growing at about 4 percent per annum throughout the 1970s and early 1980s, land scarcity soon set in (Kenya, 1979 – Pop. Census Report). Even the first generation of tea planters was already constrained by land scarcity in these densely populated highlands (cf. Silberschmidt, 1999; Orvis, 1993).

The tea established by the first generation of planters has been shared out for inheritance over time, to the extent that the competition between food and cash crops for land has denied some people a chance to own tea at all, or as much as they would like. In these circumstances, cheating and theft at tea buying centres have emerged as creative responses by under-resourced actors to mobilise resources within the dominant tea sector for their survival. The tea sector is about the only source of income in the highlands. Coffee is fast following in the tracks of pyrethrum in collapsing, leaving in its wake serious destruction of livelihoods. Theft of tea leaf through cheating farmers also feeds on the tea buying centre clerks being underpaid and operating within a national culture that tolerates distrustful tendencies in many spheres of life. Sachs (2005: 237) discusses the extent and some of the implications of countrywide distrust [often expressed in terms of corruption] to rural development in Kenya.

Although tea theft is skewed in favour of tea buying centre clerks who reap huge benefits from it, tea leaf theft is strategic in the livelihoods of 'ghost farmers' and tea buying centre *mashabiki*. This is because it allows these 'ghost farmers' who own few tea bushes or none at able to earn and function just like average tea farmers in the village. They have managed to share in the proceeds of the dominant economic activity in the village by strategically anchoring on frustrated tea buying centre clerks and intimidated farmers, whose resistance is still muted. In a sense, this theft is a form of redistribution within and between villagers in Nyamira. The transcript of a piece of popular music, reproduced below, brings out the Gusii view on corruption and exploitation.

Ekerombeta - Nyamota Nyanamba[53]

Amanyinga ane, nkiandi giankora, amanyinga ane amanyinga ane nkiandi giankora amanyinga ane nkiandi giankora.

[53] English Translation

A flea,

My blood, it has sucked it all, my blood, my blood it has sucked it all,
My blood it has sucked it all!
This flea, this porcupine; a flea and a porcupine – a flea and a porcupine
It is me, Nyamota; greetings to Nyang'au, a flea and a porcupine, yes, a flea
Yes you, a flea and a porcupine.
Potatoes, it has eaten all; potatoes, it has eaten all potatoes; yes, yes, eaten all potatoes.

Ekerombeta, n'ekerongo eke, ekerombeta nekerongo ee ekerombeta nekerongo.

Ninche Nyamota, kwani Nyamari, kwani Nyang'au, ekerombeta nekerongo ee ekerombeta, ee aye ekerombeta nekerongo.

Amarabwani, kiaria giakora, amarabwani kiaria giakora amarabwani, ee ee amarabwani kiaria giakora.

The song's core message against corruption and exploitation is anchored in natural relationships. The corrupt and exploiters are characterised as porcupines that by night eat what they have not sown and as fleas that mercilessly and continually draw their victims' blood. The song draws from the local experiences of the limited power of poor people to call attention to corruption and exploitation at local and national level in the early 1970s. Its thrust in likening the corrupt and exploiters to animals is not so much metaphoric but literally communicates the agony of victims, as their lifelines are cut and their lives disrupted. It was alleged in Sengeta that the singer of the piece, Nyamota had his songs banned from radio stations in the 1970s, for attacking the then single party regime.

Seen differently, tea leaf theft comes across as a smallholder tea sub-sector derived lifestyle that is locally embedded and socially constructed in response to shrinking physical resources, characteristic local cupidity and institutional weaknesses. The KTDA and tea buying centre management committees are too deeply entangled in the theft to combat it. Tea buying centre committee members and KTDA officials are often beneficiaries of theft in the sub-sector. Lifestyles based on theft around tea are significant in the villages of Nyamira District. Actors who follow this lifestyle are intrinsically tied up to the tea buying centres. They wake up early and go to the tea buying centre to start laying strategies for the day and to check out rumours or plans of others that may affect their undertakings. Their minds are so fixed on the tea buying centre that they are seen there even on Saturdays and Sundays when tea is usually not plucked and the centres are un-operational. These actors hover around tea buying centres like scavengers around carcases. In Chapter 9, it is argued that some of these characters lead an opportunistic lifestyle and others who may have commenced their lives here may move on to hire tea gardens and join other lifestyles in Figure 9.1.

The issue of 'ghost farmers', and the theft of tea at tea buying centres comes across as a local form of counter-tendency (cf. Arce and Long, 2000). The 'ghost farmers', *mashabiki* and tea buying centre clerks appear to be contesting social values such as honesty and commitment to the common good that are dominant locally and to shunt them aside to accommodate their avarice and desire to reorder the local economy for their own benefit. In this process the power of the KTDA clerk is harnessed afresh and re-directed to serve illegitimate interests and to intimidate farmers into 'silence' and further exploitation. The farmers' resistance is expressed mainly through enrolling with the *soko huru* dealers but that is short lived as the rules on both sides are unfavourable due to distrust (cf. Sztompka, 1999, Omosa, 2004).

Although farmers have complained to the factory directors about their problems in the tea buying centres there has not been much response. This is partly why farmers sometimes sell their tea leaf in the *soko huru* market. Perhaps this calls for a fresh look at the roles of the factory directors who are unable to play their representative roles effectively and respond to tea leaf theft in the tea buying centres and address the issue of *soko huru.* Without proper representation of farmers in decision-making bodies in the smallholder tea sub-sector, their livelihoods are in danger, through the widespread infiltration of exploitative marketing channels such as *soko huru.* The tensions between KTDA and farmers are likely to continue until KTDA practices embrace more transparency and financial disclosure. Farmers engagement with *soko huru,* sometimes on a regular basis, may require KTDA to rethink its modes and regularities of payment because farmers are keen to have more frequent incomes to run their lives. The objectives of farmers may therefore not necessarily be higher prices, but perhaps more flexible payments relevant to their multiple realities.

Governance in the Smallholder Tea Sub-Sector

The marketing problems that have mutated into the *soko huru* and the 'ghost farmer' phenomenon point to a disconnection in governance in the smallholder tea industry. This is because the stakeholder attempts to resolve the issues are weak, as evidenced in discussions by villagers in different forums including tea buying centre general meetings. Governance is understood here as multi-stakeholder negotiated formulation and implementation of rules of the game [in this case smallholder green tea leaf production and marketing] within an interdependent framework consisting of market, state and civil society (Frouws, 1997). A look at the structure of the smallholder tea sector indicates that a number of organisations are in place to serve the governance function. These include a tea sector regulator, the Tea Board of Kenya (TBK), the smallholder tea company, KTDA, and the growers' or tea farm owners' organisation, KUSSTO, which is essentially a farmers' organisation. With this organisational frame in mind, I will briefly discuss these two critical smallholder marketing problems from a governance perspective.

The problem of *soko huru* is the result of a liberalised tea industry in Kenya. Liberalisation does not however take away the regulatory powers from TBK, which licenses tea growers, marketers [of made tea] or processors. *Soko huru* therefore is a creative endeavour because the Tea Act, (Cap. 343 of the Laws of Kenya) provides this loophole in the trade of fresh tea leaf and the TBK may lack the legal capacity to tame it. The Tea Act does not anticipate trade in fresh tea leaf or provide ways to regulate it. That however, is a regulatory stance. In terms of governance, interaction between the factory directors, management, KTDA and KUSSTO may provide an avenue to resolve the problems that accelerate the *soko huru* phenomenon i.e. leaf quality enforcement and cheating on weight at the tea buying centres. This could happen because there are written rules on legitimate weight deductions for weighing bags (Tallontire, 2001). An opportunity therefore exists for KUSSTO, as the farmers' organisation, to push for these written rules and regulations to be implemented. In other words KUSSTO, as a civil society organisation, should be able to bring the problem forcefully to the attention of KTDA who employ the tea buying centre clerks. A similar opportunity exists on the part of factory directors who are elected by smallholder farmers to manage factories and whose responsibilities include supervising the tea buying centre clerks. This brings us to the crux of the matter.

Factory directors have an ambiguous role. They are elected by farmers and therefore have a representational role. However, they also sit on the board of the factory, which curtails their representational role because as board members they represent different interests, including insider management roles, which may run counter to farmers' interests. Moreover, the directors' specific roles are lost in the towering presence of KTDA and its *de facto* control of the factory workers and management that the board is supposed to supervise. In practice the representational role of directors is a mirage, for all intents and purposes, the directors are KTDA functionaries. The challenge then lies in reconfiguring their relations with KUSSTO and to work in league with it so as to better represent farmers. KUSSTO itself is largely absent in the villages as they have no local branches and leadership. In this sense local farmers' interests are poorly organised and articulated as their leadership is weak or absent. This amplifies the governance disjuncture and indicates the lack of checks and balances that provides the opportunities for some to construct their livelihoods at the expense of others. For instance, tea buying centre clerks and factory management who are aware of a lack of checks and balances may cheat farmers on many other fronts. The cheating of farmers on weight at the tea buying centres, is also a serious issue for Fair Trade, which emphasises the social conditions of production of many items of trade and attempts to achieve a wider spread of the gains made in the tea value chain (Vorley, 2003; Humphrey and Schmitz, 2001). This may pose serious problems for KTDA's marketing of made tea where products are increasingly defined in the world market according to the nature of their social and environmental conditions of production (Daviron and Gibbon, 2002). As consumers [retailers, mainly supermarkets in Western countries] insist more on disclosure of product origin and the conditions of production, it may become imperative for KTDA to audit its dealings with farmers.

The practice of 'ghost farmers' cheating other farmers on their green leaf weight is largely the result of stifled farmers' organisations and their historical domination by KTDA. As regulator the TBK has the responsibility to link up with farmers' organisations and with the KTDA to audit growers' lists in each factory. However, the magnitude of the 'ghost farmer' phenomenon appears to reflect the weakness of governance structures that should bring together the state (through the TBK) and civil society (including KUSSTO, and KTDA). Inadequate regulation means that farmers have to contend with power imbalances in tea markets that are increasingly socially constructed in diverse ways by those who have recognised loop holes in governance and seek to exploit these. Farmers are however, beginning to organise around tea buying centre committees to dislodge 'ghost farmers' from the centres. The extent of their success will obviously vary from one centre to another and on the possibility of building alliances with more visible civil society organisations that may support them and push their plight into national limelight. A higher profile civil society organisation may be able to tackle problems on many fronts drawing media attention to the issue, organising and training farmers and instigating litigation where is evidence of wrong doing (Bebbington, et al. 2006). The aim should be to change the balance of power, so that policy makers and implementers cede influence to pro-poor groups through collective action in the interest of the smallholders (Kaimowitz, 2002: 124). The smallholders' rise against 'ghost farmers' is leading to smallholders making some organisational change. At the same time the ingenuity and creativity of 'ghost farmers' is dwindling, and perhaps approaching a dead end. Such dynamic processes dominate the everyday practices of villagers in a variety of realms. These scenarios show how creativity can also be a negative force if it is applied at the expense of other farmers.

In general the tea industry regulator may be in a dilemma as a result of liberalisation rhetoric which has led to the abdication of the important duty of regulating green tea leaf trade, as stipulated in government policy (Kenya, 1999b – Sessional Paper No. 2). Issues such as clerks tampering with scales to their advantage, cheating farmers on tea leaf weight and the *soko huru* phenomenon are all within the purview of the TBK in collaboration with civil society. However, the liberalisation of the smallholder tea sector as political action creates significant uncertainty reflected in capital flows in *soko huru* which create further local livelihood uncertainties among farmers (cf. Mehta, Leach and Scoones, 2001: 2). The overarching uncertainty, especially with regard to markets and the returns thereto, have led to competition and manipulation due to power relations within the smallholder tea sub-sector. The TBC clerk emerges as powerful and able to manipulate farmers to create resources for their livelihoods, for 'ghost farmers' and other *mashabiki*. In this way the construction and organisation of markets provides differing opportunities for different people, depending on their location in the power relations and how they negotiate their positions in everyday life. Actors in the tea sub-sector network in different ways to gain a foothold and construct livelihoods. Some villagers latch on friends with farmer registration to become 'ghost farmers' while TBC committees engage with other civil society organisations to counter this. In general however, civil society organisations coalesce around high profile agendas such as political democratisation or national regime change rather than less visible issues of rural governance and the problems facing farmers (Beall, 2001).

Conclusion

This chapter has shown that smallholder tea farming is a socially constructed resource, embedded in local social reality and continually being re-worked to service a variety of livelihood ventures including those of *bona fide* farmers, 'ghost farmers', *mashabiki* and tea buying centre clerks. Pursuit of these tea-based livelihoods, stirs up a number of contests at different sites, and throws strategies and counter-strategies in conflict with one another. There are intra-household struggles for control of tea earnings and village-wide (and beyond) contests and negotiation for the control of 'stolen tea' at the tea buying centre. A key group of beneficiaries are the 'ghost farmers' who reap where they have not sown, but whose sway in the smallholder tea sub-sector cannot be ignored.

The tea buying centre clerk constitutes the locus of a double livelihood; one, in employment that is visible, the other and more important one, as the hidden face of the double-faced 'ghost farmers'. The tea buying centre clerk steals and sells tea leaf, fetching significant earnings during each working day. The 'ghost farmers' who themselves have few or no tea bushes, are an important aspect of the smallholder governance nightmare in Nyamira and perhaps in Kenya as a whole. Finally the *mashabiki* are the unruly face of smallholder tea farming. They protect the clerk and 'buy kilograms' stolen even from their own wives. In response to these influences the *soko huru* arena becomes stronger and gives the opportunity for village scouts and smallholder tea farmers to creatively construct livelihoods in hitherto unexpected ways.

Investigating the practice of 'theft of tea leaf' at the tea buying centres is methodologically challenging, because it occurs clandestinely and is anchored in relationships of significant trust and secrecy among perpetrators. This makes it difficult to get to the bottom of the issue until one is fully trusted. Theoretically, it can be seen as a counter-tendency feeding on local population pressures and governance problems in the smallholder tea sub-sector. A counter-tendency is largely a political problem that requires creative governance structures to bring together state, market and civil society organisations to tackle it. Farmers and the tea sector regulator (TBK) need to play a leading role, with the TBK leading farmers' organisations and providing more support in dealing with the double strategies of *soko huru* and 'ghost farmers'. The next chapter turns to how people seek their livelihoods by moving in and out of farming from time to time in the course of their lives.

CHAPTER 7

Does Deagrarianisation Mean Moving Permanently Away from Agriculture?

Introduction

This chapter contributes to our understanding about how villagers create resources and use them to earn a living, and does so by asking three specific questions. How and why do people move in and out of agriculture over time? Which resource creation processes ensue from these movements? And, how are livelihoods constructed in the process? In short, what holds this process together? The chapter commences by recasting the deagrarianisation debate and operationalising the concept in specific and workable terms. This is followed by an examination of the directions of deagrarianisation in Sengeta, which is derived from a detailed discussion around six themes on engagement and disengagement with agriculture, themes which emerge from the corpus of data and relate to people's life courses. These themes are discernible through a critical analysis of the data to ascertain how and why people embrace or distance themselves from agriculture as their principal means of livelihoods. The themes cover; the involvement of young men/people in their parents' fields, their movement to working off the farm; return to the land; control over land; the pursuit of respectability, and aging and land inheritance. The chapter ends by summarising the deagrarianisation process and concludes that the primacy of agriculture in rural livelihoods is gradually being undermined, but that this is occurring gradually and in a cyclical fashion as migration from rural areas is largely temporary rather than permanent and attachment to land appears to defy residence status and occupation. Both rural and townspeople are attached to the land to the same extent albeit from varying distances.

It is important to distinguish the focus of this chapter from that of the following one on 'livelihood diversification'. This is because of the blurred boundary between 'diversification' and 'deagrarianisation' within some of the literature. This chapter on deagrarianisation essentially looks at how and why people move in and out of agriculture over time, in contrast to the next chapter which looks at how and why people combine agriculture with non-agricultural activities to make their living. In both cases the creative processes of resource constitution to make a living are central to the discussions and they involve looking at the extended case studies from different dimensions in order to explain these processes. Deagrarianisation and diversification processes are not necessarily distinct and separate processes; an actor may engage in deagrarianisation at one point in time, re-enter agriculture at another point and diversify. In another scenario an actor may progressively diversify his or her livelihood until they eventually deagrarianise. These scenarios illustrate how an extended case study examined from different perspectives and at different points in time, may explain both processes of 'deagrarianisation' and 'diversification'.

Debating Deagrarianisation

Structural Adjustment Programmes (SAPs) and the accompanying neo-liberal policies and globalisation in Africa in the 1980s and 90s have led most analysts to conclude that the nature and role of agriculture in those economies is changing and to posit that the changes are deep and far-reaching. They show that the agricultural stagnation resulting from these policy changes has harmed the rural poor in Sub-Saharan Africa (SSA) by creating food shortages and higher prices, diminishing their ability to buy food and find work (Khan 2001: 8). The key argument is that agriculture's role as a source of rural livelihoods is slowly being eroded through deagrarianisation. This means that food production for self-provisioning and cash cropping (e.g. tea, cocoa and coffee production) for the market are waning in rural Africa.

Bryceson (1996: 99) has defined deagrarianisation as a process of livelihood reorientation, occupational adjustment and the spatial realignment of human settlements away from agrarian patterns. This generally implies a movement away from agriculturally-based livelihoods. Bryceson argues that deagrarianisation has proceeded in SSA through two main processes. The first is the 'derived urbanisation' of the post-independence period. This process was fuelled by the rural people's perception that urban areas offered better economic opportunities. Urban jobs sustained this and were available as a result of emerging parastatals and the Africanisation of public services and commerce. This enabled some people to move away from agriculture to urban areas, representing a first phase of deagrarianisation in the post-independence Africa of the 1960s.

The second process has to do with economic diversification and population settlement dispersal under SAPs. The oil crises of the early and late 1970s and governance problems were two factors that contributed to the crippling of most African economies in the 1980s, leading to the introduction of SAPs sponsored by donor consortia led by the World Bank and the International Monetary Fund (IMF). The results of the SAPs in many countries were civil service retrenchment and the withdrawal of subsidies for the agricultural and other sectors such as health and education, which led to increases in food and other prices (cf. Razavi, 2003: 3; Bryceson, 1999). Uncertainty led urban and rural dwellers alike to pursue household livelihood strategies consisting of a mix of subsistence activities, market oriented production, and trading – in order to spread risks of output failure (Bryceson, 1996). Unlike Bryceson, this study regards such strategies as diversification rather than deagrarianisation. Bryceson further argues that under these circumstances, low income dwellers are likely to return to rural areas, whereas the affluent might prefer to stay in cities and invest in agriculture through kin or clientage ties, creating or deepening the rural labour market and possibly creating or further supporting a deagrarianised rural population of the landless and near landless.

Return migrants to the rural areas also tend to be more educated than *in situ* rural residents of the same age, and more able to invest the skills and money that might offer non-agricultural rural employment opportunities (cf. Bryceson, 1996), a potential they share with more affluent farmers (Orvis, 1993: 34). It is important to deconstruct Bryceson's argument about urban dwellers investing in agriculture. First, when urban dwellers invest in agriculture through kin or friends they have only diversified their livelihood. Second and more importantly, the landless that they employ through kin and friends have already deagrarianised; however, the near landless only diversify their livelihood once they take the employment. Whether this ultimately leads to proletarianisation or depeasantisation (cf. Long, 1984) is another matter. The possibilities for landless and near-landless villagers to secure employment outside of their family holdings raise two key questions within the deagrarianisation debate. Do these possibilities provide permanent or temporary avenues out of self-provisioning? Second, what is the significance of rural agricultural employment to livelihoods, especially in relation to other non-farm economic activities, and how do these fit in the rural agricultural landscape?

Bryceson (1996) concludes that SSA is steadily becoming less agrarian in nature and that none of the existing theoretical approaches focuses the enquiry on the process of deagrarianisation. She suggests that 'an understanding of deagrarianisation could be pursued at two levels: as a long-term historical process and as an integral part of rural households' short-to-medium term livelihood strategies'. At the macro levels it is indeed possible to capture some of the overt and measurable manifestations of the process, such as a shrinking proportion of the population residing in rural areas and a decrease in the relative contribution of agricultural output per capita to the national economy. But such aggregate statistics mask huge variations, patterns and tendencies at local levels (cf. Bryceson, 1996). Perhaps, given identifiable trends at the macro-level the foregoing argument is accurate (see Bryceson, 2002a). But how do people encounter deagrarianisation at local levels in practice? In responding to this question Bryceson (1996; 1999; 2002a, 2002b) seems to move in the direction of livelihood diversification. The challenge, which this chapter responds to, is to provide a picture of villagers' encounters with deagrarianisation, the resource creation processes that ensue and their implications for livelihoods. As Davis and Bezemer (2004) have argued, there are a variety of socio-cultural factors that shape the rural non-farm economy such as ethnicity, gender and other social categorisations, and the extent of social capital. This is in line with Boserup's (1965) contention that agricultural change or transformation in developing countries is driven by internal factors such as population pressure. These factors appear to affect the directions and pace of deagrarianisation.

This study followed a conception of deagrarianisation that allowed for micro-level analysis that would be able to capture local variations and assess these in a macro context. To this end the study follows Meagher's (1999) conception of deagrarianisation as a movement away from agriculturally based livelihoods and an embracing of non-farm activities. Non-farm activities include agricultural wage labour, as well as non-agricultural activities and other forms of wage labour. Agricultural processing intended for sale beyond the household such as beer brewing and trade in crops/livestock produced by others, such as butchery, are categorised as non-farm activities, as they represent a move away from agricultural self-provisioning activities organised around the household farm (cf. Meagher, 1999).

Directions in Deagrarianisation in Nyamira District

People in Sengeta Village, Nyamira District were examined through extended case studies to capture their place in the deagrarianisation process. The extended cases enable us to follow people's lives through time with a view to describing and explaining how and why they moved into and out of farming at various points in their life courses. The modes of deagrarianisation that emerge reflect the heterogeneity of rural livelihood preferences and pursuits. One important outcome of this examination is the emergence of a pattern of cyclical deagrarianisation, which occurs for different reasons and is of varying lengths and depths. As indicated above the discussion is premised on life course related themes in the agrarianisation/deagrarianisation processes that emerge from the extended case studies.

Involvement in Parents' Fields

Villagers in Sengeta were initially involved in farming at their parents' fields. They did this mainly by providing household labour for their parents' farming activities and had minimal control over the activities and farm output. Their interest in farming varied greatly from one actor to the other. Some worked in their parents' fields on a transitory basis, with their minds set on school and not on the farm. As a result some of them soon left the farm for the 'White Highlands' for employment to raise money for school fees, while others worked at the plantations for longer periods mainly to raise resources for bride price, which delayed their eventual return to farming. There are also those who remained at home to work on the farms and used their parents' cattle for bride price when the time to marry arrived. Yet those who moved to the plantations and those who did not, commenced their life career through involvement in their parents' fields.

> Petro was born in 1927 into a polygamous family. He has three brothers and three sisters and a number of step brothers and sisters. His father was a herder, but the family was generally poor. As a boy he was involved in herding and clearing bushes to open new millet fields. Petro was circumcised at the age of 15. Like other young men in his village he toyed with the idea of raising his own resources to commence life. Many young men were being recruited to work in the (then) White Highlands. In 1942 he was assisted by his neighbour and uncle who already worked in the plantations, to get a job with temporary accommodation at the plantations. After working in Kericho for six years, he came back home in 1948 and started school at age 21. He supplemented his plantation work earnings by growing maize and pyrethrum to raise his school fees of nine shillings per year as his parents did not then value education.

The idea of work in one's parents' fields was becoming less taken forgranted in the 1940s, as this excerpt from Petro's case indicates. Young people were beginning to attach value to formal education, which they saw as a resource for the future. Young people often needed to work in the plantations to raise the income for school fees and this ushered in a new force in the transformation of agriculture and its place as a means of livelihood.

During the 1940s and 50s another key goal in the lives of young men after circumcision was marriage. Marriage was however strictly a function of cattle for bride price (Levine and Levine, 1966). Thus one factor strongly influencing interest in working in one's parents' fields was the possibility of inheriting cattle with which to marry. Another key retention factor was defending family land from intruders migrating from other areas that were unsuitable for their settlement. Competition between brothers for shrinking family herds to meet bride prices seems to have pushed some young men towards plantation work to raise their own resources for marriage. Some figuring that they had few or no sisters, realised that they would have to be raising cattle for bride price from outside the family farm.

In the final analysis, the need for resources for bride price and the general currency of the idea of migration to plantation areas for employment and the possibility of western patterns of consumption pulled more and more young men away from the traditional practice of working on their parents' fields. Their departure from the fields was as unplanned as was their involvement in the fields. They were involved in the fields as a matter of life course and their life courses appeared to drive them to depart for the plantations as well, mainly to seek what was lacking at home. By the 1940s, the Gusii region was securely under colonial control and the 'war economy', mainly based on raiding cattle from neighbouring clans and ethnic groups as a means of accumulating cattle had been controlled by the government. In addition, land to raise cattle was getting scarce, due to closure of the frontiers and competition from crop production (cf. Levine and Levine, 1966; Maxon, 1989). It was therefore logical for young men to look to the plantations for income to raise cattle for bride price. The extract below from Nyandika's case record underscores this choice issue.

> Nyandika joined 'egesarate', a cattle camp where old men lived with young men educating them as they took care of the cattle. He was circumcised in 1947. All the boys circumcised at the same time in any village had a leader called 'omosegi'. The leader guided and taught them while in seclusion. At the end of the seclusion period, their faces were painted with clay soil and after some partying in the village their grand fathers and / or their peers spurt 'busaa' and sour milk on the boys to bless them. The boys were then released to take care of cattle. Nyandika married his first wife from the Bosiango clan in 1951. He paid thirteen heads of cattle as the bride price. Nine of these he raised from the bride price paid for one of his sisters. He had already bought four cows and two goats from his savings from working in the tea plantations and thus was easily able to meet the bride price for his wife.

The anticipated constraints of getting cattle for bride price were at least in part overcome through leaving the farm for the plantations as this excerpt from Nyandika's case shows. The young men were moving to the plantations to search for employment to purchase cattle for bride price. Those born after Kenya's independence in 1963, followed a similar trajectory but for different reasons. For instance Angima used to work in his grandmother's fields before leaving for an urban area as shown in the extract below.

> Angima was born in 1959 to Onsinyo and Kebungo. Besides his younger brother Ombongi, he had a sister who died in 2000. He attended primary school up to standard four in 1970 when he quit for lack of school fees. His parents effectively separated in 1969 so Angima and his sister grew up in their paternal grandmother's house, mostly helping her in the fields. Their grandmother was a peasant, growing bananas, maize, beans and kales. She had occasional monetary support from her first born son who worked away in town as a mechanic and in maize and beans from two other sons in the village. It was their grandmother who organised Angima's circumcision ceremony in 1970 and that of his sister in 1974. She had to use the earnings from her bananas and kales to do this as she did not have any high value cash crop. In 1976 Angima went to live with his paternal uncle Nyagwencha who was an accomplished motor vehicle mechanic in Longisa town. Angima became an apprentice and assisted him in the workshop where he learned motor vehicle mechanics and driving.

Angima became involved in his grandmother's fields as a matter of course and like others in his generation sought to escape farming by going to work in town. In his case this was specifically to escape the poverty and abandonment that followed his parents' separation. This was different from the pre-independence generation that had sought plantation employment not to escape farming, but rather to re-enter it more powerfully after marriage. For the younger generation many of whose members had some formal education their involvement in their parents' fields was also transitory. They aimed at white collar and non-farm blue collar jobs for prestige, higher pay and town life. Even then their attachment to the land and home remained strong as will be demonstrated in due course.

Young people's involvement in their parents' fields at the start of their careers reflects the centralised patriarchal control of household labour and other resources in Sengeta village. This has been the case in both pre- and post-independence days. The patriarch arranges the household's resources according to his wishes, and most of them are organised around the family farm. This focus on the family farm has always been intended to put food on the table as well as to train the producers of the future through a form of apprenticeship on the farm. This apprenticeship appears to leave an indelible mark of farming and rural life on the apprentices as they always keep an eye on the land and return as soon as they have some money to invest on the farm or as their labour becomes irrelevant outside the farm. This may explain why all households, including those with migrants working in the formal sector in major cities and in other countries such as the Americas and Europe, still share out their land equally among all their sons for inheritance. Those in the cities and in other countries do not decline land allocations in the village. As one villager put it, "leaving out a son however rich from ancestral land allocation would be like throwing him away". Therefore, even though young people have been leaving the village for work since the 1920s[54], their attachment to ancestral land has remained fairly constant.

Migration to Work

After involvement in parents' fields, some young people moved to the plantations later, others to the towns or abroad for work. This movement represented a first transplantation of people from agriculturally based livelihoods to employment outside the family farm. In the life courses of those involved it was the first time that they were making a living outside of agriculture. This was however; largely temporary as within a span of a few years they were already on their way to the farm, for a variety of reasons, to make their living there. The reasons for departure to work have already been discussed above: the main ones were the search for income to buy cattle for bride price and to raise school fees for themselves and later some for their children. Those moving to towns and abroad went for apprenticeship /studentship and employment.

Migrants to the tea plantations in Kericho were housed in very small units that were largely meant for bachelors, this perhaps to discourage them taking their families. In any case, as one of the respondents said: "Women could not

[54] See Silberschmidt, 1999.

work as the colonial government did not give them identity cards and yet employers required the cards for one to be employed". Therefore, even though some men moved with their wives to the plantations, this only made their lives more difficult due to poor living conditions and higher consumption expenses. Creative ones such as Nyagwanga had a way of circumventing these requirements, he said: "although my wife could not be employed, she went with me to pluck tea which I weighed in under my name, so we ended up earning more". The departure of some men with their wives to work in the plantation sector suggests rising avarice and the entrenchment of the cash economy. By the 1960s people were sending their children to school in larger numbers and needed more money for their school fees, creating an incentive to maximise earnings in the plantations, in spite of the difficult working conditions. Thus sometimes movement from the farm to the plantations was total, taking away both husband and wife to make a living by working away from home.

Generally however, the difficult working conditions in the plantations therefore generally meant that migrants left their wives at home. Not many went to the plantations shortly after marriage, as a main reason for moving was to raise bride price. Whilst away working in the plantations or in towns they often changed jobs, seeking less manual and better paying, jobs. When changing jobs they mostly relied on new friendships they had developed or kinsmen in the area who provided useful information about new opportunities.

> Saulo was circumcised in 1945, and was employed in settler farms to pick pyrethrum the same year. Later his maternal uncle took him and his elder brother to Dobi farm still as pyrethrum pickers. Saulo's salary was one shilling and fifty cents per month at the first farm while on Dobi farm it was three shillings and thirty cents per month. After some time at Dobi, Saulo moved to Nyaronde where he earned six shillings per month, still doing pyrethrum work. From Nyaronde, Saulo went to Kimari where he was employed as a turn boy on trucks that carried green tea leaf to Shauji factory. As a turn boy he was taught how to drive by his driver a friendly Kuria man. As turn boy he earned twelve shillings per month. He was employed as a driver in the same company in 1951 and worked there until 1959 on a salary of fifteen shillings per month.

Saulo used his social resources and personal energy to locate better job opportunities. He rose from a pyrethrum picker, through a truck turn boy and eventually to a driver within a space of six years. He changed jobs many times relying on friendships and kinship and, in the process, his salary had in the process rose from one shilling and fifty cents to fifteen shillings. These work place manoeuvrings can be seen as an indication of commitment to, and entrenchment in, employment away from home and away from the farm as a basis of livelihood. His case illustrates the creative ways in which migrants attempted to improve their life chances at the work place by linking up with relatives and evolving friendships that yielded job opportunities.

A similar trend may be observed in the case material on those who moved to towns. Angima, with a modest formal education put in his all and within two years he was able to convincingly function as a motor vehicle mechanic as shown in the excerpt below.

> Angima became an apprentice and assisted his uncle in the workshop where he learned motor vehicle mechanics and driving. This learning was very informal, based on learning by observation and doing. Soon he could repair small faults on motor vehicles and make some money for himself. When he became good at motor vehicle repairs, his uncle started collecting payments centrally in the workshop and paying him and two other workers at the end of each working day. The work was very good and for the first time Angima bought himself a pair of shoes in 1978.

Angima's effort to learn motor mechanics and practice it within a period of two years is a remarkable feat of creativity in redeploying himself in a new field. In so doing he demonstrated his abilities to marshal his skills outside the farm and to generate a livelihood. Additionally this achievement indicates that it takes creativity to seize existing livelihood opportunities as Angima did this on the basis of social relationships with his uncle.

Overall we can conclude that some people successfully migrated from Sengeta to the plantations or towns for various lengths of periods, with the aim of raising resources for a living. It is clear that this movement was based on development of skills and deployment of kinship alliances in order to enhance livelihood opportunities in the work place. Therefore the migration to the plantations and towns involved a form of deagrarianisation, and new ways of creating resources and making a living away from home and farm. In this sense the migrants had reoriented their livelihood and residences away from agriculture (Bryceson, 1996). This was however, somewhat temporary and soon the migrants' attachment to the land and their interest in returning to it started to show.

Attachment to the land and indications of impending return

The migrants often came home to Sengeta for weekends or their annual leave and thus connected with the land more than they would if they had permanently migrated for work. These forays to the rural areas lay ground for their future investment in agriculture through spouses and kin.

> While working with Shauji tea factory Saulo developed an interest in tea growing. In 1952 he carried tea stumps from Shauji every time he went home and planted them on his farm. He showed his mother how to weed and to harvest when the crop was ready.

As they struggled to change jobs and earn more, the migrants were also thinking about their eventual return to the farms and they prepared for that eventuality in different ways. There is a seeming tendency toward agriculture, which migrants would re-engage with after accessing resources through employment. These tendencies may have been the result of strong agricultural socialisation especially through earlier involvement in their parents' fields, which defined home and kinship and prompted young men to plan to go back home to marry, inherit land and farm (cf. Hakansson, 1994).

However, with some more formal education and training employment appeared to become relatively more permanent and migration more stable. Petro's son is a case in point.

> One of Petro's sons is a school teacher in the Rift Valley and has bought a farm there. He regularly visits his parents and assists them whenever there is material or financial need. In particular he assisted with paying school fees for his younger brothers and sisters. Petro has subdivided the tea farm which he bought at Irandi for his son's inheritance. Each of them has been given 700 bushes.

While those migrants with higher education more visibly invested away from home, e.g. in land purchases, it appears that these investments were more facilitated by their membership in formal credit unions rather than a new social outlook and desire to assume cosmopolitanism. The migrants still retained moral obligations in their home villages and invested in social ties, albeit from a distance. None of them was ruled out of inheriting land and most were regularly in touch with their siblings and parents. They influenced and contributed to decision-making processes on the family farm. Some invested in better housing for their parents on the farms, although they may have calculated that upon their parents' demise the houses would become theirs. Others such as Petro's son had already inherited land including tea bushes in the village, despite his having bought his own farm elsewhere. This trend of migrants keeping one foot on the farm and the other at work in the city or abroad contradicts Iqbal's (1999) assertion that once a person leaves her or his own country, emotional attachment to the land is severed, and the individual is more likely to move in search of the greatest economic opportunity. Socialisation on the farm and cultural attachment to the land appears to have been a factor in migrant actors' emotional attachment to the land, which remained unsevered in Sengeta Village. It should be pointed out that this practice of keeping one foot on the farm and another on employment usually involved years of employment and the march back to the land was a long process. This is in line with Andersson's (2002) findings in Zimbabwe.

Migrants appear to think of home even more once they leave. Their temporary migration may suggest a decline in the importance of farming if viewed from a statistical standpoint, but in reality it is a case of "once farmers, always farmers" and it does not take much to bring out this potential for returning. In the Eastern Cape, South Africa Manona (1999) found that the migrants in towns are readily attracted back to the rural areas if there is some improvement in the infrastructure, especially electricity supply. In Sengeta Village the attachment to the land and rural living may be more of culturally inspired as the infrastructure is poor, and unlikely to improve in the coming years. However, the cell phone has enabled people in towns to stay in closer contact with rural people and to manage their affairs better. Even so, when this facility was not available, town dwellers still invested in the villages.

Some migrants appear to hold onto land for sentimental reasons. Urban Kenyans and especially those from western Kenya talk of 'home', mainly in reference to their ancestral land (Cohen and Odhiambo, 1992). They strive to have a piece of land at 'home', not so much for economic reasons as for social ones. That is where they go to for 'holidays', where they will be buried and where they carry out most of their traditional rituals such as child naming and cutting of the first hair on children's heads. This is the significance of 'place' in the livelihoods of a people. The landscape plays a role in defining and anchoring their identity. In other words people are enveloped in some sense of 'dwellingness' that links their past, present and future (Urry, 2000:139)

'Home' is also defined from a political standpoint in Kenya at least since the beginning of the 1990s. At that time there were widespread inter-tribal clashes mainly over land ownership but politically defined (Kenya Land Alliance, 2004; Abdullahi, 1997; Kahl, 1998). Those who had bought land in the former White Highlands suddenly found themselves defined as aliens, as they had moved in from distant areas and were seen to have dispossessed the 'natives'. The evictions that followed have redefined the concept of 'home' and sharpened people's appetite for inheriting ancestral land for security reasons. For example if Petro's son is evicted from the land he has purchased in Rift Valley Province where he has purchased land, he has his ancestral land to fall back on. It also means that urban homes are not as safe as home, because they may be in other people's homelands and constituencies and hence subject to inter-tribal clashes.

Thus 'home' appears to be important in terms of identity, contribution to farm organisation and food production, regardless of residence status. Overseas migrants are not only under obligation to support their parents and kin back home with money to invest on the land but also to provide ideas and decisions as to how land is to be used. As part of their sense of belonging to the village they lay claim to ancestral land for inheritance. These findings about 'home' and 'identity' and the fact that most villagers grow some food crops, even if only on a small scale, shows that the villagers do not see the market as an unequivocal ally in providing a source of food. Not even relatives in the cities and abroad fully trust the market, at least as far as their decisions and actions in Sengeta show. Even if they did, persuading those in the village to abandon farming and rely on the market would be an uphill task. In line with these findings Daley (2005b) and Russell (2003) have shown that the meagre subsistence derived by rural dwellers from the land is more than they would hope for from paid labour, and that food production and farming is a form of livelihood insurance in a seemingly turbulent market.

Back to the Land: the journey from non-farm employment to farming

At different points in their working lives, migrants return to the land and work it as if they had never been away. They actualise their attachment to the land, returning for a variety of reasons. However, their re-entry into farming meets with varying degrees of success, for a range of reasons such as lack of resources, like land and inputs. There are several scenarios in the journeys back to the land after work away from home and farm.

A common scenario in Sengeta is return upon retirement, as was the case with Nyandika. This retirement mostly occurs early, perhaps because of their attachment to land or even interest in farming. Migrants to the plantations return to Sengeta at quite a young age, mostly in their early forties. The extract below brings out Nyandika's early retirement and re-entry to agriculture.

> Nyandika had planted coffee in 1955 and tea in 1962, in both cases using earning from his employment at the tea plantations to pay for the plantings. After he had paid for the plantings they were delivered when the extension officer ensured that the field was ready. He mobilised risaga to prepare the field and to plant the tea on the day that the planting materials were delivered. It cost him about five hundred shillings to plant two thousand bushes, a sum which most villagers who had not worked outside the village or inherited many heads of cattle to sell would not have been able to afford. He said many people desired to plant tea but could not afford it. "Teachers and those of us who worked in the plantations were easily able to plant tea and coffee because we had an income". Nyandika learnt tea pruning skills at the tea plantations and has used them in the village returning from Kericho in 1960.

Retirement was not an abrupt occurrence for Nyandika; it is something he appeared to have planned by spending some weekends and annual leave days at home, investing on the land, building houses and planting tea and coffee. When he finally retired he went home to pick up farming activities that he had already started during his holidays and by proxy through kin and spouses. At retirement he smoothly fitted back into the community and re-entered farming, making his livelihood once more from agriculture.

This scenario is consistent with local understandings of employment as a temporary sojourn away from home to look for money. Permanent migration is an exception and is described with an unkind local term, *omonyamwaka*. *Omonyamwaka* means the lost one, the one without roots. A person described in this way is seen as being of limited social value, not so much for being absent on a continued basis, but more so for lacking a sufficiently deep understanding of his kin networks to invest in them. Employment is seen as valuable in the local context when the actor returns home at weekends or during annual leave so as to be with their kin, drink with them, mourn with them and support their endeavours. This linkage with family and kin while in employment provides a soft landing at retirement, especially in terms of labour mobilisation through groups or work parties. Group labour is nurtured and reciprocal, so one can only summon when locally linked and available to participate meaningfully in group activities (cf. Kongstad and Monsted, 1980). This idea of attachment to the land is further supported by reports of urban agriculture and the reliance of urban dwellers on farming in rural areas to secure food supplies to subsidise their urban livelihoods (Owuor and Foeken, 2006).

Petro's departure from work in the plantations came before his retirement and represents a different scenario of returning to the farm.

> After working in Kericho for six years, he came back home and started school at the age of twenty one in 1948. He supplemented his plantation work earnings with maize and pyrethrum growing to raise his school fees of nine shillings per year because his parents did not value education at the time.

Petro's aim of going to work in the plantations was to raise money for his school fees, but he could not raise enough due to low wages, so he returned home to go to primary school. Once in school he combined it with some farming in order to raise "the required fees of nine shillings per year". There were other cases of people who had set out to the plantations with the aim of raising their school fees money from employment. On their return to commence schooling, they all had to combine their schooling with farming to supplement their savings and to support household food provisioning. For these people school represented a basis for early return from plantation employment and a step towards re-entering farming for a second time in their life course. If they succeeded in school as Petro did, they moved into formal employment and abandoned farming for a second time. This adds another turn in the oscillations between farm and non-farm based livelihood construction. Those who were unsuccessful in school and who could not secure employment marshalled whatever resources available, particularly a wife, to commence life on the farm and start a family (cf. Silberschmidt, 1999).

The journeys from plantation employment to school that were made in the 1950s and 1960s were driven by the hope inspired by the offer of clerical jobs to Africans with basic numeracy skills. Most of the respondents from Sengeta with some formal education, such as Nyandika and Saulo, assumed more responsibilities in the plantation sector and moved beyond tea plucking. Back home teachers were required for the expanding education sector and these opportunities also encouraged people to go to school. Another factor that may have stirred interest in education among young people in the 1950s was the return of villagers who had served in the Second World War. These returnees provided a good model for villagers' and what they could achieve, as they had successfully served alongside colonial military personnel. Economic growth after the war required more skilled labour (Silberschmidt, 1999). Research from neighbouring Tanzania (Daley, 2005a: 376) shows that job opportunities increased at this time as the number of colonial settlers rose.

A final scenario in the return journeys from work to farm revolves around those villagers who returned before retirement and for reasons other than education or specifically to re-enter farming. Nyarwaru and Angima are both representative of this scenario. Both belong to the post-independence generation and had left home to escape poverty and the scrubby farming being carried out back at home. Both of them joined the informal sector rather than go to the plantations. This was in the 1970 – 1990 period when the circumstances had changed significantly from those in the 1950s and 60s. It became more popular for young people to work in the urban areas, not the plantations. Going back to the land and working in the plantations were seen as undertakings of last resort. Mung'ong'o (1998) found a similar trend in Mjombe District, Tanzania where most of those who migrated during the colonial period or just after, worked in sisal and tea plantations while those who migrated in the 1980s and 90s went to urban centres. These trends in East Africa indicate both the structural change in the economy and migration regulations in the post-independence period, but perhaps more importantly changes in lifestyles and job preferences among rural people, especially as a result of higher educational attainment.

After returning from work in an urban area Angima commenced farming on his father's land. This lasted only about two years and his father disputed his right to work the land as the extract below shows.

> When Angima came home for his grandmother's burial he did not return to Longisa again. He started to farm on his father's land, growing bananas, maize, cabbages and kale. He built a grass thatched hut and married Pauline from Mokorongosi that year, but the marriage only lasted a few years because the lady did not work hard on the farm. Neighbours laughed at her for sitting at home when Angima worked hard in the fields. She eventually left and went away to her parents. By late 1981 Angima was making good money from working the land. His father realised that and asked him to pay for the land that he used. Angima resisted but to no avail and had quit farming by August 1982.

Patriarchal authority drove Angima from the farm. This is a common feature of rural life in Gusiiland where land is inherited by sons but owned by the father into old age or even until death. Because they hold absolute title to the land, access to it by sons and others can only be negotiated. The intergenerational struggles over land may be protracted and counter-productive as in Saulo's case (see Chapter 5), where his wives and sons insisted on land inheritance and when he yielded and subdivided it his second wife and her sons disowned him and left him in relative want. Angima's negotiations only earned him a place for a compound for his house, with his father retaining control over the rest of the land until his death, mostly hiring it out for an income. This creates inequalities in the distribution of resources (Guyer, 1981). This shows that it is not only external forces such as market and policy issues that drive the deagrarianisation process (as Bryceson 1996 argues) but rather that intra- and inter-household dynamics also have an influence in sending household members in and out of farming at different times. The intervals between departure and return may vary, depending on the nature of disputes over resources and how solutions are negotiated.

Angima's stand off with his father and resultant absence from farming lasted several years. This raises questions about land registration policy. At what point should a father's land ownership cease and, when it does, how will he and his aging spouse(s) derive their livelihood? If it should remain until death, how are his adult sons to derive their livelihoods in the interim especially if they have no other means such as gainful employment outside the farm? These questions highlight the tensions between policy and reality. Policy gives rights to land to an individual but creates struggles over these same rights. These struggles over land and other resources play an important role in the deagrarianisation process as shown in Angima's case.

Yet, even the return to land and farming depends on social ties. For one to re-enter farming there is need for sufficient land and inputs. It is important to have the social relationships to access those resources not readily available. Nyarwaru on his part returned home to a state of relative poverty after the demise of both of his parents. He had lost both the inputs and the requisite social relationships after the death of his parents.

> The vehicle that Nyarwaru was working with was broken down and he came home in 2002, the same year that his father passed away. Following the passing of his father, he had the responsibility for his younger siblings. He went back to the Kisii Bus terminus to work as a tout but worked for only three months before "Michuki drove us out in February 2003" – referring to then Minister for Transport who spearheaded a campaign that streamlined public transport across the country. Nyarwaru started distilling the local brew chang'aa in October 2003 to raise some money to support his siblings, wife and children as his late parents did not leave behind much wealth for them to meet their needs.

When his parents passed on the care for his younger siblings fell on him and he had to become creative with his life. These circumstances plunged him into an 'illegal business'; *chang'aa* distillation and sales. The death of parents not only exposes children to poverty, especially if they are young at the time, but also isolates them. The networks parents used to construct a livelihood are quickly thrown off balance because reciprocity is in doubt. This is because children do not fully appreciate the subtle nuances that surround and define the flow of resources in a network. This is demonstrated by Nyarwaru's assertion that he hired *chang'aa* distillation equipment from his cousin. It means that even at that very low ebb in his life, his cousin would not let go the equipment for free. This might suggest a weakening of the kinship and extended family networks in Sengeta. The contradiction, though, is that the mere agreement by his cousin to let the equipment to him constituted significant assistance because *chang'aa* distillation is an 'illegal' activity, hence trust and kinship that may have facilitated availability of the equipment at all.

The possibility of Nyarwaru returning to farming was obstructed by lack of land and capital. Given land and capital constraints, Nyarwaru chose a business venture with the least capital outlay and the highest returns. Nyarwaru's choice of *chang'aa* brewing and sales confirms Daley's (2005b) prediction that rural dwellers lacking entrepreneurial means and educational achievement could take advantage of the increasing demand for locally produced alcohol. This is consistent with Razavi's (2003) and Mung'ong'o's (1998) assertions that the withdrawal of farm subsidies after the SAPs made agriculture difficult. Therefore, Nyarwaru's circumstances mirror the impacts of SAPs in rural Africa and indicate how deep into rural SSA World Bank and IMF policies pierce. Nyarwaru's response to the circumstances however contradicts the logic of deagrarianisation. Instead of sticking in the informal sector distilling and selling *chang'aa*, he bought a cow from his proceeds in the business and a sewing machine for his wife, spreading his investments between farming and non-farming activities. His return to marginal farming illustrates the cyclical nature of deagrarianisation (see Figure 9.1). This return to farming is a contradiction in Nyarwaru's life and may be best explained by his agricultural socialisation and thus his identity as a farmer, at least while he remained in the village. He may also have bought the cow and kept busy feeding it by the road side so as to conceal his main and 'illicit' means of livelihood in *chang'aa* distillation.

Control over land and the dilemmas around its use for a living

Land and the resources to work it are crucial to the construction of agricultural livelihoods. This is why it is often argued that policies to ensure rural people's access to land are critical to any rural development programme. However, it may be possible to have unfettered access to land and yet choose to use the land in other ways, even when it looks from the outside that farming would be the best option. In this sense deagrarianisation may result not from diminishing land availability per capita, as is often thought but perhaps from personal preferences.

Angima had struggled for the control of his father's land for a number of years without success. His father only made marginal use of it and denied Angima access. Farming was not his main means of livelihood as he relied on his traditional medical practice for a living. It was another form of patriarchal discretion, which emerges a key theme in this chapter. Angima's father reasoned that as he had the authority over the land he should mould it in ways that suited his lifestyle and aspirations.

> Angima explained that although his father was omonyamosira (medicine man) and had relied on earnings from this practice during most of his life. During his later years, beginning about 1979, his main sources of livelihood were coffee, maize growing and leasing out part of his land. His late father leased out land because he lacked the labour and inputs to invest in it. More importantly he needed easy money to finance his regular consumption of local brew, busaa and chang'aa. Additionally as he grew older many of his patients stopped seeing him and he thus turned to agriculture for a living. He led a modest life living in a grass thatched house that he built in the mid 1950s until he died in 1985.

The fact that Angima's father had title over land which he physically controlled and yet relied on a completely different activity for a living, confirms the methodological potency of extended case studies in identifying hidden realities. Traditional medical practice was a hidden livelihood. On the surface Angima's father was a farmer, part of his land was cultivated although by people who had hired it from him and another part was planted with coffee. In the lands office he was registered as a land owner. Yet these official records did not reveal that he was first and foremost a traditional healer, secondly he hired out land and thirdly he was a part-time farmer.

Even though his father had denied him land to farm, Angima had a place in father's homestead to build his hut. From Angima's descriptions his hut and that of his father's were in close proximity. This layout of the homestead may have offered a picture of harmony and cooperation between father and son and of a household where resources and responsibilities were shared. In reality however, the two individuals shared a common space but were in conflict over decision making and resource use and control. In spite of this internal reality people may have treated Angima with respect and he may have enjoyed his father's protection presumptuously [as people did not necessarily know about the bad blood between him and his father]. While those outside the household treated him with a certain respect, he did not in reality enjoy the benefits and status within the household that he might have expected. Angima's quiet struggle with his father was informed by customary practices, policy and strategic considerations. The customary practices privileged patriarchal authority and gave his father unfettered control over the land, but it also recognised his son as belonging and defined his inheritance rights. Because the Gusii inheritance rules and land registration policy mutually reinforce institutional constraints to Angima's inheritance of land, he had to act strategically by getting a place to build a hut to fully belong but push his father no further, as that could complicate inheritance if his father were to marry a new wife in protest. Policy recognises the registered title holder as the absolute owner of land and thus in the interim Angima's interests could only be negotiated informally, and intermittent harmony and cooperation with his father were the best strategy.

In general the landscape created as a result of the struggles between father and son was characteristic of agricultural households, even though the actual activities of the man and his son were not primarily agricultural; it reflected the general trend of activities in the village. The nature of deagrarianisation where farming was abandoned for some years in a villager's life course is not captured in the literature. The struggles between Angima and his father reflect this cyclical nature of deagrarianisation, but this was obscured by the landscape and by the strategic considerations in the struggles. Father did not wage an all out war against his son because he was aging and considered him the best placed to give him a decent burial, as he was his eldest son and the only one living with him at the time. Angima equally took a softer approach to wait for his inheritance from a position of strength, and for the time being his possibility to farm had to be put on hold. Other researchers have identified similar intra-household struggles over land for horticultural production in Kenya's Meru District (Dolan, 2001).

When the strategic considerations finally bore fruit and Angima effectively inherited his father's land upon the latter's demise, he lived quite similarly to his departed father.

> After his father's burial, Angima was assisted by his uncles and other village elders to demarcate their father's land equally between his brother and himself. He said of this sharing of land "now I had my own land and was comfortable, I worked for Jonathan for some time and left as I planned to farm my own land". Angima said he did not start farming immediately but instead renewed a few of the land leases his late father had established, seemingly to raise money for his local brew drink. After marrying Stella, Angima worked as a farm hand for about two years and then started a chang'aa business with his wife. Angima buys chang'aa from Sengeta across the valley, buying three canisters and hiring boys to deliver them to the house to avoid the police and chief. Once delivered his wife sells it and when it is about to run out she similarly sources her own three canisters. Besides the chang'aa business Angima deals in quarry stones from which he makes ballast for sale. He buys stones from the nearby Geita hill, which has developed into an important source of quarry stone for house construction since the 1990s. Since 1988, Angima also started slaughtering livestock around Christmas and New Year's Day and selling the meat through the front door of his main house to supplement his income.

Angima's handling of the land after inheriting it fits in with his family history. His grandfather was a traditional healer and was not known in the village for any significant change or contribution made in life other than for his *ebiranya* (magical concoctions) used against cattle rustlers. He was not a very keen or innovative farmer. Angima's father took over traditional healing and besides growing coffee which he abandoned, he only kept a traditional zebu cow. Angima followed a similar approach to farming, although he ignored traditional healing and concentrated on local brew and petty trade. As a young man he had attempted growing horticultural products for the market, but as he grew older he stuck with his family identity as custodians of tradition. This identity is not obvious from Angima's description of himself, but becomes clear from his activities. Angima's life fits Russell's (2003) assessment of Mexican peasants as having indigenous ways of life, even if they did not identify themselves as indigenous. In Angima's case he creatively picked historical family traits to live by. He was involved in *chang'aa* business, ballast making, sales and transportation during the week. During the festive December season those activities were interspersed with livestock trade or butchery. His life style revolved around making a little money here and there and spending it on local brew. This appeared to satisfy and define him in the village.

Local brew

Local brew became Angima's destiny even after gaining access to land. This business explains two issues about resource creation and livelihood construction within deagrarianisation. First it takes some people away from agriculture and enables them to create resources and make a living. Second, it spurs other forms of activities, such as leasing out land or even theft by consumers to service their habit. In the process local brew becomes a central part of local life and politics.

Angima's network of friends and thus his social identity appear to be anchored in local brew. Through sharing drink in their company he assumes his social identity (cf. Silberschmidt, 1999). This is a paradox as even though he projects an image of a custodian of culture; he also breaks with his culture by commercialising *busaa*, which was traditionally a ritual based drink. By getting hooked on both *chang'aa* and *busaa* he escapes family responsibilities such as sending children to school and identifies with those who value tradition in the form of *endagera y'abakoro* – a cultural drink, as the local brew is protectively referred to. By sticking with the cultural connotation of the brew and deconstructing it to the point of commercialising both *busaa* and *chang'aa*; Angima and his friends are able to constitute a cultural sanctuary that defends itself against a hostile government policy and at the same time makes it a viable lifestyle, viability because it has been commoditised to perpetuate production in a cash economy. Yet, its cultural connotation attracts allies in politicians who also identify with the poor, their drink and their beliefs. It is not uncommon for local politicians to caution police officers from harassing local people 'who have only set up a drink as part of a ritual'.

Silberschmidt (1999) reports finding consumption of local brew, *chang'aa* and *busaa* to be widespread in Kisii District even though it is illegal under government policy. The struggle between government and local people over local brew is a fierce one and is basically ideological. The local people see the brew as part of their culture and the government sees it as the greatest hurdle to successful farming and development. As in most ideological disputes it is a long running one. Local politicians are cautious in condemning consumption of the brew because they fear electoral reprisals if they go against local people who see the brew as part of their cultural practices. Politicians are either non-committal or pro-brew as discussed below.

> In a discussion in early June 2004, villagers drinking at Angima's homestead said that since their previous member of parliament (MP) George Anyona was defeated in the general election in 2002 they were being constantly harassed by the police. They said Anyona had protected them from police harassment, sometimes personally going to the police cells to secure their release. He used to argue that ekebundu (ritual drinking of local brew in each others' homes) was not illegal. One villager said: "good people die early, our defender Anyona passed on and we have no one to defend us". They extolled his virtues in fighting for higher producer prices for tea, pyrethrum and milk. One villager less well disposed to Anyona asked "what happened to the funds for the women's group funds, where did the late MP take them?" Others shouted at him to keep quiet saying this was politics, the late MP did not touch anybody's money. After digressing to talking about the weather, dusty roads and dust from the passing trucks the talk returned to politics and what the current MP had done for them. No response was given and as time passed the discussion became less coherent as people were getting drunk.

The way that Angima encountered resources and applied them in his life involves the convergence of his wife's lifestyle with his own. His wife had grown up in a family that specialised in the *chang'aa* trade and had worked in it since she was fifteen years old. Angima courted her while drinking in her parents' home and it was evident that the local brew economy played a central role in both of their family histories. In the brew economy income generation and social identity are intertwined: those who brew and drink (*abanywa*) are distinguished from other villagers who do not drink. *Abanywa* is a descriptive but not derogatory or condescending term, used to describe those who drink responsibly. Alcoholics who are addicted and drink habitually not giving time or resources to their families are referred to as *nyakenywa*. People known as *abanywa* are happy with the description and share their drink with each other buying a share for those who have no money, who will buy some on other days. They drink in solidarity with one another. The *abanywa* identity provides an important basis from which the Angimas have derived their livelihood and hence new ways of being (cf. Holland et al. 1998). In Chapter 9, Figure 9.1, *abanywa* are most likely to be in the lifestyles towards the left because their drinking is measured and not resource depleting like in the case of *nyakenywa* who are likely to be in the lifestyles towards the right

The local brew provides a basis for sociability and identity among *abanywa* (cf. Silberschmidt, 1999). This solidarity among *abanywa* and to some extent among *nyakenywa* drives the local brew economy. Those who have money in any one day buy for those who do not have. This gesture drives those who feel indebted to seek quick incomes to reciprocate as soon as they can. This urgency generates many hidden and short-term transactions needed to maintain a position in the local brew economy. In this environment agricultural activities such as coffee or tea husbandry take too long to offer rewards. Instead, actors go for quick returns such as distilling *chang'aa* and selling it; selling tea leaves for cash in *soko huru* (as Saulo occasionally does); leasing out land (as Angima and his late father have always done) or leasing out a few rows of tea crop to get an instant income. Some *nyakenywa* might steal utensils, bananas or maize grain from their wives or other villagers to sell and thereby get money to drink. Villagers talked of *nyakenywa* people who had perfected stealing outside of their homes to service their local brew consumption as excerpts from Joel's case below, indicate.

> Joel started petty thieving from his neighbours when he dropped out of school in 1979. Wherever a neighbour raised an alarm he could flee to his maternal grandmother's place about two kilometres away. He became more of a thief as he became addicted to chang'aa and marijuana. At one time, the members of the community broke into his mother's house to look for their belongings which they suspected Joel had stolen and found many stolen items. They set the house a blaze and the children moved from home to stay at their grandmother's place for a while.

Overall, people like Angima and his wife appear to understand the social organisation of *nyakenywa* and *abanywa* concluding that it provides continuous returns. They prioritise their *chang'aa* business over agriculture, even when they have sufficient land to work. They are entrenched in the local brew economy which defines them socially. The economy also defines their needs and how they service them, for example by purchasing most of their food rather than producing it themselves. *Chang'aa* is a full-time occupation with the business opening as early as eight o'clock in the morning and closing as late as nine o'clock in the night, seven days a week throughout the year. This leaves people like Angima's wife with no time to think of or plan to invest their profits in economic activities. They are thus entrapped in a self-perpetuating but practically sterile project.

Mung'ong'o (1998) showed that in Mjombe District in Tanzania the brewing and sale of local brew was usually a women's occupation but also that men were joining in the activity by 1995. As these cases demonstrate, men were not only increasingly dealing in local brew, but also brewing it. The reasons for this incursion into a domain that was previously exclusively a woman's livelihood are not clear: it may be lack of ingenuity or economic hardship.

Locals refer to two types of brew businesses whose names villagers have derived from BBC radio petroleum discourses. One of them is called an 'Ogoniland' drinking joint named after the Nigerian Ogoni oilfields that are not in constant operation and whose supplies are intermittent because of local conflicts. Nyarwaru's business is locally called 'Ogoniland' because he distils the *chang'aa* on his own and does not always have it in stock. His wife is not involved in the business and has time to think of alternative investments and to pressure her husband to implement them. As Nyarwaru is not involved in the *chang'aa* business daily, he is able to plan better. This type of involvement in the local brew economy may shorten deagrarianisation cycles as operators disentangle themselves and re-enter farming wholly or on a part-time basis as Nyarwaru has done. Dinah's case is similar to Nyarwaru's since she sells *busaa* only on Sundays, she is able to do other businesses, farm and educate her children.

The other type of local brew business is continuous in its nature: the brew never runs out and business runs daily. Angima's business falls into this category and is referred to as *ebisima biakuwait (Kuwait)* after the oilfields whose supply is enormous and continuous. Although the clients especially *nyakenywa,* appreciate this type of business, the priority they give to client's interests appears to be to the detriment of the household's other business. Accumulation is curtailed and any possible returning to farming delayed as there is little time to reflect and plan for the future. For those in this type of business the deagrarianisation cycle is longer and unpredictable as in Angima's case: his wife does not support him returning to farming. Angima's preference for ballast making over coffee was largely the result of his entrenchment in the local brew economy, which dominated his thoughts and actions.

The existence of two types of businesses in the local brew economy; one that supports accumulation and return to farming and another that does not, take the deagrarianisation debate beyond issues of market conditions and changing state policy. The argument that withdrawal of state agricultural subsidies as a result of SAPs (cf. Khan, 2001) denies farmers capital for farming ignores the cultural foundations of the process of deagrarianisation. The lifestyles of people such as *nyakenywa*, drive them out of agriculture even when they have the land, capital and labour required (as Angima's case shows). Lack of capital and other factors of production including land can be understood as temporary setbacks in farming. A person with an agrarian disposition will return to farming sooner, as Nyarwaru's case demonstrates. Thus there is a strong case for taking the deagrarianisation debate beyond its predominantly materialist and economistic framework to the social and cultural milieu that surrounds it, in order to capture its temporal and cyclical nature. It is cyclical because villagers experience setbacks in their farming from time to time, and move in and out of farming in that context. These rhythms are not wholly the result of economic considerations but are also defined by social, cultural and idiosyncratic factors. Angima's delayed return to farming after years of entanglement in the local brew economy shows that the amount of land owned does not explain deagrarianisation. Angima had more land than Nyarwaru, who returned to farming earlier despite being on the verge of landlessness. This earlier return to farming may be explained by a family history of farming and his personal and family circumstances that pushed him towards a more legitimate livelihood.

Nabeire ekorera – I am respectable, twists of custom and cue from a son

Social respectability is usually sought after by rural people from around middle age, when they start thinking about how their peers and other villagers view them. More importantly, because some of their children are getting married by then, they are increasingly treated with respect by daughters and sons-in-law and their siblings and parents. All of a sudden the community of respecters expands. This forces them to re-evaluate themselves with a view to positioning themselves in society in ways that indicate they deserve the respect – that they are indeed *korera.* This also means that they invest in social relationships more keenly both to reinforce their new social standing and on behalf of the next generation.

Angima's son Morinwa broke away from his parents' local brew economy married and planted tea.

> Angima's son Morinwa, planted tea bushes on half an acre of land in the year 2000 and got registered with the KTDA as a tea farmer in 2003. He earns between six and seven hundred shillings from the tea leaf every month depending on the amount of rain in the area. Morinwa explained that his father was not in farvour of planting tea on his land and he often quarrelled about it saying he was the owner of the land and had not permitted it. In an apparent departure from custom in which son learns from father, Angima took the cue from his son Morinwa and planted tea bushes on half an acre of land in 2005. In 2004, he also pruned and weeded his late father's coffee planted on his parcel of land and earned six hundred shillings from it that year. He was tired of police harassment due to dealing in chang'aa and wished to shift gradually into farming to make a living. He was getting old and did not want to continue running up and down to bribe the chief or police officers. Angima explained; "my age does not allow me to run around being chased by police officers, nabeire ekorera – I am senior – and should settle into farming". His main worry about farming was that he would have to work the land himself as his wife 'has always been a chang'aa dealer and does not even know how to handle a hoe'.

Now he is getting older, Angima evaluates himself as respectable - *ekorera,* a status he seems confident about claiming only if he re-enters farming. This is apparently how he interacts with the dominant agricultural landscape in the village and region. This way the landscape makes him as he also remakes it to match its demands. More importantly the dominant agrarian landscape comes into direct conflict with the local brew economy, forcing Angima to delay his gratification and invest in cash crops such as tea and coffee, which usually generate income monthly or irregularly respectively. Age therefore becomes a critical event which triggers the search for social conformity especially after one's children are married. The newly important goal of social conformation is not easy to attain, as Angima's case shows. It leads to a re-orientation in terms of livelihoods and landscapes: livelihood is re-oriented to fit the larger cultural and landscape picture in the village and region, in this case the status of agriculture as a respectable career. This may be the result of thoughts at the sunset of a life and the struggle to bequeath grandchildren a conventional inheritance.

Even as Angima's return to agriculture may be explained in terms of his age and maturity, it is possible that his son's strides in planting tea presented a real social model that he could not admit but which may have driven his thoughts and economic activities from then on. He rebuked his son for planting tea from the standpoint of his authority as the patriarch and figurehead of the household, but soon took his cue from him and planted tea himself. His son appears to have had an idea whose time had come, and from the cultural standpoint, Angima's response was strategic, as he asserted his status while quietly endorsing the idea. Therefore while Angima wielded traditional power, his son appears to have been wielding power in the form of knowledge that constituted the social challenge that transformed his father. This social model appears to have invoked an undercurrent of competition in farming between father and son. This competition yielded changes in terms of livelihood strategies, resources creation and the re-making of the landscape. But the power and initiative of a son is diluted, explained away or overlooked in order to privilege patriarchal authority that is founded on tradition.

In re-entering farming Angima also explained his moves in terms of government policy that was wrestling the local brew economy to the ground through raids on their business. He argued that his return to farming was due to diminishing returns from the *chang'aa* business and the consequent need to act strategically to survive. While this may have been correct, his wife did not buy the argument and said she would not quit the business soon. Perhaps Angima's idea of quitting the *chang'aa* business because of his age and his wish for respectability was more accurate. This scenario is in agreement with Bryceson's (1999) argument that the moral order of villages rests on agrarian values. As he grew older, Angima may have wanted to conform and gain social legitimacy as an elder and 'farmer'.

In leaving the *chang'aa* business, Angima may also have been disentangling himself from his wife's business in order to regain his own identity and find time for leisure and drink away from her. As Silberschmidt (1999) found out, Abagusii men like depending on women to raise cash crops from which they earn an income that they spend largely on alcohol. Therefore Angima may have calculated that his wife did not care much about farming and decided to create his own niche to generate income for his personal use. The reality however, is that Angima's wife did not involve herself in any farming (and this was not a rare case) contradicts Silberschmidt's (1999) assertion that Abagusii women controlled and managed agricultural activities and that men left farming to their wives. While most agricultural work fell on women's shoulders, some women were increasingly concentrating on small businesses in local markets, *chang'aa* businesses or even hiring tea bushes on their own to escape the dominance of their husbands. The trend was towards a separation of income generation niches rather than towards men relying exclusively on their wives to generate income or to work the land. For the deagrarianisation debate, the key implication of this scenario is that a household can no longer be seen as a unified unit of action. People may on the whole be eating from the same kitchen, but the sources of their food may be varied. As a result, deagrarianisation needs to be considered in relation to an individual adult rather than to a household. Considering deagrarianisation with regard to individual adults further underscores its cyclical nature because of the prominence of struggles over resources in households, bringing cyclical changes in fortunes and consequent movement in and out of farming. This does not mean that individual adults act in disregard of social groups to which they belong, but they act individually and in heterogeneous ways because they belong to those social groups and confront them differently.

Seen from an individual point of view, certain dynamics and struggles within and between households position individuals differently over time with regard to farming and the resources it requires. For instance, when Angima was re-entering farming, the proportion of his land available for use was smaller than it might have been if he entered farming ten years earlier when his son was younger and would only have been part of his household labour rather than a land user as was now the case. Children's ages and land inheritance are therefore two important dynamics that can sharpen struggles over resources and have implications for deagrarianisation.

Overall, Angima, Nyarwaru and other villagers who had immersed themselves in non-farm activities such as the *chang'aa* business or trading of different kinds were experiencing a social identity conflict (Bryceson, 1999). They were thus trooping back to farming in order to espouse the normative identity as 'farmers' rather than as a commitment to farming as the most viable undertaking in their scheme of things. This is particularly clear in Nyarwaru's case: at the same time as he buys a cow, he also invests in a sewing machine for his wife's use at the village shopping centre. This way he keeps one foot in a precarious farming venture and another in non-farm activities.

Aging and land inheritance: the shrinking role of farming over time

As parents age, their sons inherit the land, effectively pushing them out of farming as their source of livelihood or reducing their scope to that provided by their *emonga*. This process has to be understood in the context of rural Kenya, where there is no formal social security except for a few former civil servants who receive a small monthly pension. This is never sufficient to sustain them and their dependents through the month; the social security system in Kenya assumes that every pensioner belongs to a large caring family and has a rural home for which rent is not paid. The few pensioners in Sengeta village – mainly retired teachers and government clerical officers – receive about two thousand five hundred shillings (about twenty five euro) per month as pension, which is not enough to cover rent and food for one person.

For villagers without a formal pension, the inheritance of land by their sons pushes them into an even deeper social malaise. The extent of this malaise and its mitigation varies from household to household, largely depending on their lifelong preparation for this moment, which is not an unexpected one. Saulo's case is characteristic of the struggles that lead up to land inheritance and the livelihood constraints imposed by this stage in the life cycle in Sengeta.

> In 1999 Saulo's sons, who had no source of income, started to quarrel with him over their maintenance and to agitate for ownership of part of the tea farm. In 2001, he wanted to be baptised into the Adventist Church to avoid his sons, who came to his house when drunk and made a lot of noise. He had figured out that they would be afraid to visit him while drunk if he had been baptised as a Christian. But when Saulo asked for baptism, the church leadership demanded that he should first settle the conflicts over land amongst his wives and his sons. So he divided it between his two wives and subsequently between their several sons. This has left him with very few bushes (emonga) which he shares with his first wife. Since dividing up his land between his wives and sons his life has changed. His tea earnings have dropped from about two thousand shillings per month to a mere four to five hundred shillings. His first wife plucks both her own and Saulo's tea while he goes thatching houses or drinking. When there is no tea-plucking to be done at home she goes out to pluck tea at neighbours' farms and she is paid four shillings per kilogram of tea leaf plucked. She brings the money home and buys necessities. Saulo occasionally gets contracts to thatch houses. His second wife and her sons have abandoned him. They do not assist him with anything and she does not give him the customary food. Saulo has retreated to his first wife's house. When his sons are drunk they threaten that they will take away his emonga, but he tells them "you know my last weapon, I will curse you, inkobarama". Saulo's sons have given him problems as they did not succeed in school and get jobs and they did not learn any skills.

Two major factors appear to have prevented Saulo from accumulating resources to ease the aging and inheritance processes. Firstly, he apparently believed that investing in his children's education would enable them to get well paid jobs, perhaps buy their own land, and support him in his old age. This did not materialise because the children did not perform well in school and dropped out early. This investment of hope in tea earnings and the aborted education of one child after another seems to have drained Saulo's resources. Secondly, Saulo himself spent a lot of his resources on drinking local brew with friends. This may have been aggravated by the failure of his children to make it in school and the thought that there was nothing else he could do. Saulo's sons appear to have taken their cue from their father and took to drinking too. This apparently gave them the guts to push their father into giving them land as their inheritance. It was Saulo's decision to share his land among his wives and sons that constituted the straw that broke the camel's back.

With land now in the hands of his wives and sons, Saulo's patriarchal power had been wiped out. Suddenly, the wives and sons who had depended on him and listened to him over the years were independent of him. This scenario indicates that patriarchal power is not based on tradition or custom alone. The power is derived from the economic power that the patriarch has and which he dispenses in exchange for acknowledgement of his authority over others. Land and cattle apparently constitute the main bases of that power in Sengeta village. Once those are passed on as inheritance, the patriarch becomes vulnerable. These findings echo those of Silberschmidt (1999) that a woman's power to counteract her husband grew as her sons matured and were able to support as well as protect her. Saulo exposed himself by not holding on to the land as a way of manipulating household relations. The *emonga* that he set aside for himself appears to have been too small to support him and, predictably, some of it was in danger of being taken up by his second wife and her sons. Since his *emonga* cut across his two wives' land, they could forcibly take away the portion on their side of the land and the only weapon he had left with which to defend his *emonga* was to curse whoever touched it. The effectiveness of this weapon may not last long, as the sons' fear of their father's curse may be diminished under the influence of alcohol.

The dispossession of a patriarch such as Saulo by his own family explains why aging may be accompanied by poverty in rural areas. Saulo was not a poor man before he shared out his land for inheritance; it was the intergenerational transfer of wealth that reduced him to relative poverty. Through inheritance, his productive resources (mainly land and tea) shrank considerably overnight, predictably putting him on the road to poverty as he aged and moved out of his crafts business. His social security was likely to be greatly undermined and his survival jeopardised as he and his first wife grew older. The link between aging and poverty is often not contemplated with regard to African rural areas because it is assumed that the extended family system is strong and unchanging. Saulo's case, which is not an isolated one, challenges such assumptions. Mwamfupe (1998) had similar findings among the Nyakyusa people of Tanzania where the extended family was weakening. However, in contrast to my findings that the youth were scrambling for land to inherit, Mwamfumbe found that, faced with land scarcity, the Nyakyusa youth resorted to non-farm activities and that few of them wanted to farm even if land was available. This may have eased inter-generational tension over land unlike the situation in Nyamira.

In terms of deagrarianisation, intergenerational wealth transfer of the type that Saulo undertook leads to a shrinking role of farming in the livelihood of the aged. Although this does not constitute instant deagrarianisation, it contributes to a trend in that direction. As land is taken over by another generation, the elderly have to be creative and devise new ways by which to earn a living instead of farming.

> Saulo occasionally gets contracts to thatch houses, work which would earn him an average of four hundred shillings. However, such contracts were rare, so he has turned his attention to basket making. The demand for baskets for carrying tea leaf to the buying centres has been stable. Sometimes his friends assist him when he is in need; recently his friend who works at the tea factory gave him a hundred shillings to buy medicine for his first wife. Saulo intimated in us that his daughters are good and they do come and visit him. On their visits they usually leave him with twenty to fifty shillings, which he usually spends on busaa. Recently his sons-in-law came and gave him three thousand shillings to assist him to take his wife to hospital when she had sprained her leg, but she was healed using traditional herbs. He said the money will help to buy basic items at home and to provide him with busaa.

From the above extract it is apparent that income from crafts and handouts in cash and kind from his friends, daughters and sons-in-law have become Saulo's main means of sustaining his local brew consumption. To keep these channels open, he makes sure he misses no opportunity to show affection to his daughters, and he has also strengthened his relationship with his first wife since being abandoned by his second wife and her sons. Customarily, Saulo should have ended up with his second, younger wife upon sharing out his land, as she was more able to support him through agriculture and piece work in other people's farms. This departure from custom appears to have been resulted from a careful consideration by the second wife of the pros and cons of staying with Saulo. She apparently saw in him an extra mouth to feed rather than an investment. And not without reason, since Saulo could offer her neither the large tract of land in *emonga* nor the cattle that would traditionally be expected. Saulo's only alternative was to rely on his first wife, to anchor his family status and to secure a living through her labour.

Compared to patriarchs such as Saulo who were struggling to mitigate the effects of the intergenerational transfer of wealth, Angima and Nyarwaru were younger and were busy intensifying their farming. Although they were just moving out of *chang'aa* businesses and apparently investing their earnings from the businesses in farming, their age allowed them to farm without much intra-household tension. Therefore, while deagrarianisation was accelerating among the aged, among the middle-aged farming was gaining in importance. Deagrarianisation among the aged was not a choice but a life cycle event in which they were being rendered irrelevant in farming, while the young were seeking security in permanent crops or cattle as a launching pad for a re-entry into farming. This finding differs from others such as Mung'ong'o's (1998) that the youth lacked resources to move into full-time non-agricultural activities and therefore remained in farming. In Sengeta it was the other way round. For instance Nyarwaru had to engage in full-time *chang'aa* business in order to raise resources to re-enter farming, among other things.

In general the return to farming by the younger villagers and the strategic retention of farming by the elderly implies that deagrarianisation is not a welcome but a contested process. Hardly anybody seems to be willing to give up farming in rural areas. Explanations for this can be found in the prevailing economic and socio-cultural conditions. The economic difficulties facing rural people lead them to seek to earn a living from farming, an available and tested option. Socio-culturally, it appears that people see agriculture as a secure form of livelihood. For this reason, they invest profits made in the informal sector not in more secure business but in farming, even in precarious circumstances like Nyarwaru's. Even successful urban-based businessmen and professionals retain strong interests on the farm in Gusiiland. This is similar to Buhera urban migrants in Zimbabwe who maintained a strong presence in rural areas by building houses and claiming land not so much for economic reasons as to confirm that they belonged to a rural home area (Andersson, 2002).

The deagrarianisation process should be seen then as one that is being resisted. From a landscape-oriented perspective, it is resisted because it contradicts the dominant agricultural landscape and places those it alienates from the land in isolated and unfamiliar spaces, so that as soon as they can, they redefine themselves as farmers and re-enter farming. Landscape form is therefore a site for powerful cultural contests as well as a point of reference in oscillations between farming and non-farming livelihood. Landscape is part of the cultural dispositions imprinted in the mind, and in due course has its own influence on the direction that people take in their livelihood pursuits. This gives rise to the preference of both rural and town dwellers for inheriting land and returning to farming whenever they are out of work or have the resources to do so: a preference which explains why deagrarianisation is temporary and cyclical, as demonstrated by the various cases discussed.

Concluding Remarks

In this chapter it has been argued that actors have encountered deagrarianisation in different ways at different times. A common thread that runs through all encounters with the process of deagrarianisation is its temporal nature. Some people choose to quit farming voluntarily for a while in order to pursue certain career choices or seek resources for specific purposes. After accomplishing such objectives, they re-enter farming and continue until they run into another obstacle or choose another livelihood strategy. It appears that an actor almost always returns to farming once the intervening objective is achieved. This means, then, that deagrarianisation is a cyclical process; people go in and out of it for different reasons during the course of their lives.

People use some of the resources they generate through non-agricultural activities to re-enter agriculture. Occasionally, the return to agriculture is instantaneous, especially if it is the result of retirement or retrenchment from formal employment in town. Otherwise the transition may be long and blurred, especially if it is from informal careers such as a local brew business that may remain a part of a person's or a household's livelihood for a long time. It is in blurred transitions such as this that diversification is interlocked with deagrarianisation in a theoretically intriguing manner. However, the point that should be made is that if the transition from deagrarianisation involves a diversified livelihood, whether as a transitional phase (as sometimes seems to happen in Nyamira) or as an end result, the fluidity and complexity of rural livelihood construction is further confirmed. A number of situations that suggest cyclical transitions have been discussed in this chapter. This cyclical, non-linear, process of deagrarianisation suggests that the role of agriculture in rural livelihoods may be shrinking, but that agriculture still defines rural life in Nyamira where – as shown in chapters five and six – smallholder tea production for export is important and growing.

The extended case study of Angima demonstrated that he decisively and completely quit farming at different times and returned to it at others. It is a clear example of the cyclical, non-linear nature of the deagrarianisation process addressed here. The return to farming at different points in actors' life cycle(s) can be explained in at least four different ways. The first is in terms of culture and socialisation: in a number of cases actors appeared to value farming as a secure and respectable lifestyle. This stems from the socialisation of most actors in agricultural households and the inculcation in them of the view that farming is 'the way of life' and that it is both economical and respectable to produce as much of one's own food as possible. Younger people who can not do farm work are rebuked as lazy and as parasites. Secondly, in terms of the dominant agricultural landscape: this compels and defines lifestyles in terms of farming, even if the landscape includes non-farm activities. While actors redefine and remake the social landscape, they do this slowly and often subtly preserve its dominant characteristics, with change occurring in small, almost negligible, instalments. The overall lifestyle therefore reflects the dominant landscape. Thirdly, in terms of economic difficulties in the urban sector: these accelerate the diversification of urban livelihoods to include farming. In other words urban dwellers eventually return to farming earlier than they would do under better economic circumstances. Fourthly, in terms of socio-cultural disposition: the attachment to land and rural home is paramount among the Abagusii people regardless of occupation and residence. Both successful and marginal urban dwellers value a rural home, to which they retreat occasionally, especially during the Christmas holidays.

Deagrarianisation is therefore taking place in Nyamira in a cyclical fashion. This means that actors move in and out of farming temporarily for different reasons and for different lengths of time. Movement in and out of farming is supported and shaped by intra- and inter-household dynamics. As circumstances change, some people return to farming while others may move out of it. External macro-level and global factors also contribute to the movements into and out of farming, but such factors are not permanent either, and are often overcome, with actors re-entering farming. Actors counteract the external factors in their own ways and survive in farming, rendering deagrarianisation non-permanent. Deagrarianisation does not therefore proceed unhindered, but is checked by actor initiatives locally – some 'illegal' to raise resources and return to agriculture, and others legal but hidden, action like leasing out land or tea to survive financial strain. As Lubeck (1992) has argued, neither state intervention nor market forces have transformed African agriculture into a green revolution miracle, nor have they forced proletarianisation by blocking the reproduction of the African peasant household. Farming has therefore largely remained the main basis of livelihood in Nyamira, and although its centrality may be under threat, the threats are often temporary setbacks. In the face of more permanent threats such as land scarcity, farming is being redefined to include stall fed cattle and napier grass production, two crop seasons per year and land hiring. In the next chapter, I take up the issue of livelihood diversification with a view to distinguishing it and at times relating it to deagrarianisation, but focusing on livelihood as socially constructed and resources as constituting material and non-material aspects.

CHAPTER 8

Livelihood Diversification

Introduction

This chapter approaches the study question on how villagers create resources and use them to make their living from another angle by focusing on the question: how do villagers combine farm with non-farm activities and how are resources created and used to make a living in the process? The chapter begins with a brief discussion of the livelihood diversification literature. In attempting to answer the question, I take a historical perspective. From this perspective, as shown in Chapter 2, the people of Nyamira and Gusiiland in general have combined farm with non-farm activities since pre-colonial times. Over time however, the combinations may have changed in form and meaning for a variety of reasons, and thus the above question remains valid. I therefore identify forms of livelihood diversification in Sengeta and examine how they have come about, and what resources are created and used to make a living. To accomplish this task, I have looked at the corpus of data and identified the main themes of livelihood diversification which form the basis of discussion in this chapter. The themes include kinship, friendship and gift-giving; employment and remittances; trading; local brew production and sales; crafts and brick making and sales. Themes such as kinship, friendship and gift-giving are unusual in diversification discussions, but this links up well with my approach to resources as both material and non-material, and livelihoods as aimed at both economic and non-economic interests and goals. Some issues related to these themes, such as local brew, have been considered under deagrarianisation in Chapter 7, although from a different angle as new occupations for deagrarianising villagers. In this chapter the angle changes and the focus is on the local brew business as it complements or is complemented by farming. This only confirms the extent to which livelihoods cut across the concepts devised by experts to bracket them into various sectors. More importantly however, diversification may be transitional in the flows of actors back and forth between agrarianisation and deagrarianisation. I conclude that rural livelihood diversification is a lifelong and evolving process that does not necessarily exclusively result from structural constraints such as population pressure, land scarcity and economic downturn. Furthermore, livelihood diversification is not driven only by the actor's accumulation tendencies. To the contrary, livelihood diversification is a socially embedded process that thrives on actors' resource creation and use, and their preferences and lifestyles. Actors' interaction and negotiation within and amongst households, both locally and globally, are also part of livelihood diversification practices.

Issues in Livelihood Diversification

Rural livelihood diversification describes the phenomenon by which farm households take up non-farm activities or rely on non-farm income transfers for their living (Ellis, 2005). Ellis adds that the extent of such diversification may indicate the degree to which farming on its own can provide a secure and improving livelihood. The problem with this kind of argument is that the notion of farm household is not explained. What constitutes a farm household? Is it its mere location in a rural area? Is it to be assumed that rural households start off deriving their livelihoods exclusively from agriculture so that diversification should involve embracing non-farm activities? These questions point to the historicity and social embeddedness of livelihood change (Carswell, 2002). Looking at rural livelihood change from a historical and socio-cultural prism privileges actor preferences, lifestyles, identities and the livelihood objectives sought. This approach places actors at the core of livelihood construction rather than at the periphery of it, recognising that they cause change rather than just being caused to change.

The reasons for rural livelihood change can therefore be found not only in whether or not agriculture is working but also in what actors choose and have chosen over time, and in how their choices are changing. Even amidst scarcity it cannot be assumed that actors will respond in a predetermined manner. Therefore, for example, Scoones'(1998: 10) argument that the degree of specialisation or diversification may relate to resources available and the risks accompanying various options, only partially explains the phenomenon of livelihood change. The rest of the explanation is to be located in the social terrain in which the actor operates. In risky circumstances actors should be viewed as often weighing options and drawing on experience to make the best of their situations. And as Scoones (1998) points out, benefits accruing from particular strategies in different situations would depend on broad social norms and on internal management within the household. Household and broader social dynamics thus shape the directions of livelihood change. In shaping these changes, ideally households mediate the impacts of scarcity and other external forces.

It is because household and other socio-cultural dynamics play a role in livelihood change that diversification is not purely the result of market and policy transactions. Rather, as Francis (2000) has shown, diversified livelihood also involves all the help, transfers, exchanges and information that people have access to through social networks. She adds that some of these sources of income and livelihood may be more dependable than others and that social networks may be fallbacks rather than adequate substitutes for other forms of resources. The view that social networks constitute a fallback poses a serious methodological problem. In most rural societies social networks have been part of life since time immemorial. Yet, are they merely poor substitutes for other resources or are they part of an array of diverse and complementary resources with which actors make a living? The process of privileging certain forms of resources and lifestyles apparently brings Francis (2000) to the conclusion that at least four reasons exist for livelihood diversification, namely: responses to seasonality; means of spreading risks; strategies for accumulation, and strategies emanating from actor subcultures and other location-specific factors. The key question that emerges relates to whether processes of livelihood diversification are anchored in the preferences of actors.

Evidently pushing a structural explanation from another angle, Orvis (1993) attributes diversification to population pressure on land and the risks inherent in rain-fed, market-oriented smallholder agriculture that will compel the majority of rural Kenyan households to combine agricultural and non-agricultural activities in order to survive and attempt accumulation. This implies that diversification is inevitable among smallholders across Africa in prevailing structural circumstances. However, the nature and direction will not be uniform and should therefore be investigated with the micro-macro factors at play in mind. This is because poor farmers are not homogenous anywhere (Ellis, 2000; Khan, 2001 and Chambers, 1990). As Khan (2001: 2) has pointed out, the differences among the poor reflect highly complex interactions of human factors, markets and public policies. Such interactions with regard to livelihood diversification should be isolated and explained in ways that reflect heterogeneity in rural areas.

The scenarios emerging from this discussion point to complex and diverse processes of livelihood change, of which diversification is a part. Livelihood diversification comes across as socially constructed and is thus not an inevitable and linearly determined stage in rural change processes. In understanding this complex process, a historical approach would bring out the dynamics that shape it. In particular, looked at historically, it is possible to solve the intractable egg-chicken problem of what precedes the other non-farm or farm livelihood undertakings. It is this interaction and its contents that the rest of this chapter deals with by focusing on the forms of diversification in Nyamira District, Kenya. The forms of diversification are discussed from a historical perspective in order to capture how they have evolved over time. The study takes the view that livelihood diversification has existed in Gusiiland throughout history, and the chapter aims at deepening our understanding of change and its implications for resource creation and livelihood construction. The focus of the discussion is on the various forms of livelihood diversification that have existed throughout Gusii history, but which are changing in a variety of ways to meet changing preferences, needs and lifestyles. In a sense then, the forms of livelihood diversification are themselves changing and providing new or additional opportunities for resources creation and livelihood construction.

Forms of Livelihood Diversification

In this section the various themes of livelihood diversification identified from the case material are discussed with a view to describing and explaining the various forms of diversification. Diversification has been characterised as the combination of farming with other activities to make a living (see Ellis, 2000; 2005). This discussion goes beyond such characterisations to take a historical perspective and to focus on resources creation processes that result in the various forms of livelihood diversification. Furthermore, because the study embraces a broad definition of resources that includes both material and non-material aspects, this discussion focuses on the place of social relationships in the various forms of livelihood diversification identified. Therefore, some of the forms of diversification analysed are unusual [for instance from some economists' points of view] but the thrust of the arguments in this discussion is that actors latch on to a variety of social relationships to create resources beyond the 'farm' and to make their living. The flows of resources from outside the 'farm' are crucial to any conceptualisation of livelihood diversification, although many analysts whose work this discussion aims to transcend take such issues as kinship, friendship and gift-giving out of the diversification debate. The discussion interprets the various forms of livelihood diversification with social relationships in mind, for instance by interrogating the diverse social forces that remittances generate among recipients and the resources creation processes that accompany marriage and the exchange of bride-price and related gifts. I discuss the various forms of livelihood diversification below.

Kinship, Friendship and Gift Giving

Livelihood diversification through kinship and friendship constitute perhaps the oldest form among villagers in Sengeta and throughout the Gusii region, because it is based on customary practices that are universal to the Abagusii people. One of the commonest forms of diversification through kinship relates to bride price transfers in cattle, and allied transactions at marriage. As Kuper (1982) argues, marital rights are transferred against the payment of cattle in bride price. Nyandika's case represents a broad range of forms of bride price transfer including cattle moving from a sister's marital home to her parents' home and then to a brother's bride's or wife's natal home. Additionally the case includes bride price transfer in the case of 'woman to woman marriage', and livestock exchange between a maternal uncle and his nephew (*omosuto*) in gratitude for the uncle's use of the latter's mother's bride price for his marriage.

> Nyandika was born in 1933. He received some formal education up to standard one and when he was young they were poor, his mother did not have much property, but his dad had cattle in his first wife's bweri, which he used to graze. His father had gone to his maternal uncle and brought a cow as omosuto – a brother's gift to his sister's son to thank them for the use of that sister's bride price in his marriage. Nyandika said his father may have collected omosuto in the late 1930s. This cow stayed at his first wife's place. Nyandika's stepsister got married and the bride price of five heads of cattle and six goats added to the stock of his stepmother. Nyandika's father bought two cows from the proceeds of selling obori, which they had planted at his emonga. He shared out these two cows between his two wives. Each wife used to milk the cows equally in turns. Nyandika went to work as a tea plucker at the Kericho tea plantations in 1950. He was later promoted to tea pruning in 1952. In 1953 he became a tractor driver in Cherimo Tea Factory where he worked up to 1960 when he retired and came back home. He married his first wife from Bosiango clan in 1951, paying a bride price of thirteen heads of cattle. Nine of them he raised from the bride price for one of his sisters. He had already bought four cows and two goats from his savings from the plantations and easily completed the bride price payments.

A key question that emerges is whether in fact bride price transfer constitutes livelihood diversification. In its broadest sense, which is adopted in this study, the concept of livelihood goes beyond maximising income and putting food on the table (i.e. diversification as equivalent to choices between livelihood portfolios) to include an actor's whole lifestyle, aspirations and identity. Marriage is a major aspiration of most people in Sengeta and meeting its customary standards affects their everyday life both locally and in the diaspora, where they may go to raise income for buying cattle to eventually use for bride price. As the case material shows, marriage and the transfer of cattle in bride price constitutes 'commencing life', which has been discussed in Chapter 1. It comes across as the point at which the status of both a man and a wife changes. The man makes the transition from *omomura* (youth or warrior) to *omosacha* (mature man) and in marriage the wife changes from *enyaroka* or *omoiseke* (girl) to *omokungu* (mature woman). This transition is greatly anticipated on both sides of the marriage transaction; on the man's side for the addition of labour to the homestead and reproduction possibilities in furtherance of the lineage and on the woman's side for the transfer of bride price to enable her brother or her father to embark on a new marriage. A woman is highly respected in her natal home after marriage and the transfer of bride price (Levine, 1979; Hakansson, 1994). Hakansson (1994) adds that the state of marriage is necessary for both men and women to be considered full and mature members of the society. Marriage is thus a major aspect of livelihood and the accompanying exchanges not only further it on both sides, but also redefine actors and enhance their identities and capacities to create resources in new directions and take up new livelihood opportunities in a variety of ways.

For instance, it is clear from Nyandika's case that when he was young his mother was poor, and that what he means by poor is that she lacked milk and by extension cattle, *obotaka*. The breakthrough came with his father's collection of *omosuto* from his mother's natal home. *Omosuto* placed milk on the table for the poor woman and her children, and essentially represented livelihood diversification. But *omosuto* is not just given; it is always a struggle between uncle and nephew. According to informants, if the uncle refuses to offer the gift in peace, the nephew and his mother (if still alive) invoke a potential curse by delivering a rope and a goat and abandoning them in the homestead of the mother's brother who used her bride price to marry. If the brother ignored this, a curse could befall him which could cause a member of the homestead to commit suicide by hanging him/herself. While this could well be a myth, nobody waits to experience the curse; very often, a cow is delivered as per custom in exchange for the goat. These protracted struggles over cattle between blood relatives imply that it is an important livelihood activity, as it turned out in Nyandika's case. Similarly Kanogo (2005) has shown that the institution of bride price created protracted relations between two families that outlived the marriage itself and that had the potential of generating a host of conflict situations.

Anticipating bride-price needs and other life commencement requirements, Nyandika diversified his livelihood activities in order to acquire the cattle. As was the practice in the 1940s and 50s, Nyandika had to migrate to the tea plantations to work in order to raise the money to buy the cattle. As a livelihood objective, marriage and the transfer of bride price forces actors into different activities in order to succeed. Some of these activities take them beyond farming to non-farm activities. In a sense therefore, bride price transfer constitutes a form of livelihood diversification as well as a driving force behind diversification.

> Because she did not have a son, Nyandika's first wife 'married' Dinah in 1977 and Dinah bore two daughters and four sons. Nyandika and his first wife paid a bride price for her of six heads of cattle. Dinah grows tobacco and sells the leaves to Batigo, Nyandika's second wife. Batigo buys tobacco leaves from the village and resells them at Daraja Mbili Market, about seventeen kilometres away, every Monday and Thursday. On her part, Dinah grows coffee, tea, maize, beans and kale. Both Nyandika and his first wife treat Dinah as their eldest 'son'. They chose a man for her, to take care of her needs. The man assisted her with a cow for milk. Recently they quarrelled over school fees which he failed to pay for her children and they separated and as a result he took away his cow and a calf. With the half yearly tea bonus of December 2003, Dinah bought a cow which calved recently, so she has milk again. On Fridays Dinah brews busaa which she sells every Sunday to supplement her farm income.

From another angle, most married women in Sengeta aspire to having a son to inherit their land and extend *mwaye* – their 'lineage' – to the next generation.

Nyandika's second wife is a case in point. Firstly, when she did not give birth to a son early enough, Nyandika took a second wife. Secondly, when she still had not had a son by the time of her menopause, she arranged a 'marriage', in consultation with Nyandika, to safeguard *mwaye*. She 'married' Dinah and found an appropriate man to 'take care of her and sire children'. The man moved in with a cow and supported Dinah's children in a variety of ways before they fell out. Marriage of this kind is common and it presents new ways of earning a living that come with new relationships and networks. Dinah linked the Nyandika family to other households and facilitated the flow and creation of resources in new ways. The local brew relationship between Nyandika and Dinah, and the business links between Dinah and Nyandika's second wife Batigo represent other forms of diversification arising from the 'marriage of woman to woman'. The many branches of livelihood activity that Dinah is involved in reflect the relative independence of women in her type of marriage. Because she was not married directly by a man, she was prepared at marriage to be independent in making a living and in running her family. This independence from the control of a man has given her enough leeway to devise a variety of activities ranging from tea, tobacco and coffee growing, to trade, and local brew production and sales. Her farming includes more crops than that of many of her neighbours who did not bother to diversify. Her diversification can therefore be explained in terms of freedom to experiment and try things out without impediment from a man, rather than as a response to risk or the drive to accumulate, the motive posited by Ellis (2000), for instance. These findings agree with Hebinck and Bourdillon's (2001) argument that creativity, experience and a drive towards experimentation constitute some of the resources an actor may draw on to make a living.

Kinship-based resource creation and transfers are other important forms of livelihood diversification in Sengeta. This is also part of the history of villagers and the Abagusii people in the region. Traditionally, the Abagusii people rely on each other in homesteads, lineage and kin groups in labour provisioning for farming and herding, and in sharing farm produce and milk (see Hakansson, 1994; Silberschmidt, 1999). Nyandika relied on group labour based on neighbourhood and kin to establish tea growing. *Risaga* is based on food and drink of local brew at the end of the working day. Although fading out, this form of labour deployment is still used in the village to accomplish major tasks such as house building. These labour arrangements have evolved into groups around which other resources such as knowledge is shared. Tea planting knowledge is reported to have moved significantly within work groups as people participated in planting for the early adopters like Nyandika.

> Nyandika planted coffee in 1955 and tea in 1962, in both cases using earnings from his employment at Kericho tea plantations to pay for the plantings. He said that after he had paid for the plantings they were delivered when the extension officer had checked that the field was ready. He mobilised risaga to prepare the field and to plant the tea on the day planting materials were delivered.

The concept of work groups organised around kin groups and neighbourhood [introduced in Chapter 2] has apparently evolved into piece work on tea farms as shown in Petro's case:

> Petro has employed some people like his daughter in-law and his neighbour's two daughters-in-law, whom he pays four shillings per kilogram of tea leaf plucked and delivered to the tea buying centre. However, he weeds his tea himself, mainly in the mornings before it gets hot. He selected the three ladies, whom he described as trustworthy, in order to control the quality of tea leaf plucked and to be sure that his crop is not stolen on the way to the buying centre. These workers treat his farm as their own, counting days and starting to pluck the tea when it is ready without him reminding them. He provides them with breakfast every day they work for him and lunch if they return from the centre in time. His other son got married in church in 1991 and the family assisted him to pay the bride price. He had one cow, which he bought with earnings from his informal business, Petro gave him one cow, his brother the teacher gave him another and his paternal uncles provided one. The church assisted with transport costs. Petro's two daughters also got married through church weddings recently. The bride price paid for them was used for wedding expenses and to settle their elder brother's bride price. His teacher son provided the money for feeding visitors during the bride price negotiations. Petro's daughters and sons also buy medication for their ailing mother and often visit their father's workers, offering them gifts like sugar and cooking oil.

Labour arrangements are complex; they offer opportunities for livelihood diversification on both sides by opening up avenues for elements of free labour within paid labour utilisation, sociability on the part of the 'employer' and a flow of gifts and income to the 'employees'. The contradiction is that while labour is surplus in Sengeta, employers appear to treat employees kindly and to evolve an informal relationship with them. This is drawn from the customary practices of group labour that was recompensed with a beer party. The idea of friendship between employer and employee is consistent, whether the employees are relatives of the employer or not. This means that labour relationships are sites of mutual exchange between worker and employer rather than of labour purchase and sale as understood from a materialist viewpoint. And it is this practice of mutual exchange that makes labour arrangements a basis for livelihood diversification, as farming declines in importance as the source of income and employment.

Petro's case brings out another form of kinship-based assistance that supplements farming. This has to do with the support his sons and daughters provide, firstly for each other, especially during marriage, and secondly for their mother's medication, diet and hospitalisation. In the absence of any form of health insurance for rural dwellers outside the formal sector in Kenya, kinship support becomes the only option in times of sickness. The elderly and sick do not receive this support from a position of weakness or as a way of managing risk in a last resort action. Rather, they claim the assistance of their children when sick or in old age, believing that they are reaping the benefits of first caring for them when they were young and of investing in their education. The children do not contradict this feeling; they are often more than willing to do their best for their parents. This explains why villagers evaluate their livelihood success in terms of how their children are faring: they know that if their children are not successful in life, they will be unable to help them in old age or sickness. In the same vein and with regard to kin-based support in Zambia, Crehan (1997) indicates that the elderly turned up not for charity but for what was simply their moral due.

Although there is tension in the intergenerational flow of resources, as in the case of Saulo, in general such tensions are ironed out over time and the flow restored. This is not to overlook longstanding disputes over resources ranging from land to livestock, but to emphasise that the objective is harmony, which the patriarch seeks, even if with only one of his children. This is what emerges in Saulo's case.

> Saulo's sons give him problems as they did not succeed in school, have not learnt any beneficial skills and have no jobs. Besides, the sons drink a lot of alcohol and because they have no regular sources of income, they often turn to theft. At one time one of the sons burnt a neighbour's house after a disagreement over beer. Saulo was ordered by the village headman's court to rebuild and equip the house. The village elders decided that instead of the son being arrested, Saulo should rebuild the house. He used his own resources like money and trees to build it. He only bought grass for thatching, did the thatching on his own and bought a bed to furnish the house. At that time the son had gone into hiding. He also bailed out his other son who was about to be locked up in the police cells for stealing timber from the local dispensary. Saulo bribed the local police with two hundred shillings and they released him. None of the sons has paid bride price on their own initiative without Saulo pestering and assisting them. They hardly assist him, especially since he divided up the land for them and their mothers. His daughters often assist him with money for drink.

Saulo's case demonstrates the search for harmony in that he continued to invest in the marriage of his sons even as he courted assistance from his more amiable daughters. I deduce from these scenarios that kinship is not a given as a basis for livelihood diversification, but is created and moulded carefully over one's life course: sometimes with success, as in the case of Nyandika and Petro, and at other times with limited success, as in the case of Saulo. The key to success can be what one puts into the process of moulding the resource, for how long and how consistently. Consistent long term investment in education and training, including religious coaching, and the exertion of patriarchal authority and sanction have yielded positive results for Petro and Nyandika. This echoes Hakansson's (1994) argument that the decline of agriculture as a source of livelihood is encouraging parents in Kisii District Kenya to invest heavily in their children's education, in the hope that the children will obtain salaried jobs and support them, especially in old age.

Gifts represent another means by which villagers in Sengeta diversified their livelihoods. This is an equally historical practice because it is a longstanding custom for the Abagusii to exchange gifts in drink, food or livestock on the basis of friendship or kinship. Mayer (1950) reports for example about *embori ya ng'ina koro* – a goat that a bride gave as a gift to her maternal grandmother on the eve of her marriage. Nyandika's case demonstrates the flow of gifts along kinship lines.

> Nyandika's sister has two children who are athletes in the United States of America (USA). They came to visit Nyandika in March 2004, bringing him clothes, shoes, and a cap, and assisting him with some money to purchase fertilizer and to repay a debt which he incurred for maize seed. They also left him with some money to buy busaa and enjoy himself with friends. During the visit in March they indicated to him that they planned to leave for the USA in April 2004 and to visit again when they return from the USA in six months' time. Nyandika and other members of the Catholic Church in his village contributed money to put up the church. Nyandika pays a tithe every Sunday and also gives egetoro to the priest every Sunday. The church has helped him gain some knowledge, and kept him out of trouble. He attends the chef's barazas where they are encouraged to avoid malice and most conflicts are resolved.

This widespread engagement with gift giving in everyday life, both at home and in the churches, reflects a continuation of the Abagusii's hospitality practices in new institutions. As indicated, the traditional gift economy was based on beer, labour and livestock. This gift economy has been transformed and is also practiced through church, while the traditional forms survive in the cash economy. The main aim of the gift economy however, is solidarity and acknowledgement of belonging to the group and community. As Sherry, Jr (1983) points out, a gift allocation strategy is usually devised, assigning obligations on the basis of an actor's roles in society, e.g. in church, at the drinking place, to an uncle and to others. The focal point of gift giving in the various roles and obligations remains the cultural value of belonging to a community of interests and obligations, and the social security that comes with such belonging. This is because, as Berry (1989a) argues, in so far as resource access hinges on social identity and group membership, identity and membership are themselves resources. Villagers have to invest in social relationships as a way of creating resources.

In another way, the gift economy has been institutionalised through the merry-go-round system (*harambee or esindigisa*) in Sengeta. One villager summarised the institutionalisation of the gift economy in merry-go-round schemes as follows:

> "My wife is a member of a merry-go-round club which has sixteen members, both men and women. Each of them contributes two hundred shillings per month and

> that money is given in lump sum to one member to help solve his/her problems. The next month another member benefits, until all members are covered and the cycle is started again".

The size of the lump sum paid out varies from one club to another in Sengeta and villagers belong to as many clubs as possible, depending on their ability to pay up each month as required. The lump sum is used to buy utensils or even to pay children's school fees. The critical thing about the merry-go-round clubs is that many are unregistered and keep minimum records or none. The members meet, each gives their share and they pass it on as a lump sum to the beneficiary. They wait for a meeting again the next month. The clubs are thus built on mutual trust. The members trust that each member will honour their part of the bargain until all benefit and they start the cycle again. The notion of trust has served the little merry-go round clubs well as they are widespread and successful.

Registered Self Help Groups are larger, give loans to both members and non-members, and are more prone to problems of default and conflict. These represent a degree of commercialisation of the gift economy and another important avenue for livelihood diversification. The groups often start with friends or kin coming together and as they expand, more people join. The initial motivation is derived from the trust existing between friends and kin and the drive to help each other within a group.

> Birundu is a member of Nyabwasu Self-help Group. The group started as a gathering of their grandfather's family and the initial objective was to bring the various family members together so that they get acquainted with one another. Because they used to incur costs for food, members decided that each one of them would contribute twenty shillings. Initially any money that remained after the end of year meeting was shared out equally between members. But later members decided that the money should be kept so that if there was a problem amongst the group members, they could use the money to solve it. Later a loan scheme was commenced for members after they realised that at the end of the year they had 40,000 shillings in the account.
>
> Birundu has taken several loans from the group and has repaid them with interest. The loans were solely for paying school fees for his children. The group meeting is held once per month and since other members stay far away, like Nairobi and other towns, they send in their contributions. The group members are close relatives and they have not allowed non-relatives to join, although they can borrow. Birundu is a committee member and his sons and nephews who live in different towns in Kenya are members. They send their contributions through Western Union Money Transfer to Kisii town or through relatives coming home to visit. The members in the diaspora monitor their group meetings by mobile phone when they fail to attend in person and there are major decisions to be made. When the community decides on a project to undertake, Birundu readily joins them. "I usually do not hesitate to join hands with them. For example we

> contributed money and built Sengeta dispensary at a time when I served as a project treasurer and I held the position for a long time". Birundu was also instrumental in building Sengeta SDA Church.

The loans from self help groups enable people either to make a living from day to day as they seek other ways to repay or to start new branches of economic activity. The groups also play the role of mobilising remittances for investment in the villages as members working in various towns send their contributions to the group each month. A level of solidarity is created and the group meetings are sites of information exchange as those in the diaspora contribute to the proceedings of meetings on cell phones. In a sense, groups such as these link town and country in ways that enhance rural livelihood diversification through ideas and loans for investment in children's education and in other ventures. The process of change and diversification is not however expected to be revolutionary because the objectives of the groups are usually first and foremost social. The above-mentioned Nyabwasu case, for instance, shows that the group was initially organised around festivities and it is possible that the loan scheme may be resisted by some members in future, as they seek to meet their earlier goals of partying and socialising.

The self help groups generally help to mobilise resources informally for households. Beyond the households where most of the resources generated are utilised, self help activities such as the Nyabwasu group's, for construction of tea buying centres, primary schools and churches, constitute a site for mobilising local people to link up to resources from the government and politicians for local construction and equipment. In this sense, as Holmquist (1980) pointed out, the self help movement allows for considerable resource creation for community purposes and perhaps a redistributive effect. The self-help groups for community-wide activities and for household support begin from extended family and clan-based activities and spread benefits as they grow (cf. Mbithi and Rasmusson, 1977)

Employment and Remittances

Formal employment is the most sought after means of livelihood in rural areas. However, this does not necessarily point to the inadequacy of farming as the main means of livelihood. It only means that formal employment is largely preferred to farming. There are many reasons for this, including the higher salaries, prestige and the possibility of working away from home in urban areas that offer better infrastructure. In this section I present and discuss migrant labour from Sengeta to the tea plantations in the 1940s and 1950s, formal employment in other sectors in recent years and work in other people's farms in the village, to demonstrate how livelihood diversification has changed over time with regard to employment and remittances.

Faced with the need for an income with which to "commence life" through marriage and bride price transfer, young men from Sengeta migrated to the tea plantations in Kericho District in the 1940s and 50s to work. These were not the first batch of migrant workers from the district to go out to work; the exodus to work in railway construction and the plantations had commenced in the 1920s (Silberschmidt, 1999; Orvis, 1993). Evidence shows that from Sengeta the majority moved in the 1940s and 50s. The background to this movement was lack of a cash crop. Tea and pyrethrum had not yet been introduced in African areas and it was not until the late 1950s that coffee was allowed (Uchendu and Anthony, 1975). Livestock accumulation was also curtailed due to the collapse of the war economy following colonisation.

The migration to the plantation sector was therefore motivated by the inadequacy of farming to support village livelihoods. The local farming economy could not sustain a lifestyle in which early marriages were preceded by bride price transfers in cattle. It was imperative for young people to look outwards for income and cattle for marriage and for commencing life generally, including embracing western-style consumption patterns. The diversification was painfully slow and precarious, however, requiring that they have one foot on the farm and another on the plantation, where the pay was low. Converting this low pay into cattle was an equally long process.

> Nyandika was employed to pluck tea at the Kericho tea plantations in 1950. He was promoted to tea pruning in 1952, and became a tractor driver in Cherimo Tea Factory between 1953 and 1960 when he retired. His salary averaged fifteen shillings per month while working on the plantations. He had gone there as a result of hearing stories from other young men in his village about work on the tea plantations, and one of these men took him there. He needed to earn money to improve life for his family and be able to marry and commence life. From the earnings he bought goats which he later exchanged for cows. Through this process he managed to acquire four cows and two goats which he paid as bride price for his first wife, and then ten goats for the second wife. Asked why he retired early at the age of only twenty seven, he said "I had learned many things already by that time, from driving to pruning tea and knew that I would not fail to do my own work without being supervised brutally by white people. When I came home I continued making money from pruning people's tea here in the village". Nyandika had planted coffee in 1955 and tea in 1962, in both cases using savings from his employment on the tea plantations to pay for the planting materials.

Nyandika captures the process of converting low plantation wages into cattle. It was through such a process that one could raise bride price, normally of over ten cattle. From such a process, actors were able to raise money for enough cattle to marry several wives, as in the case of Nyandika, or to afford school fees for themselves and for their children, and to accumulate cattle and cash crops. These findings echo Orvis's suggestion (1993) that work in the plantations constituted the beginnings of accumulation because those who worked there had the income to commence cash crop production when it was eventually allowed in African areas. Deshingkar and Start (2003: 17) also report that migrant workers from Andhra Pradesh and Madhya Pradesh in India used their earnings to accumulate through investments in their farms, houses, children's education and marriages.

By the 1960s tea, coffee, pyrethrum, passion fruit and maize production had gained ground in Nyamira District. Migration to tea plantations was therefore not as imperative as was the case earlier. Those migrating went specifically to raise money for particular objectives or as a stopgap measure as they searched for better paying jobs. These villagers had by then acquired some more education and land was still fairly abundant for crop production on a reasonably small-scale basis. Excerpts from Isena's case, which are presented below, illustrate this point.

> Isena's sisters never went to school and of all his siblings, it was only his brother Petro who reached standard eight during the colonial period. Isena went to school early and sat for his Kenya Junior Secondary Examination (KJSE) in 1974. From 1975 to 1978 he worked in casual jobs in various places. He started as a van salesman in Eldoret in 1975, and then with the help of his cousin, moved to Kericho where he got a contract to pluck tea in one of the tea plantations up to 1978.
>
> In 1978 he came home and started planting his own tea, although some of his brother's tea had fallen on his land when they shared up their parents' land for inheritance. By that time he was frustrated with poorly paying short term work contracts. Over the years he had saved only four hundred shillings, which he used to purchase tea seedlings. At the same time he planted pyrethrum, which matured fast. He used pyrethrum earnings to buy more tea seedlings and planted about 2000 tea bushes. He also planted tea on a plot he had purchased in the village from his cousin, and which he has already given to his son. The money he used to buy the land was from farm earnings.
>
> "In 1979, when I was still a farmer, there was an advert in the newspapers and over the radio that teachers were being recruited. I applied and was lucky to be selected and posted to South Nyanza District, where I worked for five years before transferring to Nyamira District on health grounds".

This generation of migrant workers changed jobs more frequently and abandoned them often as they had the option of farming with better returns. Kinship was crucial in this diversification as it was the network used in employment seeking. Another important attribute of diversification in the 1970s had to do with the fact that those involved had more formal education and were able to move into formal employment easily. While moving into formal employment, they kept their agricultural investments and thus relied on diversified livelihoods longer. This became more of an accumulation strategy than was the case in the earlier years when farm investments to return to in colonial Kenya were limited. Accumulation in land and its development was therefore a possibility in latter years and was realised by those like Isena who had diversified to formal employment because they created more resources and gained more room for manoeuvre. These findings confirm those of Ellis (2005) that diversification generates resources that are deployed more flexibly. In this sense, the findings are also in line with Francis (2000) that diversification may become a strategy for accumulation. Isena's use of savings from employment to plant tea and pyrethrum may be seen as a regrounding of the farm enterprise and later in life he also used his earnings as a teacher to do zero-grazed dairy production which fed manure into his kale and napier fields, enabling him to cut fertilizer costs and reground the enterprise further (cf. Ploeg, Long and Banks, 2002).

Since the 1980s, the Kenyan economy, like those in the rest of Sub-Saharan Africa, has been shrinking under the weight of structural adjustment programmes (SAPs). Unemployment has hit rural and urban areas hard. In particular, land holdings in Nyamira and Gusiiland generally are getting much smaller to accommodate the farming interests of the rising population. Educational achievement and coverage has risen over the earlier decades but chances of gaining formal employment for tens of thousands of school leavers are low. Against this background, three livelihood diversification scenarios have emerged: First, support in remittances from those household members who have managed to get into formal employment in Kenya or abroad; second, a movement to the plantation sector of a second generation mostly with the support of retiring parents or kin; and third, work for pay in neighbours' or relative's farms in the village. I will discuss each in turn.

Remittances from members of households working away in towns and abroad form a significant part of livelihood diversification in Sengeta Village. One interesting case relates to a widow who receives substantial amounts of money and support from her children working both locally in Kenyan cities and abroad. An excerpt from her case is presented below.

> Bochaberi's second born child, who lives in the USA with her family, has been of much help to her. She paid school fees for her brother from form one to four, built a permanent house for her mother and furnished it. "She bought for me a television set, a cell phone, a radio set and a car battery to power them. In a nutshell I can say she has been very helpful. Last month, she called to inquire about my health, which worries them sometimes. She coordinates her siblings who work in Kenya to pay a worker who takes care of the tea and collect the napier grass which I buy around the village for the cattle". The siblings discuss things on cell phones and make every major decision in the home. It was their decision to put up a permanent house for their mother. They also discuss her health condition always and make decisions about her care and accruing expenses. While the one in the US bankrolls most of the actions the family takes, all Bochaberi's daughters and sons always consult with their mother and visit her frequently, except for one who is wayward. Whenever her children come home they bring her gifts such as food, clothes and money.

Kenya's economy is increasingly relying on remittances from Kenyans working abroad as a meaningful foreign exchange earner as shown below.

An Economic Intelligence Unit (EIU of London) report shows that Kenyans in the diaspora are competing neck-and-neck with such strongly performing sectors as tourism and agriculture in boosting the country's economy. Past Central Bank projections show that while tourism generates about 48 billion shillings each year, remittances from Kenyans abroad are about 50 billion shillings (*Sunday Nation*, Nairobi: Sunday October 1, 2006).

Bochaberi's everyday life is linked to remittances from her children and her lifestyle is structured around the remittances. She has a worker in the fields to take care of her tea bushes and ferry cut grass for the cattle. Her communication by cell phone, her entertainment, and housing, furnishings and consumption are largely the result of remittances. This case is typical of a livelihood that is locally situated but influenced and shaped by actors located in the village, in regional towns, in the capital city Nairobi and globally from the USA. The ideas that shape this livelihood are negotiated on the internet and over the cell phone, and what is usually implemented reflects images of North and South. Because of the variety of tastes of the various actors involved in decision making in this virtual household, Bochaberi has the opportunity to receive local Kenyan news on her television and radio, and to tune in to the Voice of America radio every evening to hear, as she put it, "what is happening in my daughter's country" – referring to the USA. She also tunes in to the BBC television news in the mornings and Cable News Network (CNN) late in the evening. These global images and sounds are for entertainment, but they also shape the way that Bochaberi looks at life and the way she presents herself in the village.

This type of household challenges the traditional definition, which assumes that members live together, eat from the same kitchen and have a dominant head that makes decisions. This is a virtual type of household with members dispersed spatially and decision-making decentralised and transacted on the internet and cell phone. The social background to decision making is mosaic and a reflection of the spatial dispersion of the membership. The contradiction in this household is that it defies customary practices where married daughters do not play a transformatory role in their natal homes (Levine, 1979; Hakansson, 1994). With the influence of Northern cultural traits, the married daughters, both those in Kenya and the one abroad, are focused on their natal home and its improvement. A possible additional explanation for this interest is located in the struggle by their mother to educate them when their late father married a second wife and sidelined them. This may have moved them closer to their mother and her status as a widow may have culminated in their united empathy for her.

A job in town or abroad for a member of a household in therefore not only reflected in remittances in cash or in kind. In other words, statistics about the number of dollars remitted are not the most important information. It is more interesting to understand the social implications for decision-making and lifestyle outcomes in the receiving household. This is because money as purchasing power or as a commodity has a minimal influence on livelihoods. But remittances in a case like this are a resource in both a material and a non-material sense, and come with the intentions, instructions, preferences and tastes of those involved. Such a resource has the potential to enter the lifeworld of actors and negotiate its space and position as if it had a life of its own, unlike money of the same face value won in a lottery for example. Therefore the importance of remittances for livelihood change and diversification lies in the manner and intent of its remission and the negotiations that ensue. This importance is located in the social forces that accompany the economic utility in the remittances in dollar value.

From another angle, the social forces (including the remitters' tastes and visions) that come with the remittances act in ways that diversify the local landscape and the livelihood of not only the recipients of the remittances but also of other actors whose landscape is reworked. Being a daughter of a school teacher from the 1930s to the 1960s and then a pioneer dairy farmer in the 1960s and 1970s, Bochaberi's attachment to cattle is nostalgic. Her children's support for the undertaking is thus a convergence of her preferences and of the children. But given that her land is not sufficient to produce the required amounts of napier grass for her three dairy cattle, she buys it from neighbours and other villagers. This has transformed the landscape as people plant the grass in different acreages to sell not only to Bochaberi but to other farmers like her, some of whom travel long distances looking for the grass for their stall fed livestock. The landscape has been reworked and land redefined in new ways to accommodate agricultural intensification as a result of an additional redefinition of napier grass as a cash crop. In this sense napier grass is recreated afresh as a resource. Scenarios like these bring out the notion of co-construction of reality through the interaction of the 'natural' and the social (Hannigan, 1995). This means that the natural environment and society are reorganised through a process of co-production by which mutual interaction takes place and alters livelihoods and the bases and manner in which they are constructed.

Compared to the combined social forces unleashed from local and international remittances in Bochaberi's case, Birundu's household handles her local remittances differently. A caption of the Birundu case is reproduced below.

> Some of Birundu's sons have acquired properties outside the village and they have put up houses there. One of them, Nyang'au stays at Mogumo with his family while Kefa lives in Nairobi and they usually come home to see their parents. Another son, Mose stays near the school where he teaches and he has acquired land there, but he usually comes home during the school holidays. "Last year Mose bought for me a mobile phone which I use nowadays to communicate with them. Initially they used to call me through their cousin near here because he

> could bring a message or I could go to his house to call them when there was need". The Birundu family is closely knit and supportive to its members, with Birundu the head of the family setting the example. He said that he often calls his children on their cellphones to find out how they are doing. They also call him to know their mother's and his health conditions from time to time. He said that "Even if they have these properties, they have every right to demand this ancestral land. With time I will divide it up for the four sons. If any of them has a shortage of maize he comes and gets his requirements. They also bring us such items as sugar and other household items whenever they visit. My daughters also do the same. I usually go to visit them, especially when I hear they have a health problem".

The flow of resources in remittances to the Birundu household is guarded. The major form of remittances is consumption items. This can be explained in terms of the strong patriarchal authority in control of the household and guarding that control by repulsing the preferences that could accompany remittances. The sons have a mission to accumulate their own land and associated property and apart from assisting in improving local household consumption, their contribution to the reconstruction of the household and livelihood is limited. Cliggett (2005) similarly found consumption-based remittances dominating in the Gwembe Valley in Zambia. Overbearing patriarchal authority may be counterproductive to the livelihood diversification process, and to rural-urban relations and negotiations among household members. Although communication has been opened up, this form of patriarchal authority seems to have stifled debate and social experimentation, and as a result dispersed the household both physically and socially. It is also possible that Birundu receives a lot more in remittances than described in the vignette, but because it has been remitted in its raw commodity form, the money remains socially neutral and essentially without noticeable effect on the livelihood and landscape, compared to Bochaberi's case, for instance. However, Birundu's sons collect some grain from their parents to consume at their places of work, which means their livelihoods are hooked to their parents' farm in some way. On the same phenomenon, Owuor and Foeken (2006) report that some townspeople in Nakuru rely on food supplies from their rural farms to subsidise their urban livelihoods.

Beyond the remittances and employment in the formal sector locally and abroad, a second generation of migrants is moving into the tea plantations for work, mainly of the blue collar type. Since the late 1990s there has been significant movement of people to the plantations, according to discussions in Sengeta Village. Even work plucking tea is not available easily and the networks of retiring parents and relatives have been useful in job seeking behaviour, as shown in the case outlined below.

> On his children Otero said: "most of my children never went beyond standard eight, except Abasi and Geoffrey who reached form four. While I was working at

Kericho, I took my two sons to school there. They reached standard seven and never wanted to continue with school. I sent Moti for training as a tailor and dressmaker, and nowadays he works at a Kericho Tea Estate, making workers' uniforms. Four of my sons are at Kericho and while I was still working there I assisted the eldest two to get jobs plucking tea and they have since been promoted. The youngest two sons went to stay with their elder brothers and I think it is their elder brothers who linked them to their present jobs. All my daughters are married except one who died recently here at home and left me with two grandchildren whom I am taking care of. They live with their grandmother in the small hut, echikoni".

All Otero's children are helpful to him whenever there is a problem in his home. They usually send money when he requests them to, but, usually they give priority to their wives and children. "Wherever they come here on vacation they buy things like sugar and other household necessities. They also bring with them their record players and we party until midnight. Like this December holidays they said they will come and visit us".

Otero's case brings out the issues shaping job-seeking behaviour in Kenya, where destiny is decided on the basis of who knows who. When he talks about assisting them in getting a job, he is essentially reverting to the gift-giving economy, where people at work develop friendship that revolves around gifts to each other in cash or in kind, so that when a colleague approaches another for a relative's job it becomes difficult to turn them down. Even if strangers could be employed, tea plantations do not advertise their low cadre job vacancies and there is a need for inside information in order to be available for a vacancy at the right time. This can only work for people who have their relatives or friends working inside to inform them and where necessary put in a word for them. This is what Otero may have done for some of his sons and what the sons appear to have done for their younger brothers. Information and the kinship networks are used as resources in securing employment and thus diversifying livelihood. This finding is in line with Cliggett's (2005: 41) finding in Zambia that Gwembe migrants relied on already established Gwembe networks in town to secure employment.

Another dimension of job-seeking networks is illustrated by Isena's case discussed earlier in this chapter. Like Otero's sons, Isena did not have a formal college education in the 1970s when he used a cousin to get a job plucking tea in the Kericho tea plantations. Social networks are critical in job-seeking behaviour and reliance on relatives and friends to get a job is a major avenue in the diaspora. A key issue emerging from these cases is that earnings in the informal sector and in blue collar sections are low and their contribution in terms of rural livelihood diversification is small. This has to do more with the low levels of education of the actors involved, and their inability to redefine life in their rural households in new ways and challenge the prevailing landscape and livelihood in any meaningful way. Although higher education does not necessarily entail social forces that transform households, if interaction between migrant actors and villagers turns out to be a dialogue of like minds, then livelihood change stalls. In the case of the Oteros, diversification has taken the form of consumption, mainly including household necessities and entertainment.

The low level of education leading to a general casualisation of labour generally undermines the amounts in remittances and the social transformational value of those remittances in rural livelihood. As a site of social experimentation and new ideas, remittances are undermined and the resulting livelihood diversification is confined largely to single households or individuals in them, compared for instance to Bochaberi's kind of diversification, which transforms landscapes and livelihood, or Birundu's, in which social welfare schemes become sites of information exchange and rural-urban exchanges and dialogue. But casualisation of labour and by extension of sections of the rural economies is not a fate that has befallen passive rural actors. Actors have come to that level through their struggles to overcome livelihood obstacles such as land scarcity and politico-economic isolation that disadvantages them in the educational system. It is in response to such obstacles that they set up different types of trade and re-engineer their traditional group labour in ways that serve local farmers.

Petro's case, discussed above, illustrates labour organisation for tea production in which he employs relatives and neighbours regularly to pluck tea for him and deliver it to the tea buying centre. Given that the labour is organised on the basis of kinship, friendship and neighbourhood, the workers and employers also access certain values in kind and in cash along the way that diversifies their livelihoods in ways that they appreciate and value. These exchanges include workers' free assistance to employers after normal working hours and gifts from workers' employed children in kind or cash. This labour arrangement, which is not uncommon and which is reflected in Nyandika's case, enables the workers to access income through their daily work.

> Nyandika has divided his parcel of land equally between his two wives. This was done by the neighbours and all his brothers. Out of this he partitioned a parcel which is his emonga – "from one end to the other for my upkeep". He grazes his cow there. He has however not partitioned his tea shamba which he has kept for the education of his younger children. They work on it and he earns a monthly income from it. He uses the money to pay for their education, buy household goods and pay a tithe to the church at Sengeta, where he worships. He has shown his eldest son's wife where to cultivate her food crops and he has also given her a few rows of the tea crop to pluck temporarily, to get an income to support herself. In return she plucks her father-in-law's tea without pay.

Nyandika manages his tea so that he ends up with labour without making any monetary payments. His labour mobilisation processes are dependent on his patriarchal authority and his ability to control and wield the tea as a resource. These findings confirm Donovan's (2001) in Kericho District where a patriarch uses his household labour for tea production and compensates them informally. Our findings in Petro's and Nyandika's cases, however, go beyond that to demonstrate that labour organisation in larger kin groups and neighbourhoods is largely beyond the farmer's control. This then brings out the larger social processes of livelihood diversification at village level.

Trading: on the open markets, kiosks and road-sides

Trade, mainly in iron products, has been a part of the Abagusii life since their arrival in their present settlement in the 1600s (Livine and Levine, 1966). However, the notion of trade has changed significantly and nowadays relates to larger and more sophisticated populations and merchandise. The nature of trade between the Abagusii and the outside world is beyond the scope of this thesis. What concerns this book is the trading that goes on because of or in spite of farming and mainly in the form of local livelihood diversification.

> Nyandika's second wife Batigo is a trader. She buys tobacco leaves locally and sells them at Daraja Mbili Market just outside Kisii Town on Monday and Thursday every week. She is well known for buying tobacco and people bring it to her in small quantities until she fills a gunny bag or two for sale at the market. After selling the tobacco at the market she buys earthen pots, mats, baskets and fish for sale by the road side at the village business centre. She said of her trade, "it keeps me busy and I make profits here and there to be able to buy things in the house like utensils, cooking oil, salt and tea. It also enables me to move out of this home to meet and discuss with other people. You know men have no problem, they can go to the market and just sit there, but as a woman I need something to do to free me from a life that revolves round the house. In the market I get to know how other people live and I relax away from plucking tea and other farm work". She started trading in 1978. She stops trading during millet weeding and harvesting time, which is a total of about five weeks each year.

The generally stated motive of this kind of trading is to make a profit, but in practice, social motives for the trading are evident. Customers do not always only come to buy, but to meet other people and talk. Traders, mainly women, have taken to trading firstly to make some money on their own and secondly, perhaps more importantly, to resist being relegated to the homestead. As Batigo points out, there is always a desire to go out and meet other people and discuss and exchange ideas. These women's struggles to liberate themselves from the homestead chores are widespread and are usually expressed in terms of their shopping every day and visits to the village centre or the nearby town. In general whatever the motives of those involved in trading in the village, their livelihoods are diversifying because of the trade. The fact that more women are trading means that they are increasingly restless about their relegation to the farm and homestead. For instance, from Nyandika's homestead, Dinah was also trading. This trend is contrary to Silberschmidt's (1999) findings that women in Kisii District, Kenya spent most of their time on the farm while men walked on the road or drank. In any event women in Gusiiland have been selling in the open air markets since the markets were established in the 1930s and 40s (Omosa, 1998:114). This notion of trading as a site of interaction with other people, to talk and exchange ideas, is similar to Perry's (2000) on rural weekly markets in Senegal which acted as bases for intra-community bonding.

The same trade as is taking place at the village centre is also undertaken on the sides of the main road near the village, especially near the tea buying centre. The tea buying centres are slowly being transformed into business centres as small restaurants and shops are set up to serve tea farmers. The businesses along the roads attract those in the immediate neighbourhoods who do not wish to walk some distance for shopping. However, wherever a kiosk or a trader's shade is put up, people assemble there at different times of the day just to talk and the traders are happy with the practice as it creates some social activity around their trade and attracts customers. The proliferation of trade around the villages is a clear indication that livelihoods are diversifying but that there are not many opportunities for the undertaking. As more and more people start trading, the goods dealt in become increasingly similar, leading to reduced sales. At that stage of competition the ability to sell on credit and the social activity around one's business are the main ways of remaining in business. Some of the traders are pushed out of business even as new ones start trading. Traders who are involved in a chain of activities, such as was the case with Nyandika's wife Batigo, survive longer in business. The fact that she carried tobacco to the larger market in Kisii town and made a profit before buying other items at lower prices for sale in the village, made her business more competitive.

Another type of business located at the village centre and near the tea buying centres is restaurant operation. The restaurant operators sell tea, *mandazi*, soda and local dishes such as *ugali* and kale or chicken. These types of businesses have existed in market centres started by the colonial government in the 1920s and 30s to service the growing demand for western goods by Africans (Omosa, 1998). In the planned markets dispersed around the countryside within about ten kilometres of each other in those days, there were usually one to two restaurants. This has changed significantly over the years. In Sengeta Village, the village shopping centre with twenty five business buildings has six operating restaurants. Most of them are run by people from within the village. An excerpt from a case study on one of the restaurant operators is reproduced below to illustrate the nature and implications of restaurant business for livelihood diversification.

> Mariko said that some of the people who owned tea were very good at paying debts in his restaurant. "Today it was payday for tea farmers and many of my customers who had eaten on credit have come and cleared their debts". Mariko makes sales of up to one thousand shillings per day and after deducting the day's expenses he usually remains with a profit of about five hundred shillings. "My main objectives are to satisfy my customers, to enlarge the business and serve a larger area. The more the customers frequent my restaurant the more I am assured

of making profits and of continuity in the business. This will enable me to meet my basic needs and assist my family in their various needs".

The business has enabled him to furnish his house, buy a goat and rent land for cultivation from Tom at one thousand shillings per year. He has already planted maize on it. Although Mariko is in business and aims at expanding it, he is always going to the farming roots of his lineage, whenever he has money to spare. Besides hiring land for cultivation from Tom, he has also rented some other land from Oino to grow wimbi for the second season and bought a tree to split and make building posts for a bigger house, as he plans to leave his current house for his younger brothers when the new one is ready. Following that line of kindness to his brothers he lent his brother two hundred shillings from the business for his own use. Mariko has ventured into the self help movement in his village, by joining Nyabwasu Group soon after starting business. He has no license to operate the business and he always closes whenever he has information that local government officers are on their way to the village. Other business people call him on his cell phone from neighbouring markets to inform him whenever they see the local authority vehicle.

Like most businesses in isolated villages, the restaurants are purely informal although the layout and food sold is as good as in the formalised businesses in bigger neighbouring markets. The restaurants are not registered as businesses and thus are not licensed by the local authorities. Neither the operators nor the workers or premises had been inspected by the department of public health at the Town Hall. The argument is that if the operators met all the licensing requirements, they would lack capital to set up the businesses in the first place. They prefer to involve themselves in a hide and seek game with the authorities over the legality of their businesses. Although this wastes their time and leads to losses, it is cheaper in their estimation than paying for the many licenses required of them. They therefore resist policy and defy authorities in order to succeed in diversifying their livelihoods. This approach is not isolated and it persists even in larger market centres where operators close down their businesses whenever they get wind of impending business inspections by authorities. Jambiya (1998) similarly found out that restaurants (*hoteli)* are common non-farm activities in rural areas in Lushoto District Tanzania, although he did not delve into their legality or illegality.

Trading also goes on from small retail shops selling household items. These shops are mainly located in the village centre although there are also some near the tea buying centres and along the roads. At the village shopping centre in Sengeta, there are a number of operational shops, most of them running informally without the required licenses, with a view to keeping operational costs low. Meshack is one of the shop operators at the village market and part of his case record is reproduced below.

Meshack started by selling kerosene in a rented kiosk at Sengeta in 2003, and the demand and turnover were high because previously people walked about three kilometres to go and buy kerosene. Having broken even with kerosene, Meshack continued with the business but added other wares by the second week. These included matches, soap, cooking fat, sugar, soda and body lotions and creams. All these he added to his business by reinvesting all his profits. All the items he sells are in small units that people in the village can afford them, as they usually do not buy in large quantities. So Meshack repacks sugar into a quarter kilogram, half a kilogram and three quarters of a kilogram to fit into the budgets of various customers according to their abilities and needs. Meshack has also come to know the cheaper brands of cooking fat that are preferred by customers because of their low prices and those are the ones he stocks. He has a knack of repackaging items such as sugar, slicing items such as soap or accessing the cheapest body creams: all with the aim of finding access to the pockets of the poor, which has been his secret of success in business. He explained that the villagers require every household item the rich require and so his challenge has been to link them to items which they need in quantities and at prices that are friendly to them, while keeping his profits low but consistent.

Fresh from succeeding in business in the village, Meshack set his sights on finding a wife. This he found in Lorna, whom he had met while working in the Matatu Industry. He married her in April 2004, although he has not paid bride price. His wife came in handy for the business because whenever he is held up at work (he is a matatu tout),she opens the kiosk and commences selling. Most of the items sold are bought from Soa Wholesalers in a town four kilometres away. He has developed a good relationship with the wholesalers and they give him the best prices. Like other business people in the village, Meshack has no licence to operate his business. He reasoned that acquiring the required papers would have taken all the capital he used to start his business and left him poorer. His approach to the law enforcement officers is similar to those of others like him – he keeps his ears to the ground and once tipped that they are on their way, he closes down quickly and escapes. His other way of escaping the law enforcers is that he mostly opens his business during the evenings when authorities have closed for the day.

Shop operation in the village market and along the roads in the village is a significant route to livelihood diversification. However, like the restaurant businesses, this is not an easy route as license requirements are a deterrent. Business people have devised their own unique ways of responding to these bottlenecks to their livelihood change. The resistance to the law and policy by those who cannot afford the licences is an indication that making a living is a struggle; a struggle against the law and against poverty. The fact that so many traders operate largely without licenses implies that the licenses are widely detested and quietly resisted. In a way the struggle involves trying to remain in business. For this reason actors attempt to unpack and repack goods in ways that respond to the nature of demand and their customers' abilities to purchase. This business ingenuity is reflective of attempts to recreate utility in ways inconceivable at the level of manufacturing industries, in order to create resources along the business chain and win the battle for survival that these traders face every day. The actors therefore quietly resist, defy or reorder the dominant policy and industrial discourse in order to deploy emerging opportunities for business and survival in changed circumstances (cf. Scott, 1985). The business creativity of repackaging items for sale according to customers' abilities and preferences is similar to Robertson's (2000) finding that women in Gikomba Market in Nairobi cleaned and polished beans using maize hulls in order to attract customers.

The direction of livelihood diversification through shops and restaurants also depends on the local styles of people gathering at a market centre or outside a shop or in a restaurant to talk and exchange information. Another important reason for coming to the shops is to listen to the radio. It is common for the restaurants to have radio sets tuned into specific stations at different times according to the tastes of the 'customers'. During the day the traders mainly tuned into the FM stations for continuous music and news. In the early evenings they tuned into to the vernacular station for news and announcements such as of local deaths and burials, to serve elderly patrons during those times of the day. From around 19 hours they were back to the FM stations to entertain the largely young clientele flocking to business premises, especially restaurants, to take tea, chat and for some to plot theft. Therefore the idea of entertainment is part of trading and 'customers' are not warned against 'idling' as is usually done in bigger towns. An elderly shop operator told me that part of the reason he set up a shop at the edge of his farm is to attract people to talk to because he could not manage to walk to the market three kilometres away everyday to meet other people. He said the shop helped him interact with other villagers and make some sales. Once again, then, the social basis of diversification is an important one. Accumulation or profiteering is not necessarily the main motive in such cases. Perry (2000) similarly found out that *loumas* (rural weekly markets) in Senegal were sites for socialising, and non-crop trade activities.

Another form of trade that is common in Nyamira District is livestock trade. In this form of trade, traders buy livestock at the lowest possible price and sell at the highest possible price in order to maximise profits. The major motivation to go into the trade is the possibility of making profits easily, depending on one's negotiation skills. But it is not an easy business, as some of the profits made must be spent on hiring people to drive the cattle on the hoof while the trader travels by public transport. This is because the trader cannot always walk to the dispersed markets tens of kilometres apart. Moreover, there are several taxes to be paid which also add to the difficulties in livestock trading. An excerpt from a case record of a livestock trader is reproduced below.

> Nyangaga said: "I started my livestock business in 1980 with a capital of five hundred shillings, which was enough to purchase one cow. I joined my stepbrother who was already doing the business. Among the people I used to go to the market with were five other people from around my home area, all of whom had started the business earlier".

"At the beginning I used to buy only cattle and I started by buying just one cow. These days I also buy and sell goats and sheep. The markets I buy and sell from are Ting'a on Mondays, Kebirigo on Tuesdays, Igare on Wednesdays, Keroka on Thursdays and Kisii on Fridays. I go to these markets on all those days and sometimes I buy a cow on my way to the market and still sell it at a profit before reaching the market. I may also buy one from a market and either sells it there at a profit, on my way back home or in the next market the following day. Through this business, I saved enough money to buy cattle, which I used to pay bride price for my wife, who takes care of the tea and small farm. I have also used the earnings from the business to pay school fees for my children and for my family's upkeep. I have used the profits to build a permanent house for myself and furnish it to my satisfaction".

Livestock trade appears to rely on friendship and kinship networks for managing the herds during movement between the markets, often through the homes of the traders. Nyangaga relied on his friends and kin to enter the business. Friends who had been in the trade longer trained him in negotiation skills, before he became an accomplished trader. To travel to all the markets mentioned one has to walk about 160 kilometres between the village and the markets each week. This is why it becomes necessary to engage people to take it in turns to drive the livestock on the hoof and to go by bus. A trader or two usually accompanies younger men driving the livestock to or from the market to supervise them and to sell along the way if the opportunity arises.

Therefore trust is important in the trade because if the supervising trader sells a colleague's livestock he should declare the price truthfully. He should also negotiate as firmly for the highest possible price as if the livestock being sold were his. Equally, during his turn to supervise – whether or not he has livestock in the herd – he should ensure that the herd is driven skilfully to avoid injuries that would cost his colleagues quick and profitable sales. These findings on the importance of trust among traders and livestock drivers are in agreement with Haan's (2000) analysis of livestock trade in the West African region, where hired people drove livestock on the hoof or transported them by truck, often across international borders, faithfully avoiding or bribing authorities and arriving safely with the livestock at appointed markets where the owner and trader would be waiting.

Through the utilisation of a variety of relationships and friendships therefore, a trader is able to make profits with which to supplement farming to earn a living. The key to success in livestock trade however, lies in the ability of a trader to negotiate without fear or favour in order to make the best out of every situation and transaction. Negotiation skills involved in bargaining, discussing and haggling constitute an invisible resource that keeps the trader afloat and also ensures that the money and energy put into trading does not go to waste. These negotiation skills differentiate success from failure in livestock trading. Those who could not stand the heat sold at a loss and soon or later threw in the towel and moved on, to do other things to earn a living. This is particularly important given that the livestock market sub-culture is very different from other settings. The normative respect between people of apparently different age groups is ignored. Insults, intimidation and obscenities rule the air in livestock markets. One reason is to intimidate newcomers and another is that "traditionally only young men herded cattle and if you have brought them to the market you befit that junior age group and will be insulted"[55]. Nyangaga's success in the livestock trade has enabled him accomplish many things that seemed to satisfy him in life.

Nyangaga said that he and other traders routinely paid the gate fees at each of the markets where they took the cattle to sell and the transaction fees once they concluded a sale. This is very important in order to secure details of the seller, so as to be covered if stolen livestock are sold. It is in the traders' interest to pay and record each transaction unless it occurred outside the market. This reduces their profits but saves them from lengthy police interrogation and possible incarceration during investigations if they bought stolen livestock. Another problem faced in the livestock trade which came up during the fieldwork, is livestock quarantine to curb infectious diseases such as foot and mouth. At such times, markets are closed and livestock movement is banned, as was the case for about six months in 2004. Trade is restricted to villages and adjacent butcheries. This affects traders and it is after such long spells of market closures that some traders lack capital to restart their trading and fall out of business. It is difficult to circumvent quarantines because it is dangerous to neighbours to bring infected animals into the village. It is in the face of such hurdles that livelihood diversification proceeds in the livestock trade.

Locally, livestock is sold to butchers who operate butcheries in several different locations. They slaughter the livestock themselves in makeshift slaughter sheds next to their butcher's shops, and sell the meat. Although he only operates seasonally, mainly during December, Angima is one of the operators of butcher's shops.

> Since 1988, Angima has slaughtered livestock – mainly cattle and goats – around Christmas and New Year's Day, and sells the meat through the front door of his main house to supplement his chang'aa and ballast income. Sometimes he relies on a livestock trader from a neighbouring village to get livestock for slaughter when he has not commenced his yearly livestock trade.

Angima is fairly successful whenever he operates the butchery because sometimes he trades in livestock and is able to estimate the net weight of the carcase at the point of purchase and estimate his profit or the lack of it. In general most butchers' shops are also informal although they liaise with meat

---

55 Livestock trader on why respect on the basis of age is ignored in livestock markets. This hostility and intimidation kept women on the periphery of the market, often getting male relatives or friends to buy or sell for them in the mainstream market.

inspectors to have the meat inspected regularly and stamped for a small informal fee. This means that they are not registered but the inspectors argue that if they ignored informal or unregistered butcheries they would endanger the lives of innocent consumers. Hence, it is morally right for them to inspect the meat and possibly let those who register businesses do their part later (discussion with a local meat inspector, 2005). This approach by the meat inspectors, whose stamps on meat consumers are keen to see before purchasing, contributes to the casualisation of butchery businesses, because the shops provide further avenues for rent-seeking.

Overall the butcheries represent a contest between policy and practice, in the course of which livelihoods are diversified and policy is ignored. To succeed in the butchery business it is necessary to cooperate with the meat inspector by offering the rent sought and to close down the business when those who enforce the business registration policy are nearby. This behaviour is not necessarily cheaper for business but it is common, perhaps because traditionally the Abagusii people have resisted government since colonial times (cf. Maxon, 1989). Another explanation is that villagers generally view government with suspicion, because it wants business premises painted regularly and prefers permanent buildings for business. According to traders it was only in 1995 that shops outside mainstream market centres were registered, with unnecessary delays and demands for bribes. The struggles and suspicion between government and villagers is therefore historical and is perceived differently. Sometimes villagers associate government with the 'land rover vehicle' – meaning the District Commissioner or the police, and therefore with coercion and oppression.

Another form of trade common in Nyamira involves fuel wood and it is common throughout the small-scale tea growing areas of the Gusii region. The decision by the tea factories management to use fuel wood in place of electricity during certain stages of tea processing in the mid 1990s was meant to reduce production costs and to give local people an opportunity to earn some money through selling their wood to the factory. In a way it was a statement that the farmers owned the factories after they were liberalised. I talk of fuel wood trade because there are hardly any dealers who consistently sell their own wood to the local tea factory. Each of the traders buys trees, processes the wood as required and then sells it to the factory at factory set prices per cubic metre of wood. Festus is one of the villagers involved in fuel wood trade and a part of his case record is reproduced below.

> The fuel wood business has helped Festus to pay a medical bill for his wife and nursery school fees for his children. It has also kept him busy and has helped him to develop a good relationship with other villagers such as those from whom he buys trees and those he hires to split the wood and to arrange it. From the profits made he has rented tea to pluck for two years, bought a cow and some chickens, and is planning to buy another cow soon to supply milk for his family.

> "I experience some problems in this business. If a tree I have bought falls on somebody's property I involve the village headman to reach an agreement on compensation. I also have a problem when I want to buy a tree and the owner has probably sold it to more than one person. Therefore, during purchasing, I usually involve the village headman and a few neighbours to be my witnesses and this is at a cost of course. Also the pay per stack (three cubic metres) at the factory has remained one thousand five hundred shillings even when the prices of trees have been rising, because the factory fixes the price. When I hire a vehicle I am required to pay upfront to the owner, they do not listen to promises to pay later. Most of the trees I buy these days are far from the road and that means more transport costs. Due to scarcity of trees their prices have been rising steadily". He said the directors who had pressed the factory to start using wood as a source of energy in the first place, should now push it again to increase payments for the wood. Festus is a member of Sarianya Self-help Group and serves as its secretary. Each member contributes twenty five shillings per week and at the end of each month they hold a merry go round, sharing the five thousand shillings raised between two of their members for their own use.

The Festus case shows that wood fuel trade has contributed to the diversification of livelihoods in the village. Not only those involved in the trade diversify, but also those whose labour is required to cut, split and transport the wood to the factory yard. New income streams have been introduced in the livelihoods of at least five groups of people. The first is wood traders whose diversification Festus represents. The second group is the chain saw owners. The chain saws are hired for felling trees and cutting them according to specifications. The chain saw owners make profits on the basis of the difference between what they are paid and their fuel, maintenance and labour costs. In other words the third group that benefits is the chain saw operators who are paid by the owners of the chain saws. The fourth group is perhaps the largest and constitutes general unskilled labour that splits the wood and those who transport the wood to the roadsides. Those who transport to the roadside may be the same people who split or they may be different groups, and they are paid by the trader. The fifth group of people in the wood fuel trade chain is the transporting truck owners and their drivers who are paid by the traders to deliver the split wood to the factory yards.

The factory managements' single act of shifting their energy policies to include supplementation of electricity with fuel wood threw the entire rural economy into a spin, with actors taking strategic positions in the trading that ensued. In the process several groups of people whose livelihoods had hitherto been dependent on farming or other activities were re-oriented to benefit from the trade. So the wood fuel trade diversified the livelihood of the various groups of people in different ways. A wood fuel trader such as Festus is the face of the wood fuel trade and represents the various business activities organised around the wood fuel trade with tea factories and the extent of livelihoods diversification in Sengeta. The money that he makes from the trade has gone into the education of his children, family consumption and accumulation in livestock. Besides, as a member of a self help group, Festus has apparently cushioned his business from collapse due to lack of capital by investing in a rotational savings scheme that may ensure that he has money to re-invest in his trading. His trade thus also enables other people to save and mobilise resources to invest in different ways, leading to other forms of diversification. An important dimension of rural change that results from trade in fuel wood has to do with the re-definition of trees as cash crops that can be relied on to gain an income as the market is expanded and predictable. The wood fuel trade has reordered the landscape in such a way that a variety of stakeholders are continually preparing to take part in the various aspects of the trade, e.g. by planting new trees or buying new chain saws and axes. This is similar to Perry's (2000) finding that rural weekly markets stimulated villagers to produce in preparation for each weekly market day.

Local Brew Production and Sales

Local brew is a historical phenomenon among the Abagusii people, especially important in their ritual practices. Over its long history, however, the local brew has been commercialised and re-packaged into an economy of a kind. Local brew includes two 'brands', namely *busaa* and *chang'aa.* Busaa is the truly traditional brew of the people that is part of all the rituals performed, including weddings, rites of passage and sacrifices to appease spirits. *Busaa* is also a major ingredient in the group labour processes as it is the main drink after a day's work. In a sense, the social life of adults among the Abagusii has always been organised around the *busaa* drink. It is alcohol content that mainly differentiates *busaa* from *chang'aa.* While *busaa* has an estimated alcohol content of up to seven percent depending on the fermentation period, on average *chang'aa* has about seventy five percent per unit (Field Discussions, 2004/5). Both *busaa* and *chang'aa* are almost fully commercialised except to the extent that they are offered free to visitors in a home during funeral rites, weddings or other private occasions. In general, these days the drinks are accessed mainly through the market in that certain villagers make the brew and sell it directly on a retail basis to consumers or wholesalers who in turn sell it to retailers. This is basically a home-based industry, because production and sales take place from actors' homesteads. In most cases a trader's living room – *eero* – is the main site for conducting sales; in a sense it is the 'bar'.

In chapter seven I discussed local brew as one of the major destinations of villagers upon deagrarianisation. In other words, I argued that actors move out of agriculture into local brew trade as a means of livelihood. In this section I argue that some people combine local brew production and sales with farming in the course of agrarianising at different moments of their life course. Other people also routinely combine local brew business with farming to earn a living, which means that local brew business constitutes an opportunity for livelihood diversification. Dinah is a case in point.

> Dinah no longer grows a lot of tobacco due to ill health. The little she grows she sells at the local market or to her step-mother-in-law Batigo, who sells it at Daraja Mbili market in Kisii Town. She now concentrates on brewing busaa. On Fridays she brews busaa which she sells on Sundays to supplement her tea, coffee and tobacco incomes. Dinah only sells beer to grown-up people; if she sells to children or students their parents usually come to quarrel with her. Most of her customers are men, even though there are a few women who drink. Dinah gets into trouble with the local chief and his assistant, because when they pass nearby, the customers run away for fear of arrest, often without paying for their drinks. She also closes her house once she learns that they are around. She finds brewing better than tea as its returns are immediate compared to those of tea. She relies on her busaa business to pay school fees for her son who is in secondary school. In 2005 he was not awarded a government bursary and she spent earnings from tea and busaa to pay his school fees.

Nyandika's daughter-in-law Dinah is representative of actors in Sengeta who use local brew as an avenue of livelihood diversification in its correct meaning – taking up other activities to supplement farming as a means of livelihood. Dinah stuck with farming, growing coffee, tea, maize, beans and some bananas, even as she was involved in tobacco growing and trade at different times of her life. She also had *busaa* ready for sale every Sunday to make some more money. Her success in diversification ventures stems from the manner in which she juggles a variety of activities at the same time, mainly by organising them carefully so that she is in the market for two days a week, selling local brew on one day and working on the farm during the rest of the week. Her involvement in merry-go-round clubs also constituted another form of diversification that enabled her to grow her proceeds from farming and other ventures and be able to pay school fees for her children. As already shown above in the discussion on 'kinship, friendship and gift giving', her independence from the control and direction of a man set her free to experiment with a number of activities and to seek success in many directions.

The Angima case represents major aspects of the local brew industry in Sengeta. Angima and his wife are major retailers of chang'aa who have made money from it which Angima has used to pay bride price as well build a house. The contradiction in this case is that although these actors live on a farm they have not been farmers and it cannot be argued that they are diversifying their livelihood from agriculture. From their trading hey days up to mid-2005, their land was rented out or left idle. It would be more accurate to say that they were diversifying their livelihood from local brew trade to agriculture.

> Angima took the cue from his son Morinwa and planted tea bushes on half an acre of land in 2005. He also pruned and weeded his late father's coffee that is on his parcel of land in 2004 and earned six hundred shillings from it that year. He said that he is tired of police harassment due to dealing in chang'aa and would like to slowly shift into farming to make a living.

Whatever the order of things, local brew trade appears for historical reasons to do with the Angimas' family histories (see Chapter 7) to have been a major livelihood avenue and is a common feature of livelihood trajectories in the village. As of 2004/5, Angima is beginning to get into farming, and he is in a sense diversifying into agriculture as he planned to slowly phase out of the local brew business. Therefore his livelihood diversification occurred as he agrarianised. His family's success in the local brew business is due to their consistency both in maintaining their supplies and in beating the police and other law enforcement officers at their game of trying to abolish the trade and consumption of local brew. Their main strategy in this has been to evade arrest or to bribe their way out (as well as their customers'), so long as they are arrested at their home. This makes their home 'a safe drinking den' and means that they get more customers and higher profits, and ultimately success. According to Robertson (2000) the state agents' efforts to abolish local brew business does not always succeed, and people's resistance is sometimes quiet and sometimes openly defiant.

Nyarwaru's *chang'aa* business is very much the same as Angima's although he is mostly at the wholesaler's end. The differences in their businesses largely relate to how they have confronted their success. While Angima has been slow to bounce back into farming, Nyarwaru has been quick to do so.

> Nyarwaru has used the money from the local brew business to pay debts, school fees for his children and family upkeep. He has bought a cow, a sewing machine for his wife, and chickens for eggs for his family, and he has repaired his house. Because he lacks enough land, the cow grazes by the roadside and he buys napier grass for it from other villagers who have a surplus. His younger brother borrowed five hundred shillings to buy maize and will refund it later.

Nyarwaru's livelihood diversification is becoming more complex than Angima's. Part of the explanation for this would be located in the varying aspirations of the men's spouses. While Angima's wife is deeply and historically entangled in *chang'aa* business, Nyarwaru's wife does not understand the trade and is aloof, preferring to do other things for a living. Her membership of the Adventist Church, which is doctrinally against alcohol consumption and handling, is the strongest statement that she is not sympathetic to her husband's occupation. Levine (1979: 25) found that the Adventist Church preaches the protestant ethic in its most exacting form and in addition demands monogamy and teetotalism. This explains Nyarwaru's purchase of a sewing machine for his wife as one way of beginning to distance himself from the chang'aa trade, and as part of his strategy of quitting the business. This is unlike the Angimas, whose history and social disposition more readily supports the trade.

The local brew economy also presented employment opportunities for some actors in Sengeta. Those employed neither owned the businesses nor the premises from where they operated. The employers hired premises, provided other start-up resources and paid the employees to carry out the business for them. A portion of the case material on such an arrangement is reproduced below.

> In 2002, Kegogwa approached Elkanah to sell local brew on his behalf at a place he rented at the Junction. Elkanah agreed to the proposal and started the work on January 15, 2002. The employer is a mason and that keeps him busy most of the time so he has no time to conduct the business. Elkanah is the one who buys chang'aa on behalf of his employer. He buys five litres of the liquor at 400 shillings from various people, not just one source. Elkanah is paid a commission of fifty shillings for each five litres he sells, plus an additional thirty shillings for lunch per working day. The business premise from which he operated is open from 8:00 AM but the closing time is not fixed; it depends on the flow of customers. Some days he closes early if there are no customers, other days business continues till past 10.00 PM.
>
> Elkanah sells in various quantities according to the preferences of customers: beer can be bought for five, ten, twenty, forty or eighty shillings. Most of his customers are men but there are also a few women. He always sells to adults to avoid quarrels with local people, who object to the sale of beer to children and students. Whenever he is arrested during police raids his employer bribes to get him out. Elkanah does not drink, is single and spends his free days helping on his parents' fields, as he eats from their kitchen. He also occasionally buys household items such as sugar, kerosene and salt for them, using his commission income. The business is not smooth however: "I undertake the business under cover behind the shop building so that many people may not know whether or not the business is on, lest they report me to the assistant chief. Mostly my customers come, buy and take the beer while standing and they move away as soon as possible. Customers who are in a group sit because they buy a large quantity say for eighty shillings, which they then share amongst themselves".

The local brew business of the type described in the excerpt presents livelihood diversification at both ends of the employment relationship. The employer aims at making a profit and therefore gaining an additional income, and this goal is reached. For his part, the employee has work and earns a commission for the amounts of brew that he sells. Thus he is able to get an income and to diversify his livelihood in some way. Besides, those who make the brew are also continually making their sales and redirecting their livelihoods accordingly. The critical point about this arrangement is that the employee agreed to bear the risks of arrest and even imprisonment in exchange for a commission. This risk taking points to the level of unemployment in Nyamira District and the extent of experimentation on the part of young people in order to earn some income. Opportunities for income-generating are also apparently lacking, prompting them to take up such high risk ventures. The fact that the employee remains in employment even after his customers are arrested severally and his premises raided a number of times by the police indicates that the business is good and he makes money both for himself and for the employer. The undertakings of these two men also indicate that the business is core to their livelihoods and that giving up would spell doom to their lives. They therefore continue with their struggles for survival, winning here and losing there, and on balance continuing to make a living. This scenario also explains the shrinking place of farming in the livelihood of these two actors and perhaps their households. If farming could earn them a similar amount of income, they might perhaps have tried it, rather than sticking it out with a business that exposes them to so much undesirable risk.

Another dimension of the local brew economy is that it depletes resources in certain livelihoods even as it enhances those of the traders. This is a debatable assertion because consumption is a choice and arguing about whether it is right or wrong, or more accurately, viable or unviable, is nether here nor there, because livelihood construction is about choices and meeting goals and aspirations in life. *Nyakenywa* - 'those who drink themselves silly' (see chapter seven) aspire to enjoy life in that way, that is the best they hope for everyday and therein rests their livelihood success. But looked at from the outside it is possible to deduce that the sacrifices on the part of family and household members to support a *nyakenywa* lifestyle are enormous and undermine food security, children's education and other household-wide aspirations. The apparent precedence of one actor's preferences over all others in a household is not a common way of life locally. Therefore, the *nyakenywa* sub-culture is not the most celebrated lifestyle in Sengeta, but it is a lifestyle for some people all the same.

Crafts: Basketry, Thatching and Ballast-making

Crafts like local brew production are a historical phenomenon. The Abagusii have been involved in crafts of different types since time immemorial, making bows and arrows, hoes and soapstone products since the 1600s when they arrived in their present settlements. Such industries have been documented by historians (Maxon, 1989; Levine and Levine, 1966) in significant detail and are beyond the scope of this thesis. The concern here is on the forms of craft making that have been commercialised in ways that they constitute alternative avenues to economic activity and income generation that supplement farming as a means of livelihood. Crafts of this kind have been in existence throughout history but have found new expressions over time and are increasingly produced for the market rather than for home use, as was the case during the pre-colonial period for instance.

A common craft in Sengeta is basketry. Beyond the fact that basket-making skills are passed on informally from generation to generation, the origins of these skills are not well known. Saulo is one of the villagers who has mastered basket-making skill and is making money out of it.

> Since 1959, Saulo gets some additional income from thatching houses. He said that thatching houses is taboo for women in Gusiiland; it's purely a male

occupation, although since 2000 contracts to thatch have become rare. This, he explained, is because of the rarity of grass for thatching owing to population pressure. The land previously left to grass has been turned over to food and tea growing, especially on the hilltops. Besides, many people prefer corrugated iron sheet roofs. Saulo also weaves baskets for sale and specialises in baskets used for chicken rearing, grain drying and storage, and for carrying green tea leaves to the buying centres.

From the extract, it is clear that Saulo makes baskets for carrying tea from the farms to the tea buying centres. This means that the widespread adoption of tea growing in Nyamira and neighbouring districts from the 1960s has redefined basketry in the region. Macro policies by both the colonial and the post-colonial governments of promoting tea production may have directly provided opportunities for Saulo and other craftspeople like him to commercialise their products and thus diversify their livelihoods. Otherwise the demand for the baskets would have been too limited to ensure a steady income from basket making. Tea growing thus spurred the growth of basketry in Gusiiland and opened up opportunities for the further development of skills, materials and products.

Basketry in the service of the small scale tea industry can be said to place producers such as Saulo firmly in the tea value chains and thus as part of the global tea processes and trade (cf. Tallontire, 2001). Saulo's survival as a basket-maker therefore hinges on specific global processes and on the 'new imperial order' that keeps such global trade like the tea trade in place (Petras and Veltmeyer, 2001). In this perspective, basket making that is geared to the service of tea production is subject to the global obstacles that face the world tea trade and its governance. Therefore, although far removed from the power games at World Trade Organisation (WTO) negotiations in major world cities, Saulo is intractably trapped in their outcomes and can be a victim of such negotiations.

Saulo also makes locally specific mats – *orwambo* (pl. *chindwambo*), used for sun drying grain such as maize and finger millet, and he makes baskets for other uses such as for storing millet grain and for keeping chickens. However, these are not as fast moving as those for handling tea leaf. A few people purchase them occasionally, especially for keeping chickens. *Chindwambo* are mainly made for women on site in their homes, as they are difficult to transport over long distances. This line of business was apparently undermined by the use of synthetic materials for sun drying grain. Given the range of basketry products that Saulo makes, he is still in business because of being able to plan his production according to demand. Basket making is an important source of income for Saulo especially after dividing up his land for inheritance by his sons and being left with limited land and tea bushes.

Basket making is closely linked with thatching houses as some of the villagers who make baskets also thatch houses. But thatching houses is another of the oldest skills among the Abagusii people. It requires comfort with heights and sobriety while at work. This was particularly important as accidentally falling from a roof top about twelve metres high could be fatal. But the work also requires the energy to balance on a roof and to withstand the hot sun while working during most of the day. It is for this reason that Mokogi is increasingly shifting from thatching houses to basket making as he gets older. Basket making is less hazardous and less demanding.

> Mokogi said, "These days I thatch houses only for my close friends and relatives who seriously value the quality of my work and strongly desire my services. This is due to the ill health I am experiencing nowadays. When I thatch I get backache, which has made me shift from thatching houses to weaving baskets for carrying green tea leaves. I sell these baskets to supplement my income from thatching and other activities. I have used the money I have been getting from thatching houses to meet the basic needs of my family, such as paying school fees for my children. I have also bought a few chickens".

The excerpt from Mokogi's case record suggests that he prefers to work for his relatives and friends. The strength of kinship and friendship as the basis for rural everyday life emerges in his approach to thatching. The best service is reserved for relatives and friends, regardless of the risks. This is further evidence that some livelihood transactions are based on kinship and friendship. Trust is highest among kin and friends, and the reasons Mokogi invests in that trust at the risk of fatal accidents relate to the strengthening reciprocal relations with those who may be of assistance to him in the future. Such these expectations are never obvious in ordinary discourse, but are subconscious, staying hidden until there is a need for assistance. Mokogi's strategies therefore bring out the two levels on which livelihood diversification works. At the first level, he uses his skills to earn an income from thatching. At a second level he creates some form of latent resources by investing in strengthening his kin and friendship networks. This will help him to diversify his livelihood in the future by drawing on the latent resources created earlier.

Ballast making is a common form of livelihood diversification and it is a new phenomenon gaining currency only recently, when more and more people began to build permanent houses both in the homesteads and in the markets. The permanent houses require ballast and because machine-made ballast is expensive for most people, many prefer ballast made locally by hand using a small sledge hammer. Angima is one of the villagers involved in ballast making.

> Besides the chang'aa business, Angima deals in quarry stones for construction. He buys stones from the nearby Geita hill which was for common use in the 1970s but has become a commercial source of quarry stone for house construction with each family that owns a portion of land there quarrying the stones and selling them or making ballast. Angima's main ballast customers include teachers who built their residential houses in the village and neighbouring ones. He said other

customers come from the market centres to buy for the construction of shop buildings.

Angima's ballast making venture serves two purposes that relate to livelihood diversification. The first relates to spying on any approaching police or other law enforcement officers as he works by the roadside, and alerting those drinking in his compound. This supports the *chang'aa* business in the background and entrenches his household's diversified livelihood. The second purpose relates to the income that he makes by selling the ballast. At least since 2004, this enables him to supplement his farming and *chang'aa* income. An interesting aspect of the ballast making venture is that selling is linked to the social networks developed over the years. Angima has sold ballast to his old friends the Jonathans and other people they put him in touch with. These social networks have been a special resource in his ballast business and thus his diversification process. It is perhaps in this sense, as Long (2001) has argued, that social relationships become 'springboards' into new branches of economic activity.

During his stint working in the tea plantation in Kericho District in the 1950s, Nyandika learnt tea pruning. He has used these skills ever since he retired in 1960 to earn extra income with which he supplements his tea and other income.

> Asked why he retired early at the age of only twenty seven, Nyandika said "I had learned many things already by that time, from driving to pruning tea and knew that I would not fail to do my own work without being supervised brutally by white people. When I came home I continued making money from pruning people's tea locally in the village". His second born son, who completed secondary education, is married, farms and prunes tea for other farmers in the village.

Nyandika prunes tea for other farmers and charges them per bush pruned. He has also trained one of his sons and more or less 'passed on the knife to him'. By training his son to continue with the skills in the village, he has set in motion another livelihood diversification process as he himself is exiting because of age. The scope for diversification as a result of the application of tea pruning skills is enormous as tea growing has spread significantly over the years and it is pruned every two to three years depending on the variety. The challenge for Nyandika's son is to quickly inherit and keep his father's network of friends to sustain the business.

Brick making was also observed to be taking place along the river valleys and by the swampy plains.

> Poris started making bricks in 1999. He made two thousand bricks and sold each at five shillings each in 2002. Later he made another four thousand bricks which he sold for twenty thousand shillings. With the income from bricks, he teamed up with his brother-in-law and bought a plot at a nearby market. The total cost of the

plot was sixty thousand shillings. He went to Nyamira Tea savings and cooperative society and took out a loan of ten thousand shillings to clear his part of the price. They then constructed a semi-permanent house on the plot, which they have leased out to business people. One wing of the house is being used as a butchery shop and the other is a grocery shop. The tenants pay them five hundred shillings per wing per month. The partners have a joint bank account into which the monthly earnings from the house are deposited. The money is a saving for improving the house. If the money increases, they plan to buy another plot.

This is another important avenue for livelihood diversification because a chain of actors are enabled to diversify. The first group of actors includes those who sell trees that are cut and used as fuel wood to fire the brick kilns. The second group is those who prepare the clay soil for brick making by moulding and fermenting it. The third group includes those who actually make the raw bricks using wooden boxes and arranging them to dry in readiness for firing. The fourth group is those who arrange the dry raw bricks into the kilns and fire them. The fifth group is those who transport bricks from the valleys to the road sides for sale. And the sixth group is of course the owners of the brick making enterprises who pay each of the foregoing actors and end up making profits after they sell the bricks. Often, most of the actors originate from one or two villages, and this has a similar diversification impact as the wood fuel trade discussed earlier. Given the scarcity of opportunities to make an income, there is an intense struggle to participate in the various aspects of brick making, especially in the less skilled tasks like cutting wood for firing and transporting bricks. Overall, brick making contributes to livelihood diversification in a variety of ways in Sengeta, especially because of the growth of the construction industry in recent years, which, as indicated in Chapter 1, is the result of the growth of tea growing and of cooperative societies. The cooperative societies offer competitive loans to members and enable them to build houses easily.

Conclusion

In this chapter it has been argued that livelihood diversification takes different forms in Nyamira District. The forms of livelihood diversification discussed are: kinship, friendship and gift giving; employment and remittances; trading; local brew production and sales, and crafts. All these forms of livelihood diversification are socio-historically constructed and embedded. Taking a historical perspective, I have shown that the various forms of livelihood diversification have existed in Nyamira since time immemorial, but that they are changing. For example, craftsmanship such as basketry is now linked to tea production and the makers have a new niche in the markets. By defining resources broadly to include material and non-material aspects, I have discussed the creation and flow of resources outside the 'farm', such as marriage and bride price exchange, as sites for livelihood diversification. This is because marriage itself constitutes non-material resources in terms of identity and also because the gifts exchanged in connection with a marriage have more significant implications for livelihood transformation than may have been the case historically, when such resources may have been locked in a series of marriages. The discussion has also emphasised the important role of social relationships in livelihood diversification and in the ensuing efforts to create resources. For instance, in locating employment, actors rely on existing kin or friendship networks. The same applies in the start-up of businesses in the villages, whether it is *chang'aa* production ventures or livestock trade. Customers for the various businesses and crafts products are also mostly located along kinship and friendship networks until the markets are expanded as experience is gained. This discussion has gone beyond existing analyses such as Ellis's (2000) that are premised on agriculture as the starting point in livelihood diversification and on a view of resources as largely material. It places the combination of farming and other activities in its historical context and shows how livelihoods and resources transcend their material aspects.

Overall, most livelihood diversification forms such as village-based businesses involving *chang'aa* and other items are informal. The casualisation of businesses and employment varies the scope of diversification significantly among villagers, but also opens up new sites for contests between the state and villagers. This implies tax and rates evasion, and rent-seeking behaviour on the part of state officials. Politics is also deployed to defend 'illegal' businesses such as *chang'aa* dealerships by labelling them as part of local customary heritage.

Remittances from Kenyans in urban areas and from abroad define local livelihood diversification in significant ways. Some of the remittances that are deployed with the missions and visions of the remitters imprinted on them involve considerable negotiation among actors located in different places but with an interest in given households. The outcomes are diversified livelihoods both at household levels and beyond, as the new activities rework the landscape with a variety of results, including redefinition of phenomena as resources, with new or additional meanings and uses. Some of the remittances and other diversification proceeds are used to intensify farming, especially through dairy production, which also means intensified napier grass production. Next, in Chapter 9, I turn to the various lifestyles on the bases of which villagers protect their livelihoods, and which they go between, depending on how they handle livelihood diversification and make a living.

CHAPTER 9

Lifestyles and the Search for Social Security in Everyday Life

Introduction

This chapter looks at how villagers organise themselves individually or in league with others to protect their livelihoods and attain the ever-shifting status of social security on their own terms and in line with their own preferences. I commence with a brief review of social security studies to bring out the debate to which the chapter contributes. Thereafter, drawing from case material presented in previous chapters, five styles of livelihood protection and thus for the pursuit of social security are discussed. The five styles through which villagers protect their livelihoods are: accumulators' lifestyle; lifestyle on the edge; lifestyle in the shadows; grey lifestyle; and, the opportunistic dependency lifestyle. These lifestyles are not so much practical ways that actors organise themselves, but rather analytical representations of their everyday life. The coherence of practices, socio-cultural dispositions, identity and organisation, that is characteristic of actors' everyday life qualifies them as emerging lifestyles in Sengeta. It is concluded that actors are always conscious of threats to their livelihoods and devise ways to mould their lifestyles in directions that help avoid disruption, but even so disruptions often occur due to 'environmental factors' beyond their control.

Social Security Studies: A Brief Review

One of the key destabilising forces of livelihood is vulnerability. Vulnerability has been defined as 'a high degree of exposure to risk, shocks and stress; and proneness to food insecurity' (Chambers, 1989; Davies, 1996; both cited in Ellis, 2000: 62). Chambers sought to distinguish poverty, which he defined as 'deprivation, lack or want' from vulnerability, described as 'defencelessness, insecurity, and exposure to risk, shocks and stress (Yamin et al. 2005). Yamin et al. argue that vulnerability and poverty are not the same – the former concept depicts the factors that drive people into poverty, keep them there and block their exit routes. In refining the concept of vulnerability, Ellis deploys two other concepts, resilience and sensitivity (Ellis, 2000). Resilience refers to the ability of an ecological or livelihood system to bounce back from stress or shocks while sensitivity denotes the magnitude of a system's response to an external event such as a shock. An Economic Commission for Africa's (ECA) definition of vulnerability makes the link with resources.

The ECA (2002) views human vulnerability as the lack of key assets, which exposes societies to increased risk of poverty. Poor people tend to have not only low incomes, but also low and unstable natural resource bases. In consequence, their livelihoods are more likely to be disrupted by prolonged drought, major crop failures, or devastating human and livestock diseases. Ellis (2000) classifies these disruptive factors, which he describes as 'livelihood mediating processes' into two; endogenous factors that include social relations, institutions and organisations and exogenous factors such as economic trends and policies, and unforeseen shocks like floods, pests and diseases. He concludes that endogenous factors modify access to resources, while exogenous factors provide the context within which actors devise livelihood strategies. Moreover, these mediating processes evolve over time, often with ruptures or stresses and strains. These conceptualisations of vulnerability begin from the premise of the inadequacies of actors and obscures how they rise from the abyss. As actors do (attempt to) climb out of the abysses of inadequacy more emphasis should be placed on their creativity and struggles.

In order to position this analysis within the dynamism and creativity of rural life, this study views vulnerability as a dynamic process. Actors juggle resources and opportunities in a variety of ways in an attempt to come out stronger and to survive the worst conditions. The challenge for them is to avoid sliding into irreversible responses to crisis, such as selling off their production assets or dissolving the family unit (Kabeer, 2002). Actors face trade-offs between their search for security and the value they give to the dignity and self respect of members, which sometimes involve choices between different kinds of 'ill-being' rather than different kinds of well-being (cf. ibid). Thought of in this manner the concept and state of vulnerability appears to more closely denote actors in search of social security. Presenting actors in this way frees us analytically from viewing them as living in the state of defencelessness and insecurity that is implicit in the concept of vulnerability.

Originally, social security programmes were designed primarily for the purposes of poverty alleviation to bridge the gap between the socially dysfunctional and what society considered the socially functional. Thus the aim was to enhance social functioning where it was lacking (cf. Siporin, 1993). Social security programmes originated in England mainly through the Elizabethan Poor Laws, which aimed at regulating labour and controlling vagrancy by using public revenues to alleviate poverty (Midgley, 1993; cf. Macarov, 1993). Midgley (1993) further argues that the link between social security and poverty has been explicit as shown in Britain's Beveridge Report of 1942 and in the United States through the Social Security Act of 1935, which captured the belief that social security would help in preventing poverty in the future.

Therefore, social security is a legacy of centuries of effort to provide people with a means of support in times of individual, social or economic distress (Dixon and Scheurell, 1993). The social norms that mould society's perceptions of social security result from an accumulation of preferences generated by a people while shaping their specific society. The institution of social security is thus part of a society's heritage, an indelible mark of her history and aspirations. This is why the British Poor Laws were essentially an acknowledgement of the Judeo-Christian traditions, in which the church assisted the poor in its vicinity. The social security programs resulting from the Poor Laws of 1601 were organised around church parishes (see Persky, 1997: 179). With these early beginnings social security has evolved considerably, first in the western world and then to other regions thereafter. This evolution has led to the development of traditions that promote and enforce patterns of beliefs, prejudices and preconceptions about social security, about its gainers and losers (Dixon and Scheurell, 1993).

Social security programs in developing countries do not reach the vast majority of the population who live in conditions of poverty and deprivation because the formal employer based programmes do not cover the vast peasant agricultural and urban informal sectors (Midgley, 1993; van Ginneken, 1999). Midgley (1993) also reveals that besides the limited reach, social security programmes in the Third World are sometimes poorly administered and ineffective, especially due to corruption. As public institutions their legitimacy and governance are too contested and personalised to guarantee long-term rights to groups in greatest need (Wood and Gough, 2006: 1697; cf. Lund and Nicholson, 2003). An exception in this African picture is South Africa where services such as pensions are beginning to provide safety nets for households of all races and in some cases reducing chronic poverty (Slater, 2002).

Kenya's formal social security system is almost entirely employer-based, leaving out those in the peasant and informal sectors, except in the health sector where some benefits are open to anyone who can pay an insurance premium to the National Hospital Insurance Fund (NHIF). The minimum premium is 160 Kenya shillings (about two US dollars) per month, which is too high for most peasants and the unemployed. Dixon and Scheurell's (1993) contend that there are village, tribal or family level informal social protection mechanisms in the Third World that interface with formal social security measures. However, in many countries, such as Kenya, the informal and formal social security institutions hardly interface in any meaningful way. Similarly, in Tanzania, the majority of the population create their security outside of formal systems (cf. Steinwachs 2002).

Consequently, social policies in developing countries relegates the poorest segment of the population (often the great majority) to 'self-help', or self-organised social security mechanisms (Nooteboom, 2003). This provokes the question: how do villagers organise themselves individually or in groups to deal with their vulnerability and attain a status of security in everyday life? This study adopts Nooteboom's (2003: 33) definition of social security as 'all ways in which individual people, households, and communities protect their livelihood and are protected socially against the shocks and stresses that threaten its continuity and stability' and then responds to the question. This definition goes beyond traditional ones by de-essentialising the role of the state in social security and the assumption that majority of citizens have reached a certain satisfactory level of living which the state would help them protect (cf. Tostensen, 2004). Therefore following this and Steinwachs' definition (2002: 4) social security should be seen as including efforts to first, protect against sudden loss of incomes and livelihoods; second, protect against the reduction of means of existence, and third, to enhance people's capability to cope with uncertainties. The task here as Kaag, *et al.* (2004: 59) argues is to focus on the multiple ways in which people try to secure their livelihood, *directly through their own efforts or indirectly through support and care from others* (my emphasis).

Styles in the Search of Social Security

This chapter discusses five identifiable lifestyles from the corpus of data and from practical observations in the field. These are not the only possible categories of lifestyle, but are representative of the social landscape. The first lifestyle, one to which villagers aspired, is the accumulators' lifestyle. In this lifestyle accumulation in terms of land, cattle and children's education, and investment in social relationships in the extended family, clan and church are fundamental. The second is the lifestyle on the edge in which accumulation has largely failed; investment in social relationships is weak and intergenerational support and relations are problematic. Third is the lifestyle in the shadows, in which activities invisible to casual observers and even researchers dominate resource creation processes. These include livestock tenant keeping, leasing out land and tea. Social relationships are invested in and they remain strong and crucial to sustaining the activities that are largely anchored on trust on both sides of transactions. The fourth is the grey lifestyle where theft, local brew, marijuana and 'corruption' in tea buying centres are the cornerstones. Social relationships remain important and those involved in this lifestyle invest heavily in them. Finally, the opportunistic dependency lifestyle consists mainly of habitual drinkers, *nyakenywa*, who rely on social relationships to get quick cash but do not invest in them. These are essentially hard working people, mainly young men hooked to local brew and easy money, that they seek through quick piece work and long-term activities that pay daily such as well and pit latrine digging.

The various styles of livelihood protection and the search for and maintenance of social security discussed in this chapter constitute analytical schemes of villagers' everyday life, not livelihood positions and strategies that actors deliberately and neatly put together. The lifestyles therefore represent a general characterisation of related attempts to protect livelihoods and search for security as observed in practice and deduced from the case material. It is not an attempt to arbitrarily box villagers into certain watertight categories; rather it is an attempt to typify their varied constructions of social security in everyday village life. In so doing, some actors may look like they fit into more than one style. This re-emphasises the view that livelihood construction and its protection from collapse is a continuous and ever-changing process. It changes in direction and in content over time, from season to season, as actors rethink their strategies, re-work, and re-style their ways around resources. As Steinwachs (2002) points out, many of these changes can be explained in terms of social change and transformation of social relationships and reorganisation of resources. Characterisations of these various emerging styles of livelihood protection and search for social security are discussed below.

Accumulators' Lifestyle

The starting point of protecting a livelihood is the actors themselves as individuals or in groups. It is in the actors that the livelihood being protected resides and it is there that the will to re-style and re-work the livelihood in new or different ways in order to avoid disruption is also located. The livelihood is defended because it serves the actor in their circumstances but may need to be reconstructed to better reflect their preferences and aspirations. Even in positions of extreme weakness and vulnerability, actors attempt to build on what they have in terms of social networks and other resources in order to slowly but surely overcome disorganising and demeaning circumstances. They are not absolutely insecure and defenceless; they have many ways out and many viable defences.

As a first line of defence, actors summon their creativity and experimentation skills to deploy their resources in ways that propel them to the status of social security, where they can meet their basic needs as well as look into the future. In looking into the future they search for security in at least two respects. Firstly, in terms of sequential time, such as the next day, week, season or year, depending on the nature and extent of security so far attained. Secondly they search for security in their old age and, by extension, through and for the next generation. Actors who have met their basic needs in the present start to consider their old age, however distant or close it may be. They may not say it to anyone, but through their actions they prepare for it in the best way they know. The aspect of the future in terms of the next generation relates to the old age terminating one generation and ushering in the next in the practical African sense of patriarchy and matriarchy. It is understood that at the termination of one generation, property is passed on. In many instances this happens as a matter of course; but blessings and curses may also be wielded at that time. For instance, when Saulo's sons are drunk they threaten that they will take away his *emonga,* but he tells them: "you know my last weapon; I will curse you, *inkobarama*". This demonstrates the issue of a curse more or less as a weapon of last resort in defence of his means of livelihood (land and tea) from encroachment by his wayward sons and wife. By contrast, the issue of blessings unites generations in preparation for and during old age and is a meaningful social action. The fear of a curse and the prospect of blessings from the aging and mostly ailing parents; the patriarch and the matriarch, encourage the younger generation to support and provide for them as far as possible, and this is usually appreciated in the term , '*monyue mache maya'* (fare thee well) a blessing for the future generation.

The crucial challenge to the protection of a livelihood lies in engagement with the future in terms of sequential time such as the following day, week, season or year. Petro's case is typical in the way he confronts the future both sequentially and inter-generationally. He started constructing his livelihood through his own initiative, which with the assistance of others in his networks of social relationships saw him go to work in the tea plantations which later saw him through school.

> In 1942, Petro's neighbour and uncle who already worked in the plantations assisted him with temporary accommodation and to get a job there. He worked in the tea estates plucking tea between 1942 and 1947 at a salary of three shillings per month but hardly saved any money for future use. While working in the tea plantations he came to appreciate how easy it was to tend the tea crop and developed an interest and aspiration to own his own tea crop in the future. After working in Kericho for six years, he came back home and started school at age 21 in 1948. He supplemented his savings from plantation work with maize and pyrethrum growing to raise his school fees, because his parents did not help pay for his education. He sat for his Common Entrance Examination (CEE) in 1954 and passed.
>
> After primary school he was employed on probation as a teacher. He worked as a teacher for two years (1956-1958) and left the job because the salary of one hundred shillings per month was too low. In 1960 he joined a cooperative society as a treasurer and later as Store Keeper for a salary of one hundred and seventy shillings per month. During that time he saved five hundred shillings with which he bought an exotic dairy cow. The cow used to produce eight litres of milk per day, but died after only two years. He has however, always kept a cow ever since. In 1969 Petro bought land at Irandi about two kilometres from his home for 1600 shillings. This money was from his tea and pyrethrum earnings, and from a bank loan. He planted 1600 tea bushes on the land and later increased it to 3000 tea bushes. One of his sons is a school teacher in the Rift Valley Province and has bought a farm there. He regularly visits his parents and assists them whenever there is material or financial need. In particular, he assisted with paying school fees for his younger brothers and sisters. Petro's daughters (one of whom is a teacher) and their husbands also assist with hospital bills and drugs occasionally.
>
> In 1970, Petro joined a group of six people each contributing five hundred shillings to start a business of buying and selling timber. "The business collapsed

> due to mistrust, the chairman ran it down but explained the collapse was due to sales on credit and defaulting customers". Petro used to be a member of several self help groups, including the Sengeta Education Group, which assisted with his hospital bills. He also used to be a member of Sengeta One Group although he never benefited from it. He quit the group earlier and it is now collapsing steadily. The group started in the late 1970s by pooling resources from about fifty villagers to buy matatu (taxi) vehicles. This was achieved without a hitch and a posho mill was purchased with the profits in the early 1980s and another in the early 1990s. Recently they sold the vehicles and there are rumours in the village that they are planning to sell the posho mills. Petro has subdivided the tea farm which he bought at Irandi for his son's inheritance. Each of them has been given 700 bushes.

Petro's spells in working as a teacher and at a cooperative society, show that he seems to have been thinking about the future in sequential terms. These thoughts evidently led him towards tea growing as a bulwark around his regular income, in case employment did not last in the face of changes. This was a wise move as the cooperative society job disappeared with the collapse of the world pyrethrum market in the late 1970s. With the tea, he had protected his regular income and with that his entire livelihood. But the act of planting tea was anchored on his social networks, directly and indirectly. Indirectly he relied on his earlier knowledge of tea from the plantations to establish his own tea. In this sense, he was building on the social networks that took him to the plantations in the 1940s in the first place. Directly he relied on his parents' and wife's labour networks – *amasaga* – for the task of tea planting. Thus in the accumulators' lifestyle social relationships are invested in and deployed from when needed.

Having survived the loss of a job by falling back on tea, Petro pursued his engagement with the future further by attempting to accumulate land and tea. He reorganised his tea and other earnings, purchased more land and planted it with tea. This enabled him to deal with the sequential future as well as the inter-generational future. In terms of the sequential future, he was able to assure a steady flow of tea income, even if the market value declined, through extensifying his production. With this accumulation he could look forward to his old age and deal with it more effectively. He used his tea earnings to send his children to school and in this way he was preparing for possible support in old age from children with formal employment and a stable income. The accumulation in land also focused on future intergenerational transfer of land and other resources. In terms of the outcomes of his children's education, some of them eventually landed formal employment as school teachers. He has finally fallen back on his purchased land to cushion himself during intergenerational transfer of wealth. This he did by dividing the bought land between his sons and leaving himself with the tea on the land he had inherited from his parents. This has assured him of a stable monthly income. Other villagers who fit this style of searching for social security include Isena who like Petro purchased land early in life and gave it to one of his sons when the time came, thus gaining more room for manoeuvre for his livelihood.

> Isena was born in 1952 and went to school early completing Junior Secondary School Exams in 1974. From 1975 to 1978 he worked in various places in casual jobs. He started as a van salesman in Eldoret in 1975, and then moved to Kericho with the help of his cousin to secure a contract plucking tea in a plantation up to 1978 when he came back home. That year he started planting his own tea, although some he benefited also from some of his brother's tea being on the land that was given to him when shared up their parents' land for inheritance. By that time he was frustrated with poorly paying short term work contracts. He had saved only four hundred shillings which he used to purchase tea seedlings. He also planted pyrethrum at the same time, which matured fast. He used his pyrethrum earnings to buy more tea seedlings and planted about 2000 tea bushes. He also planted tea on a plot he had purchased from his cousin, which he has already given to his first born son. The money he used to buy the land was from farm earnings. Isena was previously an official of the Sengeta One Self Help Group but is not keen to talk about the problems now bedevilling the organisation.

The aim of people like Petro and Isena, who typify this style is to minimise conflict and dissatisfaction in their households and avoid turbulent and disruptive struggles over resources. They do this by distributing their accumulated property to their sons for inheritance, leaving themselves secure on their inherited land.

Petro and Isena had also involved themselves in other activities beyond agriculture. Both had linked up with various people in self-help groups cum business organisations or in business partnerships. The two men had both been involved in a group that operated public transport vehicles and posho mills, but were now losing out as a result of more recent distrust in the leadership. Straddling or involvement in multiple activities appears to be the hallmark of the accumulators' lifestyle and way in which they defend a livelihood and maintain their security. The businesses that these two actors tried out ranged from posho mills, public transport and the timber business, and this indicates that they were keen in breaking into high value business, that would assure them not just higher profits but also perhaps job opportunities for their children. Following Ploeg, et al (2002) one can argue that actors in the accumulators' lifestyle attempt to ground their livelihood in new patterns of resource use and in pluri-activity to anchor themselves in off-farm income for perpetuity. These actors invest in social relationships and use them to borrow money whenever there is a need. Isena took a loan from a cooperative society to build his new permanent house and Petro received money from a self-help group for hospital bills incurred by his wife.

Isena and Petro are both practising Christians. Their participation in the church has probably moulded their children to be more compliant and shielded the parents from the waywardness that disrupted other livelihoods by children seeking their inheritance too early, leaving their parents in want or also misusing them because of local brew. In particular, Petro has received support from the church whose congregation provide finger millet for his wife's meals as she does not eat corn maize on medical counsel. Petro has invested in church affairs but also received support when he confronted death in his family and when his several children wedded in church. The church has provided food, logistics and presents and proved handy in times of need. As a large community it provides support that is varied and deep.

The church yields two forms of utility for its members in this life style. The first is ecclesiastical support, which emphasises the centrality of the patriarch and matriarch, and what is right or wrong in their eyes. This shields the parents from their children invading their means of their livelihood and instils the attitude that providing assistance in old age is a pious act. Petro has brought up his children in church and they have been exposed to God as a patriarch and their father as his representative in the family. The Adventist church in which he brought them up cherishes and teaches the Mosaic Law, particularly the Ten Commandments in Exodus Chapter Twenty. This includes one particular law that favours and protects parents and can be found in Exodus chapter twenty verse twelve: 'Honour thy father and thy mother: that thy days may be long upon the land which the Lord thy God giveth thee'. Such teachings have helped enhance Petro's patriarchal authority over his children, and to subdue them to his advantage. According to Mayer (1951) the Adventists were a powerful mission in the Gusii areas that proscribed the use of beer. This aspect of teetotalism as a way of life has also predisposed Petro's children differently from Saulo's, who drank with their parents at certain points in their lives until their father had to temporarily take refuge in baptism in the Adventist church. Second, the church provides material and non-material support in times of need, providing food and other material supplies (particularly the resources needed at times of bereavement), celebrating together during members' weddings and grieving together at times of bereavement.

Alongside the church or other religious organisation, this style of searching for social security also benefits from social relations and local community members. Petro has confronted death in the company of the extended family, neighbours and friends from the church and beyond. This support is expected because all members of these institutions make the same investment for others. The support is particularly important for actors in this style because they tend to invest handsomely with their time and money in these institutions. Petro at his early 80s is a member of the church choir, an indication of the efforts he makes in investing in the institution. While the church regularly responds to distress in members' lives, this is not always so among other networks of social relationships that actors rely on. The musician in a popular piece of Gusii music, the text of which is reproduced below, acknowledges that while many people turn up to participate in the preparations for and burial ceremonies of their neighbours and relatives there are others who create journeys out of the grieving village to avoid responsibilities.

Goika Otugute Oyomino by Master Chris Monyoncho: Kegogi New Band[56]

Ense eye tomenyete neyomoichano, naende ney'amaseko naende obosoku.

Abanto abange nkorora oyomwabo gakure, gose omoamate oye baka baike ang'e. Omongwana nigo akoimoka oroisia esafari gokwania abairi erio tamotindeka.

Ekero akoirana bwairire, nigo atindete, nario akogenda omochie oyio korwana chisegi. Oboria, embori nereo, nengoko nereo, erinde tweroserie tosoke isiko.

Baminto obwo nobosoku, ebiokoria ng'ang'e ore, korende komotuguta kwagenda esafari. Oyominto noba omwarimu, goika oimokie obokombe erio otugute oyomino.

The singer warns that it is shameful and laughable that an individual should avoid the responsibility of burying their neighbour or relative, but return later to the bereaved household and attempt to force their way into post-burial ceremonies. While this practice comes across as isolated the singer implores all, including apparently respectable people such as teachers to participate in burying their people. In Sengeta those who have no time to spare put in money to support the bereaved: community members in the diaspora send donations in cash to bereaved families when they cannot participate in the burial ceremonies. This explains the importance of networks of social relationships in this style of protecting livelihoods.

Overall in this accumulators' lifestyle actors struggle and succeed largely on their own account. Knowing the dangers of setbacks they also continually invest in social relationships as part of ordinary village life and in some cases as potential protection of their livelihoods. When things go wrong, they rely heavily on social relationships they have already built (Nooteboom, 2003). This reliance explains why they invest heavily in social relationships over time. The struggles that characterise this lifestyle relate to ensuring livelihood security in the interim and in the future. The challenges of the future that they understand and seek to confront are those of intergenerational needs and wealth transfers.

---

[56] English Translation

One must always participate in burying their own people

In this world you can't live without problems, laughter and shame

Some people support bereaved neighbours and relatives to bury their dead

But there is one of us who always creates journeys in order to avoid assisting in the burials of neighbours and relatives

Then he returns to the village in the evening drunk to cause a commotion in the home of the bereaved asking for rites food!

It is shameful to create journeys when your assistance is required, but return later to seek rites food!

Even teachers should carry implements and participate in burying their departed fellow villagers.

Success in this style appears to reside in the possibility of an actor moulding a set of social relationships and resources and deploying them in ways that assure livelihood stability through time and inter-generationally. Accumulation in land is one sure way in which these transitions over time and generation are managed successfully.

Lifestyle on the Edge: Digging in, looking inwards

The lifestyle on the edge is common in Sengeta village. The main feature of the lifestyle is that the actors have tried their utmost in supporting themselves as individuals in mainstream activities such as farming or legal trading but only succeeded to a limited extent. They have turned to low return and time-consuming activities such as crafts, thatching and peripheral trading, for example, selling by the road side. In responding to constrained cash flows they turn to unconventional cash crop marketing such as the *soko huru* for tea to get quick cash. Their investment in social relationships is limited and their returns from those relationships are low and insufficient to meet their needs. Their lifestyle may be characterised as neither a result of scarcity nor of recklessness, but of a combination of endogenous and exogenous factors. The endogenous factors include inter-generational, inter-sibling and inter-spousal conflicts over resources and, to some extent, significant local brew entrapments. These factors fracture the use of resources to bolster livelihood and in some instances drain them through litigation and counter-litigation over such resources. In a sense then, these factors expose the livelihood to insecurity and hasten the process of collapse. The exogenous factors include unfriendly market processes (such as of tea) that disadvantage the weak and poor and deprive them of resources, unfriendly local and formal dispute resolution processes and a lack of continuing education avenues in the weak educational system that engenders vicious cycles of failure. These factors constrain the availability of resources for constructing a livelihood and strangle efforts at protecting gains made by weakening the quality of the next generation in the labour market, hence undermining the interdependence between generations. Some examples from the case material will illustrate these issues.

Saulo's case best depicts a livelihood that he has historically built through creative accumulation. However when push came to shove, the interaction of endogenous and exogenous forces pushed him into a lifestyle on the edge.

> Since dividing his land for his wives and sons for inheritance, his life has changed. His tea earnings have dropped from about two thousand shillings per month to a mere four to five hundred shillings. His first wife plucks her own tea and Saulo's by herself, while he goes thatching houses and drinking. When she finishes plucking their tea, she goes out to pluck tea at neighbours' farms where she is paid four shillings per kilogramme. She uses the money to buy household necessities. Saulo only occasionally gets contracts to thatch houses and so has turned his attention more to basket making. Sometimes his friends assist him

> when he is in need, recently his friend who works at the tea factory gave him a hundred shillings to buy medicine for his first wife.
>
> Saulo's daughters are good to him, they visit him and leave him with twenty to fifty shillings for his busaa. Recently his sons-in-law visited and gave him 3000 shillings to assist him to take his wife to hospital when she had sprained her leg, although she was healed with traditional herbs. The money will assist them buy basic items at home and for his entertainment with busaa. They have only one cow at home, which his first wife takes care of. This came from his daughter's bride price. He thinks that his daughters have been very helpful in reducing poverty in his home and helping him live happily, sharing whatever he gets with his friends. None of the sons has paid bride price on their own initiative without his assistance. They hardly assist him, especially since he divided up the land for them and their mothers. His perception is that the division of the land caused his second wife and her children to disown him since he no longer has any control over his land and tea.

At the edge Saulo has tried to mould resources in a number of ways in order to protect his livelihood. First, he joined the Adventist church with a view to repulsing his wayward sons. He had however not invested much in the church institution and on his own admission, his reception there was poor and the leadership asked him to sort out disputes over resources in his household before joining the church fully. This apparently forced him out and he retreated to drinking again, just like his sons. When he did get around to dividing his land and tea for their inheritance, he found himself isolated especially by his second wife and her sons. This sent him into a second way of protecting his livelihood at the periphery. He cultivated a good relationship with his first wife and anchored himself in her house. While there, he relies on her for food and labour to work his few bushes of *emonga* tea. She also works on other people's farms plucking tea to earn money for food. While this protected his livelihood, his lifestyle remained on the edge, and he barely ekes out a living.

A third way in which Saulo seeks to protect his livelihood is by cultivating a good relationship with his daughters. This has worked significantly in the sense that they occasionally visit him and give him some pocket money for his drink. I deduce that the harder life became the more Saulo looked inwards for social support. He was able to receive some bride price for his first wife's daughter and sold off part of his land during the difficult times. This shows that he continues to negotiate and to protect his waning patriarchal authority to some extent. This explains why he used some of the money earned from selling the land to buy a cow and to contribute to payment of bride price for one of his sons. In so doing, he was seeking to rework his relationships with the sons by showing what he could offer to them. He also wanted to have some of his sons properly married, through bride price transfer to earn the status of *ekorera* in the village and attract respect. This demonstrates that a livelihood is not just about putting food on the table and increasing income, if so Saulo would have kept the money; it is also to do with self-actualisation and identity protection.

This is very close to Wallman's (1984) description of livelihood that transcends the material realms. The fifth way of protecting his livelihood is digging into his basket making and thatching, that he has done as a side line over the years. He now makes more baskets and tailors them more to the local tea trade. Although thatching and basket making do not pay well they have become central to his livelihood. At around age 80, it is inconceivable that Saulo can not retire from thatching and basket making, as he is keen on protecting his livelihood and maintaining his security.

Another actor protecting his livelihood in the same manner, even as his health is failing is Mokogi, whose case excerpt is reproduced below.

> Mokogi thatches houses but only for his close friends and relatives who seriously value the quality of his work. He suffers from ill health, and he has mostly shifted from thatching houses to weaving baskets for carrying green tea leaves. He sells the baskets to supplement his income, and to meet the basic needs for his family, such as paying school fees for his children and he also bought chickens".
>
> According to Mokogi Abagusii traditions bar women from thatching houses because it is equated with killing one's husband, that is to say if a woman went up the roof to thatch the house she is figuratively saying that her husband is as good as dead and she is crossing over to perform men's duties.
>
> "Recently, I was paid a bride price of three heads of cattle and a goat for one of my daughters. I grow passion fruits and tobacco, which I sell locally to traders who transport and resell it at Daraja Mbili market in Kisii Town. I do not transport it to the market myself because I grow only a little making it uneconomical to transport. I grow maize, bananas and beans for my own domestic use". Due to lack of contracts to thatch houses and his ill health, he passes time by making baskets. He said "I like making baskets because I do it while seated and I do not experience backache after the work". He continued: "I am constructing this semi-permanent house because the one I am currently staying in is inadequate and I want it used as a kitchen, when the new one is ready for occupation. The money I am using in this construction project is from tea leaves, tobacco leaves and passion fruit sales".
>
> As we sat and discussed, his cousin came and bought tobacco worth ten shillings to smoke. Mokogi also gave two baskets to his brother to sell for him at the tea buying centre the following day when farmers would be receiving their tea earnings. He has planted passion fruit between his pruned tea bushes. He goes against agricultural expert advice, and intercrops tea and passion fruits because he has so little land and from his experience neither crop suffers for being intercropped. As soon as he prunes the tea he plants maize in the spaces, trying to take advantage of the space before the tea forms a canopy over the ground preventing any germination underneath.

Like Saulo, Mokogi is aging but also ailing, however even though he is about 70 years old he continues to thatch houses because he also lives a lifestyle on the edge. Like Saulo he also wields custom to protect his livelihood. He argued that women are traditionally barred from thatching houses and did so arguably to protect his livelihood niche. This mirrors Saulo's wielding of his weapon of last resort; a curse from a father and patriarch to protect his *emonga* from his second wife and her sons. These two men, with similar skills have been pushed to the edge by different factors, but they protect what remains of their livelihoods in similar ways. Mokogi links up with his brother to sell baskets for him and he also sells tobacco. He does several small jobs to keep his life going and to protect his image as a patriarch and provider. This explains his construction project at his advanced age, when in other cases children appeared to support their parents to build better houses. For Mokogi as with Saulo the struggles on the edge go beyond income security to include identity protection and self-actualisation in having a home and children properly married with bride price transferred. The relative livelihood insecurity that Saulo and Mokogi struggle with confirm Okojie's (1988) findings that the elderly in sub-Saharan Africa are more insecure than often thought, especially as they are a relatively invisible population of the poor, hidden by the myth of the protective extended family. Most of the elderly operate a livelihood on the edge.

In other cases intra-household struggles over resources get sharper as the children grow up and their demands on the parents increase. For Saulo conflict over resources has driven his relationships in a variety of directions. With his sons drinking for the courage to agitate for a share of the land and tea for inheritance, Saulo embraced the church and sought baptism to avoid them. The misbehaviour of the sons after drinking also made their mothers abandon brewing, embrace the church and thus create new relationships. The sons found an unexpected and distant ally in the church which pushed their father to give them inheritance in land and settle disputes over land prior to his baptism.

The web of relationships in Saulo's household and with other external institutions such as the church shows the complexities of social management at household level. Saulo is caught up in the shifts and twists that ensue in intra-household relationships and is forced to not only seek external allies but to reorder his relationships in the family for survival as he finds himself largely abandoned and dispossessed. Saulo's abandonment by his second wife shows the process of family nucleation in Sengeta. This is occurring both because of women's increasing level of independence in Gusiiland and the greater autonomy they have once their sons reach maturity (Levine, 1979; Silberschmidt, 1999). This however does not fully explain Saulo's abandonment by the second wife because the first wife who took him in has older sons than the second wife. Perhaps this scenario might be explained by the second wife being younger and seeking a way to mould her newly acquired resources so as to improve her life. This aim may have led her to avoid Saulo whose lifestyle centred more on consumption of local brew than in accumulation. The contradiction in all these fluid relationships is that Saulo continued to reach out to his sons by helping them to pay bride price to regularise their marriages. He hoped to improve his social standing among other men in society and to win over some of his sons, even as he perfected his relationships with his first wife's daughters who assisted him. Whatever the motive in Saulo's and other household members' actions, it is clear that social relationships are fluid and may often defy logic and rationality, but still be useful for actors' preferences and strategies, as shown in Saulo's case where conflict, accommodation and avoidance are creatively interspersed in everyday life.

Inter-spousal conflict may also reach a higher level where threats of witchcraft are wielded with the aim of appropriating a social relationship in ways that may yield resources for a particular actor. The excerpt from Jason's case record, below, shows how two brothers were targeted with witchcraft in terms of poison disguised in their food or drink in what is alleged to be a struggle over tea earnings between spouses.

> In the course of my visits and discussions in the village I was informed that Jason's brother Osoro had been offered poisoned tea by his wife as he worked on the farm. The story was that she bought the poison from the market and put it in the tea. She carried the tea in a thermos flask to her husband where he was weeding tea. When Osoro went to take the tea he noticed that it smelt awful, he felt that it was not good tea. He called neighbours who also smelt the tea and said that it was mixed with poison. When he brought the tea home, he called more people to witness what had happened including his brother Jason. He took the tea and poured it on fresh grass, which quickly withered away although by that time the tea was cold – and so it was concluded that it was mixed with poison.
>
> After the incident, the allegations were brought to the attention of the village headman who presided over the case. Only family members were allowed to attend the deliberations. During the discussions Osoro requested the attendants to partition his land so that he could marry another wife. He said: "The cause of all these problems seems to be tea". Control of the tea earnings was the key issue. The woman does not work the land; only the man tends his tea and pays school fees for his children. The tea bonus (second earnings) might be the problem because the woman wants to have the money. A villager said, "Many people would have died since Osoro is not a selfish man. He usually calls people who work with him in his shamba to share whatever food is brought to him. I wanted to take the woman to the police station, but the owner refused and the evidence had already been destroyed".
>
> After the case at the village headman's court I met Osoro's mother at his homestead. She was disappointed and said: "I do not want to talk about the matter, the woman wanted to kill my son, after trying to bewitch him many times. All my sons are as good as dead; their wives want to finish them and control the tea and everything. Jason was almost killed sometime ago, but I advised him to leave the tea to his wife. He took my word seriously and he is okay now doing his own casual labour. I have told Osoro the same. He insists that he is the one who planted the tea and should be in charge. I thought people would chase that woman away for good, but they did not, they are still staying together that is all".

The excerpt shows that threats with witchcraft on Jason led his mother to advise him to turn his tea over to his wife's control in order to be safe. An attempt was made on his brother's life and that became a subject of the village headman's court case. Part of the struggle over tea earnings is because men tend to spend the money on local brew, often in total disregard of family needs. But increasingly women are interested in controlling the income, which is substantial in most households. They therefore fight for it even to the point of death. It is alleged that one man in the village had killed his wife when she insisted on a share of the tea earnings. Threats and actual deployment of witchcraft as part of struggles over household resources have also been reported in Meru District, Eastern Kenya over the income from high value French bean exports (Dolan, 2002). However, in Sengeta areas it is alleged that men go as far as committing homicide in order to defend their control over tea earnings and other household resources.

The threats with witchcraft and actual deployment have strained relationships between Osoro's mother and her daughters-in-law, with whom she was very angry. This conflict between mother-in-law and daughter-in-law over the manner in which she or her son is treated, is not uncommon, as indicated in the following a local popular song from the 1970s:

Omokungu omobe by Andrew Bundi Onyono - Eronge boka[57]

Omomura oyomo akanywoma korwa Manga agakorerwa enyangi.

Chiombe chiakorentereire,

Okanywoma omokungu ogoita mama omino, omoseria rero inchera amenyete.

Mama naba omobe nere mama.

This popular song is often played on the vernacular radio station and was produced in the 1970s, according to villagers. It is about a young man who married through a church wedding and his wife started mistreating his mother so much that she spends much time away from home. The singer sympathises with the young man saying – *chiombe chiakorentereire* – marriage has caused you trouble. This implies that the cattle-based relationship is causing trouble, but having committed to it, one must make the best of it. While Osoro's mother's anger at her daughters-in-law can be understood in the context of the dangers they posed to her sons' lives, the common aggression to mothers-in-law by daughters-in-law is a riddle. Part of the explanation can be found in the mother-in-law continuing to expect support from her sons and at the same time

[57] English Translation

A bad wife

One young man married a woman from Manga through a wedding

Marriage [cattle] has caused you trouble!

You married a woman who beats your mother and throws her out of the home.

However bad, your mother is your mother!

to control certain resources. This causes envy for their sons' wives, especially where population pressure means that resources are scarce. However conflict between a woman and her sons' wives is the exception rather than the rule in Sengeta village, as indicated by the cordial relationships between Nyandika's second wife and her daughter-in-law, and many others such as Petro's wife and her daughters-in-law who share milk cordially.

Another aspect of intra-household struggles over resources is that of co-wife rivalry. A co-wife's unloading of a husband onto another as happened with Saulo, may have caused anger between the wives, but it is not an issue on the surface. Co-wife rivalry is however common in Sengeta village and is expressed in periodic quarrels as shown in the excerpt from Bochaberi's case record, below.

> As if it happened on the day of interview, Bochaberi recalled with sullenness that after she had paid school fees for her husband through a lot of difficulties, he could walk away into the hands of another woman, leaving the burden of taking care of their children squarely on her shoulders. After the fallout Bochaberi went back to the farm again with determination and managed to educate all her children and cater for their needs.

The rivalry between co-wives mainly centred on the different burdens each had to carry, while suspecting that their husband was supporting the other more. The rivalry is about resources. These findings are similar to Dolan's (2002) from Meru District, Kenya although she found that the rivalry was expressed in terms of witchcraft threats, which was not found here. In both cases however, the aim was to protect resources and livelihood.

In general the actors operating this lifestyle on the edge are struggling to live and have not sufficiently invested in social relationships, although it is clear that they benefited significantly from them. This is shown for example in Mokogi's activities that thrive on supportive networks of social relationships. People ensconced in this style place limited emphasis on their children's education, which is often largely unsuccessful. Consumption of local brew is seamlessly weaved into their lifestyles, although they cannot be described as habitual drinkers – *nyakenywa*, they are more or less moderate and routine drinkers. Perhaps the most intractable problem in this lifestyle is that it lacks tendencies to accumulation whether in savings, land, livestock or education and this is a major part of the reason for its precariousness. It appears very likely that younger actors in this lifestyle will experience intergenerational conflicts over resources, because they have ignored accumulation and their children's education. These processes keep these livelihoods on the edge and make it harder and more complicated to protect them.

Lifestyle in the Shadows

In some cases the search for social security pales and disappears into the shadows of a conventional and regular livelihood. This essentially follows on from the significant failure of self-supporting activities and the absence of any accumulation of land, cattle or monetary savings. In the continuum of lifestyles, I am building in this chapter failure of accumulation seems to push a livelihood to operating on the edge. When an actor operating or searching for social security on the edge slips, the lifestyle no longer holds together on the edge and they land in the shadows; and begin to operate an invisible livelihood. The activities involved are subtle and invisible to a casual observer. One needs to be embedded locally to understand how resources are produced.

In the invisible livelihood in which actors the most important activities and resources are obscure from casual observation. Actors mould their resources in ways that defy local conventions and rely on higher levels of ingenuity and experimentation. They may pose as peasant farmers and appear so to their neighbours, but in practice the resources they apply to meet their critical needs or solve their most pressing problems may be largely invisible. Slater and Twyman (2003) argue that a hidden [or invisible] livelihood is not illegal or illicit. This study takes the same view of an invisible livelihood. Angima's is a case in point.

> Angima's late father owned coffee on about one and half acres but did not share earnings from the crop with them. Similarly he did not support them in any way with earnings from his herbal practice or any other income generating activities he carried out which included leasing parts of his land to tenants. Angima's most trying time in life occurred in 1972, (two maize seasons after he was circumcised) when there was a serious drought and the maize crop failed. He used to collect wild fruits from the nearby Geita forest, which had a thick natural forest and wattle trees on the edges. As the hunger intensified his father got food from a widow he had temporarily remarried and was able to support his mother and children with it.
>
> After their father's burial, Angima was assisted by his uncles and other village elders to demarcate their father's land equally for his brother and himself. He said "now I had my own land and was comfortable, I worked for Jonathan up to 1987 and left as planned to farm my own land". However, he did not start farming at that point and instead renewed a few of the land leases his late father had rolled out, to raise money for his local brew drinks. His brother lives on his land and works as a hired farm hand, and occasionally as a lumberman in the village. He is married and his wife concentrates on farming activities growing kale, maize and beans. Angima's family relies on her for vegetables, which they take on credit and pay for at the end of each week.
>
> In 1988, Angima's brother was arrested during a police raid at a chang'aa place. He was quickly taken into a Nyamira court and sentenced to five months imprisonment or a fine of five thousand shillings. Angima approached his former employer and friend Jonathan, and requested him to rent part of his brother's land in order to raise money for the court fine and get him out of prison. Jonathan agreed and hired a half an acre of land for three years at two thousand shillings per year. In 1990, Angima was attacked on his way home from drinking, by thugs

> whom he did not recognise. He sustained serious head injuries and elders recommended a surgical operation, for which, the indigenous head surgeon asked twenty five thousand shillings. Angima did not have the money and therefore sold a quarter an acre of his land for fifty thousand shillings to his cousin.

During the 1972 famine Angima's father may have appeared to casual observers to have pulled through using his income from traditional healing and the coffee crop. However, in practice the coffee crop on his farm had been abandoned for years and the failed crops on his farm were not his either, they belonged to other villagers who had hired the land from him. His healing career may have contributed, but not significantly. The real support for his livelihood and that of his mother came from an invisible source – a widow he had 'inherited'. This invisible source yielded the maize meal that many families lacked which gave rise to real hunger and famine locally. At this point in time the self-provisioning widow was his most important source of social security, but this was not common knowledge in the village. This echoes the informal risk management arrangements, such as marriage that Holzmann and Jorgensen (2001) identified as common among the poor.

The second most important source of social security for Angima's father at the time and which seems to be continued by Angima and his brother in their lifestyles is leasing out land. In leasing out land Angima's father effectively transferred the risk of food production to third parties in exchange for rental income. He was not affected when the crop failed although a casual look at his farm would have elicited sympathy. The income earned was useful during the famine period and it may well have been this money that endeared him to the widow. Fruit and berry gathering by Angima also constituted another shadowy manner in which the family protected their livelihood and found located food security during the famine period. In later years after his father passed on, Angima perfected the art of leasing out land to accumulators who pay rent for the land for a period of time ranging from a crop season to several years and worked it in the hope of getting yields whose value is exceeds the rent they paid for the land. The value is however not a market one as locally, self produced food has a premium tag on it. This is mainly derived from the unspoken views that only lazy people rely on the market for food and that home produced food is of a better quality. Leasing out land, even if it is not sufficient for own food provisioning, is thus not one of the most respectable things to do for a living in Sengeta.

Angima nonetheless leased out land to service his local brew consumption and to support his purchases of goods and services. Both he and his brother leased out land to get money whenever they were sick and needed cash in a lump sum. Their reliance on leasing out land was so entrenched that they even approached their neighbour and friend to lease their land when he had not expressed interest. This led Jonathan to lease the land, mainly to support them and because they trusted each other to the extent that neither expected the other, to turn around and claim more than they had bargained for. In this sort of transaction Jonathan comes across as a mercy tenant rather than a market based one. Land here is held like money in the bank, withdrawn whenever there is need to use it. The main contradiction in this behaviour and which underscores the unconventional nature of this lifestyle is that the land could fetch more if used for own production than if leased out. This explains in part why accumulators such as Jonathan leased land and others such as Petro even bought more rather than lease in. Contrary to these findings on land renting, Haugerud (1989) in her study in Eastern Kenya found that relatives among the Embu people who were poorer borrowed land from their better to do relatives.

Another closely related aspect of this lifestyle is leasing out tea bushes for an income. This practice, which is increasingly common in Sengeta, is as shadowy and unconventional as it is informal, turning tea production and sales from a relationship between a farmer and the tea factory to one between farmers. This mutation of tea based relationships is the result of shrinking opportunities and the search for social security. Excerpts from Ondima's case record make this point clearer.

> Ondima has been a farmer during most of his adult life, in the 1950s he owned oxen and he used to team them up with Jonathan's to plough their farms in turns. He planted tea in 1968 with the assistance of his cousin who was a tea extension officer. His cousin allowed him to plant as many tea bushes as he could, although people were allowed to plant only 2500 at the time, but he had enough land to plant about 3500 tea bushes. He used tea and milk earnings to pay school fees for his children. He has also built corrugated iron sheet roofed houses for himself and his youngest son. His other sons built theirs when they finally started working. One has retired and another was retrenched, so none of his children is presently in employment. He shared out land for their inheritance in 2000 and is left with some tea and land for planting food crops, which will eventually be turned over to them when he and their mother pass on.
>
> Ondima's earnings started dropping in 2000 soon after dividing up the land to his sons. He has to look for the easiest way to get money when he needs it especially during sickness. Sometimes he sells his goats and he able to solve a problem. Another time he requested his son who is a member of a self help group to borrow for him to pay his wife's hospital bill. Recently in 2003 he wanted to go to hospital, but needed to clear his son's debts with the self help group in case he had to borrow while he was away in hospital, so he decided to lease out some of his tea bushes to get the money. He approached some people in the village who usually hire tea bushes and they referred him to Jonathan's son. He called him to the farm and they counted nineteen rows, haggled over the price a bit and agreed on six thousand six hundred for three years. They signed an agreement before witnesses and he was paid all the money at that point.

It was a difficult decision for him to lease out his tea bushes, because as he put it one can not tell; the earnings may turn out to be more than what he's been paid, which is usually the aim of the one who rents. "I have never leased out tea bushes in my life, but when things get rough I have to live and there is nothing else to do. The money helped me to settle debts for my son and go to hospital. It is difficult to borrow so much money from any source, so only my resources such as tea can pull me out of trouble. But some people especially young people who drink too much, nyakenywa, play around with tea these days, they lease out everything and use the money for local brew. When they eventually have a problem that needs money to be overcome, they have nothing to help them".

Ondima relies on the remaining tea bushes for his day to day upkeep and hopes that he will get to the end of the lease period in August 2006 without needing to lease out more tea, as that will reduce his earnings to a bare minimum. He said, "Things have really changed, we were not allowed to lease out tea in the past, but in the last ten years one can lease all his tea and recover it later to continue farming. Now a tea bush has another form of value that did not exist in the past, it can be leased out like a rental house and reclaimed later. It is a good thing that this has happened but people have to be careful."

Ondima was for a long time socially secure and essentially was an accumulator. He invested in his children with significant success, but their retirement and retrenchment at almost the same time and their inheritance of his land complicated his livelihood pushing him to a lifestyle in the shadows. The circulation of actors from accumulators to an invisible livelihood, demonstrated in this case, underscores the fluidity of livelihoods and that nothing in their construction is permanent. Fortunes keep changing because the factors at play are both endogenous and exogenous; some are within the control of actors and others beyond it. The struggle to protect a livelihood therefore moves the pendulum in any direction, depending on the resources that an actor is able to summon and retain over his or her life course.

Like Saulo, Ondima slipped just at the point when he shared out his land and tea for inheritance. However, while Saulo had the basket making and house thatching skills, and the labour and loyalty of his first wife, Ondima lacked both and stared at his ailing wife sometimes helplessly. The struggle to break away from a farming career that is in a shambles pushes Ondima into an invisible livelihood much faster than Saulo. The interesting thing in this case is that unlike Angima, who sold his land when he faced a huge medical bill, Ondima started by having his son borrow for him from a self-help group and when pressure mounted for more resources he turned to leasing out his tea. This underlines the importance of historical factors in the way that an actor handles adversity. It shows that efforts to protect a livelihood so that it is not exposed to more insecurity are historically constructed. Angima sold his land because history of direct user attachment with it, like his father who also leased it out. He also had not developed it, so it was not worth as much as Ondima's tea. This high value development on Ondima's land cushioned him from exposing too many of his resources to handle his ill health problem. Leasing out the tea is a temporary undertaking to raise the required money to solve a problem at hand. Ondima could easily bounce back into the accumulation path in the future. The tea acts as a safety net, as a springboard able to help the actor bounce out of poverty, or at least resume gainful work (cf. Holzmann and Jorgensen, 2001). This is not the case Angima, who has shrunk his resources through irreversible land sales. This irreversibility according to Ellis, (2000) points to a more vulnerable livelihood; than Ondima's whose behaviour when faced with vulnerability is reversible with time.

To avoid people losing a key resource like land, and the intra-household tensions over land sales, songs have been composed and produced locally that warn people not to sell their land indiscriminately. One such song is reproduced below.

Titoonia Oboremo by Prof. Kenyanya & Ombui, Mosaiga Boka Boka[58]

Otakonyora n'oboremo bwabuchire okoonia oboremo kwagenda amasamba.
Gaki titoonia oboremo, engaki neike moranyore emechando.
Onye ndiria mwancha timoonia oboremo bwaino, engaki neike moranyore emechando.
Abaminto nigo tokumetie igoro y'abamura barero bachire amasamba.
Bachire amasamba batiga chinka chiabo.
Otakonyora n'oboremo bwabuchire, okoonia oboremo mwagenda amasamba.
Onye ndiria mwancha timoonia oboremo bwaino.
Engaki nere eraike moranyore emechando.

The song warns young men who sell their land and move to the tea plantations for work that there will be troubled times ahead for them because of land scarcity. The critical message in the song is that land does not increase. It points to the conflicts that may ensue after land is sold haphazardly, leaving

---

[58] English Translation

Do not sell your ancestral land

There isn't enough land so that you may sell and disappear to the plantations as you have!
Please do not sell land, with time you will face problems
If you could take heed, do not sell your ancestral land, with time you will face problems.
Compatriots we are worried about young men migrating to the plantations.
They have migrated and left homes without people!
There isn't enough land so that you may sell and disappear to the plantations as you have!
If you could take heed, do not sell your ancestral land,
With time you will face problems.

families without sufficient resources. Departure to the tea plantations after selling land is seen as a way of avoiding questions from relatives and friends about what has been done with the money acquired. Through such behaviour, the seller disguises himself in the work place, spends the money on beer and later returns home to the trouble of which the song warns. Predictably at the point of returning from 'work' in the plantations, those friends and relatives left behind will avoid the land seller who by then will be poorer. In a sense therefore indiscriminate land sales disrupts the local neighbourhood and kinship relationships in the long run. The findings on land and sensitivities over its sale or purchase, and its centrality in kinship and especially relationships between agnates, confirm Glickman's (1974) argument that the Abagusii view land as a political commodity, distributed according to a definite principle of kinship selection. Contention and protection of these selection criteria is the main basis of most conflict over land in Gusiiland.

Another of the invisible livelihood activities that characterise this lifestyle is *sagare* – livestock tenant keeping (see Chapter 10). In this practice an actor mostly an accumulator, gives a cow to another actor who has land and pasture but for a variety of reasons does not own cattle, to keep it for him as a tenant. The tenant feeds the cow, controls ticks and meets small veterinary expenses and more importantly controls the milk when the cow calves down. The owner of the cow takes away the weaned calf and may give it to another tenant to commence another tenancy cycle. When the tenant is finally able to purchase his own cattle or the owner wishes to repossess his cow, he gives reasonable notice for the tenant to plan the exit. Villagers told me that the owner of a cow already with a tenant must act with utmost morality when taking his cow away. He may not for example take away the cow soon after it has calved and the tenant only started enjoying his benefits, unless this is because of an emergency that each party appreciates. If it is just an excuse to repossess the cow to get milk for his own family, the tenant may sue at the village headman's court and recover the costs expended in taking care of the cow. Disputes of this kind are rare, as shown in the excerpt from a livestock tenant Ochiemo's case record, presented below.

> "I was born in 1942 in the Nyaura area and attended Iranya primary school up to standard eight in 1959. I lacked the fees to continue with school because my parents were poor. After leaving school I went to Kericho and worked in the plantations plucking tea between 1960 and 1963. My salary was forty eight shilling per month. In 1964, I came back home and built a three roomed grass thatched house and married my first wife in 1965, paying a bride price of four cattle and a goat. The cattle were from my sister Kemuma's bride price of five heads of cattle and a goat. After that I commenced farming, growing bananas, maize and passion fruits. I planted tea and pyrethrum in 1969, after my father divided up his land for us to inherit, and I got five acres".

"I used my tea and pyrethrum earnings to build my corrugated iron sheet roofed houses in 1978 when the tea earnings were good. I also married my second wife in that year. By then I had many cattle, some of which I had bought using my tea earnings and others from my sister Nyaboe's bride price of eight cattle. My brother took four and I kept four. In 1983 my father and mother started getting sick frequently and I sold one cow after another to pay their hospital bills. Both of them died in 1987 after I had spent most of my savings and my cattle pen was empty. My children were also going to school and needed school fees. The money I made as a carpenter and from roofing simple houses did not help much. Tea earnings were all going to school fees for children in secondary school. Even now most of the tea earnings go into school fees payments, although the children were girls and they have been married outside now and I do not see what the benefit of that education has been".

"I was without a cow here for a long time until late in 1988 when I decided to approach a friend of mine called Jonathan and asked him to give me a cow to keep for him so that my children could get milk. Jonathan is my friend because sometimes when he has small carpentry jobs I do them for him at a fair price. He agreed and gave me a cow. Luckily the cow gave birth after only two months and my children were very happy. I kept the cow for six years and gave Jonathan four calves. When one of Jonathan's sons was paying bride price in 1995, he used it to add to what he had raised".

Asked if it is not a loss to keep somebody's cow and or him to take all the calves and finally the cow, he said, "I do not think it is a loss. First, I have all the milk, the children consume the evening milk and in the morning I sell the milk. Besides, I have the manure and people do not look down upon me because my wives do not go to their homes to collect cow dung with which to plaster house walls and floors. You see the cow down there in the paddock, it is for sagare and I think it is beneficial. It is like taking a loan without interest, or my pasture is the interest. When everything returns to normal and I have money I will buy my own cattle but for now, these sagare cows have assisted me a lot, even if I cultivated all the land under pasture I could not raise crops equivalent to half the value of the milk my family consumes, let alone the amount of milk we sell. I will never regret accepting these cattle. If you ask my children, they will tell you the cow is ours, I do not go telling my children about cows, and only their mothers know the terms on which we have the cow, to avoid any future disputes."

"One of my sons in high school is doing his final year and he is promising. I hope he will pass and continue to college and help us when we get old. The younger ones in primary are also doing well. Three of my daughters completed secondary school already but did not do well. None of them is employed and they are all married". He has not received any bride price for any one of them but is hoping that will happen and perhaps enable him to own cattle again.

Ochiemo, like Ondima above, also fell out of an accumulation path due to medical bills. He had organised his life in such a way that he managed to put his children to school and improve his houses and only slipped as a result of his parent's ailments. This underlines the difference between accumulators or those like Petro who attempt to protect their livelihoods through accumulation and those whose lifestyle is organised around invisible livelihoods. For instance, Petro was able to mould his family and social relationships over time to overcome medical bills, while Ochiemo sank under their weight. Ochiemo is actually younger than Petro, but Ochiemo's accumulation up to the point when he faced adversity in the form of the medical bills was shallow and his social relationships were weak. This partly explains why he slipped into an invisible livelihood much faster than, say, Ondima. Ochiemo is representative of many actors in Sengeta who have land and pasture but, partly through factors beyond their control, have slipped to a point that they can only put milk on the table for their children through becoming tenant livestock keepers.

Tenant keeping is an ingenuous way of attempting to protect a livelihood and maintain a locally acceptable level of social security without compromising one's social standing and identity. It is rare that a tenant or owner of a cow given to a tenant reveals the transaction details to other villagers. When the cow given to a tenant originates from the village, the other villagers are left guessing whether it has been sold or not. This keeps the tenant's status intact, if not enhanced, within the meaning of cattle ownership. If the owner purchases the cow and delivers it directly to the tenant, it is even better, as ownership remains anonymous. Livestock tenancy may be turned into a hoax, but still retain the intention of protecting a livelihood. This happens when witchcraft is allegedly directed at cattle, maybe even resulting in their death. One villager told me: "My cattle have been dying a lot in the past two years, so to protect this one, I asked a friend of mine to buy it for me in the market and bring it in openly telling people that he was bringing it to me for *sagare* – to keep it for him as a tenant". This elaborate trick was intended to prevent his enemies from bewitching a cow that was thought to belong to someone else. Whether real or a hoax, livestock tenant keeping is an important way for protecting a declining livelihood and ensuring some form of social security where insecurity would otherwise occur. Levine and Levine (1966) assert that tenants are usually relatives of cattle owners, but this study established while that some tenants are relatives, they may also be trusted friends, neighbours or former employees. Trust is the key attribute sought by both parties in the livestock tenancy arrangement.

This lifestyle of invisible livelihoods is seamlessly interwoven in networks of social relationships. A key reason for this is that the lifestyle is dependent mostly on trust-based transactions such as inheriting a widow, leasing land and tea, and livestock tenancy. In all these transactions, the actor needs elaborate social relationships to locate the required 'customers' with sufficient money to lease their resources to enable them solve their problems or meet their needs. These social relationships are also required to secure good cattle to keep as tenants. The people offering the good cattle need to be trustworthy friends retained over a long period, as shown in Ochiemo's case. Before fully slipping into an invisible livelihood, a host of social relationships may delay the process and ensure social security for a time. In Ochiemo's case these included bride price based relationships and siblings. In Ondima's case it involved indirect use of a self help group loan acquired through his son. The point to be stressed is that social relationships are integral to a lifestyle in the shadows and the social security achieved in this way is largely based on such social networks.

An important observation on this lifestyle is that it is supported, and in turn supports, the accumulators' lifestyle in significant ways. This is characteristic of rural life where the economy is structured in such a way that the livelihoods of the well to do are dialectically linked to those of the relatively poorer. These structural links are simultaneously supportive and exploitative of the relatively poor. They are exploitative because the poorer are weakened and their resources siphoned at lower than usual or fair prices, but are supportive because, without them perhaps, the poorer actors could be worse off. In the cases discussed, without the money with which to pay medical bills or without much needed food and milk, the actors would have suffered livelihood insecurity. This brings the role of the state in ensuring social security into focus. One can argue that if the state intervened with free social services, including education, health and food rations or income support, then the need to apply resources in the manner described may have been prevented in some of the cases and this would hasten the recovery of the livelihoods. The notion of linking formal and informal mechanisms of social security advanced by Steinwachs (2002) therefore makes sense if only in terms of injecting more resilience into rural livelihoods and rejuvenating them over time.

Grey Lifestyle: crime and contraband in village life

In the emerging continuum of lifestyles in search of social security or the protection of livelihoods, the grey lifestyle appears to be the next logical destination of actors after failure in the invisible livelihood. This is not to imply that all those who fail in the lifestyle in the shadows or on the edge must of necessity end up in the grey lifestyle. Being 'illegal', the grey activities do not attract all those actors who would 'logically' fall into the lifestyle. The question of where the rest of those who slip through the various lifestyles in the continuum go is responded to in the next section of this chapter. The interesting thing to note with regard to this section is that some actors, having failed in their operations on the edge and in the lifestyle in the shadows, slip into the grey lifestyle in their endeavours to seek social security and protection. The social organisation of the grey lifestyle in Sengeta village has to do with crime such as theft; and, handling and trading in contraband or goods forbidden by law such as local brew and marijuana. Another aspect of the grey lifestyle relates to local 'corruption' in the small-scale tea sub-sector.

The issue of theft is common in the village discourse in Sengeta and villagers attribute it largely to 'the waywardness of the youth of these days'. However, from Joel's case record, an excerpt of which is presented below, it appears that his mother sanctions his relying on theft to protect his livelihood.

Some of the goods he was alleged to have stolen were recovered from her house and she apparently was happy with her son's lifestyle, and has benefited from it.

> Joel started petty stealing from neighbours around his home when he dropped out of school 1979. Wherever a neighbour raised an alarm he could flee home to his grandmother's place which is about two kilometres away. He started picking up the habit steadily and more frequently as he got addicted to chang'aa and marijuana. At one time, the villagers decided to break into his mother's house to look for their belongings, which they suspected Joel had stolen and they found very many of them. They set the house ablaze and for a while, Joel and his siblings moved from home to stay at their grandmother's place.
>
> Joel went to stay at his maternal aunt's home, some seven kilometres away and while there he initiated one of his cousins into the habit of stealing. Informants indicated that, "his cousin became more notorious and daring". He could steal from many homes and start selling the items cheaply, even near the owners' homesteads. At one point he was caught red handed with stolen items and the irate public set him ablaze. He was hospitalized with severe burns and he lost an arm as a result.
>
> At one time Joel was arrested, and after a stint in prison, he came back home and started brewing chang'aa and selling it himself. According to those who went to drink there, there was a lot of bhang (marijuana) left to dry in the open. The local administration officials went to arrest him after a tip off that he was engaged in illicit business and Joel engaged the three local administration police officers in a fierce battle injuring all of them. He wanted to shoot them but one local resident, an army officer on vacation at his home went and rescued the policemen and disarmed him. "He was remanded for about two weeks and then we saw him back in the village", said a villager. After leaving the remand cells he tried to behave like other people in the village, apart from selling rolls of bhang. He reared over five hundred chickens, but at night he used to take his police uniform and a pistol and go to steal. With this dirty money he was able to build a semi permanent house which stayed in until his death.
>
> A villager said: "I suspect he had a lot of money in his house which his wife used to bribe the policemen and I think that she had taken an oath not to talk to anybody about his activities". His cousin said, "As my cousin, I never socialised with him very much. I feared him since he was a very bad man. He used to collaborate with his mother a lot. Most of the stolen goods were kept at his mother's house. I even feared going to greet my aunt because Joel used to beat his wife badly and even chased away his two brothers who were staying with friends in Kisumu and Kitale, respectively. They only came home on learning about his death".
>
> His cousin said that on the night that he was killed, he allegedly went for a robbery operation, leaving his pregnant wife alone at home in the night. Along the way he picked up his cousin and another person from around his home and proceeded to where they planned to steal. His cousin had only one hand having lost the other in an irate public's blaze. That night they went to their target

homestead and tried to enter, but the dogs were very fierce, making them to retreat. The local gang advised Joel's to call off their mission as the dogs had alerted most villagers, but the Joel trio insisted that they had travelled a long way and could not return home bare handed. They proceeded to a widow's homestead and stole the only cow she had. Out of instinct, the widow woke up to check on her cow, only to find that it was not there. She raised the alarm, (egekuro) awaking neighbours who started a chase. The trio were cornered when they tried to hide in a small thicket, one managed to escape but Joel and his cousin were cornered and beaten to death.

Joel effectively lived beyond his means and his mother's poverty may have endeared her to her son's new abilities to provide hitherto unavailable necessary items. The main issue is that mother and son drank way beyond their means and urged each other on into theft. To build up his stealing career Joel recruited his maternal cousins to provide logistical support. This developed into a network of relatives relying on theft to secure their livelihood. The key point to note with regard to Joel's livelihood is that he slipped away from convention at an early point in life, when he started drinking and stealing small items with the support of his mother. At that point their livelihood was entrenched in theft and it became established in that direction with the enlisting of relatives and friends who provided weapons into the network.

Another aspect of the grey lifestyle is production and trading in marijuana. Marijuana is a high value drug and herb whose leaves and seeds are used for smoking. It can be easily produced on farms in Sengeta. Saulo's second wife planted the herb in the 1980s to sell it and get money to educate her children.

Saulo said that he used to own cattle acquired using tea earnings when his family was small and he was fairly well off, able to feed his family and join other men regularly for a busaa drink, until his second wife had a protracted court case. The second wife had planted the outlawed marijuana so that she could sell it to educate her children. One day their neighbour was caught by the police in possession of the drug and he pointed to Saulo's second wife as the one planting it. The police arrested her and prosecuted her but the case took a long time, costing the family a lot of money in travelling to see her in the cells and bribing the police and court officers. She was finally fined 3000 shillings. "That was the start of poverty in this homestead". Saulo explained that since then it had become difficult to accumulate cattle through tea earnings because of the increased consumptive needs of the large family. In addition his tea earnings have declined over the years and the land available for rearing cattle has also reduced, both due to division for inheritance.

Whether obtaining money for school fees was an excuse or not, Saulo's second wife had reached the point of combining local brew with marijuana to earn a living. This is the same point that Joel had reached when he wanted to conceal his theft career by resorting to local brew production and marijuana trading. In both cases the main issue is that they wanted to ensure the continuity of their social functioning, in other words they were searching for social security by deploying 'illegal' and 'unconventional' resources. They came to this point in their lives mainly by choice, because there were many in similar circumstances who chose to solve their problems and meet their needs in different ways. However this choice is common, because the returns are higher although the risk of arrest and imprisonment or exposure to other sanctions is also higher, as Saulo's case illustrates. Saulo estimated that the protracted court case over marijuana may have been the beginning of poverty in his family.

Angima's case better illustrates the place of local brew in protecting livelihoods in Sengeta. Angima's wife is involved wholly and exclusively in *chang'aa* trade and has completely ignored farming although Angima inherited land.

> Angima's wife has been selling chang'aa since her mother initiated her into the business when she was about fifteen years old. She had come to know her husband when he used to visit her parents' home where she used to sell chang'aa and they got into friendship and married. Since being married she has been selling chang'aa from her house everyday throughout the year. Whenever she or her husband go for the chang'aa from the distillers, they have to hire boys to carry three canisters from Sengeta to their home to avoid the police and chief as the boys are assumed to be fetching water. Once it is delivered his wife sells for him until it is about to run out then she in a similar fashion sources her own three canisters. They have alternated like that since they started the chang'aa business.
>
> Besides the chang'aa business Angima deals in quarry stones for construction, which he buys from the nearby Geita hill. Once he has bought the stones back from the hill he carts the big boulders to the side of the road just next to his house. There he sits everyday to make ballast from boulders by splitting and breaking them using a small sledge hammer. He makes about ten tonnes of ballast each year and sells each at three thousand shillings. Angima explained that his main purpose for working under the tree to make ballast is not so much to make money but to spy on the police and the chief. While seated there making ballast he keeps an eye on both ends of the road and whenever he saw the chief or a police vehicle approaching from a distance he whistles aloud, alerting customers and his wife to take off. They had evaded the police and chief many times because he is able to see them early enough while seated under the tree making ballast. If by some chance the police officers or the local chief arrive without him noticing them, they don't harass him as his work is known to be ballast making. If his customers are arrested he quickly raises two to three thousand shillings for a bribe and they are released.

Angima's wife has not known any other way of making a living other than through the local brew business. She has worked closely with her husband in it, investing even in bribing for the release of their customers, perhaps as a guarantee that of the safety of drinking in their place. Angima worked under a tree making ballast and strategically positioning himself to alert his wife and her customers about any approaching law enforcement officers. Through these means that have improvised mechanisms to keep their business afloat and whenever such improvisations failed, they circumvented policy through bribes.

Nyarwaru for his part explains his involvement in chang'aa production and sales as the only option in his life, given that he has limited land and no resources to go into any other business.

> In 2001, Nyarwaru went to Mogonga to work as a matatu tout. On this route there was no traffic police harassment, but the vehicle he was working with irretrievably broke down and he came home in 2002. In the same year his father passed away and the responsibility over his younger siblings fell totally on him, having lost both parents. He went back to the Kisii Bus terminus as a tout but worked for only three months before "Michuki drove us out in February 2003" – referring to then Minister for Transport who spearheaded a campaign to streamline public transport across the country. Nyarwaru started distilling 'chang'aa' in October 2003 to raise some money to support his siblings and his family. He did so because his late parents did not leave behind any wealth for them to meet their needs and their land is very small. He borrowed two thousand shillings from Bogiche Self Help Group, at an interest rate of twenty percent per month to start the business.

Whatever the causes, these two cases indicate that *chang'aa* production and trade emerges largely from beaten livelihoods such as Nyarwaru's (after losing his parents and having to take care of younger siblings) and Angima's (having been out of farming due to land disputes). The cases also indicate that historical factors may trap actors in this lifestyle, as with Angima's wife who came from a family specialised in the *chang'aa* trade. This confirms Francis' (2000) assertion that the livelihood strategies that people follow reflect their differing socio-cultural orientations. In both cases however, the search for social security is at the centre of decisions to embark upon or remain in the *chang'aa* trade. This also confirms Bourdieu's (1990) concept of *habitus* – especially its historical construction and the embodiment of dispositions it entails as the basis of practice.

The excerpt from Elkanah's case, below, shows how he was hired by a mason to procure and sell *chang'aa* on his behalf. Elkanah was an unemployed youth badly in need of a job and his search for it leads him to being engaged to sell *chang'aa* on behalf of a mason.

> In 2002, Kegogwa engaged Elkanah to sell local brew on his behalf at premises he rented. Elkanah started selling the chang'aa on his behalf on January 15, 2002. The employer is a mason, which keeps him busy most of the time hence; he has no time to do the business. Elkanah procures the chang'aa at 400 shillings per five litre jerrycan from various people at different times. He is paid a commission of fifty shillings for every five litres of chang'aa he sells plus an additional thirty shillings for lunch each day.

The mason seeks opportunities for growing his income by setting up a *chang'aa* business. Both Kegogwa and his employee anchor their endeavours to protect their livelihood on the illegal *chang'aa* business. The fact that the business goes on even after several police raids implies that it does meet this goal of enabling them to meet their objectives of protecting their livelihood. As Orvis (1997: 62) points out in his study in Kisii, no other rural business option in Kenya comes close to being as profitable as local brewery and sales.

Drinkers of local brew develop their own networks to protect their lifestyle in different ways including exchanging information and buying beer for each other. Choice of friends in the drinking places is therefore a delicate act of balancing kinship, trust and dependability. This is to be expected where people fear threats of the application of witchcraft in food, as was the case in the struggles over tea between spouses discussed earlier. The dynamics of buying beer are also complicated and one has to really trust people in one's group so that they do not disappear when it is their turn to buy the brew. A local song on an opportunist at a drinking place, transcribed below, brings out the realities of relationships in the drinking places.

Omosani omorimo by Isaac Ondari – Kegogi Success[59]

Mogisangio okonyakong'aina ng'a nonyachete aye,

Onyor'ekero inde n'ebusaa nario inde omosani.

Gokoigwa ekero mbwate emechando gose inde omorwaire rirorio tori gocha mwane. Ekero mbwate chibesa, ekero nde buya rirorio oseka gocha ase nde ogania ngokonye.

Rituko erimo nkagania komanya gose nomosani one ore,

ngeaka amanyinga y' eng'ondi okandora ogatama.

The song brings out a story of a man who doubted his local brew based 'friend' whom he suspected of being only apparently attracted by *busaa* and monetary assistance. He tested the friendship by putting sheep's blood on his clothes, pretending to have been injured and when his 'friend' saw him he ran away. At least three attributes of local brew based networks are brought out in this song. First, that the friendship goes beyond just buying beer but extends to other mutual assistance in cash or in kind. Second, that the relationship goes

[59] English Translation

Unfaithful friend

You, my friend who cheats that you love me, you!

Whenever I have my [*busaa*] drink that you want to share in, I am your friend.

When you hear that I have problems or I am sick, you do not visit me,

When I have money and I am okay, you smile and laugh towards me seeking assistance!

One day I tricked you to ascertain if indeed you were a friend,

I put sheep's blood on my clothes; when you saw me you ran away from me thinking I was badly injured!

beyond material exchanges to embrace the safety and welfare of actors. Third, that members of local brew based networks are not irrational and ignorant; they weigh their options and make evidence-based decisions. Relationships at the drinking places are thus being continually revised as actors find themselves uncomfortable and as new actors join networks. Actors generally seek dependable friendships and relationships, of which drinking together is just one of the objectives, not the overriding or only one. For instance, one villager told me that: "I usually drink in the afternoon after work on the farm to refresh and entertain myself, and share with my friends". He was referring to a friendship beyond the drink, especially because he liked visiting the friends and relatives in their homes. While visiting is not work, it improves people's social standing in the village as they are regarded as sociable and generous. Unless one is generous with food and drink one will rarely be visited. Therefore, villagers generally invest their time in work on their farms and in strengthening relationships through drinking and social visits.

In some cases, in order to protect their livelihoods some actors have turned to theft of tea in tea buying centres. They have become 'ghost' tea farmers and *mashabiki* (Chapter 6). This type of farmer has few or no tea bushes on their farm but relies on colluding with tea buying centre clerks to steal from *bona fide* farmers and transfer it to their accounts. In this way they are able to earn from tea that they have not grown, and in essence attain social security in an imaginative manner. These efforts to make a living at the expense of others are often referred to by other writers as corruption, but can equally be seen as creative activities on the basis of identified institutional weaknesses or loopholes. As indicated in chapter six, the tea that they bought from buying centre clerks may have been stolen from their own wives or parents, or even from themselves. Thus, protecting a livelihood through grey activities is both an act of last resort in an economy with inadequate livelihood opportunities but also one of self deception. Some of the 'ghost farmers' are also 'idlers', waking up in the mornings to go to the tea buying centres and lying in wait like hyenas [see Figure 9.1, that depicts such villagers as leading an opportunistic lifestyle]. Their choice to search for social security at the expense of others can be explained by their having recognised governance loopholes in the smallholder tea sub-sector. The sub-sector lacks sufficient rigour in standards enforcement process and inspection procedures, to ensure that farmers' rights are respected. These loop holes yield opportunities for creative actors in the villages and the tea buying centre clerks with whom they collude.

The grey lifestyle presents a variety of activities for actors in Sengeta to protect their livelihoods. 'Ghost' tea farming, theft and trading in marijuana and local brew are lucrative activities that have turned around many a livelihood. Most villagers shun these activities are shunned but many young people adopting a rebellious position and not securing formal jobs are increasingly turning into crime to secure their livelihoods. The tragedy is that crime disrupts livelihoods that are legitimately constructed, and those that rested on grey activities alike. This lifestyle, like the others already discussed, presents opportunities for some actors to attain social security, but at the cost of others, such as some *bona fide* tea farmers, whose social security it undermines.

Opportunistic Dependency Lifestyle: Nyakenywa

The opportunistic dependency lifestyle is arrived at through actors' negative linkages from the grey or shadow lifestyles and others. In the opportunistic lifestyle the actors come to the road side early in the morning, hawk-eyed for opportunities to make apparently little, but quick cash. The actors are not helpless and seated waiting for a benefactor, they move around seeking to offer little services such as helping a villager arriving from town or market to move bags or luggage into the village. They usually pose as if they are helping, and then ask for a little money. They also walk up and down the road discussing with visitors arriving in the village, imposing their assistance to show them around and then requesting for a few shillings.

Sometimes these endeavours, are successful, at other times they are not. But the fact that the actors retain these activities means that they get something out of it, to live on. Some of them may combine these activities with some farming tasks early in the morning and others by leaving the farming to their wives and returning to eat at home at the end of the day. They usually carry out their roadside activities very subtly. For example they may target their former classmates now in employment by talking to them gently and asking if there is anything they can help with. If there is nothing it is better for them and they ask for a few shillings to have a drink of local brew. They are often habitual drinkers, *nyakenywa* or strong young men, who sometimes work as diggers of wells and pit latrines. Their main characteristic is pestering friends, relatives and strangers alike, for tasks to perform for pay or for cash handouts for their local brew drink or for other needs. This brings them close to beggary, but it is difficult to define the lifestyle in this way because they mostly do some work for their money in one way or another.

Sometimes they succeed in getting something, but at other times they get nothing. Their best seasons of the year are around the Easter Weekend and the Christmas and New Year Holiday seasons. They also have better days on Fridays when people from the villages who work away come home for the weekend break and on Mondays when they return. One young man who lives this lifestyle made this comment: "There is no reason to approach anybody for a few coins now, we wait until the end of the month, and then they are able to throw coins our direction or give us some work to do". The end of the month is a good time for them. In general seeking cash handouts in Sengeta is disguised in friendship, kinship or providing a service. This distinguishes the lifestyle from beggary. This is in contrast to Northern Thailand for example where due to religious 'merit making', beggary is openly condoned and beggars use the phrase 'going to receive gifts' (Bowie, 1998).

Summary

Some of the lifestyles through which actors search for social security or protection of livelihoods discussed in this chapter are analytically conceived as following a continuum so that, simplistically speaking, once an actor fails in one they slip into the next one, as illustrated in figure 9.1. As the figure shows however, in practice the situation is more complex. There are myriad opportunities for non-linear, forward and backward linkages in the course of searching for the ever shifting social security in everyday life.

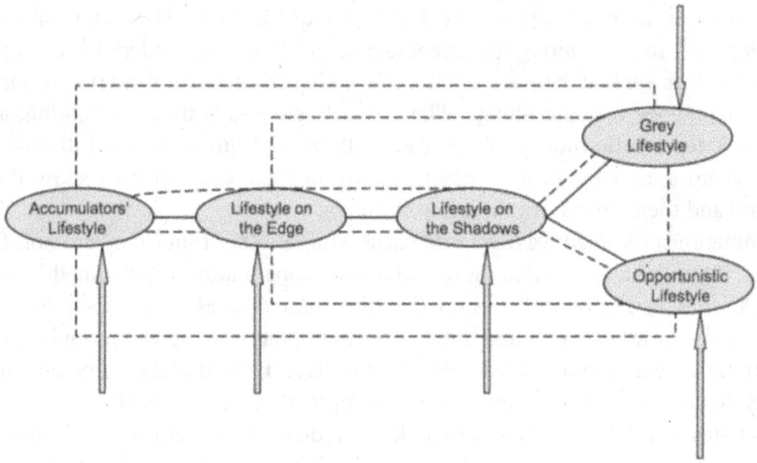

Figure 9.1 Relationships between some lifestyles for livelihood protection

Actors commence their living in any of the lifestyles shown with arrows in figure 9.1, depending on their social circumstances including the resources and opportunities they inherit. *The arrows represent starting points in reading the figure.* Upon commencement of life in any lifestyle, actors work to protect what they have, even while operating creatively with the aim of moving to preferred lifestyles: ideally from right to left on the figure, although lifestyle is a matter of personal preference and disposition. Actors often attempt to protect their livelihood through applying themselves to accumulating land, cattle and cash savings. In doing this they enlist a variety of social relationships. In the event that they slip through i.e. fail or succeed only marginally in their search for social security, they end up with a peripheral livelihood protected through what I have called a lifestyle on the edge. Here the actor essentially leads a precarious but stable and fairly conventionally organised life, relying on some social relationships but investing less in them. The notion of a continuum of lifestyles helps us explain this minimal investment in social relationships in terms of adjustment to failure, which involves ignoring some of the key attributes of the previous lifestyle, including investment in social relationships. An actor may continue searching for social security and end up building their livelihood to the point of restarting accumulation or they may slip on to the lifestyle in the shadows. Other possibilities are also open. If they slip into the lifestyle in the shadows, the use of resources is largely to the advantage of other actors, hence social relationships are core to this lifestyle, and the actor has by now accepted and adjusted to his or her weakened position in the search for social security.

This lifestyle presents opportunities for reverting to the edge or even restarting accumulation, but also for moving into the opportunistic dependency or grey lifestyles. If an actor ends up in the grey lifestyle involving themselves in theft, 'corruption' and handling contraband, they still have the possibility of going back into any other lifestyle or joining the opportunistic dependency lifestyle. Nyarwaru's case demonstrates that it is possible to commence accumulation in cattle and machinery such as a sewing machine from earnings made in grey lifestyle activities. Joel also managed to move from theft to accumulating livestock. The lines [continuous and dotted] in figure 9.1 represent the possible positive and negative linkages between lifestyles. The continuous lines represent negative linkages in lifestyles i.e. the simple trend that is common and easily discerned, of actors moving from left to right, away from the accumulators' lifestyle; the more complex positive linkages, and forward and backward movement of actors between lifestyles is represented by the dotted lines. It is here that the complexities of rural life can be found. These complexities involve the creativity through which actors move from the right to the left in fashions that may skip certain lifestyles to go on to the more ideal ones, by reworking relationships, resources and 'environments'.

The movement of actors between various lifestyles then, is a result of both their creativity i.e. their use of agency and their interaction and negotiation with their environments. Therefore the movements may be conceived as resulting in a sense from the dialectic relationships or interaction between practice and 'structure' (King, 2000: 422). The heterogeneity of lifestyles in almost homogeneous circumstances in Nyamira can be explained in terms of the varied '*habitus*' (Bourdieu, 1990) of the villagers, and their differing preferences and starting points in life. Life is thus lived in leaps and bounds facilitated by creativity to move to preferred lifestyles, but the process is often severely undermined by 'structural' factors beyond the actors' control. The climb back to preferred lifestyles, even after setbacks, indicates that creativity is viable up to a point and that *habitus* and 'structure' are continually reworked by actors. If the various lifestyles may be viewed as a representation of differentiation; this may be explained in terms of 'structural' restrictions that differentially hinder villagers' creativity and ability to build positive linkages between lifestyles. Actors in all the lifestyles anchor themselves on resource sharing through social relationships, although some lifestyles invest more in relationships than others. This anchorage in social relationships outside the market is the result of uncertainties wrought by state/external actions (cf. Mehta, Leach and Scoones, 2001). In dealing with these uncertainties, villagers calculate their strategies and end up resource sharing in the 'moral economy', regardless of their statuses in the search for social security (Schrauwers, 1999). In explaining livelihood protection, it is therefore important to keep in mind the tension between 'agency' and 'structure' and how it is reflected in actual lived experience in everyday practice in terms of diversification, differentiation and intergenerational tensions, collaboration and support in ever-changing forms.

Conclusion

In this Chapter the various lifestyles for protecting livelihoods and searching for social security have been presented. The circulation of actors around the various lifestyles has been attributed to how they use resources and particularly invest in social relationships. It has been argued that the creativity with which resources and relationships are deployed in the various lifestyles and between them is often influenced by structural factors, which actors contest and rework with varying degrees of success.

In terms of policy a critical conclusion is that intergenerational wealth transfer poses serious problems to the social security of aged parents and their adult sons and daughters. Therefore, if aged people for instance above 65 years can receive state pension payouts and release property to their adult children, intergenerational relationships would be more fruitful and resources be better deployed. Another policy front worth exploration is education which comes across as a major area of parents' investment with the hope for support in old age. When children do not succeed in school and support their parents in old age serious social security problems emerge for both parties because of wasteful investments in education. The Kenyan education system closes out average or lower grade students who may lack money to join college. There is need for a more open system as education is nearly the only ladder out of poverty especially in rural areas. Educational opportunities constitute entry points to other resource networks not just for families but also for whole villages. This issue is followed up in details in Chapter 10, where the discussion focuses on actors' efforts at redefining and re-working resources in various settings.

CHAPTER 10

Re-defining Resources in Everyday Practice

Introduction

The purpose of this chapter is to draw together the various ways in which villagers redefine and rework resources over time to reflect their changing needs, preferences and livelihood objectives. It attempts to answer the question of how villagers create resources. This question has been implicit throughout the thesis, but in this chapter it is treated explicitly, with a view to explaining how and to what extent villagers create resources. The chapter commences with an overview of resource studies and positioning this question in the debate. This is followed by a presentation of results from the study on the various ways in which villagers create resources through their creative everyday practices. A discussion of the results is then presented. It is concluded that villagers are actively engaged in reworking their circumstances with a view to creating resources through renaming and redefining phenomena in a continuous process that runs throughout their everyday practice. This process, which is hinged on human agency, is however not unlimited; it is circumscribed by natural and other socio-economic factors that are often beyond the control of actors.

An Overview of Resource Studies

Recent livelihood studies have treated resources as assets or capital, conceiving them as physical, human, social, natural and financial (Scoones, 1998; Carney, 1998; DFID, 1999, 2000; and Toner, *et al,* 2004). This approach to resource studies has been criticised for ignoring non-material aspects of resources such as identity, time, information, confidence and autonomy (Wallman, 1984; Wallman and Associates, 1996; Long, 2001). The issue of material and non-material aspects of resources is important because it brings into focus the notion of livelihood as transcending the material and encompassing the values of people and the identities that they seek. In this regard Peach and Constantin's (1972) argument that the term resources presupposes a person or groups of persons and that resources are expressions or reflections of human appraisal that brings out the creativity of people in constructing livelihoods.

This means that something is not a resource until and unless someone or a group comes to appraise it as such.

This converges with Wallman's analysis (1984) that 'we need to ask for whom and in what way an item has economic potential and whether its owners recognise that potential'. In other words, an item is not a resource in all situations, for all people. People only come to appraise something as a resource when they recognise it has utility for their purposes. This process depends on the knowledge and institutional arrangements to use the item effectively (Berry, 1989a). Peach and Constantin (1972) conclude that 'the word resource is an abstraction reflecting human appraisal and relating to a function or operation in which it may take part'. In other words it is through appraisal of phenomena and recognition of their potential to contribute to the achievement of certain tasks, meet certain needs or solve certain problems that resources evolve or are created.

Therefore, resources are created through everyday practice as phenomena are redefined as part of the process of actors dealing with problematic situations or meeting their needs. Human appraisal is the main issue here and, following the actor-oriented perspective adopted in this study, this means that resources are not obvious to every eye and are never the same before every eye, even in relatively homogeneous conditions, places or groups. It also means that resources are not constant; they change as actor preferences, lifestyles, commitments and other repertoires change. Peach and Constantin (1972) support the notion of fluidity of resources, albeit from a rather deterministic point of view, arguing that resources change with each change in human epoch. This follows the changes in functions and operations for which resources have previously been defined. Most of the literature, especially on livelihoods takes the actual processes of change of resources over time and how villagers relate to these processes for granted. The assumption is that resources are either available or unavailable and this is why the issue of 'accessibility' is emphasised. The notion of villagers creating resources implies that 'creativity' and 'ingenuity' are more interesting issues for exploration than accessibility. Accessibility seems imply that resources are static and neutral, but there is evidence that resources are dynamic. This is because creative action is situationally embedded, and is a cyclical process driven by the principle of fallibility – the idea that failure in action is always possible (Joas and Kilpinnen, 2006).

This chapter attempts to fill the foregoing gap in the literature, specifically with regard to the unexplored area of how ordinary people in villagers engage with and contribute to resource creation. In understanding how villagers engage in the reconstitution of phenomena in the processes of creating and re-creating resources through giving them meanings, there is a need to capture the forces that bring about these shifts in meanings. Some of these may be located in the interaction between political, ecological and population dynamics, on the one hand, and changing socio-cultural and actor preferences and lifestyles on the other. It is important to recognise that explanations for resource creation can not successfully be derived solely from one side of the relationship, although it is clear from discussions in this book that creativity dominates people's everyday lives as they engage with structural constraints in dynamic ways to mould resources for making livelihoods. In this sense, creativity is the prime mover in villagers' lives.

Resources then, are broadly defined as constituting both material and non-material phenomena. As such, a resource has multiple and dynamic meanings that are largely amenable to people's changing needs and circumstances, albeit through negotiation. In other words, villagers have the agency to rework resources by giving them new or additional meanings and using them as such to make their living. In so doing, villagers are struggling or negotiating with their 'environments' in order to create useful niches of resource meanings and uses in their everyday lives. Within these processes social relationships are important, both as resources in themselves in terms of conferring such direct resources as a sense of belonging or identity, respect, self esteem, social worth and security, and as bases of exchange of material resources such as bride-price or other forms of gifts. Social relationships are therefore central in resource creation and livelihood construction.

Directions in villagers' creation of resources

It has already been argued that actors create resources in their everyday practice by giving meaning to phenomena and using them appropriately. As circumstances change the meanings may also change in ways that enable different or additional uses to phenomena or perhaps their combination with others for more efficient or effective use. Looked at from this angle resources are ideas and that are constantly being refined and reworked, sometimes in open fast-moving fashions and at other times in subtle ways. These processes are part of complex everyday life and often involve certain forms of 'experimentation' with phenomena, building on experience, what is known and sometimes borrowing consciously or unconsciously from other people.

Opportunities within the market may also trigger creative re-evaluation of phenomena and how they can be moulded or used to meet such market opportunities. Interactions with the economic and physical environments continuously present problems and opportunities for experimentation and further evaluation of phenomena, ultimately leading to the reworking and reconstruction of resources in ways hitherto inconceivable. The struggles to earn a living in Sengeta village bring out a number of examples of resources creation in this manner.

Re-defining Land in Everyday Practice

Among the Abagusii, land has traditionally been a part of nature, abundant in supply and in productivity. Silberschmidt (1999) indicates that in Gusiiland during the pre-colonial period the head of the household, the husband, had access to as much land as his family could cultivate and use for grazing. Droughts were few and far apart, the soils were fertile and the rains sufficient. The colonial era however, closed in the population and ended territorial expansion by fixing boundaries with neighbouring ethnic groups. This, over time, combined with high population growth rates led to pressure on the land (Garst, 1974). The colonial period led to a variety of redefinitions of land as new crops were introduced to compete with finger millet and herding (cf. Levine and Levine, 1966). The main crops introduced include coffee in 1921, pyrethrum in 1950, tea in 1956, passion fruit in 1959 and hybrid maize in 1962 (Garst, 1974). The introduction of these crops brought about a variety of redefinitions of land, culminating in land consolidation and registration, which was largely complete in Gusiiland by the late 1960s. The excerpt below from Petro's case illustrates this.

> After working in Kericho for six years, Petro came back home and started school. Because he had not saved much money and his family did not see the value of school at the time, he raised his school fees through maize and pyrethrum growing. Petro got his first pyrethrum seedlings from neighbours and from other farmers in Nyamira District. He planted them and they multiplied, then he replanted on a larger scale. He used to sell the produce to cooperative societies but since then the value of pyrethrum collapsed when World market prices tumbled in the late 1970's and early 1980's. This led farmers to uproot the crop and start doing other things, such as planting tea, that would give them money. The government tried to persuade them to plant pyrethrum again by offering high prices for the crop but they refused, because they have not forgotten the losses they made when the market disappeared. Petro sat for his Common Entrance Examination (CEE) in 1954 and passed. After that he was employed on probation as a teacher in Chache. He worked as a teacher, for two years and left the job because the salary was too low.
>
> Petro was baptised into the Seventh Day Adventist in 1950 and married in the same year. The bride price of six heads of cattle, a bull and a goat for his wife came from his sister's bride price. The wedding expenses were low because they walked to the bride's home and to church, and back to his home. In 1951, they had their first born child, a son. He dropped out of school in form four and is now married with a number of children. Formerly he used to do lumbering for a living but is now a farmer. His father occasionally assists him in paying school fees for his children. Petro has three other sons and seven daughters.
>
> In 1960 Petro joined a pyrethrum cooperative society as a treasurer and later as Store Keeper for a salary of 170 shillings per month. During that time he saved five hundred shillings with which he bought an exotic dairy cow that produced eight litres of milk per day, but it died after only two years. He has always kept a cow ever since. The cooperative society dealt mainly in pyrethrum collection from smallholders and its sale on their behalf to the Pyrethrum Board of Kenya for export.

> In 1961 he planted tea after soil from his father's farm was examined and permission to plant granted from Kericho's Tea Research Foundation. The tea stumps for planting were given to him from Kericho on credit and he paid up after harvesting and selling the green tea leaves. He started by planting one thousand seedlings and gradually increased to three thousand bushes.
>
> In order to receive tea stumps, he prepared a seed bed complete with holes as directed by an extension officer and mobilised family, kin and neighbourhood labour (risaga) to plant early in the morning on the day the stumps were delivered from Kericho. After he was registered as a grower he developed his own 'egesa' (shade) and started to grow his own seedlings from mature tea as he had learned in the tea plantations. He initially did this for infilling dried stumps on the farm. In later years, especially after 1972, when polythene sachets were introduced for vegetative production of tea seedlings, he started selling them to other farmers. He has a tea seed bed, grows napier grass, maize, beans, tea, sugar cane and kale.

The excerpt from Petro's story shows how he has redefined the way that he uses land over time. First, because he needed school fees he planted maize and pyrethrum for sale. Later he planted tea and he has reared cattle since the 1960s. Over time Petro has taken up various crops introduced by the colonial government and these enabled him to change the uses to which he put his land. The land he previously used for growing millet and for pasture was later used for tea, pyrethrum and maize growing. Thus he has changed the meanings of land at different times in response to his cash needs and perhaps to how he wanted to be identified at different times of his life course. An indication of changes in the meanings of land is the uprooting of pyrethrum in the 1980s when prices fell. This can be explained by dwindling returns from the crop and its diminishing value as a source of income. But it can also be seen in terms of the alternative cash crop, tea, and its increasing importance at the time. The key strength of tea is that growers receive prompt monthly payments. In both ways, the act of uprooting pyrethrum was one of resistance to the pyrethrum authorities and a shift in the meaning of land use from pyrethrum to tea. The expression 'uprooting' does not only imply an act, but equally a process of abandonment of pyrethrum and disengagement with the notion that growing it represented income.

Another form of redefinition of land that is common in Sengeta relates to production of tea seedlings. As the importance of tea as a cash crop gained momentum Petro saw an opportunity to make an income by producing tea seedlings. He started this out of a personal need to infill withered bushes in his farm. After perfecting the skill he saw a business opportunity in his and neighbouring villages. The seedlings in the nursery needed regular watering and this is partly why Petro constructed a shallow well on his farm. In this sense the meaning of water also changed and it became part of his tea seedling business.

The process of redefinition of land as a resource appears to have been anchored on a number of other resources. For instance Petro relied on neighbours and other networks that took him to other parts of the district to obtain pyrethrum planting material. After acquiring some planting material he multiplied the material on his farm and then re-planted in a larger scale. Thus, he first acquired planting material by engaging with social networks and later through co-production with 'nature'. When the crop was ready, he enrolled with a cooperative society in order to sell. The creation of pyrethrum as a resource also transformed him into a member of a cooperative organisation so he could fully reap its benefits. This again illustrates how resources are not static and neutral; but rather dynamic and with the capacity to transform actors in the process of being created. In this case the production of pyrethrum sends Petro to school and leads him to become a member of a cooperative society. Similarly his tea planting efforts turned his attention to work parties as had to embrace the work groups to carry the creation of tea as a resource to fruition.

Angima and his brother redefined their land differently to be able to make a living from it. They saw it as an opportunity to make money directly by leasing it out to those who needed more land to work. They did this both as a response to emergencies and to meet regular expenditures. The excerpt below from Angima's case brings out the issue in some detail.

> After their father's burial, Angima was assisted by his uncles and other village elders to demarcate their father's land equally for his brother and himself. He said "now I had my own land and was comfortable so I worked for Jonathan for a short time as I planned to farm my own land". However he did not start farming at that point but instead renewed some of the land leases his late father had made. He did this to raise money for his local brew drink. His brother lives on his land and works as a hired farm hand, and occasionally as a rickshaw puller in the village. He is married and his wife concentrates on farming activities growing kale, maize and beans. Angima's family relies on her for vegetables which they take on credit and pay at the end of each week. In 1988, Angima's brother Ombongi was arrested during a police raid at a chang'aa place. He was taken into a Nyamira court and sentenced to five months' imprisonment or a fine of five thousand shillings. Angima approached his former employer and friend Jonathan and requested him to hire part of Ombongi's land in order to raise money for the court fine and get him out of prison. Jonathan agreed and hired a half an acre of land for three years at two thousand shillings per year. In 1990, Angima was attacked by thugs on his way home from drinking and sustained serious head injuries, so elders recommended a surgical operation. The traditional head surgeon asked for twenty five thousand shillings for the operation. Angima did not have the money, and so sold a quarter an acre of his land for fifty thousand shillings to his cousin.

Angima and his late father's practice of leasing out land rather than working it represent a shift in the meaning of land in Sengeta village. The practice is neither illegal nor rare, but shows that villagers attach different meanings to the same resource. Those who leased the land saw more benefit in working it, than Angima and his father who consistently saw less value in working it. This heterogeneity of the meanings of resources is linked to actor identity. Angima, his brother and their late father were entrapped in local brew consumption and needed quick cash from time to time, which shaped the meanings they attributed to the land. Angima sold a part of his land to his cousin to meet a medical bill. In leasing out and selling land the two brothers relied on friendship and kinship networks. Interestingly they leased to a friend, but sold to a kinsman. In so doing they followed Abagusii customary law that recognises land as belonging to the family and by extension the immediate agnates. Hence, it was acceptable to lease out land to a friend because it could be reclaimed later and thus would not leave family hands, but selling to an agnate meant retaining it in the extended family, even if ownership was transferred (cf. Levine and Levine, 1966).

Livestock Tenant-keeping and Trade

The Abagusii traditionally valued cattle for their meat, milk, traction, prestige and bride price (Levine and Levine, 1966; Silberschmidt, 1999). Bride price represents an important site for the creation of enduring relationships between families and clans, which provide particular opportunities that are of use in a variety of ways of making a living. Bride price and marriage are therefore dynamic resources in Gusiiland. Cattle as bride price are the main basis for marriage in many African societies, including among the Abagusii. Bride price transfer to consummate a marriage creates new relationships between the two families involved. Family here denotes the two extended families, which thereafter relate in ways that exclude further intermarriage between them. According to Shadle (2003) women became more valuable after 1950 because farm labouring '*risaga*' was organised around them in commercialised farming. This led to an increase in bride price. Another change came as education increasingly replaced labour as the basis of women's valuation in marriage. This also led women, particularly those with formal employment, to fetch more in terms of bride price. Villagers said that since the late 1970s bride price has increasingly taken a monetary form as opposed to cattle. They said that the bride price for a school teacher is about fifty thousand shillings and two or four nice cattle. The highest bride price that they had heard of in the area was seventy five thousand shillings and two cattle which was paid for a high school teacher in the early 1980s. Many villagers are of the view that due to general economic difficulty, bride prices are falling significantly and parents negotiate for bride price more in symbolic terms than in terms of value. The cattle transferred in bride price payments form the basis of inter-familial social links (Ouma, Obare and Staal, 2004).

The parents of the bride and groom address each other by the title *korera (pl. chikorera)*. The bride's parents and their siblings refer to the groom, his siblings and cousins as *abana* (my children) and the groom's parents and their siblings refer to the bride, her siblings and cousins in the same manner. The marriage thus creates permanent relationships between two extended families. They condole each other when bereaved, but as relatives-in-law do not do much in common in terms of ceremonies and rites (for detailed marriage relationship and kinship terms and obligations see Philip Mayer, 1950; Iona Mayer, 1965; Levine, 1979 and Hakansson, 1994). In Sengeta the meanings of cattle have been extended and represented differently in at least two ways that are quite widespread: cattle tenant keeping and livestock trade.

> Ochiemo said: "I was without a cow here for a long time until late in 1988 when I decided to approach a friend called Jonathan and ask him to give me a cow to keep for him so that my children could have milk. Jonathan is my friend, sometimes when he has small carpentry jobs I do them for him at a fair price. He agreed and gave me a cow. Luckily the cow gave birth after only two months of taking it. My children were very happy. I kept the cow for six years and gave Jonathan four calves. When one of his sons was paying bride price in 1995, he took the cow back to add to what his son had raised".

In Gusii customs, *sagare* or tenant keeping is traditionally practiced between relatives (Levine and Levine, 1966). In seeking a cow owner outside the family who was willing to let him keep a cow Ochiemo devised a new interpretation of cattle and the meanings they convey. The idea of cattle tenant keeping (as initiated by a tenant) is new, particularly as Ochiemo has no kin or affinal relationship with Jonathan that would have provided a reason to provide a cow and milk to the Ochiemo family. In this way the cattle tenant and cattle owner have shifted their meanings of cattle and created a new cattle based relationship between themselves that is not affinal and final. It is one in which the cattle owner will recover his cattle later. In this reworked relationship, the tenant has all the benefits including *de facto* ownership in the eyes of the public for the time being. The *de facto* ownership confers prestige on the tenant and enables him to use this prestige in his social functions. The tenant also provides milk to his or her family through negotiation and re-working social relationships and using his pastures. In addition to working out a new relationship, cattle ownership is reordered, in the sense that the tenant bears none of the risks of ownership such as death or theft but enjoys the benefits. This shift of benefits without risks undermines the traditional value of having large herds at home with the men having to defend or protect them from raiders (Silberschmidt, 1999). The fact that the tenant bears no major risks implies that trust plays an important role in this relationship and safeguards the interests of both parties. The undeclared aim is to maximise 'joint utility' rather than profit in this supra-market relationship (Folbre, 1986). In Nyamira the relationship between tenant and cattle owner is one of equality and respect, contrary to Cliffe's (1982) findings that such relationships are of dependency and subservience in some pastoral communities in East Africa.

The other aspect of change of the meaning of cattle is in relation to their transformation into ordinary merchandise. Actors are increasingly involved in livestock trade as a means of making their living, leading to the establishment of livestock markets around Gusiiland. Although traditionally cattle have been exchanged for other goods throughout Gusii history, the network of livestock-specific markets, the intensity of activity in those markets and the large number of traders is a recent phenomenon.

> Nyangaga explained: "I started my livestock business in 1980 with five hundred shillings, which was enough to purchase one cow. I joined my stepbrother and five other men from near my home who were already doing the business".
>
> "At the beginning I used to buy only cattle but these days I also buy and sell goats and sheep. The markets I buy and sell from are Ting'a on Mondays, Kebirigo on Tuesdays, Igare on Wednesdays, Keroka on Thursdays and Kisii on Fridays. I go to these markets on all those days. Sometimes I buy a cow on my way to the market and still sell it at a profit before reaching the market". He has educated some of his children and built a permanent house for his family with profits from this livestock trade.
>
> My discussions with other traders indicated that their number has been rising over time. One trader told me that he started trading in the company of his late father in the early 1970s and they used to walk in the company of three or four other traders, but "nowadays we are over twenty on the same route, excluding the young men we hire to drive the cattle back and forth". They attributed this growth to rising demand for meat in the urban areas, which leads traders to move to more distant markets to buy livestock cheaply and make a profit. They said that livestock are slightly cheaper in Igare and Kona markets closer to the border with the Masai, who have more livestock.

In the pre-colonial history of the Abagusii there were at least three ways to own or increase livestock ownership; through raids on neighbouring clans or tribes, bride price exchange and breeding (Levine and Levine, 1966). A fourth avenue that was not especially widespread, perhaps because the Abagusii were not particularly keen on cultivation at the time, was exchanging grain for livestock (Philip Mayer, 1951). Livestock trade as a full time job is therefore a new phenomenon in Gusiiland. Moving from one market to the other in pursuit of cheaper purchases and profitable sales of livestock has changed the meaning of cattle to the status of a commodity. These changes in meaning have been co-produced by meat consumers, livestock traders, butchers and local (regional) governments. The opportunity has been contemporaneously spotted by the butchers and livestock traders who have created a situation requiring government intervention in setting up special livestock markets across the land complete with a rates system. The transformation of livestock into a commodity for trade has created jobs in local government to run markets and allowed for a growth in livestock traders, butchers and labourers who drive the livestock to and from the markets. The livestock trade illustrates the dynamism of resources in the process of being created. The trade has helped rework local government, claim physical spaces in various markets and provide new livelihood opportunities. In this way the trade has reconstructed urban and emerging market centre landscapes in significant ways by entrenching in those spaces. The bargaining and haggling that goes on in the livestock markets appear to the outsider as almost directionless undertakings with no benchmarks, but they provide the basis on which profits or losses are made. So there is order amidst the apparent chaos, and continuous sales, purchases and the development of careers all occur (cf. Hill, 1969: 392-3).

Reclaiming and redirecting the wild into the market

Grass and trees are associated with the wild in Gusii history and life. It is only since the consolidation and registration of land under individual titles in the early 1960s, that trees and grass slowly began to fall into private hands and acquire commercial value. In Sengeta almost all trees, grass and shrubs are now in private ownership. Trees are sold at high prices, especially since the tea factory nearby started using wood as an additional source of energy, which drastically increased local demand for wood. Wood is also used locally for firewood, building, fencing, furniture and ornament.

Because people only own small pieces of land and yet wish to continue to rear cattle for milk, many have turned to semi or zero grazing their livestock. This calls for fodder to be delivered to the cattle in their stalls. This practice has turned napier grass into a new cash crop. People who plant it and have no livestock or produce it in excess have a ready market among those who have livestock and little fodder. Some farmers, especially those who do not stall feed their cattle, have sufficient napier grass. However those with more cattle and less land have turned to purchasing the grass from those who grow it for sale. A part of Petro's case record illustrates this point.

> Petro said that his earnings from the tea enabled him to acquire one cow. He feeds it on the napier grass on his land which is more than enough and also on the pasture paddocks he has established. He has shown his married sons which portions of land they can plant with their food crops like maize, finger millet, sugar cane and kale. One of his sons grows napier grass at the edges of his portion. He sells the grass to neighbours and other villagers, sometimes giving it free of charge to his father to feed his cow, when he lacks enough from his fields.

This excerpt shows that Petro usually produces as much napier grass as he needs for his cattle, but whenever he has a shortage he gets some free of charge from his son. His son grows excess grass to sell to those who do not have enough for their cattle. From this a double shift in the meaning of grass can be deduced. First napier grass "come in" from the wild and become a part of cattle culture in Gusiiland, where historically cattle were grazed on naturally growing pasturage. Second, more recently napier grass has been transformed into a new cash crop, grown by those like Petro's son who have no cattle, in order to sell. This latter development is the result of several interacting factors. These include farmers with the resources to put up zero grazing stalls and purchase the cattle, napier grass growers without cattle and, perhaps, an expanding local milk market. The critical point is that some villagers have identified an opportunity in napier grass sales and seized it to make a living, hence reworking napier grass into the market. The market has partly been built with remittances from other countries. Some farmers with a steady flow of income rear cattle and purchase napier grass for them even if they do sell the milk. Bochaberi's case, part of which is reproduced below captures this argument.

> Bochaberi's second born child, who lives in America with her family, has been of much help to her. She paid school fees for her brother from form one to four, built a permanent house for her mother and furnished it. "She bought me a television set, a cell phone, a radio set and a car battery to power them. In a nutshell she has been very helpful. Last month, she called to inquire about my health, which worries them. The children also pay a worker to take care of tea and collect the napier grass that I buy around the village for the cattle".

Bochaberi does not appear to make her own money, but appears to live mostly on remittances. A good deal of these she ploughs back into the livestock enterprise, hiring labour and purchasing napier grass. The milk produced is mostly for self consumption and part of the reason for maintaining cattle is sentimental because her family has long been linked to dairy farming. For this reason her children have decided to support her farming, and in the process they provide a market for napier grass in a way that overcomes local economic difficulties in farming.

Napier grass has also been redefined in another direction. Due to the scarcity of forests from which to collect sticks for weaving baskets, it is now common to use split mature napier grass canes for making baskets. Saulo is one of the basket makers who have moved in this direction of redefining napier grass and redirecting it into the market in another way. Part of his case record is reproduced below.

> Saulo gets some additional income from thatching houses at a fee, an occupation he has been in since 1959, although since 2000, contracts to thatch have become rare. This, he explained, is because of the rarity of grass for thatching owing to population pressure. The land previously left for grass has been turned over to food and tea growing, especially on the hill tops. Besides, many people now prefer corrugated iron sheet roofs. Saulo also weaves baskets for sale specialising in baskets for grain drying, chicken rearing, grain storage and others for carrying green tea leaf to the buying centres. Because there are no forests nowadays where the sticks can be collected for weaving baskets, he splits mature napier grass canes and weaves with them. He said people have slowly come to like baskets made from napier canes because they are lighter, although they do not last as long

> as those made from sticks. He uses the extra income from thatching houses and selling baskets to supplement his tea earnings to buy food and largely for entertainment with chang'aa and busaa in the company of friends. He sells his baskets at the village tea buying centre every end of the month when tea earnings are released by KTDA. In June and December every year he sells many baskets at the main gate to the tea factory next to the local office of Nyamira Tea Cooperative Society office where tea farmers receive their mid and end year tea payments, locally known as tea bonuses.

The transformation of napier grass into material for making baskets is a creative move especially as the split canes look so tender that only a basket maker or someone who understood the process would recognise their potential This creativity links to local small-scale tea farmers who provide the market for the baskets. As Saulo indicates the redefinition is a result of the interaction of population pressure on the land leading up to scarcity of land, the growing tea sub-sector and the need of basket makers to make a living. In a sense, Saulo's ingenuity is shaped by his own preference to continue with basket making, by the market, and the 'unkindness' of 'nature'. Thus resource creation takes place within the confines of a particular situation, hence 'situated creativity' (Joas and Kilpinnen, 2006: 323). As the providence of physical environments diminishes villagers become more creative in their everyday practice to stay ahead of unfolding constraints. If the international tea market were to collapse, as happened to pyrethrum in the past, it would have ramifications for the livelihoods of basket makers, and growers of napier who sell to them.

Related to the notion of the shrinking providence of the physical environment, is the changes in the meaning and use of trees. As already indicated, in Gusiiland trees have historically belonged to the wild and were accessible to all according to need (Silberschmidt, 1999). However this has changed over the years and people have started to grow their own trees which they use in a variety of ways, mostly for domestic wood fuel. Private production of trees of various kinds has meant that, like napier grass, trees have assumed a commodity status. An excerpt from Petro's case underscores this point.

> Petro recently sold three blue gum trees for one thousand five hundred shillings to Simion who supplies firewood to the tea factory. He also sold three cypress trees at one thousand six hundred shillings to Kennedy to make timber to use in making furniture for his house. He used the money to buy dry maize for his family and the rest he is using in meeting his own basic daily needs, and those of his family.

Petro makes a significant although intermittent income from his trees. This practice represents a shift in the ways that trees are viewed and used. Trees that may once have been grown mainly for domestic use are now being sold. This has effectively transformed trees into a cash crop. In the process new livelihood opportunities arise where none previously existed.

The change of policy in the local tea factories to embrace the use of wood as an additional source of energy provided the impetus for the transformation of trees into a cash earning opportunity. The factories provide a continuous market for the wood and this attracts a number of people in the villages to start trading in wood. The wood traders buy and collect wood from surrounding villagers until they have sufficient to economically transport to the factory. This enables those with fewer trees and without the capacity to transport timber an opportunity to sell. One of the traders involved in wood fuel trade in Sengeta village is Festus, part of whose case record is presented below.

> Festus said that the fuel wood business has helped him to pay a medical bill for his wife and nursery school fees for his children. It has also kept him busy and has helped him to improve his relationships with other villagers, especially those from whom he buys trees and those he hires to split the wood and arrange it. From the profits he has hired tea bushes to pluck for two years, bought a cow, some chickens and was planning to buy another cow soon to supply milk to his family.
>
> "I experience some problems in this business, such as the pay per stack (three cubic metres) at the factory that has remained at one thousand five hundred shillings even though the price of trees has been rising. When I hire a vehicle I am required to pre-pay the owner, they do not listen to promises to pay later. Most of the trees I buy these days are far from the road and that means more transport costs. Their scarcity means that their prices have been rising steadily". The factory directors, who pressed the factory to start using wood as a source of energy in the first place, should now push to increase prices for the wood.

The opening up of tea factories to wood as a source of energy provides opportunities for local people to sell their wood. This was negotiated by factory directors who are farmers' representatives in the factory management. They recognised it would provide an opportunity for local people with trees to make additional income. They argued that that factory energy expenditure should not all go to the state run electricity power company; but that some should instead trickle to the local farmers. This approach resonated with the local people and they responded by supplying the wood at set prices. This has increased the market for trees and created a new trade in them. Trees have been redefined as a cash crop, like tea although they take much longer to mature. The prices initially set per unit of wood may have been good when supplies were abundant but with scarcity setting in the prices are now being contested. This is important because wood fuel incurs heavy transport costs in relation to its value (Cline-Cole, et. al. 1987). However the scarcity of trees and their rising prices engender major contradictions in this trade, because land is becoming scarcer while at the same time the factory requires more wood. It is unlikely that the available farm land will support factory's needs in the coming years. Contrary to this, Patel *et al.* (1995) argue that the sub-division of land and incentives from well developed markets may lead to increased tree cover in smallholder areas in Kenya.

Leasing out tea bushes

The excerpt from Festus's case record (above) shows that he has hired tea bushes from another farmer, using profits from his wood fuel trade. His intention in hiring the tea is to further strengthen his livelihood by moulding the tea to improve its yields, so that he will earn a profit. Another side of this transaction is captured by part of Ondima's case, presented below.

> Ondima explained that it was a difficult decision for him to lease out his tea bushes, because the earnings from it may turn out more than he receives in rent (which is the aim of the one who rents). "I have never leased out tea bushes in my life, but when things get rough I have to live and there is nothing else to do. The money I received helped me to settle debts for my son and go to hospital and it is difficult to borrow as much money from any other source, so only my resources such as tea can pull me out of trouble. But some people especially young people who drink too much, nyakenywa, play around with tea these days, they lease out everything and use the money for local brew. When they eventually have a problem needing money to overcome, they have nothing to help them".

On the other side of the tea leasing transaction, that of the tea owner, the driving force is to get an immediate income to solve an urgent problem, such as seeking medical attention, or for routine expenditure such as on local brew consumption. Whatever the reason the interesting thing to note is that tea is redefined through this transaction. The tea bush becomes available for transfer to a third party at a fee, reducing the long wait for a cash return on the leaves. In this redefinition the value of the tea to the owner shifts from the leaf to the whole bush and land. For emergency expenditure there are many avenues for securing credit in the villages, if one planned their lives differently, but even amidst such opportunities as loans from self help groups the redefinition of tea and its leasing out persists. For instance Nyamira Tea Savings and Cooperative Society, with an office near Sengeta, offers emergency and other loans to tea farmers who save with the society as this explanation from an official, below, indicates.

> The field officer explained: "tea farmers who enrol as members of the society receive their monthly, half-yearly, and annual earnings through the society. Such farmers have a right to take development loans according to the level of their savings in the society and their ability to repay on the basis of their tea earnings. We also offer small loans for purchasing a solar lighting system and mobile phones, which we usually procure for members. Other loans we offer to members are for school fees and for medical bills, which also depend on ability to repay within the next twelve months. Membership is growing every month and farmers are taking loans especially for school fees, which we pay directly to schools by cheque. We have no major problems in loan repayment as we operate a check

system on the members' monthly tea earnings. We have recently opened up membership to non-tea farmers so that traders and teachers have become members even if they have no tea".

Formal and informal opportunities for emergency loans are abundant in Nyamira District. The preference of leasing out tea and land then is best explained in terms of Ondima's assertion that "*It is difficult to borrow much money from any source, so only my resources such as tea can pull me out of trouble*". It seems the motive is to play with one's resources in order to solve one's problems. The starting point in solving one's problems or meeting needs centres upon an actor and their resources, as argued in chapter nine. Only when such internal solutions fail, do people start going for loans of different kinds. This implies that villagers placer great value on their own creativity in rearranging their own resources before they seek solutions to their problems externally in informal or formal lending institutions.

Harnessing local brew: busaa and chang'aa

Among the Abagusii, local brew particularly *busaa* is traditionally used for entertainment in labour organisation during *risaga* (Levine and Levine, 1966; Orvis, 1997). It is also used in homes to entertain visitors and is drunk during rituals and other ceremonies. Over the years however, additional forms of the brew such as *chang'aa* have been introduced and are increasingly available for sale. The beginnings of the commercialisation of local brew are not clear. Silberschmidt (1999) and Orvis (1997) discussed the entrenchment of the practice in Gusiiland since the 1970s. Commercial local brew is widely available in Sengeta and has increasingly become a means of livelihood for some people, as this excerpt from Angima's case shows.

> Angima's wife was initiated into the chang'aa business when she was about fifteen years old. She got to know her husband when he visited her parents' home where she used to sell chang'aa and that is how they got into friendship and marriage. Since she got married she has been selling chang'aa from her house everyday of the year. She buys the drink in twenty litre canisters, from the distillers, and hires boys to carry the canisters from Sengeta to their home to avoid the police and chief as the boys are assumed to be fetching water. Once the chang'aa is delivered she sells it. When it is about to run out Angima sources his three canisters in a similar fashion. They have alternated like that since they started the chang'aa business.

The excerpt above raises two interesting points about the commercialisation of local brew in Nyamira that need to be highlighted. First it provides evidence that some people have taken up local brew production and sales as a full time job. This implies that the process of commercialisation is largely complete and people such as Angima's wife fully rely on the local brew business. Second is that the practice of commercialising local brew represents a shift in its meaning from a drink for rituals and home entertainment to a commodity. Commercialisation has led to the local brew being reworked and redefined in order to put it in the market. It should be noted that there are no special bars where this brew is sold and consumed in Gusiiland, rather it is sold and consumed in the physical spaces of the sellers' houses and compounds, which have been redefined to accommodate customers. This means that the privacy of traders or sellers has been reorganised to accommodate strangers in their homes who come regularly for the drink. These redefinitions, reorganisation and reworking of relationships and space to accommodate customers and the local brew in the market, represent a major recreation of local brew as a resource, through changing its meaning and meanings of phenomena around it.

Re-inventing situations for information exchange

The commercialised local brew has also helped redefine the way people communicate with each other and exchange ideas locally. The drinking place has become one of the major sites for information exchange. Drinking has also become part of leisure and entertainment and thus an important way in which time is invested outside the home and farm. A part of Nyandika's case record makes these issues clearer.

> Nyandika mostly takes busaa with his friends as part of socialising and says sharing the little he has with others is a blessing. While drinking with friends, they share information on different subjects.

Nyandika invests time and other resources in busaa drinking for purposes of socialising, sharing and exchanging information. He depicts the drinking place as a forum for receiving new ideas and offering any that he may have to his friends. Other villagers who do not drink have their own forums for information exchange locally. The three excerpts from case records on Jason, Birundu and Frederick show various ways in which villagers have re-invented sites for information exchange and communication.

> Jason attends the chief's barazas (public meetings) for lessons on improved farming. The chief facilitates arbitration of land boundary disputes at the baraza. Jason sometimes goes to the roadside to catch up on the latest news from peers and friends.
>
> Birundu catches the latest news and gossip from his age mates and friends at the shops and at funeral ceremonies.
>
> Frederick makes phone calls from a private telephone shop at the market. He also receives calls from his sister-in-law at the tea buying centre in the evenings when his friend who has a cell phone comes there to chat with other villagers and to listen to the radio in the restaurant. A cousin to his wife also sends text messages to him through his nephew's cell phone.

The three excerpts indicate that people devise different ways to communicate and to receive information. The market centres, shops along the roads and landmarks such as tea buying centres are major focal points of informal meetings where information is exchanged. In the process these sites have been bestowed with new meanings as information exchange sites. It is evident that the cell phone and radio have been relocated from the privacy of owners' pockets and homes to these sites, to make them more complete for information exchange. Informal creation of sites for information exchange and leisure such as these may conjure up images of idle talk by the roadside, but they constitute important forums that have been constituted creatively to serve local interests and autonomy.

Evolution of formal education as a resource

Education is another resource that has been redefined in a number of ways over time. In the 1940s and 1950s, people such as Petro's parents did not value their children's education and sending children to school was often seen as losing labour from the fields. However, Petro viewed education as useful and made his own efforts, including going to work in the tea plantations to secure his school fees. He also did some farming in order to top up his savings from plantation work and complete his schooling. In seeking education at the time and apparently with his parent's opposition, Petro was seeking to improve himself. He was investing in education for his own benefit as an individual and perhaps for his family in the future. Petro's parents apparently had other thoughts about their old age care and did not foresee the possibility of support from educated children. Since that time children's education and their eventual employment have come to be viewed as major resources.

> Petro explained that his son is a school teacher in the Rift Valley where he lives with his family. "He has bought a piece of land there using a loan from a cooperative society. He usually comes at the end of the month and assists in financial matters, such as buying medicine, sugar, salt and small things for the house and paying school fees for his younger siblings. My other son married through a church wedding in 1991 and the family assisted him to pay bride price. He had one cow which he bought using earnings from his informal business, I gave him another, his brother the teacher contributed one and my two brothers provided him with another".

Most people in Sengeta seemed to be preoccupied with their children's education, either presently or historically. Those whose children have completed school and secured employment recall with nostalgia how they had worked hard to educate them. Those with children still in school describe with pain how they find it difficult to raise the ever increasing secondary school fees for their children. In so doing they are shifting their attention from the farm to their educated children as a long term resource. Their struggle is to successfully mould their children's education into that resource, often under difficult circumstances.

> "Nyakeenga and I differed when he promised to pay school fees for my daughter who was in secondary school but then failed to do so. I have been growing tobacco which I pluck, dry and take to sell at Daraja Mbili Market on Mondays and Thursdays. The money I earn is used to pay my daughter's school fees", lamented Dinah.

Education for children is greatly prized, for at least two reasons. First, given that land resources in the villages are dwindling, the children need an education in order to support themselves outside the village and off of the farm in the future. Second, parents hope that if their children are educated and able to secure employment they will support them when they are in need or in old age. This is particularly evident in the way that employed people from the villages who support their siblings, parents and relatives are praised and thanked in public fora, such as churches, drinking places and burial ceremonies. Successful completion of school is looked forward to with hope by many people.

> Ochiemo said, "One of my sons in high school is doing his final year and he is promising. I hope he will pass and continue to college and help us when we get old. The younger ones in primary are also doing well. Three of my daughters completed secondary school already but did not do well. None of them is employed and all are married". He said he has not received any bride price for any one of them but is hoping that will happen, perhaps enabling him to own cattle again.

Notwithstanding Kenya's high rates of unemployment, a child performing well in school is already considered promising and a potential resource for the parents in old age. This reflects the absence of a formal social security arrangement for smallholder farmers and informal sector workers in Kenya. Ochiemo thought of one of his sons as a long-term resource worth investing in, in order to benefit in old age, and considered his married daughters as a short-to -medium term resource in terms of bride price, which might possibly enable him own cattle again. In general parents define their children, on the basis of custom and experience, as constituting various kinds of resources in the short medium and long-term.

Recapitulation and Discussion

The findings on the processes of reworking and redefining resources over time offer some insights about the state of affairs in rural people's attempts to position themselves in social action around resources. It is clear from the findings that villagers continually assess their circumstances and are on the lookout for opportunities to improve the resources at their disposal. The findings also suggest that the way in which villagers' redefine and rework resources is shaped by multiple external factors and processes. For instance, the reworking and redefining of land as a resource is linked to its increasing scarcity in the region. Nyamira is a land-scarce district with an average population density of 609 to the square kilometre and an average farm size of 0.45 hectares (Kenya, 2002, Nyamira District Dev. Plan 2002 – 2008). This pressure on the land, which had already set in by the 1940s (see Maxon, 2001) may partly explain the high creativity with which land is reworked and redefined. Scoones and Wolmer (2003) argue that land is a key livelihood resource because it can *inter alia* act as security, as a means to gain access to other livelihood options, and as a lever for other forms of investment and linkage. Land scarcity in Nyamira makes people more responsive to the external factors that threaten their livelihoods, evident in the rapid switch to other crops in the wake of the collapse of the international pyrethrum market in the 1980s. Daley (2005b) recorded a similar response to the same problem in Tanzania. In Nyamira the emergence of tea helped drive this change more quickly as it gave villagers a different production option that met their social objectives, especially with regard to their regular need for income for school fees, a need that may not have been so widespread previously. Pressure on the land and people's increasing need for regular income may also have contributed to the transformation of land into an item for lease to meet cash needs on the one hand, and the social objectives of farming for those who rented the land, on the other. On both sides of the transaction the actors seek autonomy in terms of applying their own resources to resolve their problems, rather than go into debt by borrowing. Land is therefore a fluid resource, changing in meaning and use according to the changing needs and preferences of villagers. This is contrary to the conventional view that peasants farm the land according to prevailing external interventions, such as extension. For example, the recovery of pyrethrum prices coupled with extension campaigns have not been sufficient to persuade Nyamira farmers back into pyrethrum growing. This is partly because land is scarce and the competing crop, tea, is permanent. Tea can be leased out or informally mortgaged and the regular income it provides, although low compared to that from pyrethrum, better meets social and economic objectives whether these be payment of school fees, or cash for drinking parties, food or other needs.

Livestock tenant keeping can be seen as a way of redistributing wealth in the form of milk, but also in terms of prestige. While Levine and Levine (1966) had found that cattle owners only take relatives as tenants, the findings in this study indicate that this practice has been reworked and that tenants now also include relatives, friends and former workers. Thus cattle ownership has been reordered and stretched beyond immediate familial relations. This extends the risks that the cattle owner bears in the relationship with regard to crime and witchcraft (cf. Silberschmidt, 1999). Acceptance of such risks, implies that cattle owners have fewer avenues for accumulation and also have to be more creative in reworking relationships and trust. Equally some villagers have transformed cattle into commodities and trade in them in the market. This can be explained in terms of dwindling rural opportunities, as resources become scarce at the same time as need for income rises. The trading is developing slowly and within the means and objectives of local people. It is not as fast moving and capital intensive (involving trucks to transport the cattle) as it is elsewhere, such as parts of West Africa (cf. Haan, 2000). The returns from the trading have been useful to traders and interest in the occupation is increasing.

The interaction between pressure on the land and entrenched villagers' objectives in cattle rearing has increasingly transformed napier grass into a cash crop. The hardy nature of the grass means that it can be produced on the margins such as by the road side, or on sandy and marshy areas. The amount one produces does not matter as buyers move around buying from different people until they have enough. This allows people to produce on small patches of land. Napier grass has also been redefined as a raw material for basket making through basket makers' attempts to retain their craft and the ready market presented by small-scale tea growers who use the baskets to carry their leaves to the buying centres. Trees have slowly assumed a cash crop status as people buy and sell them locally. The big leap in this transformation however, arrived with the change of policy in tea factories to supplement electricity with wood fuel. This has not only provided opportunities for villagers to sell their trees but also created another category of traders dealing in wood fuel. These traders saw the opportunity of buying wood locally and selling in bulk to the tea factory. The major contradiction in this resource creation is that with land scarcity and four tea factories in the district to supply wood fuel to, there is no future in this business. Soon or later the trees will run out and the factories will return wholly to electric power. This provides a powerful reminder that nature has its own limits and that opportunities for resource creation, actor creativity and social action are not unlimited. However, following Boserup (1965), Patel *et al.* (1995) suggest that population pressure and market expansion could spur tree growing among smallholder farmers. This argument would further stretch the argument made in this book about the co-production of resources and challenges the prediction made here that there is no future sourcing wood fuel in land scarce areas like Sengeta.

Leasing out tea bushes has been explained in terms of raising emergency income for paying hospital bills or sourcing quick income for routine expenditure, such as on local brew. Villagers prefer to handle their needs and problems by moulding their own resources in different ways before exposing themselves to borrowing from external sources. Redefining tea bushes as an item for leasing is a new phenomenon in Gusiiland and represents an attempt to find personal solutions to problems before looking outwards. This underscores the high value that actors place on their autonomy. This transformation of tea bushes is partly a result of the liberalisation of the small-scale tea sector that freed farmers from government control and allowed them to engage with other tea markets beyond those run by the state (cf. Kenya, 1999b, Sessional Paper No. 2 on the Liberalisation and Restructuring of the Tea Industry). Leasing tea bushes is thus an opportunity that has been partly facilitated by policy changes that allowed the practice to take place in the open and without sanctions, although it is not officially encouraged.

The local brew, which is one reason for seeking money through leasing out tea, provides a forum for sociability, information exchange and leisure. Villagers also spend time in church and at work on the farm or elsewhere; but in terms of information exchange, informal venues such drinking points, burial ceremonies and shopping centres are the most important in Sengeta. Recreating these venues for information exchange depends on the preferences of villagers, their perceptions of the information that is useful to them and how they choose to get it. The villagers have created and worked out venues for their information exchange that are casual, but which also accommodate their social relationships and modern avenues such as radios and cell phones. Thoughts about communicating with villagers ought therefore, to take into consideration their simultaneously casual yet structured manners of information exchange that appear to be linked with their work schedules and quest for autonomy.

Preoccupation with children's education is evident in Sengeta. The usual explanation for this and the struggles to raise school fees, often under difficult conditions, is that children who are educated and subsequently employed will be of help to their parents in their old age or times of need. Given the flows of assistance to siblings and parents from those in employment it is clear educated children have become a major resource. Education is a way of moulding a resource (children) so that it will later yield desired outcomes such as school fees and other assistance for siblings and relatives. One way for a rural poor family to climb out of poverty is to successfully educate their children and hope that at least one of them secures formal employment. This gives their parents respect in the community as well as providing a stream of resources to parents as well as siblings and other relatives. Therefore, children's education is not just for their own good or improvement, but is a family investment undertaken in the hope of constructing a ladder out of poverty and disrespect. Viewing children as resources, especially in terms of support during sickness and in old age, is partly the result of the customary practice of intergenerational interdependence within the extended family setting and partly a result of a lack of any formal social security system for the majority of Kenya's population. Investment in formal education has been identified as an important attempt by rural people to overcome poverty in Western Kenya (Marenya, et al. 2003) and in other countries such as India (Deshingkar and Start, 2003). Marenya et al. (2003) present education as a virtuous cycle, where 'a good education enables people to access lucrative labour markets in the formal non-farm rural economy, the proceeds from which they reinvest in their children and their farms'. They argue that secondary school enrolments in western Kenya is rising in spite of close to tenfold increase in the cost of education between 1989 and 2002, and that this reflects the socio-economic importance placed on education and the increasing recognition of the importance of education for climbing out of poverty. In this sense, education constitutes a resource pursued in different ways by different villagers. Hoddinott (1992) also found among the Luo of western Kenya, children are a dependable source of support in terms of money, goods and assistance with domestic tasks in old age. A change in state policy that embraces welfare mechanisms could significantly alter parents' discourses about their children as fallbacks in times of sickness and old age.

Concluding Remarks

This chapter has shown that villagers are active in reworking and redefining their circumstances to create resources in a variety of ways. Resources are renamed and thus created for new or additional uses that facilitate livelihood construction. This process of resource creation hinges on the creativity of actors and the continuous scanning of their environment for new or more rewarding opportunities that enhance their preferences, self-respect and autonomy. Inherent in these processes is the use of social relationships in clarifying definitions and opportunities, and in the actual use of the resources created.

This chapter also argues that villagers' avenues for resource creation are not unlimited. Natural and other factors such as institutional arrangements often circumscribe resource creation processes, leading to situated creativity. For example, the future of the wood trade and even tea and napier grass growing are limited by land constraints and local population pressure. Will the local basket making craft die and China fill the gap? When viewing children's education as a resource there is an inherent tension between 'structure' and agency, in the sense that the Kenyan economy may not provide the jobs required. The assumed value of children's education is to some extent dependent on a resilient job market, without which the value of education as a resource may remain chimerical. The definition of children as a resource for the extended family is partly a product of the current levels of social security provision. A change in this state of affairs might have a significant effect on social practices and discourses over children and the support that parents expect them to offer later in life. Human agency and social action must therefore be seen within the reality of natural and socio-cultural constraints that are often beyond the control of actors. Chapter 11 summarises the research findings presented in this book and reflects on some of their key theoretical and policy implications.

CHAPTER 11

Resources and Livelihoods: Looking Forward

The introductory Chapter raised the intriguing question: "how are we to understand the continued survival and apparent social functioning of rural people amidst officially acknowledged absolute poverty?" The question had a rhetorical function and in seeking to answer it, I took the view that rural people construct their livelihoods in ways that are largely invisible to policy makers. This book is about the creativity of ordinary rural people. It seeks to unravel the diverse ways in which such villagers create resources and use them to make their living in a variety of ways and with different results.

Various theoretical perspectives in the literature can be drawn upon to address the principal question in this book, namely: how do villagers in Nyamira District, mid south-western Kenya, create and use resources to make a living and with what results? The actor-oriented perspective emphasises that actors have agency, that is, the knowledge and capacity to act creatively and strategically. The perspective points towards the notion that villagers create resources through their everyday practices, but does not deal with the specific processes through which this happens. Livelihood approaches stress the centrality of resources, expressed in terms of various 'capitals' to the lives of poor people. The approaches thus emphasise that poor people interact in various ways with resources to make their living. However, they define resources narrowly from a materialist and economics perspective, focusing on issues of (un)availability and (in)accessibility. They do not deal with how resources come into being as social, rather than natural elements, or the roles of actors in such processes. The landscape perspective takes the view that livelihood is co-produced by nature and human action, and that the landscape is co-produced through human actions upon 'nature', undertaken in pursuit of livelihoods. The perspective thus recognises a dialectical relationship between 'nature' and humans. Not all resources, however, are the result of this relationship; furthermore the dynamics on both sides are not fully accounted for. As Urry (2000:138) has shown, the view or appearance of a landscape can deceive. In practice, a landscape is the result of social experience; and includes what has gone into creating it, both the struggles and the cooperation. While the dynamics on the natural side of the equation are largely beyond the scope of this study, I proceeded to consider the socio-cultural context of social action and to 'privilege' creativity in the resource moulding processes. Therefore, this book emphasises the creativity involved in the acts of defining and using resources to make a living. Yet, this emphasis recognises the reality of creativity being situational since human agency is not unlimited.

Resources are fluid, that is, they unfold and are often transformed by actors. The livelihood – resources nexus in everyday practice implies that material and non-material resources are equally central to making a living. Non-material resources include social relationships, but are also constituted on the basis of those relations. Issues such as identity, self-esteem, intergenerational respect and interdependence are both relational and constitutive of non-material resources. Non-material resources are socio-culturally constructed and differ between 'fields', or contexts of social action (Crossley, 2001: 87). Yet, social actors do not necessarily stick to the 'rules' and 'timelessness' of socio-economic structures; they renegotiate their relations with other individuals by manipulating common understandings about the situations in which they operate (King, 2000: 421). This explains for instance, why 'ghost farmers' silently infiltrated the TBC committee elections to get their supporters elected, pose as helpers or employees of the TBC clerk and buy glasses of tea for farmers from neighbouring kiosks. All this is done to legitimise their 'illegitimate' positions in the buying centres. The shifts and calculations that villagers make around friendships and through gift exchanges in local brew-drinking places is also negotiated on the bases of re-working kin relations and embracing emerging needs in a cash economy based on the consumption of local brew.

One thread that runs throughout the entire book is how villagers rely on social relationships to create and use resources to make their living. This book seeks to describe and explain this process. At the outset the research question is specified and elaborated as being located in a setting that is described in official Kenyan governmental discourse, and within the meaning of development experts, as one of extreme poverty. Chapter 1, contrasts this discourse with villagers' socially embedded efforts to create resources for 'commencing life' in terms of marriage and bride price exchange. The setting of the research is elaborated in Chapter 2, which discusses the historical construction of the Nyamira landscape with a view to locating the villagers of Sengeta in it. This is done through available secondary data, which do not provide a complete picture, although they do allow a detailed charting of the spatial setting of the study. Using concepts from the actor-oriented, livelihood and landscape perspectives, the study problem is further amplified in Chapter 3. The main outcome of the discussions in Chapter 3 is that villagers do have a certain restricted, capability to create resources through situated creativity in everyday practice (Long, 1992, 2001; Joas and Kilpinnen, 2006). The methodological process for exploring the study question is provided in Chapter 4. An important aspect of the methodological approach is the emphasis on the extended case study method to capture resource creation and use practices from a historical, social and cultural perspective. This enables me to bring out the variety that exists in the processes through which livelihoods are constructed and to map the various lifestyles people deploy for protecting their livelihoods.

Chapters 5 and 6 present the findings relating to resource creation and livelihood construction organised around smallholder tea production, which is the dominant economic activity in Nyamira District. The study shows that migrant labour to the tea plantations in the former 'White Highlands' during the colonial period played an important role in the uptake of smallholder tea farming. The remoulding of traditional work parties, *risaga* helped spread interest in tea, especially among the kin of these 'pioneers'. After taking up tea farming, villagers moulded it in diverse ways in order to make their living, reflecting their preferences and lifestyles and defying the formal view of tea as a government dominated resource. An important finding is how tea earnings percolate into and support social networks through local brew drinking, church, cultural ceremonies, gift exchanges, labour exchanges and rites. Some villagers have successfully moulded tea and tea earnings into accumulation in land, cattle and children's education, leading to what they describe as 'successful lives'. Others have moulded their tea into entertainment in local brew and related consumption leading to low accumulation in children's education and eventually to what they refer to as 'not so successful lives'. From the villagers' perspective the success or failure of livelihood is socially embedded. For example, a patriarch evaluates his life together with those of his entire family, including grown up and married children, especially sons. If the children are comfortable, respectful and supportive to the parents, then the livelihood of the patriarch is successful, and vice versa. This extends the meaning of livelihood beyond material wellbeing to include symbolic and social capitals like good social relationships, intergenerational harmony, identity and self-esteem. These non-material livelihood preferences imply that sharing of resources is crucial to livelihood pursuits and actors' evaluations of their success.

Beyond the tea farm, villagers face a variety of problems that present new opportunities for resource creation and livelihood construction. The overzealous enforcement of leaf quality by the KTDA tea buying centre clerks, and their practice of cheating farmers on the weight of their tea leaf has turned farmers towards alternative markets (*soko huru)* for their leaf. The *soko huru* has two implications for resource creation and livelihood construction. First, as adherence to quality is not so important in *soko huru,* it provides an opportunity for villagers to recreate value in poor quality leaf resulting from weather conditions such as drought or hailstones. *Soko huru* also allows villagers to mould their tea leaf into cash earnings on a daily basis if they choose; unlike the regular KTDA buyers who pay only once a month. This allows villagers to run their lives in different, hitherto unthought-of, ways. Second, *soko huru* has created an opportunity for village scouts who mobilise people to sell their tea leaf in that alternative market. The village scout mobilises farmers to support his claim for commissions from the *soko huru* dealers and has thus relied on his social ties with other villagers to create a resource in the form of commissions.

Villagers embraced *soko huru* in an off and on fashion to resist those who wiled power in the regular market and in to moderate their relations with them in some way. The tea buying centre clerks' practice of cheating farmers on their tea leaf weight is linked to the phenomenon of *mashabiki;* the clerks' handlers who also 'purchase kilograms stolen' from farmers. Some of the *mashabiki* do not grow any tea and are 'ghost farmers' who have falsified farmer registration in the tea buying centre. Other *mashabiki* are tea growers but still 'buy stolen kilograms'. The *mashabiki* phenomenon envelops and enables 'ghost farmers' to create resources in tea and make a living from it, even if they are actually not tea farmers. In the same way, the tea buying centre clerks have transformed their work situations into sites for theft and have shown ingenuity in creating new resources that help form the basis of their livelihoods. Non-ghost farmer *mashabiki* rely on reworking their social relationships with tea buying centre clerks to secure more kilograms and a higher income. Irrespective of outsiders' possible moral appraisal of the corruption involved these processes are all based on relationships of trust and secrecy and require close-knit social ties. These findings show that the governance of smallholder tea and the tea subsector in general is weak and could be strengthened.

Another important issue is deagrarianisation, which is covered in Chapter 7. It is clear from the case material that villagers disengage with farming from time to time, and for a variety of reasons. Yet, from an actor-oriented perspective this process is by no means unilinear, villagers also return to agriculture at different times in their life course. The persistent return to agriculture even when land is becoming scarce can be explained in terms of socio-cultural dispositions and socialisation, the prevailing agricultural landscape and economic difficulties in urban areas. Deagrarianisation is the result of intra- and inter-household dynamics including land scarcity and disputes, aging and inheritance, and emigration. During deagrarianisation episodes, villagers create resources through formal and informal employment in urban and rural areas. In rural areas local brew production and sales are an important avenue for resource creation and making a living. In some instances, this becomes a full time job and a basis for temporary deagrarianisation. Social relationships are central in villagers' efforts to secure formal and informal jobs in and outside the villages and in running local brew businesses. Yet deagrarianisation does not proceed unhindered. It is checked by actor initiatives and resistance, and people re-enter farming even under difficult circumstances. This evidence challenges conventional views about the linear nature of deagrarianisation. It shows instead that people move in and out of agriculture as they rework their contexts and re-orient their capabilities and opportunities in diverse ways.

This brings us to the question of how villagers combine farming with other activities to make a living, which is dealt with in Chapter 8. It is recognised that in trying to diversify, villagers are seeking new or additional opportunities to create resources and make a living. Therefore, the various forms of diversification are identified, described and explained. The discussion departs from conventional analyses of diversification such as Ellis' (2000) because the cases show that diversification is a historical process and that actors work and rework resources differently, transforming the diversification process itself. The forms of diversification discussed result from villagers moulding opportunities in new ways to create resources. For instance, villagers exchange resources through kinship, friendship and gift giving thereby creating and maintaining relationships on the basis of which additional resources are created. Bride-price exchange creates a host of other exchange processes that extend over many generations. Labour exchange has found mixed anchorages in kinship and cash economies. Formal employment and remittances provide another form of diversification. Remittances often generate social forces that transform the landscape and engender further diversification by providing employment opportunities for some people in emerging activities such as dairy farming and napier grass sales. Trading by the road-side, in kiosks and in open-air markets is another form of diversification. Although this is a historical phenomenon, the range of goods and services involved has changed over time, in response to changing lifestyles and local needs.

Local brew production is also, in some instances, combined with agriculture to make a living. This is a negotiated form as it is 'illegal' but bribery and the cultural veil and discourse thrown around it ensures its continued existence. A final form of diversification is crafts, ballast and brick making. Crafts mainly include basket making and thatching houses. These involve approaching familiar phenomena in new ways such as weaving baskets for carrying tea leaf and making them with split napier canes as opposed to sticks that have disappeared with the forests. This illustrates how livelihood diversification is a socially constructed historical process, as the forms of diversification themselves transform through time.

Livelihoods can be (re)constructed and consolidated in different ways. So, how do villagers protect their livelihoods? How do they search for social security in everyday life? These issues are discussed in Chapter 9, which deploys the concept of lifestyle to characterise the various ways in which villagers protect their livelihoods. The lifestyles presented are analytical representations of observed everyday practices in Sengeta. Several lifestyles are distinguished. The first is the accumulators' lifestyle where people strive to accumulate through land, cattle and children's education, and invest in social relationships – both ecclesiastical and secular. When faced with difficulties they first attempt to resolve them on their own before involving relatives and friends. Their accumulation gives them room for manoeuvre in protecting their livelihoods. If they fail to protect them effectively, they fall into a lifestyle on the edge, where accumulation has largely failed and investment in social relationships is weakened, although they still benefit from relationships in sustaining their livelihoods. This lifestyle is defined by the reality or possibility of experiencing intergenerational conflict over resources.

A villager may then slip into a lifestyle in the shadows, in which livelihood is protected largely through 'invisible activities' such as leasing out land and/or tea, and tenant keeping. Social relationships are highly crucial in this lifestyle for locating 'customers' and maintaining relationships of trust that sustain livelihood protection. Villagers in this lifestyle invest in social and symbolic capital. The grey lifestyle may beckon those who fail to protect a livelihood in the lifestyle of the shadows. In this lifestyle the main activities are crime such as theft and corruption, and the production and/or sale of local brew and marijuana. Here social relationships are crucial, but are sometimes ignored. Finally, there is the opportunistic dependency lifestyle. In this lifestyle villagers invest less in social relationships but emphasise them to get quick cash, by doing piece work for short periods of time before disappearing back to local brew drinking places. These people, who are mainly *nyakenywa,* are usually by the roadsides and to a casual observer they may pass for idlers, but they are usually hawk-eyed for opportunities to protect their livelihoods. The opportunities include a cash handout from a relative or a friend or some brief piecework like giving directions to a stranger. Such people often operate on the margins by choice, because of the primacy they attach to local brew consumption. Overall the analysis shows how villagers continually struggle to construct their livelihoods and do so with mixed results, they move in and out of these lifestyles through both negative and positive linkages.

Analysis of the ways in which villagers differently create resources in these cases leads to the conclusion that their creativity is socially, culturally and economically situated. This means that some structural conditions are impenetrable and any creativity eventually meet a dead end. Such tensions between agency and structure are discussed in Chapter 10, which presents fluctuations in natural and economic environments as restricting creativity in some instances, while in others enhancing people's room for manoeuvre in their endeavours to create resources and make a living. For instance when trees are scarce and there are no sticks for weaving baskets, demand for the baskets from the smallholder tea sub-sector provides opportunities for weaving baskets using napier grass canes.

Resource Creation, Livelihood and Lifestyle: Some Reflections

This book has shown that villagers create or mould resources through creative everyday practices. They do this by naming and renaming phenomena and in the process they endow them with new or additional meanings and uses. This process is socially embedded and hinges on the quality of social relationships that villagers enlist from within, and beyond, their households. As a socially constructed process, it implies co-creation in league with others in an interactive process. This study extends the notion of co-creation to include creation in league with 'nature', with other individuals, with groups or institutions (such as markets or state agencies). This is clear in the example of poor quality tea leaf being transformed into a resource through collective action by farmers, village scouts and *soko huru* dealers and networks, a practice which only emerged in the context of policy liberalisation, which threw up opportunities for the emergence of multiple tea markets.

Co-creation of resources also leads to livelihoods being a shared undertaking and process. In using the resources created, villagers emphasise sharing with each other in diverse arenas, including family, church, drinking place, ceremonies and rites. Livelihood cannot then be separated from social life including the relationships that people build, how they spend their time after work and, indeed, their sense of belonging, and autonomy. Sharing constitutes a form of identity affirmation and is a central theme in resource creation and making a living. The striking importance attached to a sense of belonging and acceptance within the extended family and locality, which 'makes one feel alive' is arguably as, or perhaps even more, important than putting food on the table (Wallman, 1984). Therefore, struggles in rural life are arguably motivated both by material and non-material satisfaction.

This brings us to the realisation that resource creation and livelihood construction are like two sides of the same coin (cf. Wartena, 2006: 76). How can the linkage between the two be understood? The concept of lifestyle as conceived in Chapter 3 and developed in subsequent chapters provides this link. Lifestyle connotes an actor's preferences, disposition, identity, primary resource creation and use processes, social relationships, and use of time and information. These concepts have been weaved into the discussion throughout the book and were expounded in detail in Chapters 9 and 10. Throughout, the concept of lifestyle has been used to represent the social constructions around which villagers secure their livelihoods and struggle to avoid disruptions. Lifestyle therefore embodies creativity in terms of showing what villagers do to remain afloat in their circumstances, in other words how they live everyday. Lifestyle also implies the constraints of creativity because it also represents what emerges from negotiations and struggles with 'environments' in, for example, the context of actor preferences, dispositions and identity. This concept of lifestyle resonates well with Bourdieu's (1990) *habitus*, which represents creativity as tied to the specific socio-cultural fields that an actor engages with (Dalton, 2004: 613). For instance, villagers in Nyamira evaluate their livelihoods in terms of intergenerational respectability and support. Resource creation and livelihood construction need to be understood in the context in which they take place.

In Nyamira livelihood diversification involves many clashes with the state. These include practices around local brew production and sales, market rates and business permits. This shows how the livelihood directions pursued by villagers in Nyamira are constrained by wider policies. The conventional policy discourse that local brew is 'illegal' needs to be reconciled to the reality that local brew has been an important arena for resource creation and livelihood construction in Nyamira for a long period of time (cf. Orvis, 1997). Local efforts at livelihood protection reflect the nature of relations between villagers and the state and with other actors in diverse sites beyond their villages. These efforts are largely informal and socially constructed within extended family and clan/neighbourhood circles. The conventional belief that African rural society provides adequate social security through informal socio-cultural arrangements is misplaced. The extended family system is under strain especially due to increased family nucleation and migration.

However, people continue to struggle to anchor onto social relationships through which they can construct and protect livelihoods; and to creatively coin social arrangements to take care of them from cradle to grave. The retreat to social relationships as a basis for resource creation and livelihood construction amidst 'wider development discourses and practices' implies that the social embeddedness of livelihoods, are not a remnant of 'village ethics' but the result of villagers' interactions with the external environments, including the state (Schrauwers, 1999: 105-107). A case in point was the emergence of many sorts of savings clubs [merry-go-rounds] in the 1990s, in response to the introduction of charges for education and health and the collapse of farmers' cooperative societies due to SAPs. These merry-go-round clubs constitute strategies for creating additional resources and securing livelihoods that are based on existing, intergenerational, relations of trust.

Creativity in social relationships also faces an institutional challenge. For instance cyclical deagrarianisation is based on widespread and continuous attachment to the land. This is largely the result of socialisation about ancestral land as 'home', from a socio-cultural and physical security perspective that has become more deeply entrenched in response to the nationwide land politics of the 1990s (Abdullahi, 1997; Cohen and Odhiambo, 1992). This notwithstanding the movement towards non-farm activities and migration to other places also reflects local land scarcity. Therefore institutional and natural factors are both constraints that put creativity under pressure and demonstrate that human agency is not unlimited. Counter-tendencies such as 'ghost farmers' indicate that the institutional leash on creativity can often be overcome through intuitive and unconventional practices. The location of these counter-tendencies *inter alia* in the smallholder tea sector, the brainchild of the Kenyan government, which has historically maintained a watch over it, indicate a disconnection of governance (Due, 1969; Steeves, 1978; Nyangito, 2000 and Gitu, 2004). These governance problems have permitted the emergence of 'ghost farmers' and *soko huru* and this emergence implies that there is much competition over tea, which is an important resource for livelihood construction. This leads some people to create livelihoods at the expense of others as checks and balances in the subsector have weakened. At the same time the quick income from emergent markets, like *soko huru,* facilitates the maintenance of viable everyday livelihoods and moves tea farming beyond entrepreneurship to a form of 'reinvented moral economy', in which people often do not seek the highest returns in an economic sense (Schrauwers, 1999: 107).

Overall the results presented in this book indicate a continuous tension between agency and structure in everyday life and that neither aspect should be over-emphasised. Long's (2001: 16) contention that actors have the capacity to process their social experiences and to devise ways of coping with life, even under the most extreme forms of coercion, extends the role of agency in social action beyond realistic limits. While it is true that actors do survive even under conditions of extreme coercion, this survival should be understood as dynamic, resulting from the interaction of many factors, and not simply driven by agency. A look at the *soko huru* phenomenon shows that it results partly from actor ingenuities and partly from institutional changes (in terms of liberalisation policies in the tea subsector). *Soko huru* enables farmers to negotiate with the KTDA from a position of strength, to secure attention and seek to shift the balance of power in tea markets. Markets, like other institutions, are socially constructed and continually reworked to create space for moulding resources, providing diverse opportunities for making and protecting livelihoods. Engaging with such actor – structure tensions with an open mind, enables us to illuminate the multiple dimensions of problems, instead of focusing on and privileging one angle at the expense of another.

Complexity, Uncertainty and the Future

Reality in rural areas such as Nyamira is in constant flux. That fluidity is partly a result of complex and often 'invisible' rural livelihoods, knowledge, policies and governance that are all trapped in uncertainty. Uncertainty 'describes a situation where 'we don't know what we don't know' (Mehta, et al, 2001: 2). Given the findings of this study, that villagers create and co-create resources and use them to make their living in diverse ways, how do we deal with the conventional wisdom and 'official discourse' organised around powerlessness, inaccessibility, laziness, passivity and unavailability that is used to depict the poor and their circumstances? The findings confirm that social life is always provisional and continually being worked and reworked. In a sense, this means that making a living is like tending a garden, it remains unfinished business, a continuous process. Creativity sometimes leads to unintended consequences or unexpected happenings. In other words, life is not linear and predictable; rather it continually unfolds through actors' situated creativity and its futures and outcomes are less than certain. This confirms uncertainty as the "reality of living in an emergent world, where every moment gives birth to new possibilities and new categories, where existing items constantly create, dissolve and reconfigure themselves, meshing with others to make new entities and new classes of things"(Rocheleau, 2001: 86). This all occurs through and within socially embedded processes.

Therefore, knowledge and learning about the rural poor needs to be recast in a process of iteration that privileges the everyday experiences of rural people and positions their actions in ensuing negotiations of expertises – both scientific and lay (Scoones, 1999). This process constitutes and simultaneously gives rise to a 'pro-poor science' that values and supports poor people's preferences, aspirations and initiatives (Kaimowitz, 2002). This science begins with poor people's creativity and should form the basis for formulating and implementing policies that are relevant, legitimate and relate to the multiple realities of poor people. This challenges conventional notions of and approaches to planning. It suggests that blueprint planning is particularly misplaced. One alternative forward is indicative planning that is anticipatory, flexible and responsive to changing realities, and the multiple activities that constitute livelihoods.

Implications for policy

Chapter 1 began with a litany of policy statements about absolute poverty and its causes. The rural poor, counted as every seven in ten people (67 percent) in Nyamira District, are depicted as incapable of accessing food, shelter, clothing, health and education. I have shown in this book that in making a living, villagers attempt to meet such needs and many others (such as 'proper' marriage, identity, self-esteem and intergenerational support) by themselves. In pursuing these goals villagers mould resources in diverse ways through creative everyday practice and use them to meet their objectives to their satisfaction. This implies that some rural people are poor only in terms of the way development experts define them. The expert definition and the attribution of poverty need to be revisited so as to include actor attributes and especially to deconstruct the official Kenyan view that the poor are lazy. This view appears to follow logically from the flawed notion of resources as being material, available or unavailable, accessible or inaccessible: a view that depicts resources as 'already processed' and static. This is paternalistic and ignores poor people's creativity and capabilities to process and negotiate reality.

It has been shown that the policy environment in the smallholder tea industry is weak, allowing a lack of checks and balances that leads to 'theft of tea' at the tea buying centre, and the unruly tea market, *soko huru*. The governance and regulatory structures in the sector require reinvigorating and strengthening especially the roles of the TBK and KUSSTO. Activities based on the presumed shrinking role of agriculture in rural economies should prepare to contend with the socio-cultural and landscape dominance of agriculture in those areas. Promotion of rural non-farm employment (RNFE) programmes should recognise this, and take it into account. It also means that such programmes should recognise the constraints and gaps that exist within the policy environment in which important small-scale rural traders, such as cattle traders, butchers, kiosk operators and local brew producers and sellers operate. Finally, the assumed social security of the elderly within extended families is crumbling. Land laws recognise the holder of a property title as the legitimate owner for as long as they live and do not relinquish those rights. This uncovers the difficult practical problem of what happens to a patriarch's grown-up children who may have families and no other means of making a living except a claim on their father's insufficient land. If they take up the land how does the patriarch or matriarch make a living? Intergenerational conflict over resources increasingly threatens to displace the elderly in Kenya's rural areas where unemployment is the rule, and employment the exception. These complex and continually changing contexts and processes of resource creation and livelihood construction imply that rural development policy needs to be more adaptive. In particular, it should be less prescriptive, because of the uncertainty that surrounds everyday living, leaving experts with a misguided and incomplete comprehension of these happenings.

From commencing life to locating resources and opportunity

I started this book by explaining how marriage presents a highly challenging time for many Abagusii villagers and represents the actual commencement of life, through the search for resources in the form of cattle for bride-price. This takes villagers in many different directions including migration to find work and income to finance emerging needs. Over time more people have had to 'marry' before they obtain the resources to pay the bride-price. This reflects the changing circumstances of life in Nyamira. Whether they commence life and marriage through payment of bride-price or they postpone it (which, as shown in chapter 9, is becoming increasingly common), villagers set off in life along any one of five observable lifestyles, which provide the basis on which they attempt to secure their livelihoods in diverse ways. Everyday life is a struggle to defend resource creation and use opportunities in particular lifestyles and to rework circumstances into improved prospects for the future or to move into other preferred lifestyles. The struggles in everyday life also proceed on the basis of social relationships and resource sharing, which depend on peoples' socio-cultural and historical orientations, and local and macro level dynamics. Personal preferences, disposition and experience interact in dynamic ways to shape movements between lifestyles that can be used to represent and profile villagers' everyday practices.

In Chapter 4, I indicated my implication in the study, having been born and raised in Nyamira. I am therefore a product of ordinary villagers' motions, from commencing life at marriage through bride-price exchange to struggles in everyday life to invest in tea growing and children's education. The education of children and their possible formal employment constitute important ladders out of poverty. My father commenced life and marriage using his sister's brideprice in the early 1940s. Thereafter he teamed up with one of his brothers to acquire a plough and a pair of trained oxen. Working in turns between their fields in wider work groups, he produced maize for the market and by 1963 had enough money to secure tea stumps for planting, his friendship with a tea extension officer enabling him to plant over three thousand stumps at once. Using tea earnings, he invested in his children's education, bought more land in the village and in the former White Highlands, engaged in dairy farming, retail trade and participated in several self-help groups. I had the opportunity of growing up on a mixed farm organised around tea; plucking tea during weekends and school holidays. In those days there were no 'ghost farmers', *mashabiki* or *soko huru*. The TBC clerk was less influential because quality control was mostly done in the farms by the patriarchs and matriarchs who, being first generation tea growers, wielded unquestionable power in the farms. In a sense I have seen tea farming unfold in Nyamira over the past three decades and in the process, my parents used me as 'free' family labour, invested in my education and eventually look up to me to support them in their old age. My father contributed cattle for my marriage as he did for all his other sons. In retrospect, I can see that he did this partly to redirect our sisters' bride price to our marriages and to weave a relationship between us and our sisters, but also to bind our commencement of life to his magnanimity to strengthen our loyalty to him. It is tea earnings that enabled him to do this and to disperse his sons to the former 'White Highlands', while he remained at home with most of his tea and sufficient room for manoeuvre in his old age. When family land was being shared out for inheritance I was in Wageningen and only participated in the family meeting through a cell phone connection. I was allocated land and tea; although to date I am not a registered tea farmer! I have brought some of these experiences of my life in Nyamira and in tea farming in particular to bear on this study. The changes that have taken place in the smallholder tea sub-sector are better understood in the context of economic change and liberalisation, family nucleation, land scarcity and even the political democratisation that informs the struggles between the KTDA and farmers. But farmers' choices on how to sustain or improve their various lifestyles and what resources to use in doing this cannot be fully understood if we do not include the everyday relevance of creating and recreating the social relationships as resources for actively participating in these struggles.

Bibliography

Abdullahi, A.M. (1997) 'Ethnic Clashes, Displaced Persons and the Potential for Refugee Creation in Kenya: A Forbidding Forecast'. *International Journal of Refugee Law,* 9 (2): 196 – 206.

Adams, R. (2010) *The Short Guide to Social Work.* Bristol: The Policy Press.

Adato, M. and R. Meinzen-Dick (2002) Assessing the Impact of Agricultural Research on Poverty using the Sustainable Livelihoods Framework. IFPRI, FCND Discussion Paper no. 128. Washington DC: IFPRI.

Alderson-Smith, G. (1984) 'Confederations of Households: Extended Domestic Enterprises in City and Country'. In: Long, N. and B. Roberts (Eds.) *Miners, Peasants and Entrepreneurs: Regional Development in the Central Highlands of Peru.* Cambridge: Cambridge University Press.

Alumira, J.D. (2002) Rural Household Investment Behaviour – Implications for Technology Targeting and Development Pathways: A Case Study of the Semi-Arid Tropics of Zimbabwe. A Paper Presented at the CGIAR International Social Research Conference Cali, Colombia 11-14 September.

Andersson, J.A. (2002) Going Places, Staying Home: Rural-Urban Connections and the Significance of Land in Buhera District, Zimbabwe. PhD Thesis. Wageningen: Wageningen University.

Arce, A. (2003) 'Value Contestations in Development Interventions: Community Development and Sustainable Livelihood Approaches'. *Community Development Journal* 38 (3): 199-212.

Arce, A. and P. Hebinck (2002) 'Life Styles and the Livelihood Framework: Problems and Possibilities for Development Studies'. Wageningen: Department of Social Sciences – Rural Development Sociology (Unpublished Paper).

Arce, A. and N. Long (2000a) 'Reconfiguring modernity and development from an anthropological perspective'. In: Arce, A. and N. Long (Eds.) *Anthropology, Development and Modernities: Exploring discourses, countertendencies and violence.* London & New York: Routledge.

Arce, A. and N. Long (2000b) 'Consuming modernity: mutational processes of change'. In: Arce, A. and N. Long (Eds.) *Anthropology, Development and Modernities: Exploring discourses, counter-tendencies and violence.* London & New York: Routledge.

Ashley, C. and S. Maxwell. (2002) 'Rethinking Rural Development' ODI Briefing Paper, March. London: ODI.

Bagchi, D.K. et al. (1998) 'Conceptual and Methodological Challenges in the Study of livelihood Trajectories: Case-studies in Eastern India and Western Nepal'. *Journal of International Development,* 10: 453 – 468.

Bates, R.H. (1989) *Beyond the Miracle of the Market: The Political Economy of Agrarian Development in Kenya.* (New edition, 2005) New York: Cambridge University Press.

Baumann, P. (2000) 'Equity and Efficiency in Contract Farming Schemes: The Experience of Agricultural Tree Crops'. London: Overseas Development Institute.

Beall, J.O. (2001) 'From Social Networks to Public Action in Urban Governance: Where Does Benefit Accrue?' *Journal of International Development,* 13: 1015 – 1021.

Bebbington, A., L. Dharmawan, E. Fahim and S. Guggenheim (2006) 'Local Capacity, Village Governance, and the Political Economy of Rural Development in Indonesia'. *World Development, 34 (11): 1958 – 1976.*

Berry, S. (1989a) 'Access, Control and Use of Resources in African Agriculture: An Introduction.' *Africa* 59 (1): 1-5.

Berry, S. (1989b) 'Social Institutions and Access to Resources'. *Africa* 59 (1): 41- 55.

Berry, S. (1993) *No Condition is Permanent: The Social Dynamics of Agrarian Change in Sub-Saharan Africa.* Madison: Wisconsin University Press.

Blowfield, M. (2004) 'Ethical Supply Chains in Cocoa, Coffee and Tea Industries'. *GMI,* 43 (Autumn): 15 – 24.

Borsch-Supan, A. and R. Schnabel (1998) 'Social Security and Declining Labour- Force Participation in Germany'. *The American Economic Review* 88 (2): 173- 178.

Boserup, E. (1965) *The Conditions of Agricultural Growth: The Economics of Agrarian Change Under Population Pressure.* London: George Allen & Unwin Ltd.

Bourdieu, P. (2000) 'Making the Economic Habitus: Algerian Workers Revisited'. *Ethnography,* 1 (1): 17 – 41.

Bourdieu, P. (1990) *The Logic of Practice.* Stanford: Stanford University Press.

Bowie, K.A. (1998) 'The Alchemy of Charity: Of Class and Buddhism in Northern Thailand'. *American Anthropologist, New Series,* 100 (2): 469 – 481.

Brown, L.H. (1968) *Agricultural Change in Kenya: 1945 – 1960.* Stanford: Stanford University Press.

Bryceson, D.F. (2010) 'Africa at Work: Transforming Occupational Identity and Morality'. In: D.F. Bryceson (Ed.) *How Africa Works: Occupational Change, Identity and Morality.* Rugby: Practical Action Publishing.

Bryceson, D.F. (2002a) 'The Scramble in Africa: Re-orienting Rural Livelihoods'. *World Development,* 30 (5): 725 – 739.

Bryceson, D.F. (2002b) 'Multiplex Livelihoods in Rural Africa: Recasting the Terms and Conditions of Gainful Employment'. *Journal of Modern African Studies,* 40 (1): 1 – 28.

Bryceson, D.F. (2000) Rural Africa at the Crossroads: Livelihood Practices and Policies. Natural Resource Perspectives No. 52, April. London: ODI.

Bryceson, D.F. (1999) Sub-Saharan Africa Betwixt and Between: Rural Livelihood Practices and Policies. ASC Working Paper 43/1999. Leiden: African Studies Centre.

Bryceson, D.F. (1996) 'Deagrarianisation and Rural Employment in Sub-Saharan Africa: A Sectoral Perspective'. *World Development* 24, No. 1: 97-111.

Burawoy, M. (1998) 'The Extended Case Method'. *Sociological Theory,* 16: 4 – 33.

Carlsen, J. (1980) *Economic and Social Transformation in Rural Kenya.* Uppsala: Scandinavian Institute of African Studies.

Carney, D. ed. (1998) Sustainable Rural Livelihoods: What Contributions can we make? London: DFID.

Carswell, G. (2000) Livelihood Diversification in Southern Ethiopia. IDS Working Paper 117. Sussex: IDS.

Chambers, R. (1995) 'Poverty and Livelihoods: Whose Reality Counts?' *Environment and Urbanization,* 7 (1): 173 – 204.

Chambers, R. (1990) Micro-environments Unobserved. Gatekeepers Series No. 22. London: International Institute for Environment and Development.

Chirwa, E. et al. (2005 'Walking Tightropes: Supporting Farmer Organisations for Market Access'. *Natural Resources Perspectives,* 99 (September). London: The Overseas Development Institute.

Chitere, P.O. and Ontita, E.G. (1991) 'Village Communities in Kenya with Emphasis on Kabras Area'. In P.O. Chitere and R. Mutiso (Eds.) *Working with Rural Communities: A Participatory Action Research in Kenya.* Nairobi: University of Nairobi Press.

Clayton, E.S. (1961) 'Small-Scale Cash Crop Production in a Developing Economy'. *Economic Development and Cultural Change,* 9 (4): 618 – 624.

Cliffe, L. (1982) 'Class Formation as an "Articulation" Process: East African Cases'. In H. Alavi and T. Shanin (Eds.) *Introduction to the Sociology of "Developing Countries".* London: Macmillan Education Ltd.

Cliggett, L. (2005) 'Remitting the Gift: Zambian Mobility and Anthropological Insights for Migration Studies'. *Population, Space and Place,* 11: 35 – 48.

Climo, J.J. (2000) 'Eldercare as "Woman's Work" in Poor Countries'. *Journal of Family Issues,* 21 (6): 692 – 713.

Cline-Cole, R.A., J.A. Falola, H.A.C. Main, M.J. Martimore, J.E. Nichol and F.D. O'Reilly (1987) Wood Fuel in Kano. A Final Report of the Rural Energy Research Project, Buyero University. Kano: Department of Geography, Buyero University.

Cohen, D.W. and E.S.A. Odhiambo (1992) *Burying SM: The Politics of Knowledge and the Sociology of Power in Africa.* London: James Currey.

Cohen, D.W. and E.S.A. Odhiambo (1989) *Siaya: The Historical Anthropology of an African Landscape.* Nairobi: Heinemann Kenya.

Cosgrove, D.E. (1984) *Social Formation and Symbolic Landscape.* Wisconsin: The University of Wisconsin Press.

Cosgrove, D.E. (1997) 'Spectacle and Society: Landscape as Theatre in Premodern and Postmodern Cities'. In: Groth, P. and T.W. Bressi (Eds.) *Understanding Ordinary Landscapes.* New Haven and London: Yale University Press.

Cowen, M. (1984) 'Early Years of the Colonial Development Corporation: British State Enterprise Overseas during Late Colonialism. *African Affairs,* 83 (330): 63 – 75.

Crehan, K. (1997) *The Fractured Community: Landscapes of Power and Gender in Rural Zambia.* Berkeley, Los Angeles & London: University of California Press.

Crossley, N. (2001) 'The Phenomenological Habitus and Its Construction'. *Theory and Society,* 30: 81 – 120.

Daley, E. (2005a) 'Land and Social Change in a Tanzanian Village 1: Kinyanambo, 1920s – 1990'. *Journal of Agrarian Change,* 5 (3): 363 – 404.

Daley, E. (2005b) 'Land and Social Change in a Tanzanian Village 2: Kinyanambo in the 1990s'. *Journal of Agrarian Change,* 5 (4): 526 – 572.

Dalton, B. (2004) 'Creativity, Habit, and the Social Products of Creative Action: Revising Joas, Incorporating Bourdieu'. *Sociological Theory,* 22 (4): 603 – 622.

Daviron, B. and P. Gibbon (2002) 'Global Commodity Chains and African Export Agriculture'. *Journal of Agrarian Change,* 2 (2): 137-161.

Davis, R.J. and D.J. Bezemer (2004) 'The Development of the Rural Non-Farm Economy in Developing and Transition Economies: Key Emerging Conceptual Issues'. Chatham, UK: Natural Resources Institute.

Deneulin, S. (2006) 'Individual Well-being, Migration Remittances and the Common Good.' *The European Journal of Development Research,* 18 (1): 45 – 58.

Deshingkar, P. and D. Start (2003) 'Seasonal Migration for Livelihoods in India: Coping, Accumulation and Exclusion'. ODI Working Paper 220. London: Overseas Development Institute.

DFID (1999) Sustainable Livelihoods Guidance Sheets Sections 1-4. London: DFID.

DFID (2000) Sustainable Livelihoods Guidance Sheets Sections 1-5. London: DFID.

Dixon, J. (2000) 'A Global ranking of national social security systems'. *International Social Security Review* 53 (1): 109-122.

Dixon, J. and R.P. Scheurell (1993) 'Social Security: A Cross-cultural Perspective – Introduction'. *Policy Studies Review* 12 (1): 85-91.

Dolan, C.S. (2001) 'The 'Good Wife': Struggles over Resources in the Kenyan Horticultural Sector'. *The Journal of Development Studies* 37(3): 39-70.

Dolan, C.S. (2002) 'Gender and Witchcraft in Agrarian Transition: The Case of Kenyan Horticulture'. *Development and Change* 33(4): 659-681.

Donovan, M. (2001) 'The Intimate Geography of Family Farms'. *Comparative Studies in Society and History,* 43 (2): 273 – 297.

Dorward, A, N. Poole, J. Morrison, J. Kydd and I. Urey (2003) 'Markets, Institutions and Technology: Missing Links in Livelihoods Analysis'. *Development Policy Review* 21(3): 319-332.

Drinkwater, M. (1994) 'Knowledge, Consciousness and Prejudice: Adaptive Agricultural Research in Zambia'. In I. Scoones and J. Thompson (Eds.) *Beyond Farmer First: Rural People's Knowledge, Agricultural Research and Extension Practice.* London: Intermediate Technology publications.

Due, J.M. (1969) 'They Said it couldn't be done, Two Agricultural Development Projects in Kenya'. *Canadian Journal of African Studies,* 3 (3): 595 – 613.

ECA – Economic Commission for Africa (2002) Harnessing Technologies for Sustainable Development. ECA Research Report. Addis Ababa: ECA.

Egoz, S., J. Bowring and H.C. Perkins (2006) 'Making a 'Mess' in the Countryside: Organic Farming and the Threats to Sense of Place'. *Landscape Journal,* 25 (1-06): 54 – 66.

Ellis, F. (2005) 'Small Farms, Livelihood Diversification, and Rural-Urban Transitions: Strategic Issues in Sub-Saharan Africa. A Paper for the Conference on the Future at the International Food Policy Institute, Washington, DC.

Ellis, F. (2000) *Rural Livelihoods and Diversity in Developing Countries.* Oxford: Oxford University Press.

Ellis, F. and M. Kutengule (2003) 'Livelihoods and Rural Poverty Reduction in Malawi'. *World Development,* 31 (9): 1495 – 1510.

Emerson, R.M., R.I. Fretz and L.L. Shaw (1995) *Writing Ethnographic Fieldnotes.* Chicago and London: The University of Chicago Press.

Eriksen, T.H. (2004) *What is Anthropology?* London: Pluto Press.

Folbre, N. (1986) 'Hearts and Spades: Paradigms of Household Economics'. *World Development* 14(2): 245-255.

Francis, E. (2000) *Making a Living: Changing Livelihoods in Rural Africa.* London and New York: Routledge.

Francis, E. (2002) Rural Livelihoods, Institutions and Vulnerability in South Africa. Working Paper no. 02 – 30, Development Studies Institute, London: DESTIN, LSE.

Freeman, D.B. (1985) 'The Importance of Being First: Pre-emption by Early Adopters of Farming Innovation in Kenya'. *Annals of the Association of American Geographers,* 75 (1): 17 – 28.

Frouws, J. (1997) 'The Changing Parameters of Social Regulation and Governance in Agriculture'. In de Haan, H. and N. Long (Eds.) *Images and realities of Rural Life: Wageningen Perspectives of Rural Transformations.* Assen: Van Gorcum.

Garst, R.D. (1972) The Spatial Diffusion of Agricultural Innovations in Kisii District, Kenya. Unpublished Ph.D. Thesis, Department of Geography, Michigan State University.

Garst, R.D. (1974) 'Innovation Diffusion among the Gusii of Kenya'. *Economic Geography,* 50 (4): 300 – 312.

Ginneken, van W. (1999) 'Social Security for the Informal Sector: A New Challenge for the Developing Countries'. *International Social Security Review,* 52 (1): 49 – 69.

Gitu, K.W. (2004) 'Agricultural Development and Food Policy in Kenya: Building a Case for Support'. An Unpublished Paper Prepared for Food and Agriculture Organisation (FAO).

Glickman, M. (1974) 'Patriliny among the Gusii and the Luo of Kenya'. *American Anthropologist, New Series,* 76 (2): 312 – 318.

Gluckman, M. (1949) 'The Village Headmen in British Central Africa: Introduction'. *Africa,* 19 (2): 89-94.

Groth, P. (1997) 'Frameworks for Cultural Landscape Study' In Groth, P. and T.W. Bressi (Eds.) *Understanding Ordinary Landscapes.* New Haven & London: Yale University Press.

Guyer, J. (1981) 'Household and Community in African Studies'. *African Studies Review, 24 (2/3) June - September: 87-137.*

Haan, L.J. de (2000) *Livelihood, Locality and Globalisation.* Nijmegen: Nijmegen University Press.

Haan, L. de and A. Zoomers (2003) 'Development Geography at the Crossroads of Livelihood and Globalisation'. *Tijdschrift voor Economische en Sociale Geografie,* 94 (3): 350 – 362.

Haan, L. de and A. Zoomers (2005) 'Exploring the Frontier of Livelihood Research'. *Development and Change* 36 (1): 27-47.

Hakansson, N.T. (1994) 'The Detachability of Women: Gender and Kinship in Processes of Socioeconomic Change among the Gusii of Kenya'. *American Ethnologist,* 2 (3): 516 – 538.

Hall, A.D. (1936) *The Improvement of Native Agriculture in Relation to Population and Public Health.* London: Oxford University Press.

Hannafin, M.J., K.M. Hannafin, S.M. Land and K. Oliver (1997) 'Grounded Practice and the Design of Constructivist Learning Environments'. *Educational Technology Research &Development,* 45 (3): 101-117.

Harris, J. (2002) 'The Case for Cross-Disciplinary Approaches in International Development'. *World Development* 30 (3): 487-496.

Haugerud, A. (1984) Household Dynamics and Rural Political Economy among Embu Farmers in Kenya Highlands. PhD Thesis, North West University, Ann Arbor: University Microfilms International.

Haugerud, A. (1989) 'Land Tenure and Agrarian Change in Kenya'. *Africa* 59 (1): 61-90.

Haugerud, A. (1995) *The Culture of Politics in Modern Kenya.* Cambridge & New York: Cambridge University Press.

Haynes, J. (2008) *Development Studies.*Cambridge: Polity Press.

Hebinck, P. and M. Bourdillon (2001) 'Analysis of Livelihood', In M. Bourdillon and P. Hebinck (Eds.) *Rural Livelihoods in Zimbabwe*. Harare: Weaver Press.

Heyer, J. (1981) 'Agricultural Development Policy in Kenya from the Colonial Period to 1975', In: Heyer, J., P. Roberts and G. Williams (Eds.) *Rural Development in Tropical Africa.* London & Basingstoke: Macmillan Press Ltd.

Heyer, J. and J.K. Waweru (1976) 'The Development of Small Farm Areas' In Heyer, J., J.K. Maitha and W.M. Senga (Eds.) *Agricultural Development in Kenya: An Economic Assessment.* Nairobi: Oxford University Press.

Hill, P. (1969) 'Hidden Hausa Trade'. *Man, New Series, 4(3): 392-409.*

Hoddinott, J. (1992) 'Rotten Kids or Manipulative Parents: Are Children Old Age Security in Western Kenya?' *Economic Development and Cultural Change,* 40 (3): 545 – 565.

Holland, D.D., D. Skinner, W. Lachicotte, Jr. and C. Cain (1998) *Identity and Agency in Cultural Worlds.* Cambridge, Massachusetts: Harvard University Press.

Holliday, A. (2002) *Doing and Writing Qualitative Research.* London: Sage Publications Ltd.

Holmquist, F. (1980) 'Defending Peasant Political Space in Independent Africa.' *Canadian Journal of African Studies,* 14 (1): 157 – 167.

Holzmann, R. and S. Jorgensen (2001) 'Social Risk Management: A New Conceptual Framework for Social protection, and Beyond'. *International Tax and Public Finance,* 8: 529 – 556.

Humphrey, J. and H. Schmitz (2001) 'Governance in Global Value Chains'. *IDS Bulletin,* 32(3): 1-14.

Hyden, G. (1980) *Beyond Ujamaa in Tanzania: Underdevelopment and the Uncaptured Peasantry.* London: Heinemann Educational Books Limited.

Hyslop, G. (1972) 'Some Musical Instruments of Kenya'. *African Arts,* 5 (4): 48 – 55.

Iqbal, M. (1999) 'Are we Losing our Minds?' *Options Politiques,* September: 34 – 38.

Jambiya, G. (1998) 'The dynamics of Population, Land Scarcity, Agriculture and Non-Agricultural Activities: West Usambara Mountains and Lushoto District, Tanzania'. ASC Working Paper 28/1998. Leiden: African Studies Centre.

Joas, H. and E. Kilpinnen (2006) 'Creativity and Society'. In J.R. Shook and J. Margolis (Eds.) *A Companion of Pragmatism.* Malden & Oxford: Blackwell Publishing.

Jones, S. (1999) 'From meta-narratives to flexible frameworks: an actor level analysis of land degradation in Highland Tanzania'. *Global Environmental Change,* 9 (1999): 211-219.

Kaag, M. *et al.* (2004) 'Ways Forward in Livelihood Research'. In D. Kalb, W. Pansters and H. Siebers (Eds.) *Globalisation and Development: Themes and Concepts in Current Research.* Dordrecht: Kluwer Academic Publishers.

Kabeer, N. (2002) Safety Nets and Opportunity Ladders: Addressing Vulnerability and Enhancing Productivity in South Asia. Overseas Development Institute, Working Paper no. 159. London: Overseas Development Institute.

Kahl, C.H. (1998) 'Population Growth, Environmental Degradation, and State Sponsored Violence: The Case of Kenya, 1991 – 93'. *International Security,* 23 (2): 80 – 119.

Kaimowitz, D. (2002) 'Towards a Pro-poor Forest Science'. *IDS Bulletin,* 33 (1): 123 – 126.

Kamuzora, F. (2004) 'The Need of System Thinking in Development Management: Some Evidence from Two Interventions'. In: Kamuzora (Ed.) *Understanding Complexities of Livelihoods Systems for Sustainable Poverty Reduction.* Bradford: Bradford Centre for International Development.

Kanogo, T. (2005) *African Womanhood in Colonial Kenya 1900-50.* Oxford: James Currey.

Kearney, M. (1996) *Reconceptualizing the Peasantry: Anthropology in Global Perspective*. Boulder and Oxford: Westview Press.

Kenya Land Alliance (2004) 'The National Land Policy in Kenya: Addressing Historical Injustices.' Issues Paper No. 2/2004. Nakuru: Kenya Land Alliance.

Kenya, Republic of (1965) African Socialism and Its Applications to Planning in Kenya, Sessional Paper No. 10, 1965. Nairobi: Government Printer.

Kenya, Republic of (1979) National Development Plan: 1979 – 1983. Nairobi: Government Printer.

Kenya, Republic of (1979b) The Tea Act, Cap. 343 of the Laws of Kenya. Revised Edition 1991. Nairobi: Government Printer.

Kenya, Republic of (1984) National Development Plan: 1984 – 1988. Nairobi: Government Printer.

Kenya, Republic of (1986) Economic Management for Renewed Growth, Sessional Paper No. 1, 1986. Nairobi: Government Printer.

Kenya, Republic of (1987) District Focus for Rural Development. Nairobi: Government Printer.

Kenya, Republic of (1989) National Development Plan: 1989 – 1993. Nairobi: Government Printer.

Kenya, Republic of (1994) Nyamira District Development Plan: 1994 – 1996. Nairobi: Government Printer.

Kenya, Republic of (1996) Economic Reforms for 1996 – 1998: The Policy Framework Paper. Nairobi: Government Printer.

Kenya, Republic of (1999a) Population and Census. Nairobi: Central Bureau of Statistics.

Kenya, Republic of (1999b) Sessional Paper No. 2 on the Liberalisation and Restructuring of the Tea Industry: Reforms in the Tea Board of Kenya and Privatisation of the Kenya Tea Development Authority. Nairobi: Government Printer.

Kenya, Republic of (1999c) National Poverty Eradication Plan, 1999 – 2015. Nairobi: Government Printer.

Kenya, Republic of (2002) Nyamira District Development Plan: 2002 – 2008. Nairobi: Government Printers.

Kenya, Republic of (2005) Geographic Dimensions of Well-being in Kenya: Who and where are the Poor? A Constituency Level Profile, Vol. 2. Nairobi: Ministry of Planning and National Development, Central Bureau of Statistics.

Kenyanchui, S.S.S. (1992) 'European Settler Agriculture' In W.R. Ochieng' and R.M. Maxon (Eds.) *An Economic History of Kenya* (pp. 110 – 127). Nairobi: East African Educational Publishers.

Khan, M.H. (2001) Rural Poverty in Developing Countries: Implications for Policy. Washington: International Monetary Fund.

King, A. (2000) 'Thinking with Bourdieu Against Bourdieu: A 'Practical' Critique of the Habitus'. *Sociological Theory,* 18 (3): 417 – 433.

Kitching, G. (1980) *Class and Economic Change in Kenya: the making of an African Petite-Bourgeoisie.* New Haven & London: Yale University Press.

Kofi, T.A. (1977) 'Peasants and Economic Development: Populist Lessons for Africa'. *African Studies Review,* 20, No. 3 (December): 91-119.

Kongstad, P. and M. Monsted (1980) *Family, Labour and Trade in Western Kenya.* Uppsala: Scandinavian Institute of African Studies.

Korf, B. (2004) 'War, Livelihoods and Vulnerability in Sri Lanka'. *Development and Change* 35 (2): 275-295.

Kuper, A. (1982) *Wives for Cattle: Bridewealth and Marriage in Southern Africa.* London: Routledge & Kegan Paul.

Leach, M., R. Mearns and I. Scoones (1999) 'Environment Entitlements: Dynamics and Institutions in Community-Based Natural Resources Management'. *World Development,* 27(2): 225-247.

Leeuwis, C. (1989) 'Marginalization Misunderstood: Different Patterns of Farm Development in the West of Ireland'. *Wageningse Sociologische Studies* 26, Wageiningen: Wageningen Agricultural University.

Leonard, D.K. (1991) *African Successes: Four Public Managers of Kenyan Rural Development.* Berkeley & Los Angeles: University of California Press.

Levine, R.A. and B.B. Levine (1966) *Nyansongo: A Gusii Community in Kenya.* New York: John Wiley & Sons.

Levine, S. (1979) *Mothers and Wives: Gusii Women of East Africa.* Chicago & London: The University of Chicago Press.

Levine, S. (1980) 'Crime or Affliction? Rape in an African Community'. *Culture, Medicine and Psychiatry,* 4: 151 – 165.

Leys, C. (1971) 'Politics in Kenya: The Development of Peasant Society'. *British Journal of Political Science,* 1, (3): 307-337.

Long, N. (2001) *Development Sociology: Actor Perspectives.* London: Routledge.

Long, N. (2001b) 'The Power of Music: Issues of Agency and Social Practice'. Rural Development Sociology Group, Wageningen: Wageningen University.

Long, N. (2000) 'Exploring local/global transformations: a view from anthropology', In Arce, A. and N. Long (Eds.) *Anthropology, Development and Modernities: Exploring Discourses, Counter-tendencies and Violence.* London and New York: Routledge.

Long, N. and M. Villareal (1994) 'The Interweaving of Knowledge and Power in Development Interfaces'. In Scoones, I. and J. Thompson (Eds.) *Beyond Farmer First: Rural People's Knowledge, Agricultural Research and Extension Practice.* London: Intermediate Technology Publications.

Long, A. and Ploeg, J.D. van der (1994) 'Endogenous Development: Practices and Perspectives'. In: Ploeg, J.D. van der and A. Long (Eds.) *Born from Within: Practice and Perspectives of Endogenous Rural Development.* Assen: Van Gorcum.

Long, N. (1992) 'From paradigm lost to paradigm regained? The case for an actor-oriented sociology of development', In Long, N. and A. Long' (Eds.) *Battlefields of Knowledge: The Interlocking of Theory and Practice in Social Research and Development.* London & New York: Routledge.

Long, N. (1968) *Social Change and the Individual: A Study of Social and Religious Responses to Innovation in a Zambian Rural Community.* Manchester: Manchester University Press.

Lonsdale, J. (1967) 'New Perspectives in Kenya History: A Review Article'. *African Affairs,* 66 (265): 348 – 353.

Lubeck, P.M. (1992) 'The Crisis of African Development: Conflicting Interpretations and Resolutions'. *Annual Review of Sociology* 18: 519-540.

Lund, F. and J. Nicholson (2003) 'Introduction: A New Approach to Social Protection'. In: F. Lund and J. Nicholson (Eds.) *Chains of Production, Ladders of Protection: Social Protection for Workers in the Informal Economy.* Durban: School of Development Studies, University of Natal.

Macarov, D. (1993) 'Social Security as Poverty's Guardian'. *Policy Studies Review* 12 (1/2): 92-101.

Mandi, J.W. (1971) Kenya Tea Development Authority, Tea Cultivation Manual. Nairobi: Kenya Tea Development Authority & Government Printers.

Manona, C. (1999) 'De-agrarianisation and the Urbanisation of a Rural Economy: Agrarian patterns in Melani Village in the Eastern Cape'. ASC Working Paper 32/1999. Leiden: African Studies Centre.

Marenya, P.P., W. Oluoch-Kosura, F. Place and C.B. Barrett (2003) 'Education, Nonfarm Income, and Farm Investment in Land-scarce Western Kenya'. *BASIS Briefs,* 14 (February): 1-4. Madison: Department of Agricultural and Applied Economics, University of Wisconsin.

Marsden, T., J. Banks, H. Renting and J.D. van der Ploeg (2001) 'The Road Towards Sustainable Rural Development: Issues of Theory, Policy and Research Practice'. *Journal of Environmental Policy and Planning;* 3: 75 – 83.

Mason, J. (2002) *Qualitative Researching, Second Edition.* London: Sage Publications Ltd.

Maxon, R.M. (2002) 'Colonial Conquest and Administration'. In Ochieng', W.R. (Ed.) *Historical Studies and Social Change in Western Kenya: Essays in Memory of Professor Gideon S. Were pp. 93-109.* Nairobi: East African Educational Publishers.

Maxon, R.M. (2001) 'Where Did the Trees Go? The Wattle Bark Industry in Western Kenya, 1932 – 1950'. *The International Journal of African Historical Studies,* 34 (3): 565 – 584.

Maxon, R.M. (1989) *Conflict and Accommodation in Western Kenya: The Gusii and the British, 1907 – 1963.* Rutherford, Madison & Teaneck: Fairleigh Dickinson University Press.

Maxon, R.M. (1992) 'The Establishment of the Colonial Economy' In W.R. Ochieng' and R.M. Maxon (Eds.) *An Economic History of Kenya* (pp. 63 – 74). Nairobi: East African Educational Publishers.

Maxon, R.M. (1976) 'Gusii Oral Texts and the Gusii Experience under British Rule'. *The International Journal of African Historical Studies,* 9 (1): 74 – 80.

Maxon, R.M. (nd) 'Early Gusii Resistance to British Rule 1905 – 1914, (KNA 967.6203 Max.).

Maxwell, S. (1999) 'The Meaning and Measurement of Poverty' ODI Policy Briefing Paper, Number 3, February. London: ODI.

Mayer, Iona (1965) 'From Kinship to Common Descent: Four-Generation Genealogies among the Gusii'. *Africa,* 35 (4): 366 – 384.

Mayer, Philip (1950) 'Privileged Obstruction of Marriage Rites among the Gusii'. *Africa,* 20 (2): 113 – 125.

Mayer, Philip. (1951) Two Studies in Applied Anthropology in Kenya. London: His Majesty's Stationery Office for the Colonial Office.

Mbithi, P.M. and R. Rasmusson (1977) *Self-Reliance in Kenya: The Case of Harambee.* Uppsala: Scandinavian Institute of African Studies.

Meagher, K. (1999) If the Drumming Changes, the Dance also Changes: Deagrarianisation and Rural Non-Farm Employment in the Nigerian Savanna. ASC Working Paper 40/1999. Leiden: African Studies Centre.

Mehta, L., M. Leach and I. Scoones (2001) 'Editorial: Environmental Governance in an Uncertain World'. *IDS Bulletin,* 32 (4): 1 – 9.

Midgley, J. (1993) 'Social Security and Third World Poverty: The Challenge to Policymakers'. *Policy Studies Review* 12 (1/2): 133-143.

Mironga, J.M. (2005) 'Effect of Farming Practices on Wetlands of Kisii District, Kenya'. *Applied Ecology and Environmental Research,* 3 (2): 81 – 91.

Mung'ong'o, C.G. (1998) 'Coming Full Circle: Agriculture, Non-Farm Activities and the Resurgence of Out-Migration in Njombe District, Tanzania'. ASC Working Paper 26/1998. Leiden: African Studies Centre.

Murphy, R. (1995) 'Sociology as If Nature Did Not Matter: An Ecological Critique'. *The British Journal of Sociology* 46 (4) December: 688-707.

Murray, C. (1998) Changing Livelihoods in Qwaqwa: Research Questions and Methods of Study. Working Paper 1, Multiple Livelihoods and Social Change, IDPM, University of Manchester.

Murray, C. (2002) 'Livelihoods Research: Transcending Boundaries of Time and Space'. *Journal of Southern African Studies,* 28 (3) September: 489-509.

Mwabu, G. and J. Wang'ombe (1997) 'Health Service Pricing Reforms in Kenya'. *International Journal of Social Economics,* 24 (1/2/3): 282-293.

Mwamfupe, D. (1998) 'Changing Village Land, Labour and Livelihoods: Rungwe and Kyela Districts, Tanzania'. ASC Working Paper 29/1998. Leiden: African Studies Centre.

Narayan, D. and D. Nyamwaya (1996) 'Learning from the Poor: A Participatory Poverty Assessment in Kenya'. Washington, DC: World Bank.

Netting, R.M. (1993) *Smallholders, Householders: Farm Families and the Ecology of Intensive, Sustainable Agriculture.* Stanford: Stanford University Press.

Niger-Thomas, M. (2001) 'Women and the Art of Smuggling'. *African Studies Review,* 44 (2) September: 43-70.

Nooteboom, G. (2003) A Matter of Style: Social Security and Livelihood in Upland East Java. PhD Thesis, Catholic University of Nijmegen.

Nyairo, J. and J. Ogude (2005) 'Popular Music, Popular Politics: *Unbwogable* and the Idioms of Freedom in Kenyan Popular Music'. *African Affairs,* 104 (415): 225 – 249.

Nyangito, H.O. (2000) Policy and Legal Framework for the Tea Sub-sector and the Impact of Liberalisation in Kenya. KIPPRA Policy Paper No. 1. Nairobi: KIPPRA.

Nyangito, H.O. and J.H. Kimura (1999) Provision of Agricultural Services in a Liberalised Economy: The Case of the Smallholder Tea Subsector. Discussion Paper No. 16. Nairobi: Institute of Policy Analysis and Research (IPAR)

Ochieng', W.R. (1974) *A Pre-Colonial History of the Gusii of Western Kenya C.A.D. 1500 – 1914.* Nairobi: East African Literature Bureau.

Odhiambo, W.H.O., H.O. Nyangito and J. Nzuma (2004) Sources and Determinants of Agricultural Growth and Productivity in Kenya. KIPPRA Discussion Paper No. 34. Nairobi: KIPPRA.

Ogot, B.A. (2002) 'Historical Portrait of Western Kenya up to 1895'. In Ochieng', R. (Ed.) *Historical Studies and Social Change in Western Kenya: Essays in Memory of Professor Gideon S. Were,* pp. 13-28. Nairobi: East African Educational Publishers.

Okojie, F.A. (1988) 'Aging in Sub-Saharan Africa: Toward a Redefinition of Needs Research and Policy Directions'. *Journal of Cross-Cultural Gerontology, 3: 3-19.*

Okoth-Ogendo, H.W.O. (1976) 'African Land Tenure Reform'. In Heyer, J., J.K. Maitha and W.M. Senga (Eds.) *Agricultural Development in Kenya: An Economic Assessment.* Nairobi: Oxford University Press.

O'Leary, Z. (2004) *The Essential Guide to Doing Research.* New Delhi: Vistaar Publications.

O'Loughlin, T. (2011) 'The Missionary Strategy of the Didache'. *Transformation,* 28(2) April: 77-92.

Omoka, W.K. (1991) 'Effect of Community Power on Local Development Projects in Kakamega District'. In Chitere, P.O. and R.M. Mutiso (Eds.) *Working with Rural Communities: A Participatory Action Research in Kenya,* pp. 79-87. Nairobi: Nairobi University Press.

Omosa, M. (2004) The *Soko Huru* Trade: Network Building, Informal Contracts and Compliance Failure in the Marketing of Green Leaf Tea in Rural Kenya. Working Paper No. 540, IDS, University of Nairobi.

Omosa, M. (2003) The Interplay between Commodity Markets and Rural Livelihoods: A Focus on the Tea Industry in Rural Kenya. Working Paper No. 538, IDS, University of Nairobi

Omosa, M. (1998) Re-conceptualising Food Security: Interlocking Strategies, Unfolding Choices and Rural Livelihoods in Kisii District, Kenya. PhD Thesis, Wageningen University, Wageningen.

Orvis, S. (1997) *The Agrarian Question in Kenya.* Gainesville: University Press of Florida.

Orvis, S. (1993) 'The Kenyan Agrarian Debate: A Reappraisal'. *African Studies Review,* 36 (3) December: 23-48.

Orvis, S.W. (1989) The Political Economy of Agriculture in Kisii, Kenya: Social Reproduction and Household Response to Development Policy. PhD Thesis, The University of Wisconsin – Madison.

Otieno, W. (2002) Armillaria root rot of tea in Kenya: Characterisation of the pathogen and approaches to disease management. Ph.D. Thesis, Wageningen University

Ouma, E.A., G.A. Obare and S.J. Staal (2004) 'The socio-economic dimensions of smallholder livestock management in Kenya and its effects on competitiveness of crop-livestock systems'. *Uganda Journal of Agricultural Sciences* 9: 31 – 37.

Owuor, S. and D. Foeken (2006) 'Surviving in the Neighbourhoods of Nakuru Town, Kenya'. In P. Koenings and D. Foeken (Eds.) *Crisis and Creativity: Exploring the Wealth of the African Neighbourhood.* Leiden and Boston: Koninklijke Brill NV.

Panelli, R., O. Stolte and R. Bedford (2003) 'The Reinvention of Tirau: Landscape as a Record of Changing Economy and Culture'. *Sociologia Ruralis,* 43 (4) October: 379 – 400.

Patel, S.H., T.C. Pinckney and W.K. Jaeger (1995) 'Smallholder Wood Production and Population Pressure in East Africa: Evidence of an Environmental Kuznets Curve'. *Land Economics,* 71(4): 516-530.

Peacock, J.L. (1986) *The Anthropological Lens: Harsh Lights, Soft Focus, Second Edition.* Cambridge: Cambridge University Press.

Persky, J. (1997) 'Retrospectives; Classical Family Values: Ending the Poor Laws as they knew them'. *The Journal of Economic Perspectives,* 11 (1): 179-189.

Perry, D. (2000) 'Rural Weekly Markets and the Dynamics of Time, Space and Community in Senegal'. *The Journal of Modern African Studies,* 38 (3): 461 – 486.

Petras, J. and H. Veltmeyer (2001) *Globalization Unmasked: Imperialism in the 21st Century.* Halifax: Fernwood Publishing Ltd.

Picchi, A. (1994) 'The Relations between Central and Local Powers as Context for Endogenous Development'. In: Ploeg, J.D. van der and A. Long (Eds.) *Born from Within: Practice and Perspectives of Endogenous Rural Development.* Assen: Van Gorcum.

Ploeg, J.D. van der (1994) 'Styles of Farming: an Introductory Note on Concepts and Methodology'. In: Ploeg, J.D. van der and A. Long (Eds.) *Born from Within: Practice and Perspectives of Endogenous Rural Development.* Assen: Van Gorcum.

Ploeg, J.D. van der (2003) *The Virtual Farmer: past, present and future of Dutch Peasantry.* Assen: Royal Van Gorcum.

Ploeg, J.D. van der, A. Long and J. Banks (2002) 'Rural Development: The state of the art – Introduction'. In: Ploeg, J.D. van der, A. Long and J. Banks (Eds.) *Living CountrySides – Rural Development Processes in Europe: The State of the Art.* Doetichem: Elsevier Bedrijfsinformatie BV.

Ploeg, J.D. van der, et al. (2000) 'Rural Development: From Practices and Policies towards Theory'. *Sociologia Ruralis,* 40, (4): 391 – 408.

Poate, C.D. and P.F. Daplyn (1993) *Data for Agrarian Development.* Cambridge: Cambridge University Press.

Ray, C. (1999) 'Endogenous Development in the Era of Reflexive Modernity'. *Journal of Rural Studies,* 15 (3): 257 – 267.

Razavi, S. (2003) 'Introduction: Agrarian Change, Gender and Land Rights'. *Journal of Agrarian Change,* 3, (1&2) January and April: 2-32.

Reddy, S. and J. Vandemoortele (1996) User Financing of Social Services: A Review of Theoretical Arguments and Evidence. New York: UNICEF.

Roberts, J. (1965) 'Kenya's Pop Music'. *Transition,* 19: 40 – 43.

Robertson, C.C. (2000) *We Only Come Here to Struggle: Stories from Berida's Life.* Bloomington and Indianapolis: Indiana University Press.

Rocheleau, D. (2001) 'Complex Communities and Relational Webs: Uncertainty, Surprise and Transformation in Machakos'. *IDS Bulletin,* 32 (4): 78 – 87.

Rodney, W. (1973) *How Europe Underdeveloped Africa.* Nairobi: Heinemann Publishers.

Russell, J.W. (2003) 'Land and Identity in Mexico: Peasants stop an Airport.' *Monthly Review,* 54 (9): 14 – 25.

Sachs, J.D. (2005) *The End of Poverty: How we can make it happen in our lifetime.* London: Penguin Books Ltd.

Saugeres, L. (2002) 'The Cultural Representation of the Farming Landscape: masculinity, power and nature'. *Journal of Rural Studies,* 18: 373 – 384.

Schrauwers, A. (1999) '"Its Not Economical": The Market Roots of a Moral Economy in Highland Sulawesi, Indonesia'. In Li, T.M. (Ed.) *Transforming the Indonesian Uplands.* London and New York: Routledge and Taylor & Francis Group.

Scoones, I. (1998) Sustainable Rural Livelihoods: A Framework for Analysis. IDS Working Paper 72. Sussex: IDS.

Scoones, I. (1999) 'New Ecology and Social Sciences: What Prospects for a Fruitful Engagement?' *Annual Review of Anthropology,* 28: 479 – 507.

Scoones, I. and W. Wolmer (2003) 'Endpiece: The Politics of Livelihood Opportunity'. *IDS Bulletin,* 34 (3): 112 – 115.

Scott, J.C. (1985) *Weapons of the Weak: Everyday Forms of Peasant Resistance.* New Haven and London: Yale University Press.

Scott, J.C. (1976) *The Moral Economy of the Peasant: Rebellion and Subsistence in Southeast Asia.* New Haven: Yale University Press.

Seur, H. (1992) Sowing the Good Seed: The Interweaving of Agricultural Change, Gender Relations and Religion in Serenje District, Zambia. PhD Thesis. Wageningen: Wageningen Agricultural University.

Shackleton, S., C. Shackleton and B. Cousins (2000) Re-valuing the Communal Lands of Southern Africa: New Understandings of Rural Livelihoods. Natural Resource Perspectives No. 62, November. London: ODI.

Shadle, B.L. (2003) 'Bridewealth and Female Consent: Marriage Disputes in African Courts, Gusiiland, Kenya.' *Journal of African History,* 44: 241 – 262.

Shankland, A. (2000) Analysing Policy for Sustainable Livelihoods. Research Report 49, Sustainable Livelihoods Programme, IDS, University of Sussex.

Sherry, Jr. J.F. (1983) 'Gift Giving in Anthropological Perspective'. *The Journal of Consumer Research,* 10 (2): 157 – 168.

Silberschmidt, M. (1999) *Women forget that Men are the Masters: Gender Antagonism and Socio-economic Change in Kisii District, Kenya.* Uppsala: The Nordic Africa Institute.

Silberschmidt, M. (2001) 'Disempowerment of Men in Rural and Urban East Africa: Implications for Male Identity and Sexual Behaviour'. *World Development,* 29 (4): 657 – 671.

Siporin, M. (1993) 'The Social Workers' Style'. *Clinical Social Work Journal,* 21 (3): 257-270.

Slater, R. and C. Twyman (2003) 'Hidden Livelihoods? Natural Resource- Dependent Livelihoods and Urban Development Policy'. Working Paper 225. London: Overseas Development Institute.

Slater, R. (2002) 'Differentiation and Diversification: Changing Livelihoods in Qwaqwa, South Africa, 1970 – 2000. *Journal of Southern African Studies,* 28 (3): 559 – 614.

Slee, B. (1994) 'Theoretical Aspects of the Study of Endogenous Development'. In: Ploeg, J.D. van der and A. Long (Eds.) *Born from Within: Practice and Perspectives of Endogenous Rural Development.* Assen: Van Gorcum.

Soper, R.C. (1974) 'New Radiocarbon Dates for Eastern and Southern Africa'. *The Journal of African History,* 15 (2): 175 – 192.

Stake, R.E. (2003) 'Case Studies'. In Denzin, K.N. and Y.S. Lincoln (Eds.) *Strategies of Qualitative Inquiry.* Thousand Oaks, London & New Delhi: Sage Publications, Inc.

Stebbins, R.A. (2001) *Exploratory Research in the Social Sciences.* Thousand Oaks, London & New Delhi: Sage Publications.

Steeves, J.S. (1978) 'Class Analysis and Rural Africa: The Kenya Tea Development Authority'. *The Journal of Modern African Studies,* 16 (1): 123 – 132.

Steinwachs, L. (2002) 'Extending Health Protection in Tanzania: Networking Between Health Financing Mechanisms'. Social Security Policy Development Branch ESS Paper No. 7. Geneva: International Labour Organisation.

Stewart, J. (2004). *Stewart's Quotable Africa.* Johannesburg: Penguin Books (South Africa) Limited.

Street, J. (2003) 'Fight the Power: The Politics of Music and the Music of Politics'. *Government and Opposition,* 38 (1): 113 – 130.

Sussman, M.B. (1975) 'The Four F's of Variant Family Forms and Marriage Styles'. *The Family Coordinator,* 24 (4) October: 563-576.

Swift, J. and K. Hamilton (2001) 'Household Food and Livelihood Security' In: S. Devereux and S. Maxwell (Eds.) *Food Security in Sub-Saharan Africa.* London: ITDG Publishing.

Swynnerton, R.J.M. (1966) 'Natural Resources that Govern the Future'. *African Affairs,* 65 (258): 40 – 54.

Swynnerton, R.J.M. (1962) 'Agricultural Advances in Eastern Africa'. *African Affairs,* 61 (244): 201 – 215.

Swynnerton, R.J.M. (1954) A Plan to Intensify the Development of African Agriculture in Kenya. Nairobi: Government Printer.

Sztompka, Piotr (1999) *Trust: A Sociological Theory.* Cambridge: Cambridge University Press.

Talbott, I.D. (1992) 'African Agriculture' In: R.W. Ochieng' and R.M. Maxon (Eds.) *An Economic History of Kenya.* (pp. 75-91). Nairobi: East African Educational Publishers.

Talbott, I.D. (2002). 'The Origins of Small-holder Tea Production in Western Kenya' In R.W. Ochieng' (Ed.), *Historical Studies and Social Change in Western Kenya: Essays in Memory of Professor Gideon S. Were* (pp 141-157). Nairobi: East African Educational Publishers.

Tallontire, A. (2001) 'The Implications of Value Chains and Responsible Business for the Sustainable Livelihoods Framework: Case Studies of Tea and Cocoa'. An Unpublished Paper for the Natural Resources and Ethical Trade Program. London: Natural Resources Institute.

Tea Board of Kenya (2004) Fact Sheet on Kenya Tea. Nairobi: Tea Board of Kenya.

Timberlake, L. (1985) *Africa in Crisis: The Causes, the Cures of Environmental Bankruptcy.* London: Earthscan.

Toner, A., T. Franks, I. Goldman, D. Howlett, F. Kamuzora, F. Muhumuza and T. Tamasane (2004) 'Translating Sustainable Livelihoods into Practice: A Comparison of Livelihoods-oriented Development Interventions in Tanzania, South Africa and Uganda'. In: Kamuzora (Ed.) *Understanding Complexities of Livelihoods Systems for Sustainable Poverty Reduction.* Bradford: Bradford Centre for International Development.

Tosh, J. (1980) 'The Cash Crop Revolution in Tropical Africa: An Agricultural Appraisal'. *African Affairs,* 79 (314): 79 – 94.

Tostensen, A. (2004) 'Towards Feasible Social Security Systems in Sub-Saharan Africa'. Working Paper Number 2004: 5. Chr. Michelsen Institute for Development Studies and Human Rights, Bergen, Norway.

Toufique, K.A. (2001) Sustainable Rural Livelihoods in Bangladesh. Research Report 45, Sustainable Livelihoods Programme, IDS, University of Sussex.

Tsuruta, T. (2003) 'Popular Music, Sports, and Politics: A Development of Urban Cultural Movements in Dar es Salaam, 1930s – 1960s'. *African Study Monographs,* 24 (3): 195 – 222.

Velsen van, J. (1967) 'The Extended Case Method and Situational Analysis'. In: A.L. Epstein (Ed.) *The Craft of Social Anthropology.* London: Tavistock.

Vorley, B. (2003) Food Inc.: Corporate Concentration from Farm to Consumer, A Summary. London: UK Food Group.

Uchendu, C.C. and K.R.M. Anthony (1975) *Agricultural Change in Kisii District, Kenya.* Nairobi: East African Literature Bureau.

Uphoff, N. and C.M. Wijayaratna (2000) 'Demonstrated Benefits from Social Capital: The Productivity of Farmer Organisations in Gal Oya, Sri Lanka'. *World Development,* 28 (11): 1875 – 1890.

Urry, J. (2000) *Sociology beyond Societies: Mobilities for the Twenty-first Century.* London and New York: Routledge.

Wallman, S. (1984) *Eight London Households.* London and New York: Tavistock Publications.

Wallman, S. and Associates (1996) *Kampala Women Getting By: Wellbeing in the Time of AIDS.* London: James Currey.

Wartena, D. (2006) Styles of Making a Living and Ecological Change on the Fon and Adja Plateaux in South Benin, ca. 1600 – 1990. PhD Thesis. Wageningen University, Rural Development Sociology.

Watson, E.E. (2003) 'Examining the Potential of Indigenous Institutions for Development: A Perspective from Borana, Ethiopia'. *Development and Change,* 34 (2): 287-309.

Wekesa, P.W. (2004) 'The Politics of Marginal Forms: Popular Music, Cultural Identity and Political Opposition in Kenya'. *Africa Development,* 29 (4): 92 – 112.

Were, G.S. and D. Nyamwaya (1986) *Kisii District Socio-cultural Profile.* Government of Kenya. Nairobi: Lengo Press.

Whitehead, A. (2002) 'Tracking Livelihood Change: Theoretical, Methodological and Empirical Perspectives from North-East Ghana'. *Journal of Southern African Studies,* 28, (3) September: 575-598.

Wood, G. and I. Gough (2006) 'A Comparative Welfare Regime Approach to Global Social Policy'. *World Development,* 34 (10): 1696 – 1712.

Yamin, F., A. Rahman and S. Huq (2005) 'Vulnerability, Adaptation and Climate Disasters: A Conceptual Overview'. *IDS Bulletin,* 36 (4) October: 1 – 14.

Yin, R.K. (1981) 'The Case Study Crisis: Some Answers'. *Administrative Science Quarterly,* 26 (1): 58 – 65.

Yin, K. R. (1994) *Case Study Research: Design and Methods*, Second Edition. London and New Delhi: Sage Publications.

Zeleza, T. (1989a) 'Kenya and the Second World War 1939 – 1950' In: Ochieng', W.R. (Ed) *A Modern History of Kenya 1895 – 1980 in Honour of B.A. Ogot.* Nairobi: Evans Brothers Ltd.

Zeleza, T. (1989b) 'The Establishment of Colonial Rule 1905 – 1920' In: Ochieng', W.R. (Ed) *A Modern History of Kenya 1895 – 1980 in Honour of B.A. Ogot.* Nairobi: Evans Brothers Ltd.

Glossary of Gusii, Kiswahili and Contextual English

Words	
Ababania	Prophets
Abairi	Relatives
Abakoro	Forebears
Abanto	People
Abanyaisaga	Farm work group [party] members
Abanyibi	Rain makers
Abanywa	Responsible beer [local brew] drinkers
Amache	Water
Amanyinga	Blood
Busaa	Domestic beer brewed from finger millet and maize
Bweri	Cattle pen
Chang'aa	Locally distilled liquor [about 75 per cent alcohol content]
Chiombe	Cattle
Chinsaga	Spider weed
Chirobia /chibese	Money
Chisegi	Fights [wars]
Chisokoro	Ancestors
Division	Administrative unit [above location] in Kenya
	Magical concoctions for arresting or repelling thieves, witches or other intruders
Ebitinge	Ankle Rings
Echikoni	Kitchen
Eeri	Bull
Egesicho	Hide or Skin [used to make clothing]
Egetoro	Support [in money or in kind]
Ekegeni	Party
Ekegusii	Gusii Language
Ekerero	[Invented] maternal grandmother's first visit to see a specific grandchild. May occur for each of her daughters' children if resources allow, but usually the emphasis is on the first born child of each daughter. During such visits *korera* on both sides exchange gifts mainly provided by the child's parents.
Ekegoro	Sandy hilltops (usually covered by fine grass, *ekenyoru*)

Ekerombeta	Flea
Ekerongo	Porcupine
Ekerubo	Lowland or plains
Ekenyoru	Fine Grass for thatching houses
Ekerisio	Taking turns to herd a group's [clan or neighbourhood] cattle
Embori	Goat
Emechando	Difficulties / Trouble
Emeotoro	Arm rings
Emonga	Patriarch's private land [set aside from wives' land and sons' inheritances]
Enchage	Zebra
Engoge	Baboon
Eng'ondi	Sheep
Engoro	Original progenitor and source of prosperity and life in Gusii mythology
Engubo	Hippo
Ensoko	Water fountain or spring
Enyangi	Wedding
Enyang'au	Hyena
Enyaroka	Initiated girl
Enywomo	Marriage
Erongori	Porridge / Gruel
Esasati	Broad grass from marshy areas used for thatching houses
Esindigisa	Merry-go-round
Gesarate	Cattle camp in which cattle from a group of people in an area were guarded by young men and where elders occasionally went to educate the young men. Camps were organised around *ekerisio* groups.
Harambee	Funds drive for a common cause ['Pulling together' – rallying call for Kenya's first president
Huru	Liberal [free or independent]
Inka	Home
Korera	Title by which a man's and his wife's parents address each other.
Location	Administrative unit [below division] in Kenya
Mama	Mother
Mandazi	Sweet dough baked in different shapes. They are a variation of doughnuts.
Matatu	Public Service Vehicles
Mwaye	Her [his] house or lineage
Mzee	Elder [Patriarch]
Ng'ina koro	Grandmother

Nyakenywa	Habitual [irresponsible] beer [local brew] drinkers
Obokima / Ugali	Maize or millet meal
Oboremo	Land
Obori	Finger millet
Obosoku	Shame
Obotaka	(1) Poverty (2) Lacking in milk
Obwamate	Sense of community
Omochie	Homestead
Omogisangio	Peer [may refer to a friend in another context]
Omoiseke	Initiated girl
Omokungu	Married woman
Omomura	Young man
Omonyamosira	Medicine-man
Omonyamwaka	A permanent migrant or one who takes many years to return home
Omosacha	A man
Omosani	Friend
Omosegi	A leader [teacher] of a group circumcised boys in seclusion
Omosuto	A man's gift in cattle to a sister's son to appreciate use of that sister's bride price for his marriage
Ororera	Umbilical cord
Orwambo	A mat woven with sticks and sealed with cow dung for use to sun dry grain
Ototo	Pig weed [*amaranthus hybridus*]
Rinagu	Night Shade [*Solonum nigram]*
Rituko	Day
Risaga	Work party (group)
Sagare	Cattle tenant keeping
Shabiki	Supporter or handler
Soko	Market
Sub-location	Administrative unit [below location] in Kenya
Tente	Swampy [marshy] land
Wimbi	[Obori] finger millet

Author Index

Subject Index

REGNUM EDINBURGH 2010 SERIES
Series Listing

David A. Kerr, Kenneth R. Ross (Eds)
Mission Then and Now
2009 / 978-1-870345-73-6 / 343pp (paperback)
2009 / 978-1-870345-76-7 / 343pp (hardback)

No one can hope to fully understand the modern Christian missionary movement without engaging substantially with the World Missionary Conference, held at Edinburgh in 1910. This book is the first to systematically examine the eight Commissions which reported to Edinburgh 1910 and gave the conference much of its substance and enduring value. It will deepen and extend the reflection being stimulated by the upcoming centenary and will kindle the missionary imagination for 2010 and beyond.

Daryl M. Balia, Kirsteen Kim (Eds)
Witnessing to Christ Today
2010 / 978-1-870345-77-4 / 301pp

This volume, the second in the Edinburgh 2010 series, includes reports of the nine main study groups working on different themes for the celebration of the centenary of the World Missionary Conference, Edinburgh 1910. Their collaborative work brings together perspectives that are as inclusive as possible of contemporary world Christianity and helps readers to grasp what it means in different contexts to be 'witnessing to Christ today'.

Claudia Währisch-Oblau, Fidon Mwombeki (Eds)
Mission Continues
Global Impulses for the 21st Century
2010 / 978-1-870345-82-8 / 271pp

In May 2009, 35 theologians from Asia, Africa and Europe met in Wuppertal, Germany, for a consultation on mission theology organized by the United Evangelical Mission: Communion of 35 Churches in Three Continents. The aim was to participate in the 100th anniversary of the Edinburgh conference through a study process and reflect on the challenges for mission in the 21st century. This book brings together these papers written by experienced practitioners from around the world.

Brian Woolnough and Wonsuk Ma (Eds)
Holistic Mission
God's plan for God's people
2010 / 978-1-870345-85-9 / 277pp

Holistic mission, or integral mission, implies God is concerned with the whole person, the whole community, body, mind and spirit. This book discusses the meaning of the holistic gospel, how it has developed, and implications for the church. It takes a global, eclectic approach, with 19 writers, all of whom have much experience in, and commitment to, holistic mission. It addresses critically and honestly one of the most exciting, and challenging, issues facing the church today. To be part of God's plan for God's people, the church must take holistic mission to the world.

Kirsteen Kim and Andrew Anderson (Eds)
Mission Today and Tomorrow
2010 / 978-1-870345-91-0 / 450pp

There are moments in our lives when we come to realise that we are participating in the triune God's mission. If we believe the church to be as sign and symbol of the reign of God in the world, then we are called to witness to Christ today by sharing in God's mission of love through the transforming power of the Holy Spirit. We can all participate in God's transforming and reconciling mission of love to the whole creation.

Tormod Engelsviken, Erling Lundeby and Dagfinn Solheim (Eds)
The Church Going Glocal
Mission and Globalisation 2011 / 978-1-870345-93-4 / 262pp

The New Testament church is... universal and local at the same time. The universal, one and holy apostolic church appears in local manifestations. Missiologically speaking... the church can take courage as she faces the increasing impact of globalisation on local communities today. Being universal and concrete, the church is geared for the simultaneous challenges of the glocal and local.

Marina Ngurusangzeli Behera (Ed)
Interfaith Relations after One Hundred Years
Christian Mission among Other Faiths 2011 / 978-1-870345-96-5 / 334 pp

The essays of this book reflect not only the acceptance and celebration of pluralism within India but also by extension an acceptance as well as a need for unity among Indian Christians of different denominations. The essays were presented and studied at a preparatory consultation on Study Theme II: Christian Mission Among Other Faiths at the United Theological College, India July 2009.

Lalsangkima Pachuau and Knud Jørgensen (Eds)
Witnessing to Christ in a Pluralistic Age
Christian Mission among Other Faiths 2011 / 978-1-870345-95-8 / 277 pp

In a world where plurality of faiths is increasingly becoming a norm of life, insights on the theology of religious plurality are needed to strengthen our understanding of our own faith and the faith of others. Even though religious diversity is not new, we are seeing an upsurge in interest on the theologies of religion among all Christian confessional traditions. It can be claimed that no other issue in Christian mission is more important and more difficult than the theologies of religions.

Beth Snodderly and A Scott Moreau (Eds)

Evangelical Frontier Mission

Perspectives on the Global Progress of the Gospel

2011 / 978-1-870345-98-9 / 312pp

This important volume demonstrates that 100 years after the World Missionary Conference in Edinburgh, Evangelism has become truly global. Twenty-first-century Evangelism continues to focus on frontier mission, but significantly, and in the spirit of Edinburgh 1910, it also has re-engaged social action.

Rolv Olsen (Ed)

Mission and Postmodernities

2011 / 978-1-870345-97-2 / 279pp

This volume takes on meaning because its authors honestly struggle with and debate how we should relate to postmodernities. Should our response be accommodation, relativizing or counter-culture? How do we strike a balance between listening and understanding, and at the same time exploring how postmodernities influence the interpretation and application of the Bible as the normative story of God's mission in the world?

Cathy Ross (Ed)

Life-Widening Mission

2012 / 978-1-908355-00-3 / 190pp

It is clear from the essays collected here that the experience of the 2010 World Mission Conference in Edinburgh was both affirming and frustrating for those taking part - affirming because of its recognition of how the centre of gravity has moved in global Christianity; frustrating because of the relative slowness of so many global Christian bodies to catch up with this and to embody it in the way they do business and in the way they represent themselves. These reflections will—or should—provide plenty of food for thought in the various councils of the Communion in the coming years.

Beate Fagerli, Knud Jørgensen, Rolv Olsen, Kari Storstein Haug and Knut Tveitereid (Eds)

A Learning Missional Church

Reflections from Young Missiologists

2012 / 978-1-908355-01-1 / 239pp

Cross-cultural mission has always been a primary learning experience for the church. It pulls us out of a mono-cultural understanding and helps us discover a legitimate theological pluralism which opens up for new perspectives in the Gospel. Translating the Gospel into new languages and cultures is a human and divine means of making us learn new 'incarnations' of the Good News.

REGNUM STUDIES IN GLOBAL CHRISTIANITY

(Previously GLOBAL THEOLOGICAL VOICES series)

Series Listing

David Emmanuel Singh (Ed)
Jesus and the Cross
Reflections of Christians from Islamic Contexts
2008 / 978-1-870345-65-1 / 226pp

The Cross reminds us that the sins of the world are not borne through the exercise of power but through Jesus Christ's submission to the will of the Father. The papers in this volume are organised in three parts: scriptural, contextual and theological. The central question being addressed is: how do Christians living in contexts, where Islam is a majority or minority religion, experience, express or think of the Cross?

Sung-wook Hong
Naming God in Korea
The Case of Protestant Christianity
2008 / 978-1-870345-66-8 / 170pp

Since Christianity was introduced to Korea more than a century ago, one of the most controversial issues has been the Korean term for the Christian 'God'. This issue is not merely about naming the Christian God in Korean language, but it relates to the question of theological contextualization - the relationship between the gospel and culture - and the question of Korean Christian identity. This book demonstrates the nature of the gospel in relation to cultures, i.e., the universality of the gospel expressed in all human cultures.

Hubert van Beek (Ed)
Revisioning Christian Unity
The Global Christian Forum
2009 / 978-1-870345-74-3 / 288pp

This book contains the records of the Global Christian Forum gathering held in Limuru near Nairobi, Kenya, on 6 – 9 November 2007 as well as the papers presented at that historic event. Also included are a summary of the Global Christian Forum process from its inception until the 2007 gathering and the reports of the evaluation of the process that was carried out in 2008.

Young-hoon Lee
The Holy Spirit Movement in Korea
Its Historical and Theological Development
2009 / 978-1-870345-67-5 / 174pp

This book traces the historical and theological development of the Holy Spirit Movement in Korea through six successive periods (from 1900 to the present time). These periods are characterized by repentance and revival (1900-20), persecution and suffering under Japanese occupation (1920-40), confusion and division (1940-60), explosive revival in which the Pentecostal movement played a major role in the rapid growth of Korean churches (1960-80), the movement reaching out to all denominations (1980-2000), and the new context demanding the Holy Spirit movement to open new horizons in its mission engagement (2000-).

Paul Hang-Sik Cho
Eschatology and Ecology
Experiences of the Korean Church
2010 / 978-1-870345-75-0 / 260pp

This book raises the question of why Korean people, and Korean Protestant Christians in particular, pay so little attention to ecological issues. The author argues that there is an important connection (or elective affinity) between this lack of attention and the other-worldly eschatology that is so dominant within Korean Protestant Christianity.

Dietrich Werner, David Esterline, Namsoon Kang, Joshva Raja (Eds)
The Handbook of Theological Education in World Christianity
Theological Perspectives, Ecumenical Trends, Regional Surveys
2010 / 978-1-870345-80-4 / 759pp

This major reference work is the first ever comprehensive study of Theological Education in Christianity of its kind. With contributions from over 90 international scholars and church leaders, it aims to be easily accessible across denominational, cultural, educational, and geographic boundaries. The Handbook will aid international dialogue and networking among theological educators, institutions, and agencies

David Emmanuel Singh & Bernard C Farr (Eds)
Christianity and Education
Shaping of Christian Context in Thinking
2010 / 978-1-870345-81-1 / 374pp

Christianity and Education is a collection of papers published in *Transformation: An International Journal of Holistic Mission Studies* over a period of 15 years. The articles represent a spectrum of Christian thinking addressing issues of institutional development for theological education, theological studies in the context of global mission, contextually aware/informed education, and academies which deliver such education, methodologies and personal reflections.

J.Andrew Kirk
Civilisations in Conflict?
Islam, the West and Christian Faith
2011 / 978-1-870345-87-3 / 205pp

Samuel Huntington's thesis, which argues that there appear to be aspects of Islam that could be on a collision course with the politics and values of Western societies, has provoked much controversy. The purpose of this study is to offer a particular response to Huntington's thesis by making a comparison between the origins of Islam and Christianity.

David Emmanuel Singh (Ed)
Jesus and the Incarnation
Reflections of Christians from Islamic Contexts
2011 / 978-1-870345-90-3 / 250pp

In the dialogues of Christians with Muslims nothing is more fundamental than the Cross, the Incarnation and the Resurrection of Jesus. Building on the *Jesus and the Cross*, this book contains voices of Christians living in various 'Islamic contexts' and reflecting on the Incarnation of Jesus. The aim and hope of these reflections is that the papers weaved around the notion of 'the Word' will not only promote dialogue among Christians on the roles of the Person and the Book but, also, create a positive environment for their conversations with Muslim neighbours.

Ivan M Satyavrata
God Has Not left Himself Without Witness
2011 / 978-1-870345-79-8 / 260pp

Since its earliest inception the Christian Church has had to address the question of what common ground exits between Christian faiths and other religions. This issue is not merely of academic interest but one with critical existential and socio-political consequences. This study presents a case for the revitalization of the fulfillment tradition based on a recovery and assessment of the fulfillment approaches of Indian Christian converts in the pre-independence period.

REGNUM STUDIES IN MISSION

Series Listing

Kwame Bediako

Theology and Identity

The Impact of Culture upon Christian Thought in the Second Century and in Modern Africa

1992 / 978-1870345-80-2 / 508pp

The author examines the question of Christian identity in the context of the Graeco–Roman culture of the early Roman Empire. He then addresses the modern African predicament of quests for identity and integration.

Christopher Sugden

Seeking the Asian Face of Jesus

The Practice and Theology of Christian Social Witness in Indonesia and India 1974–1996

1997 / 1-870345-26-6 / 496pp

This study focuses on contemporary holistic mission with the poor in India and Indonesia combined with the call to transformation of all life in Christ with micro-credit enterprise schemes. 'The literature on contextual theology now has a new standard to rise to' – Lamin Sanneh (Yale University, USA).

Hwa Yung

Mangoes or Bananas?

The Quest for an Authentic Asian Christian Theology

1997 / 1-870345-25-5 / 274pp

Asian Christian thought remains largely captive to Greek dualism and Enlightenment rationalism because of the overwhelming dominance of Western culture. Authentic contextual Christian theologies will emerge within Asian Christianity with a dual recovery of confidence in culture and the gospel.

Keith E. Eitel

Paradigm Wars

The Southern Baptist International Mission Board Faces the Third Millennium

1999 / 1-870345-12-6 / 140pp

The International Mission Board of the Southern Baptist Convention is the largest denominational mission agency in North America. This volume chronicles the historic and contemporary forces that led to the IMB's recent extensive reorganization, providing the most comprehensive case study to date of a historic mission agency restructuring to continue its mission purpose into the twenty-first century more effectively.

Samuel Jayakumar

Dalit Consciousness and Christian Conversion

Historical Resources for a Contemporary Debate 1999 / 81-7214-497-0 / 434pp

(Published jointly with ISPCK)

The main focus of this historical study is social change and transformation among the Dalit Christian communities in India. Historiography tests the evidence in the light of the conclusions of the modern Dalit liberation theologians.

Vinay Samuel and Christopher Sugden (Eds)

Mission as Transformation

A Theology of the Whole Gospel

1999 / 978-18703455-13-2/ 522pp

This book brings together in one volume twenty five years of biblical reflection on mission practice with the poor from around the world. This volume helps anyone understand how evangelicals, struggling to unite evangelism and social action, found their way in the last twenty five years to the biblical view of mission in which God calls all human beings to love God and their neighbour; never creating a separation between the two.

Christopher Sugden

Gospel, Culture and Transformation

2000 / 1-870345-32-0 /152pp

A Reprint, with a New Introduction, of Part Two of Seeking the Asian Face of Jesus

Gospel, Culture and Transformation explores the practice of mission especially in relation to transforming cultures and communities. - 'Transformation is to enable God's vision of society to be actualised in all relationships: social, economic and spiritual, so that God's will may be reflected in human society and his love experienced by all communities, especially the poor.'

Bernhard Ott

Beyond Fragmentation: Integrating Mission and Theological Education

A Critical Assessment of some Recent Developments in Evangelical Theological Education

2001 / 1-870345-14-2 / 382pp

Beyond Fragmentation is an enquiry into the development of Mission Studies in evangelical theological education in Germany and German-speaking Switzerland between 1960 and 1995. The author undertakes a detailed examination of the paradigm shifts which have taken place in recent years in both the theology of mission and the understanding of theological education.

Gideon Githiga

The Church as the Bulwark against Authoritarianism

Development of Church and State Relations in Kenya, with Particular Reference to the Years after Political Independence 1963-1992

2002 / 1-870345-38-x / 218pp

'All who care for love, peace and unity in Kenyan society will want to read this careful history by Bishop Githiga of how Kenyan Christians, drawing on the Bible, have sought to share the love of God, bring his peace and build up the unity of the nation, often in the face of great difficulties and opposition.' Canon Dr Chris Sugden, Oxford Centre for Mission Studies.

Myung Sung-Hoon, Hong Young-Gi (eds.)

Charis and Charisma

David Yonggi Cho and the Growth of Yoido Full Gospel Church

2003 / 978-1870345-45-3 / 218pp

This book discusses the factors responsible for the growth of the world's largest church. It expounds the role of the Holy Spirit, the leadership, prayer, preaching, cell groups and creativity in promoting church growth. It focuses on God's grace (charis) and inspiring leadership (charisma) as the two essential factors and the book's purpose is to present a model for church growth worldwide.

Samuel Jayakumar

Mission Reader

Historical Models for Wholistic Mission in the Indian Context

2003 / 1-870345-42-8 / 250pp

(Published jointly with ISPCK)

This book is written from an evangelical point of view revalidating and reaffirming the Christian commitment to wholistic mission. The roots of the 'wholistic mission' combining 'evangelism and social concerns' are to be located in the history and tradition of Christian evangelism in the past; and the civilizing purpose of evangelism is compatible with modernity as an instrument in nation building.

Bob Robinson

Christians Meeting Hindus

An Analysis and Theological Critique of the Hindu-Christian Encounter in India

2004 / 987-1870345-39-2 / 392pp

This book focuses on the Hindu-Christian encounter, especially the intentional meeting called dialogue, mainly during the last four decades of the twentieth century, and specifically in India itself.

Gene Early

Leadership Expectations

How Executive Expectations are Created and Used in a Non-Profit Setting

2005 / 1-870345-30-4 / 276pp

The author creates an Expectation Enactment Analysis to study the role of the Chancellor of the University of the Nations-Kona, Hawaii. This study is grounded in the field of managerial work, jobs, and behaviour and draws on symbolic interactionism, role theory, role identity theory and enactment theory. The result is a conceptual framework for developing an understanding of managerial roles.

Tharcisse Gatwa

The Churches and Ethnic Ideology in the Rwandan Crises 1900-1994

2005 / 978-1870345-24-8 / 300pp

(Reprinted 2011)

Since the early years of the twentieth century Christianity has become a new factor in Rwandan society. This book investigates the role Christian churches played in the formulation and development of the racial ideology that culminated in the 1994 genocide.

Julie Ma

Mission Possible

Biblical Strategies for Reaching the Lost

2005 / 978-1870345-37-1 / 142pp

This is a missiology book for the church which liberates missiology from the specialists for the benefit of every believer. It also serves as a textbook that is simple and friendly, and yet solid in biblical interpretation. This book links the biblical teaching to the actual and contemporary missiological settings with examples, making the Bible come alive to the reader.

Allan Anderson, Edmond Tang (Eds)

Asian and Pentecostal

The Charismatic Face of Christianity in Asia

2005 / 1-870345-43-9 / 596pp

(Reprinted 2011)

(Published jointly with APTS Press)

This book provides a thematic discussion and pioneering case studies on the history and development of Pentecostal and Charismatic churches in the countries of South Asia, South East Asia and East Asia.

I. Mark Beaumont

Christology in Dialogue with Muslims

A Critical Analysis of Christian Presentations of Christ for Muslims from the Ninth and Twentieth Centuries

2005 / 1978-1870345-46-0 / 228pp

This book analyses Christian presentations of Christ for Muslims in the most creative periods of Christian-Muslim dialogue, the first half of the ninth century and the second half of the twentieth century. In these two periods, Christians made serious attempts to present their faith in Christ in terms that take into account Muslim perceptions of him, with a view to bridging the gap between Muslim and Christian convictions.

Thomas Czövek,

Three Seasons of Charismatic Leadership

A Literary-Critical and Theological Interpretation of the Narrative of Saul, David and Solomon

2006 / 978-1870345-48-4 / 272pp

This book investigates the charismatic leadership of Saul, David and Solomon. It suggests that charismatic leaders emerge in crisis situations in order to resolve the crisis by the charisma granted by God. Czovek argues that Saul proved himself as a charismatic leader as long as he acted resolutely and independently from his mentor Samuel. In the author's eyes, Saul's failure to establish himself as a charismatic leader is caused by his inability to step out from Samuel's shadow.

Jemima Atieno Oluoch

The Christian Political Theology of Dr. John Henry Okullu

2006 / 1-870345-51-4 / 137pp

This book reconstructs the Christian political theology of Bishop John Henry Okullu, DD, through establishing what motivated him and the biblical basis for his socio-political activities. It also attempts to reconstruct the socio-political environment that nurtured Dr Okullu's prophetic ministry.

Richard Burgess

Nigeria's Christian Revolution

The Civil War Revival and Its Pentecostal Progeny (1967-2006)

2008 / 978-1-870345-63-7 / 347pp

This book describes the revival that occurred among the Igbo people of Eastern Nigeria and the new Pentecostal churches it generated, and documents the changes that have occurred as the movement has responded to global flows and local demands. As such, it explores the nature of revivalist and Pentecostal experience, but does so against the backdrop of local socio-political and economic developments, such as decolonisation and civil war, as well as broader processes, such as modernisation and globalisation.

David Emmanuel Singh & Bernard C Farr (Eds)
Christianity and Cultures
Shaping Christian Thinking in Context
2008 / 978-1-870345-69-9 / 260pp

This volume marks an important milestone, the 25th anniversary of the Oxford Centre for Mission Studies (OCMS). The papers here have been exclusively sourced from Transformation, a quarterly journal of OCMS, and seek to provide a tripartite view of Christianity's engagement with cultures by focusing on the question: how is Christian thinking being formed or reformed through its interaction with the varied contexts it encounters? The subject matters include different strands of theological-missiological thinking, socio-political engagements and forms of family relationships in interaction with the host cultures.

Tormod Engelsviken, Ernst Harbakk, Rolv Olsen, Thor Strandenæs (Eds)
Mission to the World
Communicating the Gospel in the 21st Century: Essays in Honour of Knud Jørgensen
2008 / 978-1-870345-64-4 / 472pp

Knud Jørgensen is Director of Areopagos and Associate Professor of Missiology at MF Norwegian School of Theology. This book reflects on the main areas of Jørgensen's commitment to mission. At the same time it focuses on the main frontier of mission, the world, the content of mission, the Gospel, the fact that the Gospel has to be communicated, and the context of contemporary mission in the 21st century.

Al Tizon
Transformation after Lausanne
Radical Evangelical Mission in Global-Local Perspective
2008 / 978-1-870345-68-2 / 281pp

After Lausanne '74, a worldwide network of radical evangelical mission theologians and practitioners use the notion of "Mission as Transformation" to integrate evangelism and social concern together, thus lifting theological voices from the Two Thirds World to places of prominence. This book documents the definitive gatherings, theological tensions, and social forces within and without evangelicalism that led up to Mission as Transformation. And it does so through a global-local grid that points the way toward greater holistic mission in the 21st century.

Bambang Budijanto
Values and Participation
Development in Rural Indonesia
2009 / 978-1-870345-70-4 / 237pp

Socio-religious values and socio-economic development are inter-dependant, inter-related and are constantly changing in the context of macro political structures, economic policy, religious organizations and globalization; and micro influences such as local affinities, identity, politics, leadership and beliefs. The book argues that the comprehensive approach in understanding the socio-religious values of each of the three local Lopait communities in Central Java is essential to accurately describing their respective identity.

Alan R. Johnson

Leadership in a Slum

A Bangkok Case Study

2009 / 978-1-870345-71-2 / 238pp

This book looks at leadership in the social context of a slum in Bangkok from a different perspective than traditional studies which measure well educated Thais on leadership scales derived in the West. Using both systematic data collection and participant observation, it develops a culturally preferred model as well as a set of models based in Thai concepts that reflect on-the-ground realities. It concludes by looking at the implications of the anthropological approach for those who are involved in leadership training in Thai settings and beyond.

Titre Ande

Leadership and Authority

Bula Matari and Life - Community Ecclesiology in Congo

2010 / 978-1-870345-72-9 / 189pp

Christian theology in Africa can make significant development if a critical understanding of the socio-political context in contemporary Africa is taken seriously, particularly as Africa's post-colonial Christian leadership based its understanding and use of authority on the Bula Matari model. This has caused many problems and Titre proposes a Life-Community ecclesiology for liberating authority, here leadership is a function, not a status, and 'apostolic succession' belongs to all people of God.

Frank Kwesi Adams

Odwira and the Gospel

A Study of the Asante Odwira Festival and its Significance for Christianity in Ghana

2010 /978-1-870345-59-0 / 232pp

The study of the Odwira festival is the key to the understanding of Asante religious and political life in Ghana. The book explores the nature of the Odwira festival longitudinally - in pre-colonial, colonial and post-independence Ghana - and examines the Odwira ideology and its implications for understanding the Asante self-identity. Also discussed is how some elements of faith portrayed in the Odwira festival can provide a framework for Christianity to engage with Asante culture at a greater depth.

Bruce Carlton

Strategy Coordinator

Changing the Course of Southern Baptist Missions

2010 / 978-1-870345-78-1 / 268pp

This is an outstanding, one-of-a-kind work addressing the influence of the non-residential missionary/strategy coordinator's role in Southern Baptist missions. This scholarly text examines the twentieth century global missiological currents that influenced the leadership of the International Mission Board, resulting in a new paradigm to assist in taking the gospel to the nations.

Julie Ma & Wonsuk Ma

Mission in the Spirit:

Towards a Pentecostal/Charismatic Missiology

2010 / 978-1-870345-84-2 / 312pp

The book explores the unique contribution of Pentecostal/Charismatic mission from the beginning of the twentieth century. The first part considers the theological basis of Pentecostal/Charismatic mission thinking and practice. Special attention is paid to the Old Testament, which has been regularly overlooked by the modern Pentecostal/Charismatic movements. The second part discusses major mission topics with contributions and challenges unique to Pentecostal/Charismatic mission. The book concludes with a reflection on the future of this powerful missionary movement. As the authors served as Korean missionaries in Asia, often their missionary experiences in Asia are reflected in their discussions.

S. Hun Kim & Wonsuk Ma (eds.)

Korean Diaspora and Christian Mission

2011-978-1-870345-91-0 / 301pp

As a 'divine conspiracy' for Missio Dei, the global phenomenon of people on the move has shown itself to be invaluable. In 2004 two significant documents concerning Diaspora were introduced, one by the Filipino International Network and the other by the Lausanne Committee for World Evangelization. These have created awareness of the importance of people on the move for Christian mission. Since then, Korean Diaspora has conducted similar research among Korean missions, resulting in this book

Jin Huat Tan

Planting an Indigenous Church

The Case of the Borneo Evangelical Mission

2011 / 978-1-870345-99-6 / 343pp

Dr Jin Huat Tan has written a pioneering study of the origins and development of Malaysia's most significant indigenous church. This is an amazing story of revival, renewal and transformation of the entire region chronicling the powerful effect of it evident to date! What can we learn from this extensive and careful study of the Borneo Revival, so the global Christianity will become ever more dynamic.

Bill Prevette

Child, Church and Compassion

Towards Child Theology in Romania

2012 / 978-1-908355-03-4/ 377pp

Bill Prevett comments that "children are like 'canaries in a mine shaft'; they provide a focal point for discovery and encounter of perilous aspects of our world that are often ignored." True, but miners also carried a lamp to see into the subterranean darkness. This book is such a lamp. It lights up the subterranean world of children and youth in danger of exploitation, and as it does so travels deep into their lives and also into the activities of those who seek to help them.

Samuel Cyuma

Picking Up the Pieces

The Church and Conflict Resolution in South Africa and Rwanda

2012 / 978-1-908355-02-7/ 411pp

In the last ten years of the 20th century, the world was twice confronted with unbelievable news from Africa. First, there was the end of Apartheid in South Africa, without bloodshed, due to responsible political and Church leaders. The second was the mass killings in Rwanda, which soon escalated into real genocide. Political and Church leaders had been unable to prevents this crime against humanity. In this book, the question is raised: can we compare the situation in South Africa with that in Rwanda? Can Rwandan leaders draw lessons from the peace process in South Africa?

GENERAL REGNUM TITLES

Vinay Samuel, Chris Sugden (eds.)
The Church in Response to Human Need
1987 / 1870345045 / xii+268pp

Philip Sampson, Vinay Samuel, Chris Sugden (eds.)
Faith and Modernity
Essays in modernity and post-modernity
1994 / 1870345177 / 352pp

Klaus Fiedler
The Story of Faith Missions
1994 / 0745926878 / 428pp

Douglas Peterson
Not by Might nor by Power
A Pentecostal Theology of Social Concern in Latin America
1996 / 1870345207 / xvi+260pp

David Gitari
In Season and Out of Season
Sermons to a Nation
1996 / 1870345118 / 155pp

David. W. Virtue
A Vision of Hope
The Story of Samuel Habib
1996 / 1870345169 / xiv+137pp

Everett A Wilson
Strategy of the Spirit
J.Philip Hogan and the Growth of the Assemblies of God Worldwide, 1960 - 1990
1997 /1870345231/214

Murray Dempster, Byron Klaus, Douglas Petersen (Eds)
The Globalization of Pentecostalism
A Religion Made to Travel
1999 / 1870345290 / xvii+406pp

Peter Johnson, Chris Sugden (eds.)
Markets, Fair Trade and the Kingdom of God
Essays to Celebrate Traidcraft's 21st Birthday
2001 / 1870345193 / xii+155pp

Robert Hillman, Coral Chamberlain, Linda Harding
Healing & Wholeness
Reflections on the Healing Ministry
2002 / 978-1- 870345-35- 4 / xvii+283pp

David Bussau, Russell Mask
Christian Microenterprise Development
An Introduction
2003 / 1870345282 / xiii+142pp

David Singh
Sainthood and Revelatory Discourse
An Examination of the Basis for the Authority of Bayan in Mahdawi Islam
2003 / 8172147285 / xxiv+485pp

For the up-to-date listing of the Regnum books see www.ocms.ac.uk/regnum

regnum

Regnum Books International

Regnum is an Imprint of The Oxford Centre for Mission Studies
St. Philip and St. James Church
Woodstock Road
Oxford, OX2 6HR
Web: www.ocms.ac.uk/regnum

Robert Hillman, Coral Chamberlain, Linda Harding
Healing & Wholeness
Reflections on the Healing Ministry
2002 / 978-1- 870345-35- 4 / xvii+283pp

David Bussau, Russell Mask
Christian Microenterprise Development
An Introduction
2003 / 1870345282 / xiii+142pp

David Singh
Sainthood and Revelatory Discourse
An Examination of the Basis for the Authority of Bayan in Mahdawi Islam
2003 / 8172147285 / xxiv+485pp

For the up-to-date listing of the Regnum books see www.ocms.ac.uk/regnum

regnum

Regnum Books International

Regnum is an Imprint of The Oxford Centre for Mission Studies
St. Philip and St. James Church
Woodstock Road
Oxford, OX2 6HR
Web: www.ocms.ac.uk/regnum